The Cambridge Companion to Florence B. Price

Active in Chicago during the first half of the twentieth century, Florence B. Price was an African American composer, pianist, organist, and music teacher, and a central figure in the early twentieth-century wave of Black composers of art music in the US. Price's aesthetic engaged with Black music of the enslavement period, and her gendered racial identity deserves careful consideration, while her geography and era distinguish her trajectory from those of her European and Anglo-American counterparts. This companion introduces readers to archives and sources on Price, the style and genre of her music, and her artistic communities and reception. It contextualizes Price's music and life in relation to the sociocultural climate of her time, the Black classical scene to which she belonged, and the compositional aesthetics that informed her craft. It offers an alternative view of music's capacity to uplift and amplify underrepresented voices.

SAMANTHA EGE is an award-winning musicologist and internationally recognized concert pianist. She is the author of *South Side Impresarios: How Race Women Transformed Chicago's Classical Music Scene*. Her albums spotlight underrepresented composers, and encompass collaborations with Castle of our Skins and the BBC Philharmonic.

ALEXANDRA KORI HILL is a musicologist, editor, and freelance writer. She specializes in American culture, Black composers, and music of the nineteenth and twentieth centuries. Kori is the assistant editor for I CARE IF YOU LISTEN, powered by American Composers Forum, and serves as the 2025–2026 Provostal Postdoctoral Fellow at the University of Cincinnati's College-Conservatory of Music. Her work has appeared in the *New York Times*, Sirp, and program notes for major American orchestras.

Cambridge Companions to Music

Topics

The Cambridge Companion to Ballet
Edited by Marion Kant

The Cambridge Companion to Blues and Gospel Music
Edited by Allan Moore

The Cambridge Companion to Caribbean Music
Edited by Nanette de Jong

The Cambridge Companion to Choral Music
Edited by André de Quadros

The Cambridge Companion to Composition
Edited by Toby Young

The Cambridge Companion to the Concerto
Edited by Simon P. Keefe

The Cambridge Companion to Conducting
Edited by José Antonio Bowen

The Cambridge Companion to Eighteenth-Century Opera
Edited by Anthony R. DelDonna and Pierpaolo Polzonetti

The Cambridge Companion to Electronic Dance Music
Edited by Hillegonda C. Rietveld and Toby Young

The Cambridge Companion to Electronic Music, second edition
Edited by Nick Collins and Julio D'Escriván

The Cambridge Companion to the 'Eroica' Symphony
Edited by Nancy November

The Cambridge Companion to Film Music
Edited by Mervyn Cooke and Fiona Ford

The Cambridge Companion to Folk Music
Edited by Ross Cole

The Cambridge Companion to French Art Song
Edited by Stephen Rumph

The Cambridge Companion to French Music
Edited by Simon Trezise

The Cambridge Companion to Global Rap
Edited by Richard Bramwell and Alex de Lacey

The Cambridge Companion to Grand Opera
Edited by David Charlton

The Cambridge Companion to Hip-Hop
Edited by Justin A. Williams

The Cambridge Companion to Jazz
Edited by Mervyn Cooke and David Horn

The Cambridge Companion to Jewish Music
Edited by Joshua S. Walden

The Cambridge Companion to K-Pop
Edited by Suk-Young Kim

The Cambridge Companion to Krautrock
Edited by Uwe Schütte

The Cambridge Companion to the Lied
Edited by James Parsons

The Cambridge Companion to *The Magic Flute*
Edited by Jessica Waldoff

The Cambridge Companion to Medieval Music
Edited by Mark Everist

The Cambridge Companion to Metal Music
Edited by Jan-Peter Herbst

The Cambridge Companion to Music and Romanticism
Edited by Benedict Taylor

The Cambridge Companion to Music in Australia
Edited by Amanda Harris and Clint Bracknell

The Cambridge Companion to Music in Digital Culture
Edited by Nicholas Cook, Monique Ingalls and David Trippett

The Cambridge Companion to the Musical, third edition
Edited by William Everett and Paul Laird

The Cambridge Companion to Opera Studies
Edited by Nicholas Till

The Cambridge Companion to Operetta
Edited by Anastasia Belina and Derek B. Scott

The Cambridge Companion to the Orchestra
Edited by Colin Lawson

The Cambridge Companion to Pop and Rock
Edited by Simon Frith, Will Straw and John Street

The Cambridge Companion to Recorded Music
Edited by Eric Clarke, Nicholas Cook, Daniel Leech-Wilkinson and John Rink

The Cambridge Companion to Rhythm
Edited by Russell Hartenberger and Ryan McClelland

The Cambridge Companion to *The Rite of Spring*
Edited by Davinia Caddy

The Cambridge Companion to Schubert's 'Winterreise'
Edited by Marjorie W. Hirsch and Lisa Feurzeig

The Cambridge Companion to Serialism
Edited by Martin Iddon

The Cambridge Companion to Seventeenth-Century Opera
Edited by Jacqueline Waeber

The Cambridge Companion to the Singer-Songwriter
Edited by Katherine Williams and Justin A. Williams

The Cambridge Companion to the String Quartet
Edited by Robin Stowell

The Cambridge Companion to the Symphony
Edited by Julian Horton

The Cambridge Companion to Tango
Edited by Kristin Wendland and Kacey Link

The Cambridge Companion to Twentieth-Century Opera
Edited by Mervyn Cooke

The Cambridge Companion to Video Game Music
Edited by Melanie Fritsch and Tim Summers

The Cambridge Companion to Wagner's *Der Ring des Nibelungen*
Edited by Mark Berry and Nicholas Vazsonyi

The Cambridge Companion to *West Side Story*
Edited by Paul R. Laird and Elizabeth A. Wells

The Cambridge Companion to Women Composers
Edited by Matthew Head and Susan Wollenberg

The Cambridge Companion to Women in Music since 1900
Edited by Laura Hamer

Composers

The Cambridge Companion to Bach
Edited by John Butt

The Cambridge Companion to Bartók
Edited by Amanda Bayley

The Cambridge Companion to Amy Beach
Edited by E. Douglas Bomberger

The Cambridge Companion to the Beatles
Edited by Kenneth Womack

The Cambridge Companion to Beethoven
Edited by Glenn Stanley

The Cambridge Companion to Berg
Edited by Anthony Pople

The Cambridge Companion to Berlioz
Edited by Peter Bloom

The Cambridge Companion to Brahms
Edited by Michael Musgrave

The Cambridge Companion to Benjamin Britten
Edited by Mervyn Cooke

The Cambridge Companion to Bruckner
Edited by John Williamson

The Cambridge Companion to John Cage
Edited by David Nicholls

The Cambridge Companion to Chopin
Edited by Jim Samson

The Cambridge Companion to Debussy
Edited by Simon Trezise

The Cambridge Companion to Elgar
Edited by Daniel M. Grimley and Julian Rushton

The Cambridge Companion to Duke Ellington
Edited by Edward Green

The Cambridge Companion to Gershwin
Edited by Anna Celenza

The Cambridge Companion to Gilbert and Sullivan
Edited by David Eden and Meinhard Saremba

The Cambridge Companion to Handel
Edited by Donald Burrows

The Cambridge Companion to Haydn
Edited by Caryl Clark

The Cambridge Companion to Liszt
Edited by Kenneth Hamilton

The Cambridge Companion to Mahler
Edited by Jeremy Barham

The Cambridge Companion to Mendelssohn
Edited by Peter Mercer-Taylor

The Cambridge Companion to Monteverdi
Edited by John Whenham and Richard Wistreich

The Cambridge Companion to Mozart
Edited by Simon P. Keefe

The Cambridge Companion to Arvo Pärt
Edited by Andrew Shenton

The Cambridge Companion to Florence B. Price
Edited by Samantha Ege and Alexandra Kori Hill

The Cambridge Companion to Ravel
Edited by Deborah Mawer

The Cambridge Companion to the Rolling Stones
Edited by Victor Coelho and John Covach

The Cambridge Companion to Rossini
Edited by Emanuele Senici

The Cambridge Companion to Schoenberg
Edited by Jennifer Shaw and Joseph Auner

The Cambridge Companion to Schubert
Edited by Christopher Gibbs

The Cambridge Companion to Schumann
Edited by Beate Perrey

The Cambridge Companion to Shostakovich
Edited by Pauline Fairclough and David Fanning

The Cambridge Companion to Sibelius
Edited by Daniel M. Grimley

The Cambridge Companion to Richard Strauss
Edited by Charles Youmans

The Cambridge Companion to Stravinsky
Edited by Jonathan Cross

The Cambridge Companion to Michael Tippett
Edited by Kenneth Gloag and Nicholas Jones

The Cambridge Companion to Vaughan Williams
Edited by Alain Frogley and Aiden J. Thomson

The Cambridge Companion to Verdi
Edited by Scott L. Balthazar

The Cambridge Companion to Wagner
Edited by Thomas S. Grey

Instruments

The Cambridge Companion to Brass Instruments
Edited by Trevor Herbert and John Wallace

The Cambridge Companion to the Cello
Edited by Robin Stowell

The Cambridge Companion to the Clarinet
Edited by Colin Lawson

The Cambridge Companion to the Drum Kit
Edited by Matt Brennan, Joseph Michael Pignato and Daniel Akira Stadnicki

The Cambridge Companion to the Electric Guitar
Edited by Jan-Peter Herbst and Steve Waksman

The Cambridge Companion to the Guitar
Edited by Victor Coelho

The Cambridge Companion to the Harpsichord
Edited by Mark Kroll

The Cambridge Companion to the Organ
Edited by Nicholas Thistlethwaite and Geoffrey Webber

The Cambridge Companion to Percussion
Edited by Russell Hartenberger

The Cambridge Companion to the Piano
Edited by David Rowland

The Cambridge Companion to the Saxophone
Edited by Richard Ingham

The Cambridge Companion to Singing
Edited by John Potter

The Cambridge Companion to the Violin
Edited by Robin Stowell

The Cambridge Companion to Florence B. Price

Edited by

SAMANTHA EGE
University of Southampton

ALEXANDRA KORI HILL
University of Cincinnati

Shaftesbury Road, Cambridge CB2 8EA, United Kingdom

One Liberty Plaza, 20th Floor, New York, NY 10006, USA

477 Williamstown Road, Port Melbourne, VIC 3207, Australia

314–321, 3rd Floor, Plot 3, Splendor Forum, Jasola District Centre,
New Delhi – 110025, India

Cambridge University Press is part of Cambridge University Press & Assessment, a department of the University of Cambridge.

We share the University's mission to contribute to society through the pursuit of education, learning and research at the highest international levels of excellence.

www.cambridge.org
Information on this title: www.cambridge.org/9781009169394

DOI: 10.1017/9781009169387

© Cambridge University Press & Assessment 2026

This publication is in copyright. Subject to statutory exception and to the provisions of relevant collective licensing agreements, no reproduction of any part may take place without the written permission of Cambridge University Press & Assessment.

When citing this work, please include a reference to the DOI 10.1017/9781009169387

First published 2026

A catalogue record for this publication is available from the British Library

A Cataloging-in-Publication data record for this book is available from the Library of Congress

ISBN 978-1-009-16939-4 Hardback
ISBN 978-1-009-16937-0 Paperback

Cambridge University Press & Assessment has no responsibility for the persistence or accuracy of URLs for external or third-party internet websites referred to in this publication and does not guarantee that any content on such websites is, or will remain, accurate or appropriate.

For EU product safety concerns, contact us at Calle de José Abascal, 56, 1°, 28003 Madrid, Spain, or email eugpsr@cambridge.org

Contents

List of Figures [*page* xi]
List of Tables [xii]
List of Musical Examples [xiii]
List of Contributors [xiv]
Foreword [xvii]
NAOMI ANDRÉ
Acknowledgments [xxii]
Chronology [xxiv]

Introduction [1]
SAMANTHA EGE AND ALEXANDRA KORI HILL

PART I ARCHIVES AND SOURCES [7]

1 Listening for Florence "Bea" Price [9]
   SAMANTHA EGE

2 Hidden Figures and Black Music Historiography: Florence Price's Story and Rae Linda Brown's Scholarship [27]
   CARLENE J. BROWN AND C. E. AARON

3 Price and the Black Concert Tradition in the United States [47]
   LOUISE TOPPIN

PART II GENRE AND STYLE [63]

4 New Analytical Approaches for Florence Price Scholarship [65]
   JANE FORNER AND ELLIE M. HISAMA

5 Reflections of Price in the Mirror of Her Art Songs [85]
   MINNITA DANIEL-COX

6 The Concert Spirituals: Price as Griot-Composer [105]
   ELEKTRA V. CARTER

7 The Solo Keyboard Works [124]
GWYNNE KUHNER BROWN AND JOE WILLIAMS

8 Price and the Violin: Between Virtuosity and Vernacularity [144]
KATHARINA UHDE AND R. LARRY TODD

9 Concertos and Chamber Works: The African American Idiom in Texture and Form [173]
ALEXANDRA KORI HILL

10 Symphonies to Tone Poems [193]
DOUGLAS W. SHADLE

PART III COMMUNITY AND RECEPTION [215]

11 The Influence of Harry T. Burleigh [217]
RAE LINDA BROWN

12 Black Feminist Bonds between Florence Price, Marian Anderson, and Margaret Bonds [228]
ELIZABETH DURRANT

13 The Critical Reception of Florence Price [247]
LUCY CAPLAN

14 When Things Don't Fall Apart: The Myth of Black Cultural Rediscovery and the Afterlife of Florence Price [266]
TAMMY L. KERNODLE

Select Bibliography [286]
Index [291]

Figures

1.1 Florence Price pictured composing at the piano in her summer house in St. Anne, Illinois. Photographs Florence B. Price Family, ca. 1910–1950, Personal Materials, 1905–1953, series I, box 2, folder 2, Florence Beatrice Smith Price Papers Addendum (MC 988a), Special Collections, University of Arkansas Libraries, Fayetteville. [*page* 12]

1.2 Inside Price's abandoned summer home. Photograph by Timothy G. Nutt (2010). Used by permission of Timothy G. Nutt. [17]

1.3 Outside Price's abandoned summer home. Photograph by Timothy G. Nutt (2010). Used by permission of Timothy G. Nutt. [23]

1.4 Florence Price and her daughter Florence Louise Robinson admiring flowers outside the summer house in St. Anne, Illinois. Photographs Florence B. Price Family, ca. 1910–1950, Personal Materials, 1905–1953, series I, box 2, folder 2, Florence Beatrice Smith Price Papers Addendum (MC 988a), Special Collections, University of Arkansas Libraries, Fayetteville. [23]

8.1 Carl Flesch, *The Art of Violin Playing*, vol. 1, p. 30. [156]

13.1 This photograph of Lillian Evanti and Florence Price appeared in the *Pittsburgh Courier*, accompanied by a caption that emphasized both women's musical achievements, as well as Evanti's respect for Price: "Mme. Lillian Evanti, famous operatic and concert singer (left), greeting Mrs. Florence B. Price, the foremost woman composer of our group. During a recent visit to 'A Century of Progress' in Chicago, when she was completing plans for a country-wide tour, Mme. Evanti in an interview paid high tribute to the work of Mrs. Price." ("Evanti Praises Woman Composer," *Pittsburgh Courier*, October 13, 1934.) [248]

14.1 Bay Area Women's Philharmonic concert program, March 11, 1988. [281]

14.2 Bay Area Women's Philharmonic concert program, February 11, 1989. [282]

Tables

6.1 Price's concert spirituals and pseudo-spirituals using Randye Jones's categories of Negro spirituals. [*page* 111]
8.1 "I'm Workin' on My Buildin'" in songbooks, recordings, and Price's *Two Traditional Negro Spirituals* (1940, published 1949). [148]
8.2 Formal plan of Florence Price's Violin Concerto No. 2. [164]
8.3 Formal plan of Price's Violin Fantasy No. 1. [164]
9.1 List of known and extant concertos and chamber works by Florence B. Price. [177]
10.1 Florence B. Price, orchestral works. [194]

Musical Examples

4.1 Extensions of (024) chords in Price, "Song of the Open Road" from *Four Encore Songs*; piano part shown in m. 2, m. 4, m. 5, and m. 6. [*page* 72]
4.2 Price, "Bewilderment," m. 51–end. [73]
4.3 Price, "Beside the Sea," m. 30–end. [74]
4.4 Price, "Songs to the Dark Virgin," mm. 19–24. [77]
5.1 "What's the Use?," mm. 23–28. [89]
5.2 "Don't You Tell Me No," mm. 26–33. [95]
5.3 "Brown Arms," mm. 13–17. [99]
5.4 "Brown Arms," mm. 20–26. [100]
6.1 Price, "Peter Go Ring dem Bells," mm. 13–15. [114]
6.2 Pentatonic opening statement of Price's "City Called Heaven," mm. 1–8. [117]
6.3 Price, "I'm Going to Lay Down My Heavy Load," mm. 8–12. [119]
6.4 Price, "I'm Going to Lay Down My Heavy Load," mm. 37–39. [120]
7.1 Price, *Offertory*, mm. 10–11. [128]
7.2 Price, Suite for Organ No. 1, "Fantasy," mm. 42–50. [132]
7.3 Price, *Fantasie Nègre* No. 2, in G minor, mm. 1–11. [134]
8.1 Florence Price, "I'm Workin' on My Buildin'" (No. 2 of *Two Traditional Negro Spirituals*). [153]
8.2 "I'm Workin' on the Buildin'" as sung by Ollie Gilbert on October 28, 1969 (US-Wc, Cat. #1041 [MFH #724]). [154]
8.3 Schubert, "Ave Maria," with Mikhail Zacharewitsch's B-portamenti (marked with a line above an x) and one finger slides. [157]
8.4 Price, Violin Concerto No. 2, mm. 17–32. [168]
9.1 Price, Violin Concerto No. 1, 1st movement, motives 1 and 2, mm. 23–29. [183]
9.2 Price, Violin Concerto No. 1, cadenza II to recapitulation, m. 189. [184]
9.3 Tchaikovsky, Violin Concerto, cadenza to recapitulation, mm. 212–219. [184]
9.4 Price, Concerto in One Movement, two-piano reduction, mm. 1–9. [187]

Contributors

C. E. AARON is a writer and alumnus of the Yale Institute of Sacred Music. From 2018 to 2020, they catalogued Rae Linda Brown's papers for library acquisition. They currently work as data coordinator for Minnesota Public Radio's YourClassical Class Notes program, which provides free in-classroom concerts and lesson plans for music educators.

CARLENE J. BROWN is Professor of Music and Chair of the Music Department at Seattle Pacific University (SPU), Seattle. She is a board-certified music therapist and director of the SPU music therapy program. She is also dedicated to preserving the legacies of two extraordinary African American scholars: Florence Price and Rae Linda Brown.

GWYNNE KUHNER BROWN is Professor of Music at the University of Puget Sound in Tacoma, Washington. She edited G. Schirmer's 2023 edition of William L. Dawson's *Negro Folk Symphony* and is the author of *William L. Dawson*, a volume in the American Composers series of the University of Illinois Press.

RAE LINDA BROWN was Professor of Music at the University of Michigan, University of California, Irvine (where she served as the Robert and Majorie Rawlins Chair of the Department of Music), Vice President at Loyola Marymount University, and Provost at Pacific Lutheran University. She is the author of *The Heart of a Woman: The Life and Music of Florence B. Price*.

LUCY CAPLAN is Assistant Professor of Music at Worcester Polytechnic Institute. She is the author of *Dreaming in Ensemble: How Black Artists Transformed American Opera*. Her writing also appears in the *Journal of the Society for American Music*, *American Studies*, and *Women and Music*, as well as the *New Yorker*, *Opera*, and *Opera News*.

ELEKTRA V. CARTER is a freelance singer, musicologist, and voice teacher based in Chicago, Illinois. They have held academic positions at Murray State University and Georgia Southern University. As founding president of the International Florence Price Festival, Carter organized two music festivals dedicated to the preservation of Price's legacy.

MINNITA DANIEL-COX is Professor of Music at the University of Dayton. Her work on Paul Laurence Dunbar led to the establishment of the Dunbar Music Archive and glossary and the Dunbar Library and Archive (supported by the National Endowment for the Humanities and Mellon Foundation). A performing scholar, she has presented her scholarship around the world.

ELIZABETH DURRANT is a musicologist, singer, and PhD student in Black studies and music at Yale University. Her work appears in the *Journal of the American Musicological Society*, *Journal for the Society of American Music*, and the volume *Four Centuries of Women's Musical Salons: A Cross-Cultural History* (edited by Rebecca Cypess and Jacqueline Avila).

SAMANTHA EGE is a musicologist, pianist, and author of *South Side Impresarios: How Race Women Transformed Chicago's Classical Music Scene*. Her writing appears in the *New York Times*, *Journal of the American Musicological Society*, *American Music*, and *Women and Music*. Her albums include world premieres of Florence Price, Undine Smith Moore, and Julia Perry.

JANE ISABELLE Forner is a musicologist whose work focuses on contemporary opera in Europe and North America. Her publications examine intersections of race and gender, cross-cultural operatic composition, and political interpretations of myths in contemporary music and media. She is currently a lecturer at the University of Toronto.

ALEXANDRA KORI HILL is a musicologist from Cincinnati, Ohio. She is assistant editor for I CARE IF YOU LISTEN, powered by American Composers Forum, and the 2025–2026 Provostal Postdoctoral Fellow at the University of Cincinnati College-Conservatory of Music. Her work appears in the *New York Times*, I CARE IF YOU LISTEN, Cincinnati Public Radio's *Classics for Kids* blog, and program notes for major orchestras and organizations.

ELLIE M. HISAMA is Distinguished Professor at the University of Toronto and Professor Emerita of Music at Columbia University. A social historian and music theorist, she is the author of *Gendering Musical Modernism* and served as the Edward T. Cone Member in music studies at the Institute for Advanced Study.

TAMMY L. KERNODLE is the Park Creative Arts Professor and University Distinguished Professor at Miami University in Oxford, OH. She is the author of *Soul on Soul: The Life and Music of Mary Lou Williams*. Her scholarship appears in numerous anthologies and peer-reviewed journals. She is a past president of the Society for American Music.

DOUGLAS W. SHADLE is Associate Professor of Musicology at the Vanderbilt University Blair School of Music. He is the author of *Orchestrating the Nation: The Nineteenth-Century American Symphonic Enterprise* and *Antonín Dvořák's New World Symphony*.

R. LARRY TODD is Arts and Sciences Professor at Duke University. His books include *Mendelssohn: A Life in Music* and *Fanny Hensel: The Other Mendelssohn*. He studied piano at Yale University, and has issued with Nancy Green the Mendelssohns' cello works. He has co-authored *Beethoven's Cello: Five Revolutionary Sonatas and Their World*.

LOUISE TOPPIN is Professor of Music (Voice) at the University of Michigan and was previously Distinguished Professor of Music and Department Chair at the University of North Carolina, Chapel Hill. She has published twelve collections of music by African American composers and has received international acclaim for her operatic, orchestral, oratorio, and recital performances.

KATHARINA UHDE is a violinist-musicologist and practice-based researcher. She holds positions at Valparaiso University and LMU Munich. She is the author of *The Music of Joseph Joachim*, coeditor of two books, and has edited for Bärenreiter two compositions by Joseph Joachim. She has won prizes in competitions and released several CDs.

JOE WILLIAMS is a sound liberator, pianist, composer, educator, and curator from Tacoma, WA. Their inaugural album, *Life's Sweet Shadows*, features soprano Ellaina Lewis performing works by Richard Thompson. Williams was awarded the 2022 Paul Charosh Independent Scholar Fellowship of the Society for American Music for their contribution to this companion.

Foreword

NAOMI ANDRÉ

Regaining her place in the sun, Florence "Bea" Price (1888–1953) is changing the trajectory of how we think about music. Despite her accomplishments in the 1930s and 1940s with major performances of her works by the Chicago Symphony, Marian Anderson, and others, to many it seems as though Price dropped out of mainstream consciousness by the early 1950s and into near obscurity after her death in 1953. Yet the history of people of color, especially women, seems to toggle between that which is known and that which is unseen, as if placed just slightly out of sight.

Fortunately, there is a long-standing practice of recovery and writing ourselves into history. From Phillis Wheatley, Maria Stewart, Ida B. Wells-Barnett, Zora Neale Hurston, Audre Lorde, Toni Morrison, and many contemporary women writing today, there is a deep history of having Black women sustain these narratives. Several authors in this collection contribute to this history (and this is heroically showcased in the final chapter by Tammy L. Kernodle) and provide evidence to illustrate how Price's music continued to be appreciated in arenas that celebrated Black musical talent, primarily in historically Black colleges and universities (HBCUs). In the current scene today, this knowledge is moving from "margin to center" and finally the mainstream is catching on.[1] Price has become almost like a "tipping point," a critical call to action, for music aficionados, audiences, and scholars who yearn for a more diverse canon of classical concert music.[2] In the wake of #MeToo, #BlackLivesMatter, and anti-racism movements, Florence Price has emerged as a musical "Hidden Figure."[3]

Through recent scholarship and recordings, Florence Price is emerging from the shadows. With the groundbreaking biography in 2020 by Rae Linda Brown (published posthumously and edited by Guthrie P. Ramsey, Jr.) *The Heart of a Woman: The Life and Music of Florence B. Price*, an uptick in the availability of Price's scores, and a few recent GRAMMY recognitions (winner in 2022 for *Price: Symphonies Nos. 1 & 3*; winner in 2023 for *Price, Montgomery, Coleman*; and nominated in 2024 for *Price: Symphony No. 4 – Dawson: Negro Folk Symphony*), it is now more possible than ever to listen to, perform, and study Price's music.⁴ Price has become an iconic figure who helps us mark the difference between the way music history used to be told (when she was an invisible presence) and now the beginning of a new music historiography where she is a critical pillar for understanding music in the United States during the first half of the twentieth century.

The 2016 book and movie *Hidden Figures* dramatically illustrated how skewed our general understanding has been of Black contributions to mathematics, engineering, and the development of early space technology. Years earlier, Ralph Ellison powerfully wrote about a related, and even more encompassing, situation in *Invisible Man*. Published in 1952, one year before Price died, Ellison outlined not just the poignant situation of Black talent being hidden, but also of the tragic reality that many Black folks have not been taken seriously enough to achieve their full potential. Relegated to a parallel reality, Black talents in classical art music have been hidden in the shadows. Along with other Black musicians born in the nineteenth century, much of Price's career has belonged to a *shadow culture*. This narrative is part of a history occurring concurrently, adjacently, to the mainstream white classical musical tradition. It exists on the margins of non-Black spaces as it happens out of sight from the gaze of most white consumers. It is a place of opportunity that features an intersection of western European and white American musical traditions with Black experiences and musical cultures. Far from being lesser than or inferior to the mainstream, the shadow culture Price belonged to reveals a richer and more complex tapestry of music in the first half of the twentieth century in the United States than the conventional narrative we have been told.⁵

In the 1980s only a few people who studied music in school curricula and attended concerts knew who Florence Price was. This was the time when I was in college studying music and there were virtually no names of women composers mentioned. In fact, this was a time when music people were asking out loud, in prominent academic conferences, gatherings, and classrooms: Where were the women? And by women, most people meant white women.

Such questions were connected to larger initiatives in the academy at the dawn of the age of multiculturalism in educational agendas. Virginia Woolfe emerged as a mainstream presence with her important words about women needing to have some independence with a little space and means of their own – a notable goal, though not fully achievable for all. In musicology's related sister discipline, pioneering art historian Linda

Nochlin rerouted questions about "why no great women composers" (raised by music educator Carl Seashore in 1940) when she outlined how the leading institutions were designed by and for men.[6] Institutions of training and pedagogy were not environments where women were permitted to study, teach, or be cultivated into artists. Put starkly, traditional art schools were places where women disrobed and were visually consumed as objectified artistic models.

The early 1980s marked the third decade after Florence Price's death (in 1953) and fifty years after she first made national news with her successful wins (in both the piano and orchestral categories) at the Rodman Wanamaker Music Contest. Her awards led to the world premiere of her Symphony No. 1 in E minor with the Chicago Symphony Orchestra in 1933; this made her the first African American woman to have a symphony performed by a major national orchestra. The 1980s also marked an important interest in Price in the mainstream academy. Rae Linda Brown finished her doctorate in music at Yale University in 1987, having completed a PhD dissertation on the music of Florence Price. In addition to being an early in-depth exploration of Price's work, it was one of the first dissertations on a Black composer to come out of a music department at an Ivy League academic institution.

I entered the Harvard music department in the fall of 1989 and would be the first Black woman to receive a PhD in that department. Famed musicologist Professor Eileen Southern (the first Black tenured professor at Harvard University) had retired a few years earlier and I did not have the honor of being able to study with her. But later in my career, I had the pleasure of meeting and sharing a few meals and treasured conversations with Rae Linda Brown. My first job, at the University of Michigan, began just a few years after she left and moved to another academic institution. Though the numbers were not large, being trained outside of the space of HBCUs, I had the very good fortune of seeing a few other Black women musicologists who have been pioneering figures in the discipline at conferences and symposia. This continues to be a precious community and has included Marva Carter, Eileen M. Hayes, Yvonne Kendall, Tammy L. Kernodle, Maureen Mahon, Mellonee V. Burnim, Portia Maultsby, Gayle Murchison, Gayle Robinson-Oturu, Kira Thurman, Louise Toppin, and Josephine Wright. It is joyful to report that these pathbreaking scholars are still active and this cohort is growing. Included in this newer generation are Samantha Ege and Alexandra Kori Hill, the trailblazing, energetic scholars who had the vision and drive to conceive of and nurture this collection through.[7]

This *Cambridge Companion to Florence B. Price* builds on the wealth of orchestral, vocal, chamber, and solo instrument (primarily piano and organ) repertoire in Price's output. It signals the wealth of methodologies and academic inquiries from a wide range of scholar-performers that Price and her music have already generated. Belonging to such a venerable series, this first Cambridge Companion devoted to an African American woman composer will hopefully encourage the inclusion of additional figures who have been hidden in the shadows of mainstream musical cultures. While this volume represents a highpoint in Price scholarship, may it also mark an auspicious beginning and lay the foundation as we "hold fast to dreams" yet to come.[8]

Notes

1. I use this phrase to reference bell hooks and her 1984 book *Feminist Theory: From Margin to Center*.
2. The expression "tipping point," popularized by Malcolm Gladwell (2000), was already around earlier; see MaryAnne M. Gobble "Defining the Tipping Point," *Research Technology Management* 62, no. 6 (2019): 53–56.
3. Several essays in this collection reference the 2016 book (Margot Lee Shetterly) and film (directed by Theodore Melfi) *Hidden Figures*, which outline the history of three Black women mathematicians who advanced American spaceflight (Katherine G. Johnson, Mary W. Jackson, and Dorothy Vaughan).
4. Recent recordings of Price's work that have had Grammy recognition: Yannick Nézet-Séguin conducting the *Philadelphia Orchestra, Price: Symphonies Nos. 1 & 3* (Deutsche Grammophon, 2021); Michael Repper conducting the New York Youth Symphony, *Works by Florence Price, Jessie Montgomery & Valerie Coleman* (Avie, 2022); and Yannick Nézet-Séguin conducting the Philadelphia Orchestra, *Florence Price Symphony No. 4 – William Dawson, Negro Folk Symphony* (Deutsche Grammophon, 2023). Though many of the scores are in need of closer editing, many are available through Schirmer. *The Heart of a Woman: The Life and Music of Florence B. Price*, by Rae Linda Brown, edited and with a foreword by Guthrie P. Ramsey, Jr. (Urbana: University of Illinois Press, 2020).
5. For more information about "shadow culture narratives," see my book *Black Opera: History, Power, Engagement* (University of Illinois Press, 2018), especially pages 9–13, and Naomi André et al., "Shadow Culture Narratives: Race, Gender, and American Music Historiography," *Journal of the American Musicological Society* vol. 73, no. 3 (Fall 2020): 711–784, especially "Introduction," 712–718.

6. Carl E. Seashore "Why No Great Women Composers?" *Music Educators Journal* 26, no. 5 (March 1940): 21–88; Linda Nochlin "Why Have There Been No Great Women Artists?" in *Women, Art, and Power* (Harper and Row, 1988), 145–178.
7. This list deliberately highlights the Black women who have been critical in creating a supportive academic music community. My apologies for inadvertent omissions. I beg the indulgence of the Black men and other scholars of color who have been generous and helpful. And I thank the significant larger music academic community who have been critical for helping to expand the range of those whose voices are heard and welcomed into the academy.
8. "Hold Fast to Dreams" is one of Florence Price's solo vocal works (with piano accompaniment) from 1945. It is based on Langston Hughes's poem "Dreams" written in 1922 and first published in the May 1923 issue of *The World Tomorrow*.

Acknowledgments

The first full-length monograph on Florence Beatrice Price was published in June 2020, presenting a watershed though bittersweet moment in Price scholarship. The book, titled *The Heart of a Woman: The Life and Music of Florence B. Price*, arrived almost nine decades after Price made history as the first African American woman to have a symphony performed by a major US orchestra. It arrived three years after its author, Rae Linda Brown, passed away with illness. Price is now experiencing a revival that neither she nor her foundational scholars are around to witness. Thus, it is with deep attentiveness to the historical complexities and sensitivities, as well as the present-day pertinence and urgency of the Price narrative, that we have strived to shape this companion.

We have many people to thank for their support and guidance through this process. We express thanks to Kate Brett at Cambridge University Press for her support of this project and her recognition of a need for an edited volume on Florence Price. To our anonymous reviewers, whose feedback encouraged further clarity and directness in the purpose of our project. To the University of Arkansas, Fayetteville Special Collections' librarians and archivists: Timothy Nutt, for the care and attention he and his colleagues give to Price's materials; and Casiday Long and Tyler Schroeder, for scanning and uploading digital copies of Price's manuscripts for easier access. To Sarah Fritz, for introducing us to Ashley Berke (chief communications officer with the Philadelphia Orchestra and Ensemble Arts); to Ashley, for organizing our interviews with Philadelphia Orchestra principal librarian Nicole Jordan and music and artistic director Yannick Nézet-Séguin; and to Nicole and Yannick, for their fierce advocacy and attention to detail in their preparation and performance of Price's music.

To Naomi André, who was a solid mentor and donated her time and support for us and this project, thank you! To our contributors C. E. Aaron, Carlene J. Brown, Rae Linda Brown (posthumously), Lucy Caplan, Elektra V. Carter, Minnita Daniel-Cox, Elizabeth Durrant, Jane Forner, Ellie M. Hisama, Tammy L. Kernodle, Gwynne Kuhner Brown, Douglas W. Shadle, R. Larry Todd, Louise Toppin, Katharina Uhde, and Joe

Williams. You all are amazing! Thank you for giving your expertise and time to analyses of Price's music and life. We are honored to share this book with you. We are grateful, also, that through Jean Snyder (who sent Rae Linda Brown's unpublished paper on Price and Harry T. Burleigh to Samantha with the author's permission in spring 2017), Carlene J. Brown, and Laurie Matheson of the University of Illinois Press we were able to include Rae Linda Brown's voice alongside the new generations of Price scholars that she continues to inspire.

Thank you to our friends and colleagues who gave feedback on our individual chapters; our friends and mentors who kept the fire burning when we hit a bump in the road; and to our family members who supported us through all the highs and lows of our careers.

This book is dedicated to Florence Price and all the scholars, performers, teachers, and listeners who never forgot her and what she created. With this book, we are ensuring it won't be easy for future generations to forget again.

Chronology

1888	As confirmed in the composer's handwritten records and other primary sources, Florence Beatrice Price is born Florence Beatrice Smith on April 9, 1888, in Little Rock, Arkansas. Her parents are dentist Dr. James H. Smith and businesswoman and educator Florence Irene Smith (née Gulliver).
1896	The US Supreme Court's decision in the case of *Plessy* v. *Ferguson* rules in favor of legalized racial segregation and upholds the law of "separate but equal."
1903	Florence Beatrice Smith enrolls at the New England Conservatory of Music in Boston.
1905	Robert Sengstacke Abbott founds what will become one of the highest circulating Black-owned newspapers in the United States, the *Chicago Defender*.
1906	Florence Beatrice Smith graduates from the New England Conservatory of Music with a double major in organ performance and piano pedagogy and returns to Arkansas.
1906	Florence Beatrice Smith teaches in segregated schools, beginning with a short stint at Cotton Plant–Arkadelphia Academy in Cotton Plant, Arkansas.
1907	Florence Beatrice Smith teaches at Shorter College in North Little Rock, Arkansas.
1909	An interracial cohort, which includes W. E. B. Du Bois, Ida B. Wells, Mary Church Terrell, and Mary White Ovington, founds the National Association for the Advancement of Colored People (NAACP).
1909	James Henry Anderson founds another of the nation's soon-to-be leading Black newspapers, New York's *New Amsterdam News*.
1910	Dr. James H. Smith passes away on May 6. Florence Irene Smith is appointed the administrator of Dr. Smith's estate. Their children Florence Beatrice and Charles W. H. Smith (dates as yet unknown) receive five dollars each and the balance goes to Mrs. Smith.

1910	Florence Beatrice Smith becomes head of the music department at Clark Atlanta University in Georgia.
1911	Florence Irene Smith leaves Little Rock for Indianapolis, Indiana, and racially passes as a white woman, leaving her family and former life behind her.
1912	Florence Beatrice Smith returns to Little Rock and marries the lawyer Thomas Jewell Price, who is six years her senior.
1913	This year marks the fiftieth anniversary of the Emancipation Proclamation. On January 1, 1863, President Abraham Lincoln issued an executive order declaring the freedom of all enslaved persons in Confederate states. (This anticipated the passing of the Thirteenth Amendment in 1865.)
1914	The assassination of Austrian archduke Franz Ferdinand by Bosnian Serb Gavrilo Princip on June 28 sets World War I (1914–1918) in motion as Austria–Hungary subsequently declares war on Serbia.
1914	The Price family welcomes Thomas "Tommy" Campfield Price, Jr., who is born on September 20.
1916	The first wave of the Great Migration begins, spanning the next two and a half decades, during which millions of African Americans move en masse from the rural South to the urban North and West in search of greater freedoms and opportunities.
1917	The United States declares war on Germany on April 6 and enters World War I.
1917	The Price family welcomes Florence Louise Price, who is born on July 6.
1917	Chicago's burgeoning Black concert scene leads *Chicago Defender* music critic Nora Holt to proclaim a "Chicago Renaissance." Growing networks of Black classical music-makers (to which Florence Price will eventually belong) will deeply influence the era retrospectively termed (and foreseen by Holt) as the Black Chicago Renaissance.
1918	Nora Holt founds the Chicago Music Association (CMA), which will become the first branch of the National Association of Negro Musicians (NANM, founded in 1919).
1919	This year witnesses the Red Summer: White mobs and Black protestors clash across the United States, leading to race riots in Elaine (Arkansas), Chicago, and several other cities.

1919	Nora Holt cofounds the National Association of Negro Musicians. The inaugural convention takes place on July 29–31 and coincides with the Chicago Race Riots.
1919	Thomas Price and fellow Little Rock lawyer Scipio Africanus Jones take on one of the most well-known cases in Arkansas history, stemming from the Elaine Race Riot of 1919. They represent the first twelve Black men convicted by the court after Philips County grand jury charged 122 Black men with the crime of inciting the race riots.
1920	Florence Price appears in the minutes of the July 27–29, 1920, NANM convention as a member from Arkansas.
1920	The Nineteenth Amendment is ratified on August 18, granting women the right to vote. The persistence of de jure racial segregation means that white women are the primary beneficiaries and Black women remain politically disenfranchised, particularly in the South.
1920	The Prices' firstborn, Tommy, passes away on September 28. His death certificate cites malarial fever as the cause and pneumonia as a contributing factor. He is five years, eleven months, and twenty-eight days old at the time of death.
1921	The Price family welcomes Edith Cassandra Price, who is born on March 29.
1925	Alain Locke publishes his edited anthology *The New Negro: An Interpretation*, a monumental text that encapsulates the spirit of the New Negro Movement and Harlem Renaissance.
1926	Florence Price wins second place in the Holstein Prizes of *Opportunity* magazine for her piano suite *In the Land o' Cotton*.
1927	Florence Price wins second place in the Holstein Prizes of *Opportunity* magazine for her piano suite *Memories of Dixie Land*.
1927	The Price family joins the Great Migration and leaves Little Rock, Arkansas, for Chicago, Illinois.
1928	Florence Price becomes a member of the Chicago-based R. Nathaniel Dett Club of Music and Allied Arts, a chartered member of NANM.
1929	The Great Depression ensues, lasting for a decade and disproportionately impacting the African American population.
1931	Florence Price receives an honorary mention in the Rodman Wanamaker Music Contest for her solo piano work *Cotton Dance*.

1931	On January 19, Florence Price divorces Thomas J. Price and receives sole custody of Florence Louise and Edith Cassandra.
1932	Florence Price wins the piano category and orchestral category of the Rodman Wanamaker Music Contest with her Sonata in E minor and Symphony No. 1 in E minor, respectively. She receives honorable mentions for an orchestral suite called *Ethiopia's Shadow in America* and *Fantasie Nègre* No. 4 in B minor for solo piano.
1933	On June 15, Price becomes the first African American woman to have a symphony performed by a major national orchestra when the Chicago Symphony Orchestra gives the world premiere of her Symphony No. 1 in E minor at the Auditorium Theatre. The concert belongs to the Negro in Music program of the 1933 Chicago World's Fair Century of Progress Exposition, and is conducted by Frederick Stock and underwritten by Maude Roberts George (then president of the CMA) at a cost of $250.
1933	On July 23, a program of Florence Price's works is presented at the Illinois Host House as part of a showcase of local composers at the Chicago World's Fair. She performs her solo piano works and is joined by NANM and CMA friends and colleagues for the performance of her vocal and chamber works.
1934	On June 24, Price debuts her first piano concerto, the Concerto in One Movement, at Chicago Musical College's Orchestra Hall. Part of the school's sixty-seventh commencement ceremony, Price performs with the CMC orchestra.
1934	On October 12, the Woman's Symphony Orchestra of Chicago performs Price's Concerto in One Movement at the Ford Symphony Gardens, with Margaret Bonds as the piano soloist and conducted by Ebba Sundstrom. The concert forms part of the 1934 Chicago World's Fair Century of Progress Exposition.
1935	On May 6, the Franklin D. Roosevelt administration launches the Works Progress Administration (WPA, and renamed the Work Projects Administration in 1939) to counter the devastating rates of unemployment, exacerbated by the Great Depression. The WPA supports thousands of artists, including Florence Price, in their creative and intellectual endeavors.
1935	Florence Price becomes the first African American member of the white association, the Chicago Club of Women Organists (founded in 1928).

1937	On July 15, Florence Price and Clarence Cameron White present a WPA concert of their works at the Federal Music Project Building in Chicago. The program opens with White's *Suite for String Quartet* (1919) and is followed by Price's octet *The Wind and the Sea* (1934), *Fantasie Nègre* No. 4 in B minor for solo piano (1932), and Piano Quintet in E minor (1936).
1939	On April 9, Marian Anderson sings on the steps of the Lincoln Memorial in Washington, DC, after the Daughters of the American Revolution block her from performing at Constitution Hall on the grounds of her race. A crowd of 75,000 people attend the historic concert and millions of radio listeners tune in. Anderson closes with Florence Price's concert spiritual "My Soul's Been Anchored in the Lord."
1939	Germany invades Poland on September 1, 1939, marking the onset of World War II (1939–1945).
1939	Florence Price completes her first violin concerto, Violin Concerto No. 1 in D major.
1940	In August 1940, Florence Price is honored by her fellow Chicago musicians at NANM's convention, held in Chicago, for her contributions to musical life in the city.
1940	In November 1940, Eleanor Roosevelt attends a rehearsal of Florence Price's latest symphony (No. 3 in C minor) in Detroit, given by the Detroit WPA Orchestra, and praises Price in her "My Day" column for the *Atlanta Constitution*.
1941	On September 18, Florence Price writes to conductor Sergei Koussevitzky of the Boston Symphony Orchestra, explaining that despite her fame in the Midwest, she is unknown on the East Coast. Price hopes Koussevitzky will help champion her orchestral works. She receives no response.
1941	On December 7, Japan launches a surprise attack on Pearl Harbor, which subsequently draws the United States into World War II. African Americans fight in a segregated US military, which will foment the "Double 'V'" victory campaign in which Black soldiers will demand the same democracy they fought for abroad in their own United States.
1943	On July 5, Florence Price writes to Koussevitzky again. This time she begins forthrightly, stating the handicaps of her sex and race and imploring him to look and listen beyond any prejudice. She asks him, again, to examine her scores. He does not respond.

1943	On November 6, Florence Price sends a third letter to Koussevitzky. She advocates even more fiercely for her work and reiterates her plea for consideration, but to no avail.
1943	On December 8, NANM and CMA past president and *Chicago Defender* music critic Maude Roberts George passes away. Price biographer Rae Linda Brown notes that by the end of the decade Florence Price's coverage in the *Chicago Defender* steadily decreases. This is, in part, due to deaths and departures of stalwarts such as George. Florence Louise Robinson (née Price, the eldest daughter) will later take up the mantle of promoting her mother's works.
1947	On February 11, Price's Concerto in One Movement (two-piano version) is performed by members of the Musicians Club of Women.
1949	On February 9, Price's Suite for Brasses (also known as Suite for Brass or Octet for Brass and Piano) is premiered by members of the Musicians Club of Women.
1951	Price's *String Quartet on Negro Themes* premieres in February at Carey Temple AME Church; she later revises the title to *Five Folksongs in Counterpoint*. Her chamber work *Sea Gulls* premieres on May 14 as part of a Lake View Musical Society program.
1952	Florence Price completes her second violin concerto, the single-movement Violin Concerto No. 2.
1953	On February 18, members of the Chicago Symphony Orchestra perform Price's *Suite of Negro Dances*, broadcast on Chicago's WGN-TV, Channel 9.
1953	In May 1953, Florence Price prepares for her first professional trip to Europe, but illness stalls her plans.
1953	Florence Price passes away at St. Luke's hospital from a cerebral hemorrhage due to hypertensive cardiovascular disease on June 3. She is subsequently buried in an unmarked grave at Chicago's Lincoln Cemetery.

Introduction

SAMANTHA EGE AND ALEXANDRA KORI HILL

On July 5, 1943, Florence B. Price closed her second letter to the Boston Symphony Orchestra's conductor, Serge Koussevitzky, with the assertion, "I have an unwavering and compelling faith that a national music very beautiful and very American can come from the melting pot just as the nation itself has done. . . . Will you examine one of my scores?" She had already conquered the Midwest, first with the 1933 Chicago Symphony Orchestra debut of her Symphony No. 1 in E Minor, then with further high-profile performances of her works by the Woman's Symphony Orchestra of Chicago and the Detroit WPA Symphony Orchestra.[1] Now, her sights were set on that ever-elusive East Coast symphonic debut.

As Price advocated for her place and pertinence in the making of a national music via her correspondence with Koussevitzky, she foregrounded the "handicaps" of her race and sex, which set her apart from the white male norm of the classical music world. "I am a woman; and I have some Negro blood in my veins." This was, however, less a plea for sympathy and more an upfront declaration of her identity, for which she did not apologize. Wishing to be "judged on merit alone," Price proceeded to share the brilliant insights that she brought to her craft, highlighting, most notably, the way in which her Southern upbringing – as a daughter of Little Rock, Arkansas – shaped her understanding of what she called "real Negro music."[2]

Although Price's letters to Koussevitzky went unanswered, her voice persisted in various pockets of classical music-making, encompassing Black churches, HBCUs, Black classical music clubs, and the repertoire of countless African American vocalists and instrumentalists. Such communities took seriously Price's "unwavering and compelling faith that a national music very beautiful and very American can come from the melting pot just as the nation itself has done" and found alignment with their own advocacy of a more socially just world.

The Cambridge Companion to Florence B. Price emerges from this history of Black classical music community building and sits within three major strains of musicological research: (1) score analysis; (2) positivistic study of composers and repertoires; and (3) cultural, critical, and semiotic analysis of music. This is because Price is a composer who requires all three: her music, particularly her instrumental works, are understudied; the first biographical monograph, Rae Linda Brown's *The Heart of a Woman*, only appeared in 2020; and methods from Black music studies, gender studies, and Black feminist theory help illuminate Price's distinct experience as a Black woman building a composing career in segregated America. As her music is heard by more and more people, it is imperative that listeners and performers have access to close analyses of Price's repertoire, her life, and her times.

The Cambridge Companion to Florence B. Price is structured from the position that Price's style – African American and Western tonalities, rhythms, and forms in Western classical genres – is an aesthetic fact, not an epistemological quandary. As a composer with stylistic commonalities with the first generation of Black composers (such as R. Nathaniel Dett and Clarence Cameron White) identified by Eileen Southern, Price participated in an aesthetic nationalist movement with precedents in Europe just a few decades before her birth. While the "merging" of "Black" music and "white" classical music was (and still is) considered unique, rare, or strange, Price's application of juba rhythms, varied repetition, and art-song settings of Negro spirituals is little different from Johannes Brahms's arrangements of Hungarian folk dances; Béla Bartók's incorporation of Hungarian tonalities and polyrhythms in his aesthetic; or Wolfgang Amadeus Mozart's evocation of Ottoman *mehterân* bands in the final movement of his fifth violin concerto.

Classical composers have always found inspiration and ideas in folk and popular genres; they were never siloed off from the traditions and trends of their day. Yet, due to our rigid conceptions of race, gender, class, and culture, such practices are typically foregrounded when applied by racially minoritized composers and treated as a conceptual problem. This text, however, relishes the stylistic and aesthetic insights Price's style provides for our understanding of idiomatic diversity in American classical music specifically and classical music more broadly.

The Cambridge Companion to Florence B. Price is not unique in this regard; musicologists such as Brown, Helen Walker-Hill, Marcia J. Citron, Mildred Denby Green, Barbara Garvey Jackson, and more have challenged our understanding of classical music because of *whom* these scholars studied and *how* they studied them. Through their various publications, upon which subsequent generations of scholars, performers, and scholar-performers have built, these women asserted that the picture of the

American musical landscape was incomplete without Price, her contemporaries, and antecedents.

Their output rewrote the narrative of women's significance in the American concert tradition and in some cases fed the foundations of Price's posthumous legacy. For Brown, Walker-Hill, Green, and Jackson, in particular, assembling and recovering the building blocks of Price's biography were essential – work that we, as the editors of this companion, are fortunate to build on, rather than redo. Like our predecessors, we continue to engage the broader cultural and aesthetic questions that can be answered and should be explored through her music. Whether drawing upon elements of her biography for interpretations or centering African American music aesthetics in discussion of her works, Price scholarship thrives when the scholarly tools used are multidimensional – just like Price's style. In a time when studying biography and historical context may seem less than thrilling, it remains an essential element in studies of composers, as it provides the launch pad for the exciting, illuminating facets of a person's creative output.

It is also especially urgent in the work on minoritized composers, who are either under-documented, have archival materials that remain unpublished, or are relegated to "the first," as Price was initially. Studying biography does not mean absorption of material; it means the continued pursuit of verification of detail and observation when new or conflicting information appears. Cultural, semiotic, and analytic theorizing is not twisting material for one's own sake; it is considering how compositions can enhance our knowledge about style, culture, and the time in which those ideas were crafted.

This book is a reminder of the importance of studying composers from the angle of biography, cultural and social context, and semiotic analysis, simultaneously. We need, as Brown notes, "to *know* about these women ... to understand something of the prevailing ideologies and social contexts in which they created," and, might we add, to understand the theoretical, cultural, and personal significance of their works.[3]

And now, here we are. Across the fourteen chapters of this volume, authors from an array of intellectual and artistic backgrounds – cultural history, musicology, music theory, music therapy, performance, and social activism – have examined Price's multifaceted life and melting-pot practice through perspectives that value all that she was and all that she did. While Price may have wished for Koussevitzky to listen only to her music, not to society's prejudices and preconceptions around her Black womanhood, the authors here choose to recognize issues of race and gender as ongoing points of navigation and negotiation for Price, and as necessary intersectional dimensions to consider in the study of her trajectory. Their goal is not to reduce Price to her identity but to enlarge our capacity to hear the vitality of her compositional voice.

Thus, in the vein of other studies on Black women's intellectual histories, the authors of this companion have shown how Price's musical pursuits and ideas were shaped by a life "lived at the crossroads of race, gender, and justice."[4] With overlapping points of focus, throughout the volume, on historiographical unsilencing,[5] musical analysis, and sociocultural dynamics, each author has pushed Price scholarship into a new era, benefiting immensely from the scholarly and creative interventions and innovations that came before.

In Part I ("Archives and Sources"), Samantha Ege, Carlene J. Brown and C. E. Aaron, and Louise Toppin show how the study of biography can highlight and rectify historical gaps and archival silences. Ege opens with a critical analysis on how to "hear" Price's presence in the archive; Brown and Aaron use Rae Linda Brown's search for Price to highlight the limits and possibilities of the archive and the importance of oral history; and Toppin shows the depth of detail in the archive on the United States' Black concert tradition.

Part II ("Genre and Style") looks like a typical analysis section, but each author thoroughly integrates aspects of cultural context, analysis, and theory in their chapter. Jane Forner and Ellie M. Hisama explore new and community-oriented analytic approaches to Price's music. Minnita Daniel-Cox weaves Price's biography into her analysis of the composer's art songs, focusing on settings of poetry by Paul Laurence Dunbar, Langston Hughes, and Price herself. Elektra V. Carter situates Price's concert spirituals within Negro-spiritual performance, study, and theorization explored by Price's contemporaries and modern-day pedagogues.

Gwynne Kuhner Brown and Joe Williams use music analysis and Black feminist theory in their discussion of Price's solo keyboard works. Katharine Uhde and R. Larry Todd place Price's violin fantasies and second violin concerto in conversation with the stylistic and technical precedents of her contemporary, Clarence Cameron White; and Alexandra Kori Hill continues the discussion with a focus on Price's use of African American idioms in her concertos and chamber works. Douglas W. Shadle's chapter closes this section, offering a summary of Price's symphonies and tone poems that provides a rich, comprehensive narrative of her orchestral writing.

Part III ("Community and Reception") is squarely within the arena of social and cultural analysis, beginning with Rae Linda Brown's essay on Harry T. Burleigh's impact on Price and her contemporaries. Next is Elizabeth Durrant's Black feminist analysis of the working relationship between Price, Marian Anderson, and Margaret Bonds, followed by Lucy Caplan's perceptive look at the Black press as a method of recognition, preservation, and remembrance. Tammy L. Kernodle closes the volume with a linchpin: Price was never forgotten, and the work of past and present generations should serve as a model to retain and renew her memory from this point forward.

Revealed across these chapters is the reality that Price scholarship is a communal endeavor and must continue to take shape as such. As the gender studies scholar Katherine McKittrick reminds us, "when we are doing our very best work, we are acknowledging the shared and collaborative intellectual praxis that makes our research what it is."[6] On the one hand, this perspective is at odds with the territorial nature of academia, which asserts expertise by diminishing that which came before. On the other hand, this complements the ways in which Price's legacy has reached us today. Communities, especially those from underrepresented backgrounds, are what helped reverse Price's inaudibility and invisibility in mainstream concert halls and music classes. Communities are what countered the impact of gatekeepers such as Koussevitzky and others. And communities are what will sustain the groundswell of interest in Price today.

So, what does it look like for new research to remain in dialogue with the past; to express evolving knowledge in a creative duet with the intellectual genealogies undergirding these paths; to evince a melting pot of inspiration over siloed discourses? As the coeditors of this volume, we hope that our readers identify in *The Cambridge Companion to Florence B. Price* one such example.

Notes

1. The WPA was the Works Progress Administration, launched in 1935 and renamed Work Projects Administration in 1939.
2. Florence Price to Serge Koussevitzky, July 5, 1943, box 50, folder 4, Serge Koussevitzky Archive, Music Division, Library of Congress, Washington, DC.
3. Rae Linda Brown, *The Heart of a Woman: The Life and Music of Florence B. Price* (Urbana: University of Illinois Press, 2020), 2 (emphasis in original).

4. Mia Bay, Farah J. Griffin, Martha S. Jones, and Barbara D. Savage, "Introduction," in *Toward an Intellectual History of Black Women*, edited by Mia Bay, Farah J. Griffin, Martha S. Jones, and Barbara D. Savage (Chapel Hill: University of North Carolina Press, 2015), 1.
5. Brittney C. Cooper writes about "historiographical silences" in *Beyond Respectability: The Intellectual Thought of Race Women* (Urbana: University of Illinois Press, 2017), 123.
6. Katherine McKittrick, *Dear Science and Other Stories* (Durham, NC: Duke University Press, 2021), 31.

PART I

Archives and Sources

Respect the materials. Respect the voice.
 I would love for people to really understand the importance of respecting the composer's voice ... to be curious and ask questions and really try to understand it from a different perspective. And if you don't – if you can't get those answers – go directly to the publisher or the source materials and try to find an answer.

It is so important that when you're approaching any underrepresented composer, any composer of color, that you look at them with curiosity ... wanting to understand who they are as a person, and who they are on paper.
 —Nicole Jordan, principal librarian of the Philadelphia Orchestra

1 Listening for Florence "Bea" Price

SAMANTHA EGE

> Musicians are part of the political and cultural ethos of their time. To claim that they as individuals transcend it is nonsensical. They are also artists; the best of them are on a constant quest to refine their craft, create meaning and beauty, and communicate to those willing to listen, read or see. If they are successful, the art forms they create will be part and parcel of the times in which they live and also contain an element of universality that speaks to generations and cultures beyond their immediate context.
> —Farah Jasmine Griffin, *In Search of Billie Holiday* (2001)[1]

> I feel deeply thankful for progress, but satisfaction – no, not satisfaction. I am never quite satisfied with what I write. I don't think creators ever are quite satisfied with their work. You see there is always an ideal toward which we strive and ideals, as you know, are elusive. Being of the spiritual essence they escape our human hands, but lead us on, and I trust, upward in a search that ends, I believe, only at the feet of God, the One Creator, and source of all inspiration.
> —Florence B. Price (1936)[2]

When Florence B. Price passed away on June 3, 1953 (only two months after her sixty-fifth birthday), the lack of ceremony around such a momentous loss to the art world – that is, few obituaries in the local or national press, no publicized funeral, and no headstone for her burial site at Chicago's Lincoln Cemetery – belied her political and culture-making impact. It was in no way a measure of the immense influence she exerted as a Black female composer operating in the pre-civil-rights epoch of the early twentieth century. Even Price's death certificate gave no indication of the wondrously creative life she had once led. In the box that read "USUAL OCCUPATION (Give kind of work done during most of working life, even if retired)," the hospital's informant wrote "HOMEMAKER." And in the box next to it, headed "KIND OF BUSINESS OR INDUSTRY," the response simply stated, "HOME."[3] The bluntness of these words, harshened by their capitalized spellings, shunted Price's once dynamic musical life into a narrative of quiet, walled-in, and stereotypically female domesticity. In fact, it seemed to foreshadow the ways in which various institutions – from the classical mainstream performance sphere to the academy – would similarly enact bold and blunt negations of Price's legacy.

In the years that followed her death, Price was actively unremembered in ways that served, as Kira Thurman unpacks, "to maintain certain kinds of public memories."[4] And by "certain kinds" Thurman means the Eurocentric and androcentric lineages of the classical tradition, which Loren Kajikawa identifies as the "'possessive investment' in classical music that perpetuates, or is at least complicit with, white supremacy."[5] It was this "act of forgetting," Thurman argues, "that made it possible for listeners to feel a sense of discovery and novelty each time a Black musician performed on stage."[6] The same extended to Price as a composer and the tedious "discovery" discourse that patterned the mainstream press coverage of her twenty-first-century revival. As Tammy L. Kernodle further elaborates in Chapter 14, this discourse repackaged revelatory personal discoveries of Price's life and music as a dominant cultural narrative that overlooked more than half a century of Price's classical music champions – Marian Anderson, Abbie Mitchell, Etta Moten, Margaret Bonds, Leontyne Price, Grace Bumbry, Helen Walker-Hill, Althea Waites, Rae Linda Brown, Karen Walwyn, Louise Toppin, Maria Thompson Corley, William Chapman Nyaho, Michelle Cann, Artina McCain, Leah Claiborne; the list goes on. These histories omitted from the dominant narrative of Price's revival attest to the very deliberate act and determined effort of Black unremembrance in the wider public sphere.

With significantly less pernicious motive, however, Price's legacy was also affected by the dwindling of her intimate circle of similarly musical Black female practitioners of her generation – Race women (as I identify them) – in other words, Black female thought leaders who worked in service of their communities. First, there was Estella C. Bonds, the mother of Margaret Bonds and a builder of Black classical communities, who, upon Price's 1927 move to Chicago, was one of the first local musicians to introduce the newly arrived composer to the city's vibrant Black concert scene. Then, there was Maude Roberts George, a Black society woman, soprano, and civic leader. George served presidential terms in the National Association of Negro Musicians (NANM) and the Chicago Music Association (CMA); Price belonged to both. Entwining with the musical activities of club life, George also assiduously documented Price's activity in the nationally prominent Black periodical *The Chicago Defender* and, furthermore, underwrote the cost of Price's 1933 symphonic debut with the Chicago Symphony Orchestra. However, with the Bonds mother-and-daughter duo relocating to New York City in 1939 and George withdrawing from public life soon after and passing away in 1943, it is unsurprising, as Rae Linda Brown observes, that through the decade that followed "Price's name appears less frequently in the *Chicago Defender* as a composer and almost never as a performer."[7] Not only was Price without two of her most stalwart advocates in the last decade of her life, but ill health, coupled with a retiring (i.e., introverted) personality, also compounded the difficulties she faced in keeping her name afloat.

Indeed, this aspect of Price's narrative is shrouded in complexity and paradox; she is simultaneously unremembered and upheld, silenced and sounded, Columbus-ed (i.e., discovering that which is already there) and counterclaimed. Thus, to find Price in it all, I return to the informant's language, re-interrogating their designation of Price as "HOMEMAKER" and their ascription of Price's industry as "HOME." Doing so recalls an image in the Price archives of the University of Arkansas, Fayetteville, that shows the composer in her later years, at her summer home – a bungalow in a historically Black locale on the outskirts of St. Anne, Illinois – where she was known to write, rest, and escape the bustle of the city. There, she is seated at the grand piano with an orchestral score splayed across the instrument's desk as she pencils in ideas and revisions (Fig. 1.1). The photograph shows that home, for Price, also encompassed the political and cultural realms that she inhabited, realms that she wrote into her scores, generating artistic commentaries on her social environment. It exhibits Price as a world-maker in her insatiable pursuit of an ever-elusive artistic truth.

If the Oxford English Dictionary defines a "homemaker" as "a person who runs his or her household; one skilled at domestic tasks; a housewife or househusband," then this photograph additionally evinces Price *at home* in the network of race-proud, gender-conscious Black women, whose leadership nurtured Chicago's civically grounded Black concert scene (i.e., "a person who *runs* . . . her household"). It shows her *at home* in the taught conventions of the Western classical tradition and vernacular potentials of a national school of music (i.e., "one skilled at *domestic* tasks" [domestic: "existing, occurring, or produced inside a particular region or country"]). It further displays her *at home* in the era of the Black Chicago Renaissance and wedded (both de facto and de jure) through the intersections of race, gender, class, and geography to the political and cultural conditions of her milieu (i.e., "a *housewife*").[8] And today, we find her *at home* in a new era of recovery, rendering our work – as listeners, readers, performers, scholars, theorists, and fans – a form of house*keeping*. In search of Price, then, I treat "HOME" and "HOMEMAKER" as launch pads for digging deeper into the composer's past and into the implications for our present.

Figure 1.1 Florence Price pictured composing at the piano in her summer house in St. Anne, Illinois. Photographs Florence B. Price Family, ca. 1910–1950, Personal Materials, 1905–1953, series I, box 2, folder 2, Florence Beatrice Smith Price Papers Addendum (MC 988a), Special Collections, University of Arkansas Libraries, Fayetteville.

Literary and scholarly precedents for this kind of recovery work exist in the Black feminist and womanist texts of Farah Jasmine Griffin's *In Search of Billie Holiday*, Alice Walker's "In Search of Zora Neale Hurston," and Imani Perry's *Looking for Lorraine: The Radiant and Radical Life of Lorraine Hansberry*.[9] Griffin, Walker, and Perry clearly distinguish between the narrative of their own personal discovery and devotion to the protagonists at hand and the project of cultural recovery– of course spurred on by, but not conflated with, the former – that seeks to reconstruct, restore, and rehear lineages and legacies along interpretative lines that assert how the past may inform the present. "In search of" and "looking for" are not modes of Columbus-style exploration, but modes of dialogue. Building on this work, my chapter therefore advances "listening for Bea" as another complimentary mode.

Price's daughter, Florence Price Robinson, explained that Bea is the name she was always known by. The name you know is her professional name. She was always referred to affectionately as BEE [*sic*]. Many who claimed to know her well would say, "Florence and I have been friends for years." Then others would know this was not the case because no close friend ever called her Florence.[10]

In listening for Bea, then, I encourage us to hear Price in a different way: to enact a kind of recovery work – rather than (re)discovery work – that interrogates some of the assumptions or myths around who Price was and what she achieved. I proffer a web of considerations for the realities that lay behind her seemingly more guarded "professional name," behind the surface-level use of "HOMEMAKER" and "HOME," and behind the "rediscovered" Black artist trope. I say "realities" in the plural because what I write here is less a singular, definitive biographical portrait and more a composite of interpretations, evocations, and provocations that engage with the metacognitive act of listening to how we listen. The practice of listening is not an objective sensory act in the slightest. It is a deeply layered and highly politicized experience impacting, both historically and today, on hearings and rehearings, as well as mishearings and unhearings, of Black women's voices. Listening for Bea thus proceeds with this awareness, stepping in and outside of the archives and sources for a balance of closer hearings and broader deliberations.

On Hearing Price Played

And thus your music moved me, thrilled me;
Gently first, in paeans of joy
It swept into my soul.
And then it rose, crescendo on crescendo
Until this very heart of mine
Did surge and strain as anchored ship in storm;
Tossed and billowed and at length o'er flowed
In soothing flood of harmony,
And softly then it spread o'er all
In blessed wealth of soul,
Its benediction sweet.
        —"On Hearing Helen Hagan Play" by Joseph Seamon Cotter, Jr.[11]

In the absence of recordings that capture her speaking voice or her performances at the piano or organ, we come closest to hearing Price through the snippets she afforded journalists in interviews, the theses she advanced in her academic essays, the day-to-day adventures she documented in fragmented diary entries, and the commentaries of her craft, worldview, and personal experiences that she penned in letters – much of which can be found in the home of her Arkansas archives and across collections housed in the Center for Black Music Research at Columbia College, Chicago. Of course, none of these sources capture Price's exact manner of speaking, but this is where her scores enter the frame, as sonic imprints not only of what she wished to say, but of what she wished for us to hear, vividly, as her unequivocal voice. We might, additionally, consider her scores as "sites of cultural memory," to quote Guthrie P. Ramsey, Jr.; and we might further consider the ways in which performance transforms her musical manuscripts – that is, these "sites of cultural memory" – into "living photographs, rich pools of experiences, and a cultural poetics upon which theoretical and analytical principles can be based."[12] I argue that performing Price, or hearing Price played, enacts a transhistorical dialogue that, to reiterate Griffin, allows Price to speak to generations and cultures beyond her immediate context. This is, after all, how Price's music reached me.

To paraphrase the story of my own personal discovery:

I first met Florence Price . . . in the autumn of 2009. I was an undergraduate exchange student at McGill University in Montreal, and as I sat in my professor's early 20th-century music course . . . it became clear these meetings were meant to happen.[13]

Just as the African American poet Joseph Seamon Cotter, Jr., was inspired by the virtuosic piano playing of Price's contemporary Helen Eugenia Hagan – the first Black woman to graduate from the Yale School of Music and the earliest known Black woman to write a piano concerto – so was I by Price's *Fantasie Nègre* No. 1 in E minor, recorded by musicologist-pianist Helen Walker-Hill. Price's *Fantasie* "moved me, thrilled me . . . swept into my soul" and overwhelmed me with a "soothing flood of harmony."[14] As I have written elsewhere:

on hearing the broad and bold opening E minor chord of Price's Fantasie Nègre No 1, my purpose and further potential sounded into existence. The shimmering cascade of notes that followed descended into a lower melody that belonged to the Negro spiritual Sinner, Please Don't Let This Harvest Pass. The tune was unfamiliar but I immediately recognised its poignancy as a song of the enslaved. I was awash in Price's musical palette of classical colourings and folkloric hues.[15]

As first impressions led to repeated listenings of Walker-Hill's recording and my own study of the score, made possible by Walker-Hill's edited collection *Black Women Composers: A Century of Piano Music (1893–1990)*, I came to hear Price's first *Fantasie* as evidence not only of how she articulated voice, but also of how she articulated place, home, and belonging – all of which are prominent motifs throughout her story.

Two years after arriving in Chicago on the wave of the Great Migration that saw thousands of African Americans flee the deadly strictures of the Jim Crow South for the promised lands of the urban North and West, Price wrote *Fantasie Nègre* No. 1 in E minor, completing the work on February 9–10, 1929. Its direct Negro spiritual quotation harbored vestiges of the rural South, while the inscription beneath its title – which read "To My Talented Little Friend, Margaret A. Bonds" – entwined the influence of her new urban environment. This dedication to Bonds signaled Price's growing community and sense of home in Chicago. Furthermore, the work's longer form and more virtuosic writing – in comparison to her earlier, shorter salon-esque works – showed Price engaging musical ideas on a larger scale. In sum, *Fantasie Nègre* symbolized the ways in which these new surroundings imbued Price with the capacity to envision and realize her craft even more expansively.

However, if 1929 was the year of *Fantasie Nègre* – a pivotal moment in Price's upward trajectory to the status of the most prominent Black woman composer of her generation – it was also the year that marked the onset of the Great Depression, which affected Price deeply. Although Price had grown up in Arkansas's Black elite and married a man deemed worthy of her middle to upper social class (the lawyer, Thomas Jewell Price), the years of the decade-long Great Depression hammered home the precarity of Black capital. African American wealth building already had to weather the unstable grounds fomented by centuries of white supremacy. But a widespread economic crisis was enough to turn the smallest cracks into the deepest chasms, and during this period none were more affected than African Americans.

Against this backdrop, Price turned to the home of Estella Bonds. The Bonds South Side abode at 6652 South Wabash Avenue was, as Elizabeth Durrant illustrates in her chapter, a haven, intellectual hub, and creative sanctuary for all in need. It was in and around this space that Price wrote and revised several compositions, such as her Symphony No. 1 in E minor, *Ethiopia's Shadow in America*, Sonata in E minor for solo piano, *Fantasie Nègre* No. 2 in G minor, *Fantasie Nègre* No. 3 in F minor, and *Fantasie Nègre* No. 4 in B minor. The Bonds family home granted Price the financial stability and personal autonomy that, as Kernodle writes more broadly of those whose artistic, intellectual, and community-building work took shape in these spaces, "allowed women to become important agents of black culture and peripherally in the long struggle for racial equality in America." Kernodle asserts:

When we tune our ears to hear beyond clichés, gendered expectations, social conventions and canonic markers, we will discover that the real place of a woman is not only in the home, but also within the groove.[16]

Let us spend a little time listening for Price in the groove of her Chicago, for it is notable that in 1940 Eleanor Roosevelt remarked of the composer, "She is a colored woman and *a native of Chicago*, who has certainly made a contribution to *our* music" (emphasis added).[17] Oblivious to Price's Southern heritage, Roosevelt underscored a Chicago genesis that was at once fictional yet indicative of the efficacy of Price's Midwestern reinvention and acclimation to her adopted city. One question arises, however: Was Price equally at home in the "our" of Roosevelt's "our music" reference? Or was Price an intrinsic outsider made honorary guest by the First Lady's affirmation? In a nation-building project where, from the outset, "manhood and whiteness were the undisclosed, but always assumed, norms of liberal equality" (later to be explicitly codified in law, as Saidiya Hartman notes of a slavery-era United States), Roosevelt's comment invoked the ambivalence of Black female belonging and the precarious conditionality of Black women's equal participation, whether in the concert hall or on the political stage.[18] The First Lady's remarks find a contemporary parallel in the headline for Micaella Baranello's 2018 *New York Times* piece: "Welcoming a Black Female Composer into the Canon. Finally."[19] Here "the canon" becomes a substitute for "our music," while the passive "welcoming" is performed by the undisclosed, but always assumed, norm of white patriarchy. Thus, it is because of Price's ambivalent treatment in the wider national conversation that listening for Bea in her Chicago becomes all the more pertinent an endeavor.

Chicago's racially segregated makeup galvanized an ethos of self-sufficiency and self-help vis-à-vis the iniquities perpetuated by the dominant populace, giving rise to a robust culture of classical music-making and, as a whole, transforming "the Black Belt of racial isolation" into the "Black Metropolis of manifested racial progress," as Christopher Robert Reed puts it.[20] There, in the Black Metropolis of South Side Chicago, Price was actively welcomed. Those who formed the Black classical music community of her South Side locale embraced her as *theirs* without erasing her Great Migration journey. Her creative activity and compositional output both fueled and fed into the Black Metropolis's formation of the New Negro Movement, engendering a Black Chicago Renaissance. This was, as Darlene Clark Hine describes, "a dynamically prolific period of African American creativity in music, performance art, social science scholarship, and visual and literary artistic expression," which spanned from the early decades of the twentieth century to the 1950s.[21] And it was through an array of what Guthrie P. Ramsey calls "community theaters" (in tandem with "sites of cultural memory") – from Maude Roberts George's "News of the Music World" columns in the *Chicago Defender* to the musical patronage of the Black church, from the meetings of NANM and the CMA to the musical soirées of the Bonds salon – that Price both was claimed by and laid claim to a Black classical music inheritance.[22]

On hearing Price played during my studies in Montreal, these were the "living photos, rich pools of experience, and cultural poetics" that I sensed in her *Fantasie Nègre*, suggesting to me a deeper history beneath classical music's normative clichés, expectations, conventions, and canons. Moreover, her music gave me a sense of home and belonging as a Black woman in the classical world.

Coincidentally, it was also around this period that Price's music alerted Vicki and (the late) Darrell Gatwood to a vital history – one that had been nesting, all this time, in their recently purchased and severely dilapidated bungalow outside of St. Anne, Illinois (Fig. 1.2), which had been Price's former summer home. The composer's unplayed grand piano still stood

Figure 1.2 Inside Price's abandoned summer home. Photograph by Timothy G. Nutt (2010). Used by permission of Timothy G. Nutt.

(although it was tragically stolen merely weeks before archivists from the University of Arkansas reached the location). But it seems the Gatwoods heard Price through the ghostly remnants of the abandoned and vandalized property. They came across her handwritten scores – around 300, which were miraculously intact for the most part, in spite of mildew, mold, water damage, and being strewn on the ground by vandalizers. The Gatwoods were particularly attentive to her compositional stamp: Florence B. Price. Rather than dismissing or even disposing of what they saw, the couple subsequently conducted their own investigative work, leading them to establish contact with the Arkansas archivists Timothy G. Nutt and Tom Dillard. As Nutt and Dillard recalled in a subsequent talk, "They [the Gatwoods] told us that the house was full of materials. The things that they had pulled out the most and that they had deemed most significant were the music materials. And so they had gathered them in various suitcases and boxes and so this is the collection that greeted us when we got to their house."[23] Price's name had been unknown to the new owners; the Gatwoods listened and thus her music moved them.

On Reconstructing *Fantasie Nègre* No. 3

> [W]ith these pieces we now can finish this story. We can talk about what a sustained career looks like for an American composer, for a female composer, for an African American composer of the South. So, for somebody who grew up at a time pre-Reconstruction, through the Jim Crow era, to teaching in segregated schools, to her daughters being near lynched, to coming to Chicago and being part of Chicago's music scene and arts scene, to being a nationally recognized composer to this day, is a pretty serious story. And the University of Arkansas Special Collections is going to be the heart of that story.
> —Rae Linda Brown in an interview with James Greeson[24]

In my work as a Black feminist scholar-performer, I assert that the "art of the Black feminist scholar-performer encompasses the conviction that there is a history of classical music (i.e., Western art music) to be told both from a Black woman's vantage point and the subsequent dialogue between research and repertoire."[25] My recordings of Price's music evince this dialogue, which particularly fueled my second album of Price's solo piano music, titled *Fantasie Nègre: The Piano Music of Florence Price*.[26] In the early stages of that project, I envisioned the album opening with the first

Fantasie, recreating for new listeners the experience that I had had a decade earlier, wherein this work served as my window into the dynamic world of Bea. I then wanted to feature the entire set of *Fantasies*: No. 2 in G minor, No. 3 in F minor, and No. 4 in B minor. These works had been recovered from Price's summer home and, due to their unpublished state (unlike the first *Fantasie*), were neither logged nor preserved in any institutional record.

Unlike the second and fourth *Fantasies*, which were fully scored from beginning to end, the third *Fantasie* appeared incomplete, with only two pages visible. Still, Trevor Weston's 2011 reconstruction of Price's Concerto in One Movement at the suggestion of Rae Linda Brown – which was later recorded by pianist Karen Walwyn and the New Black Music Repertory Ensemble under conductor Leslie B. Dunner – encouraged me to see if I, too, could find the missing pieces of yet another pianistic puzzle.[27] I went to the Price archives at the University of Arkansas to locate the works for my *Fantasie Nègre* album.[28]

As I perused Price's handwritten *Fantasies* in the archives, they were everything I hoped they would be: brilliant, soulful, demanding, and rewarding. Each intertwined Black folk idioms with highly rhapsodic writing, blending virtuosity and vernacularity in a way that Katharina Uhde and R. Larry Todd further elaborate on in their contribution to this volume. Across the second, third, and fourth *Fantasies* I could hear Price's "unwavering and compelling faith," as she put it, "that a national music very beautiful and very American can come from the melting pot just as the nation itself has done."[29] Yet, each *Fantasie* was also distinct in character. I noted how No. 1 stood apart from the others with its direct spiritual quotation and folk-dance evocations. No. 2 in G minor seemed far more introspective and capricious; the influence of the German Romantic tradition was undeniable and gave me a glimpse into the more intense and introspective side of Price's compositional personality. As I studied the original and complete version of No. 4 in B minor, I was struck by its colossal and rhapsodic character (which is attenuated in the revisions and abridgments that she made to the work later down the line, as shown in John Michael Cooper's edition for G. Schirmer). The fourth *Fantasie* was a clear forerunner of Price's Concerto in One Movement. There was, however, a significant challenge with the third *Fantasie*, as I could not see any further music beyond the opening two pages of the score.

My process of listening and looking for the remaining sheet music that would, I hoped, complete the piece aligned with that of Saidiya Hartman in her monumental *Wayward Lives, Beautiful Experiments*, where she employs what she describes as "a mode of close narration, a style which places the voice of narrator and character in inseparable relation so that the vision, language, and rhythms of the wayward shape and arrange the text."[30] As a scholar-performer, my method resembled a "mode of close narration" as I imagined Price's subsequent musical ideas after the first two pages of the incomplete score. This process placed me and Price in "inseparable relation" so that the "vision, language, and rhythms" of the composer would shape and arrange my approaches, analyses, and interpretations. It aligned with Nicole Jordan's call, as the principal librarian of the Philadelphia Orchestra, to "respect the materials" and "respect the voice" when working with Price's scores.[31]

I also drew parallels with Imani Perry's *Looking for Lorraine*, which illuminates the life and loves of the playwright and radical intellectual Lorraine Hansberry. Perry describes her book as less a biography and more "a genre yet to be named – maybe a third person memoir," again reiterating the close narrational method of Hartman's description. Like Hartman's, Perry's articulation of her process resonates deeply with mine. Perry asks her reader, rhetorically, "But why did I believe this book ... had to be written?" For Perry, the answer lies in the obvious: "Hansberry was the first Black woman to have her play produced on Broadway and the first Black winner of the prestigious Drama Critics' Circle Award." Indeed, Price's accolade as the first Black woman composer of international renown mirrors the historic rationale to recover more of her life and work. But Perry adds another dimension. "There is something quieter but no less important too," she writes. "In these pages I want to catch a likeness of her to give the reader a sense of the sweet and intimate parts of her: what made her smile and raised her ire, what drove her passions and how she loved."[32] I shared a similar impetus for wanting to present Price's four complete *Fantasie Nègre* compositions for solo piano. Why did I believe the incomplete music had to be located? Well, I believed it would tell me – us – more of the composer's inner life – that is, the multifarious ways in which she existed, mattered, and thrived.

The four *Fantasies* were, to Price, some of her most important compositions. When asked to list her "Worthy unpublished works" amid her symphonies, piano concerto, chamber music, select organ pieces, and a large-scale vocal composition ("The Wind and the Sea"), she wrote "Four Fantasies for Piano."[33] Price did not distinguish between one *Fantasie* or the other; instead, she spoke of them collectively, as if in one breath. And in sounding them all, as she intended, I hoped to catch something of a likeness, as Perry set out to do in looking for Lorraine.

Perry no doubt drew inspiration from Alice Walker's 1975 "Looking for Zora," an essay that captures Walker's intimate historiographical work around the legacy of author and folklorist Zora Neale Hurston. Therein, Walker recounts the process of locating Zora's unmarked grave, demonstrating that in listening closely we may enact a process of collaging the scattered fragments of Black women's inner lives and posthumous resonances, bringing them into context and giving richly textured voice to a past we have yearned to hear.

In her essay, Walker recalls how:

Finding the grave seems positively hopeless. There is only one thing left to do:
"Zora!" I yell as loud as I can . . ., "Are you out here?"
"Zora," I call again, "I'm here. Are you?"[34]

This is how it felt listening for Bea in the missing pages of the third *Fantasie*. To locate the rest of the music, which I believed (or hoped) was simply mixed in with other manuscripts from that part of the archive, I had to call in hope of hearing a response. Moreover, I had to think as Price might have. Just like her other *Fantasies*, she opens the third one with a grandiose minor-key statement, stately tempo, and maestoso character. The second page then leaps into a more dance-like rhythm; her F minor-key solemnity melts into A♭ major-key optimism. But in the final bar, after a descending figuration in the inner voice, the piece stops, cut off in mid momentum by the abrupt end of the page.

Judging by Price's compositional choices in the other *Fantasies*, I expected to find loose pages of music that immediately returned to the original key of F minor, but I could not locate any scores that resembled this pattern. I subsequently discarded that idea in order to hear Price differently, and more accurately. I reexamined the manuscript and realized that there was more to say in the relative major key of A♭. I then looked for pages that continued in this key and found sheets that could plausibly complete the work. There was a string of pages that corresponded in style, key, and mood.

Was this what Price intended as her *Fantasie Nègre* No. 3?

I was in multiple minds about how to proceed with the recording: Was it better to record only the first two pages, leave out the third *Fantasie* altogether, or acknowledge that in the absence of Price's own authoritative voice to correct my work I would have to trust my own? I decided on the latter. After my research trip to Arkansas, I went back home, eager to play through the third *Fantasie* on my own piano. As I sat at my instrument, sounding the notes, shaping the phrases, and feeling history come to life under my fingers, I heard Bea's voice so clearly. The written record had told me Price's third *Fantasie* was incomplete, but in listening for Bea in the home of her Arkansas archives, I heard otherwise.

Coda

In recounting my individual relationship with Price's music and the process of my reconstructive work on the third *Fantasie*, I hope to have exemplified ways of parsing the journeys of personal discovery and cultural recovery. What I found in the archives – that is, what was new to me – was already there. For this reason, the BBC's coverage of my recovery work continues to sit uncomfortably. To explain, an article with the headline "Florence Price: Forgotten Work by Pioneering Composer Rediscovered" – note the recurrence of the "rediscovery" trope – used the pull quote "gathering dust" from a sentence that read, "She [Ege] quickly found pages of manuscript that seemed [to] match the first two sheets of *Fantasie Nègre* No. 3 just 'gathering dust' in a box on a shelf."[35] "Gathering dust" were not my words but the words of the reporter who interviewed me for this piece. Their depiction made me seem like an Indiana-Jones-style explorer, wading into a mysterious room, finding tattered sheets on a shelf draped in cobwebs and cloaked in dust. Well, that is not the reality of the institutional archive. The Gatwoods, the Arkansas archivists, and Rae Linda Brown had already done the exploratory groundwork and necessary organizing of the materials. All I had to do was look at what was already there in the dust-free folders of the Price materials and listen, not for my own individual story, but for the story of the artist – for the narratives, experiences, and encounters she communicated through her art forms.

I close by juxtaposing the image of the run-down summer home, obscured by overgrowth, and the image of Price and her daughter Florence Louise admiring the tenderly cultivated hydrangeas that once hugged the bungalow's external wall (Figs. 1.3 and 1.4). Across these time frames, we are reminded that the house was always there. It did not come into existence upon being identified by the Gatwoods in 2009. It was always there. Furthermore, Price's homemaking endowed us with a rich archive, now maintained by the University of Arkansas's upkeep. And so, our recovery work cannot stop at the juncture of personal discovery, as the subsequent contributions to this volume show. Each chapter that follows enacts the recovery work of tending to the overgrowth of assumptions and myths that obscure our understandings of Price's life and hinder our

Figure 1.3 Outside Price's abandoned summer home. Photograph by Timothy G. Nutt (2010). Used by permission of Timothy G. Nutt.

Figure 1.4 Florence Price and her daughter Florence Louise Robinson admiring flowers outside the summer house in St. Anne, Illinois. Photographs Florence B. Price Family, ca. 1910–1950, Personal Materials, 1905–1953, series I, box 2, folder 2, Florence Beatrice Smith Price Papers Addendum (MC 988a), Special Collections, University of Arkansas Libraries, Fayetteville.

hearings of her music. Price's upward search and striving for the ever-elusive creative, intellectual, and spiritual ideals that impelled her craft inevitably ended with her death. But the recovery of so many previously unlocated materials enables us to carry on the composer's legacy with renewed purpose and intent, as Rae Linda Brown remarked in her keynote speech at the 2015 Florence Price Music Festival at the University of Arkansas: "And so, the end of this story is now really the beginning ... It is, however, for the next generation of music scholars to delve through the music, to study it, to perform it, to record it, and to tell the rest of the story."[36]

From here, a new era of Price scholarship proceeds, indebted to all that came before.

Notes

1. Farah Jasmine Griffin, *In Search of Billie Holiday: If You Can't Be Free, Be a Mystery* (New York: Random House, 2001), 132–133.
2. Goldie M. Walden, "Keep Ideals in Front of You; They Will Lead to Victory, Says Mrs. Florence B. Price," *Chicago Defender*, July 11, 1936, 7.
3. Medical Certificate of Death, box 1, folder 20, Florence Beatrice Smith Price Papers Addendum (MC 988a), Special Collections, University of Arkansas Libraries, Fayetteville.
4. Kira Thurman, *Singing Like Germans: Black Musicians in the Land of Bach, Beethoven, and Brahms* (Ithaca, NY: Cornell University Press, 2021), 14.
5. Loren Kajikawa, "The Possessive Investment in Classical Music: Confronting Legacies of White Supremacy in U.S. Schools and Departments of Music," in *Seeing Race Again: Countering Colorblindness across the Disciplines*, edited by Kimberlé Crenshaw, Luke Charles Harris, Daniel Martinez HoSang, and George Lipsitz (Berkeley: University of California Press, 2019), 156.
6. Thurman, *Singing Like Germans*, 14.
7. Rae Linda Brown, *The Heart of a Woman: The Life and Music of Florence B. Price* (Urbana: University of Illinois Press, 2020), 238.
8. Quotations from Oxford English Dictionary online, accessed July 27, 2025, www.oed.com. Emphasis added.
9. Originally published under Alice Walker, "In Search of Zora Neale Hurston," *Ms. Magazine* (1975): 74–89; Imani Perry, *Looking for Lorraine: The Radiant and Radical Life of Lorraine Hansberry* (Boston, MA: Beacon Press, 2018).
10. Florence Price Robinson to Mary Hudgins, October 14, 1967, box 1, folder 7, Florence Beatrice Smith Price Collection (MC 988), Special Collections, University of Arkansas Libraries, Fayetteville.

11. This is the final stanza in Cotter's two-verse poem. Joseph Seamon Cotter, Jr., "[60] On Hearing Helen Hagan Play," in *Joseph Seamon Cotter, Jr.: Complete Poems*, edited by James Robert Payne (Athens, GA: University of Georgia Press, 1990), 99.
12. Guthrie P. Ramsey, Jr., *Race Music: Black Music Cultures from Bebop to Hip-Hop* (Berkeley: University of California Press, 2003), 4.
13. Samantha Ege, "Their Music Lit a Fire in Me: Three Pioneering Composers Gave Pianist Samantha Ege a Sense of Place and Purpose," *The Guardian*, November 19, 2021, G2, 11.
14. Helen Walker-Hill and Gregory Walker, *Kaleidoscope: Music by African-American Women*, Leonarda, 1995, LE 339.
15. Ege, "Their Music Lit a Fire in Me," 11.
16. Tammy L. Kernodle, "A Woman's Place: The Importance of Mary Lou Williams' Harlem Apartment," NPR, September 12, 2019, https://tinyurl.com/y7tkdrhy.
17. Eleanor Roosevelt, "My Day: Visiting WPA Music Projects," *Atlanta Constitution*, November 15, 1940, 38.
18. Saidiya V. Hartman, *Scenes of Subjection: Terror, Slavery, and Self-Making in Nineteenth-Century America* (New York: Oxford University Press, 1997), 118.
19. Micaela Baranello, "Welcoming a Black Composer into the Canon. Finally." [Originally titled "Once Overlooked, Now Rediscovered"], *New York Times*, February 9, 2018, https://tinyurl.com/4c633sw4.
20. Christopher Robert Reed, *The Rise of Chicago's Black Metropolis, 1920–1929* (Urbana: University of Illinois Press, 2011), 6.
21. Darlene Clark Hine, "Introduction," in *The Black Chicago Renaissance*, edited by Darlene Clark Hine and John McCluskey, Jr. (Urbana: University of Illinois Press, 2012), xv.
22. Ramsey, *Race Music*, 4.
23. Tom Dillard and Timothy G. Nutt (undated), OHV, Major Figures in American Music, Oral History of American Music, in the Music Library of Yale University, https://archives.yale.edu/repositories/7/archival_objects/3538627.
24. Rae Linda Brown and Jim Greeson, "Dr. Rae Linda Brown on the Florence Price music discovery," Vimeo (July 2014), https://vimeo.com/99915411.
25. Samantha Ege, "The Art of the Black Feminist Scholar-Performer," *American Music* 40, no. 4 (2022): 487.
26. Samantha Ege, *Fantasie Nègre: The Piano Music of Florence Price*, Lorelt (Lontano Records Ltd.), 2021, LNT 144.
27. New Black Music Repertory Ensemble, Leslie B. Dunner, Karen Walwyn, *Florence B. Price: Concerto in One Movement and Symphony in E Minor*, Albany Records, 2011, TROY1295.
28. Ege, *Fantasie Nègre*.

29. Florence Price to Serge Koussevitzky, July 5, 1943, box 50, folder 4, Serge Koussevitzky Archive, Music Division, Library of Congress, Washington, DC.
30. Saidiya Hartman, *Wayward Lives Beautiful Experiments: Intimate Stories of Social Upheaval* (London: Profile Books, 2019), xiii–xiv.
31. Nicole Jordan, principal librarian of the Philadelphia Orchestra, interview with the coeditors on July 24, 2023.
32. Perry, *Looking for Lorraine*, 1 and 8.
33. Correspondence, 1929–1953, series I, box 1, folder 1, Florence Beatrice Smith Price Papers Addendum (MC 988a), Special Collections, University of Arkansas Libraries, Fayetteville.
34. Walker, "In Search of Zora Neale Hurston," 8.
35. Mark Savage, "Florence Price: Forgotten Work by Pioneering Composer Rediscovered," BBC News, March 8, 2021, www.bbc.co.uk/news/entertainment-arts-56322440.
36. Carlene J. Brown, afterword to Rae Linda Brown, *The Heart of a Woman*, 242.

2 | Hidden Figures and Black Music Historiography

Florence Price's Story and Rae Linda Brown's Scholarship

CARLENE J. BROWN AND C. E. AARON

> There are a lot of contradictions in this story. . . . I had some facts, but the facts didn't make sense, given the time period. There was a story and I needed to tell it. I needed to bring her from invisibility to visibility and document her life and her music so that her legacy could be a lived legacy. She needed to be included in the history books.
> —Rae Linda Brown, personal papers on Florence Price

The 2016 film *Hidden Figures* tells the true story of three brilliant Black women mathematicians – Katherine Goble Johnson, Dorothy Vaughan, and Mary W. Jackson – who made history as part of the team that launched astronaut John Glenn into orbit. Based on Margot Lee Shetterly's book *Hidden Figures: The American Dream and the Untold Story of the Black Women Who Helped Win the Space Race*, the film offers several themes and storylines that were prominent in the early 1960s. Race, gender, and discrimination shape the narrative around the extremely bright and talented minds of Johnson, Vaughan, and Jackson.

I [Carlene J. Brown] went to see the film at the theater with my sister, the distinguished Florence Price scholar Rae Linda Brown. The movie clearly resonated with her strongly; she was very quiet as we left the theater. When I asked her what she thought, the only comment she offered was that the movie was profound and spoke directly to her.

In reading Rae Linda's manuscript for what would become the first monograph on Florence Price, it became clear that Rae Linda saw much of Price's life story in the "hidden figures" of the film. Like Johnson, Vaughan, and Jackson, Price was highly educated and brilliant, yet was held back from achieving fame on a national level because of what she also understood as her "two handicaps – those of sex and race."[1] The "handicaps" – that is, sexist and racist systemic barriers – did not hinder any of these Black women's impressive accomplishments, but it did hamper their opportunities and their due credit.

The term "hidden figures" has entered into scholarship within Black studies to succinctly refer to the unseen and boundaried careers of Black professionals, especially within the circles of composers from the United States. For example, in referencing Rae Linda Brown's and Barbara Garvey Jackson's scholarship on Price's legacy, Douglas W. Shadle writes, "It's the kind of story that I think is all too rare in classical music, where we see the composers as these hidden figures occupying secretive spaces."[2] The irony is, however, that during her lifetime Price was truly seen and heard in the Black churches, concert halls, and living rooms through the early twentieth-century Black Chicago Renaissance era. Yet, at the same time, within the white mainstream she was hidden – kept from reaching her highest ideals as an established composer for national symphony orchestras. With her death came the "invisibility" of her music. Because most of her works were not published, nor were they formally archived, her music was largely distributed among family and friends, stacked away: hidden.

Uncovering the legacy of Florence Price, un-hiding this figure of Western art music, involves tracing the contributions of several dedicated scholars, most notably Mildred Denby Green, Barbara Garvey Jackson, Althea Waites, and Rae Linda Brown. This chapter shows that the art of Black music historiography is well documented in their scholarship and writings. We begin our examination by first contextualizing Brown's contributions within the lineage of Black music histories that preceded hers, several of which had mentioned Price, but few of which made her the main focus of their scholarship. We then narrate how Brown first encountered Price and discuss which resources she employed in beginning to fill the gap of research surrounding Price, especially the archives at the University of Arkansas established by Price's daughter, Florence Louise Price Robinson, in collaboration with Barbara Garvey Jackson. We also chronicle Brown's work advocating for Price's music, ensuring its place in the concert hall as well as the archive.

Finally, we outline in greater detail Brown's methodologies for studying Price, noting how she combined the traditional academic tools used to study pre-1600 European music with the communally based tools of relationship building. With this combination, Brown was able to reconstruct from the gaps in written documentation and interweave the personal memories of Price's loved ones to create the first-ever full-length biography of Florence Price, *The Heart of a Woman*. Brown's work demonstrates that to uncover the hidden figures of Black music history one must consider the central role of trust and rapport within Black communities. Thus, through the lens of her scholarship, we examine the art of Black music historiography, using her and her work as a case study for how to construct the life story of a hidden figure like Price.

Price Scholarship in the New Negro Era

In 1936, three systematic studies of Black music in the United States were published and each mentioned Florence Price. One was an article-length treatment in *Etude* magazine by composer Shirley Graham Du Bois;[3] the second, a brief monograph by cultural critic Alain Locke;[4] and the third, a substantial volume by pianist Maud Cuney-Hare.[5] These publications fell within a few years of Price's success with her Symphony No. 1 in E Minor, the first known symphony written by a Black American woman, and among the first three notable symphonies written by Black American composers (the other two being by her peers William Grant Still and William Levi Dawson). Price's symphony won the top Wanamaker Prize in 1932, garnering her widespread recognition.

Cuney-Hare's mention of Price in *Negro Musicians and Their Music* is the briefest of the three. The aim of the text seems to have been the inclusion of as many figures in Black American music-making as possible, favoring breadth over depth. Price features in Cuney-Hare's listings of the winners of various prizes, so her name appears in two places: her Holstein second prize in 1926 for *In the Land O' Cotton* and her 1927 piece *Memories of Dixieland*; and the aforementioned Wanamaker Award for her symphony in E minor. Cuney-Hare also mentions Price's training at New England Conservatory, where Cuney-Hare herself had trained as a pianist.[6]

Mentions of Price are thus brief and surface-level, but Cuney-Hare's framing of her study merits more discussion. In her preface she writes,

> The Negro, a musical force, through his own distinct racial characteristics has made an artistic contribution which is racial but not yet national. Rather has the influence of musical stylistic traits termed Negro, spread over many nations wherever the colonies of the New World have become homes of Negro people. These expressions in melody and rhythm have been a compelling force in American music – tragic and joyful in emotion, pathetic and ludicrous in melody, primitive and barbaric in rhythm.[7]

Cuney-Hare attributes specific rhythmic and melodic features to "distinct racial characteristics." Her description references the suggestion that Afro-diasporic musics have distinct traits similar to those of African musics, a suggestion which is not problematic in itself. But her analysis does not thread such a needle of nuance, opting instead to paint Black musics in a positive light with a rather broad brush, suggesting "a distillation of these attributes in ideal form, a generative principle, an essence."[8]

Guthrie P. Ramsey, Jr., in discussing the essentialism prevalent in early twentieth-century Black music historiographies, writes, "When black writers did discuss an African legacy, their work showed how much of the racial pseudo-science of the day they had unknowingly internalized."[9] Cuney-Hare's text certainly internalizes this way of thinking, despite how well-intentioned her arguments are.

Furthermore, Cuney-Hare's euphemistic mention that "the colonies of the New World have become homes of Negro people" elides how exactly most African people came to reside in the Americas, suggesting a desire to avoid the uncomfortable reality of enslavement and its aftermath. As Ramsey notes, she "seem[s] engaged in a precarious balancing act by promoting black achievement and carefully discouraging backlashes from white society, whose negative reactions could collectively frustrate African-American social advancement."[10] Social advancement, in Cuney-Hare's estimation, is brought to fruition by "a rising group of talented composers of color who are beginning to find a listening public," facilitating "the development of an American symphonic, operatic and ballet school led for the moment by a few lone Negro musicians of vision and high ideals." This line of thinking exemplifies Cuney-Hare's alignment with what Ramsey terms "the 'rhetoric of the New Negro,'" writers of which "advanced the ideals and goals that characterized their movement – chief among them economic, social, and cultural equity with white citizens – to be achieved through the creation and dissemination of great works of literary, musical, and visual art."[11] While it is easy to critique Cuney-Hare's argument through twenty-first-century eyes, we cannot forget that she was writing in the era of Jim Crow segregation with a view to bridge the partitioned worlds of Black and white.

The "New Negro" title originates from Alain Locke's anthology of the same name, exemplifying the ideals that Ramsey lists. Locke, like Cuney-Hare, opens his volume with an argument for the importance of African American music for American music at large: "Negro music is the closest approach America has to a folk music, and so Negro music is almost as important for the musical culture of America as it is for the spiritual life of the Negro." He later adds, "the Negro has been the main source of America's popular music, and promises, as we shall see, to become one of the main sources of America's serious or classical music, at least that part which strives to be natively American and not derivative of European types of music." Then he moves into the "racial pseudo-science" discussed by Ramsey, writing, "If Negro music is to fulfill its best possibilities, Negroes must become musical by nurture and not rest content with being musical by nature ... the Negro must look to his musical laurels, and not go to sleep on his great heritage. A great folk music deserves and demands a great classical music." In this passage, Locke not only assumes an inherent, essential musical ability for Afro-diasporic people, but also assumes that skill in an oral music-making tradition transfers automatically to skill in a written one.

When Locke mentions Florence Price, it is to discuss her E-minor symphony alongside the first symphonies of her peers Still and Dawson. But while he praises the latter two for their "symphonic music in Negro idiom," he describes Price's symphony as an example of "the straight classical idiom and form," writing that "Mrs. Price's work vindicates the Negro composer's right, at choice, to go up Parnassus by the broad high road of classicism rather than the narrower, more hazardous, but often more rewarding path of racialism. At the pinnacle, the paths converge, and the attainment becomes, in the last analysis neither racial nor national, but universal music."[12] Leaving aside the impossibility of "universal music," his use of the word "vindicates" paints a sheen on his critical implication that Price did not write "in Negro idiom" because it would have been too difficult for her to do so.[13]

Shirley Graham's discussion of Price's symphony, like Locke's, also discusses the first symphonies of Still and Dawson. However, unlike Locke, Graham does not disparagingly compare Price's symphony with those of her peers. Rather, she lauds the identity of Price herself: "The truth is that Dawson's is the third symphony by a Negro, which in the last four years has been played by a reputable orchestra in this country. And one of these symphonists is a woman! Florence B. Price." Graham's prose carries an undercurrent of excitement on behalf of her race and sex, such as in this passage: "every one of those original [symphony score] sheets which were handled revealed clearly that the composer was one who had been carefully trained, had pored over many scores, and knew instruments. Which stirred the reflection that his [sic] parents could sing only spirituals. Spirituals to symphonies in fifty years! How could they even attempt it?" While Graham shares some underlying beliefs with Cuney-Hare and Locke regarding Black musical essentialism, her purpose differs. Instead of trying to argue Black American music as truly American music, she offers this as a given and seeks to demonstrate "the natural laws of evolution and development" driving "this seeming phenomenon" of Black Americans going from "spirituals to symphonies" in a short period of time.[14] Graham's undeniably positivist approach largely reflects its time.

Price's Legacy in the Post–Civil Rights Era

While glimmers of the positivist approach manifest in later scholarship, Black music studies by the 1970s had largely moved away from that impulse. The focus had shifted, rather, to one Ramsey describes in his foreword to Rae Linda Brown's Price biography as "more compensatory," – that is, "the discovery of *hidden figures* [emphasis added] and the providing of supporting materials that also provided context."[15] In some cases, this maintained an evolutionary paradigm. That paradigm, for example, seems to inform Mildred Denby Green's opening of her 1983 volume *Black Women Composers: A Genesis* – a text significant for containing one of the first biographies of Price. Green begins with a lengthy history of women in Western European art music traditions, and a history of women in the African continental music tradition(s), before a mere two-page summary of what seems to provide the direct context for her book's subject: the musical activity of Black American women.[16] Granted, at the time of her writing, in the early 1980s, feminist musicology was just emerging; perhaps the broad history of "women making music" (per the title of one 1980 volume launching feminist musicology) seemed more necessary at that point than it does to a reader now.

Eileen Southern's 1971 *The Music of Black Americans*, by contrast, demonstrates a more transparent view of the construction of history, creating a narrative that mostly eschews cause and effect language. The first paragraph of the 1983 edition's preface ends with her naming, as foci, "the social, political, and economic forces in American history that helped to shape the development of Negro music and to determine the course it took." "Development" could suggest an evolution paradigm, and "determine" could suggest thinking that is, well, deterministic. However, "helped to shape" nuances the idea somewhat, and naming "social, political, and economic forces" helps resist the notion of a mystic essence of Black music.

Southern's preface offers both a classic mode of thinking and a newer, more poststructuralist model: "Since the immediate purpose of the present work is to record the facts of history, which must precede esthetic and stylistic evaluation, I have not tried to make explicit a definition of black American music." Contra the New Musicologists, whose movement was in its beginnings in the early 1980s (a decade after Southern's landmark text), Southern resists the notion of doing history through criticism, defaulting instead to what New Musicology might construe as an old-fashioned focus on "facts" and documentation. However, there is a progressive strain of thinking in her refusal "to make explicit a definition of black American music." Rather than define, Southern's aim is "gathering together the strands that have made up the fabric of this music in the United States," in order to "provide a solid and useful basis for discussion of the question of its definition." As Southern writes at another point in the preface, "It is not to be assumed that the history of Afro-American music as presented here is necessarily complete." Opting for discussion rather than definition resists a closed canon of Black American music, suggesting instead something far more porous and open-ended.[17]

One additional component of Southern's preface that holds particular importance for understanding Black music studies reads as follows: "I reserve a special measure of gratitude for my fellow Negro musicians, who responded graciously to my requests for biographical information, pictures, and other kinds of data." Southern refers here to stories from people – often classified as ethnography – as, instead, historical data. Similar expressions of gratitude were written by Mildred Denby Green, as she referenced in her preface that she "consulted several prominent musicians for names of black women composers whom they knew either personally or through their music," while thanking composers and their loved ones "who responded to requests for interviews, biographical information, and other materials."[18] In other words, both of these foundational scholars in Black music studies name the importance of oral history to Black music historians, a theme which will be examined more in depth near the end of this chapter.

The Revolutionary Era of Rae Linda Brown

Rae Linda Brown (1953–2017) carried many of the threads of Green, and even more so of her mentor Eileen Southern, to her own understanding of Black music research. Brown was, without question, Price's most dedicated biographer to date; she ultimately spent her entire academic career researching, publishing, and promoting the life story and music of Price. Belonging to the "second generation" of Black American music scholars, Brown synthesized traditional Western European musicological methods with the oral and personal history gathering techniques grounded in the Black community.

Brown's study of Price began when she was a master's degree student in music and African American studies at Yale University in the late 1970s. For her master's thesis, she cataloged the music in the James Weldon

Johnson (JWJ) Memorial Collection of Negro Arts and Letters in Yale's Beinecke Rare Book and Manuscript Library. The collection was itself a compilation of collections, in which Brown discovered a large assemblage of music by African American composers, her first significant research discovery. However, no one had cataloged the music, so no one knew what was there. These composers were *hidden* from the public, within difficult-to-access, uncataloged academic repositories, with little information on them and no recordings to be heard. Some of their music was published but had fallen out of print; however, most was not published at all. Brown received permission to catalog the JWJ Collection, and the project was published in 1982.[19] She shared in her unpublished papers that she "felt a big accomplishment because I was able to reclaim a part of African American history."

While Brown worked on her research project, she came upon a composition by "Florence B. Price," a name that she did not know but which instantly intrigued her. Here was the Symphony No. 3 in "presentation copy" – a beautifully handwritten manuscript, a full symphony by a woman composer about whom she knew nothing about. Included with the symphony was a portrait of Price, with a typewritten and hand-signed note attached: "To Carl Van Vechten with deep appreciation for your untiring interest in a race struggling for a place in the sun."

After completing her master's degree, Brown entered Yale's doctorate program in musicology in 1980. She sought advice about a dissertation topic and was encouraged and mentored by the esteemed musicologist, educator, and author Eileen Southern to pursue a topic related to African American studies. Brown stated that the discovery of Price's symphony "haunted her.... Who was Florence Price, what else did she write? Why did I not know anything about her? How could an African American woman who wrote a symphony, that ended up in one of the most distinguished libraries in all the world, just disappear from our knowledge, from our purview, and understanding of American music?" The quest to uncover the life and music of this pioneer began in earnest for Rae Linda Brown.

Early research toward answering these questions led her almost immediately to Barbara Garvey Jackson's important 1977 article "Florence Price, Composer" in *Black Perspectives in Music*, a publication founded and edited by Brown's mentor, Eileen Southern. Brown contacted Jackson and a long-term friendship began: "Barbara tolerated my million questions, about which we had few answers, but importantly she became a mentor, a friend ... family." Brown considered Jackson's article as seminal in her early investigation of Price's life and work; "it provided the most important information to date on Price's parents and her early years in Little Rock."

Barbara Garvey Jackson (1929–2022) was a professor of music at the University of Arkansas, Fayetteville, from 1954 to 1956 and 1961 to 1991. Jackson was also the founder, editor, and publisher of *ClarNan Editions* (now a subdivision of *Classical Vocal Reprints*), established in 1984, specializing in publishing historic music by women composers. In later years, Brown's relationship with Jackson would prove personally and professionally rewarding as Jackson's press allowed them to ensure Price's music would reach as many artists and scholars as possible.

Jackson shared with Brown what she knew to date on Price, recounting how, in the 1960s, she received an invitation to offer a paper on women composers at the Arkansas State Music Teachers Association. Mary Dengler Hudgins of the Arkansas Historical Society suggested that Jackson include Florence Price, a name that she did not recognize. Hudgins had done preliminary investigations on Price and her family through historical records, and she had traced the career of one of Little Rock's successful alumni to an elementary school in Chicago, Illinois, newly named in Price's honor. At this time, Hudgins was also in contact with Florence Robinson, Price's daughter, who was living in Chicago.

In Jackson's early research, she read passages from newspaper and journal writings referencing Price and developed her own relationship with Florence Robinson. Although they ultimately never met in person, Robinson and Jackson corresponded to the extent that Jackson was able to gain a fuller picture of Robinson's mother.

Through the supportive efforts of both Hudgins and Jackson, Florence Louise Price Robinson (1917–1975) donated her mother's papers to the University of Arkansas, Fayetteville, in 1974. The university states "when [Florence B.] Price died, her orchestral music, most of which was unpublished, was inherited by of [sic] her daughter, Florence Price Robinson. Robinson encountered great difficulty finding performance outlets for her mother's music, which fell into obscurity. . . . The papers consist of correspondence of Price and her daughter, Florence Price Robinson, diary fragments, programs, and photographs."[20] Given Price's early history in Little Rock, Arkansas, the university welcomed the family collection, a significant start of repositories on Price's life and music.

In addition to Jackson's scholarship, Brown also came across Price's work recorded in biographical dictionaries and bibliographies that listed the composer's published teaching pieces for piano and organ and vocal music. But Brown found that Price, along with most African American composers outside of jazz, was omitted from scholarly texts and histories.

In her personal, unpublished papers, Brown wrote: "I started thinking about the invisibility of this black woman, who grew up in the segregated south, yet went on to one of the best music conservatories in the nation [the New England Conservatory of Music], returned to the segregated south, but ended up having her orchestral music performed by a leading American orchestra." She continued, "my role is to write her biography and tell her story, through her music."

Brown decided to focus her doctoral dissertation on the discussion of Price's Symphony in E Minor (1932), the Concerto in One Movement (1934), and the Symphony in C Minor (1940). Her research thus far allowed her to write on American nationalism of the 1930s, the Woman's Symphony Orchestra of Chicago, the WPA orchestras of the 1940s, an overview of American art music in the twentieth century, a brief biography of Price, and a list of her known compositions. She also included issues of race and gender, what type of support Price had as a woman composer, and considerations concerning the social, economic, and political forces that had an impact on the creative endeavors of Black Americans. Through these interconnected lenses, Brown conveyed a deep respect for Price's brilliance as a pianist, organist, composer, mother, wife, and a contributing member of the Black Chicago Renaissance scene of artists in the 1930s and 1940s.

Outlining her process and the challenges for collecting and organizing information on Price, Brown wrote about the glaring void in texts on American music:

If Black musicians were considered, it was in the context of jazz, but not in mainstream American music history. The difficulty in locating available resources is partly to blame for the omission of Afro-Americans from general music histories.... For example, Price is included in some nine books on music or cultural criticism, fifteen articles, three dissertations, and nineteen biographical dictionaries and bibliographies. However, her vast musical output (about 300 [compositions]) remains largely unknown because her scores are scattered throughout the country in libraries and private collections.... Contemporary newspapers, music journals, and black journals, such as the *Crisis* and *Opportunity*, which documented the activities of prominent black Americans, were used for gleaning information on Price's background and, in many cases, were the only sources available to document awards, dates of performances, and reviews.[21]

In summarizing this stage of her research process, Brown wrote:

2 Hidden Figures and Black Music Historiography   37

Gathering data for research in Afro-American music presents certain unique challenges to the researcher for the researcher must use imagination and persistence in seeking out scores and biographical information, rarely found in the most obvious places. For example, much Afro-American music, including the scores of Price, still remains in private collections. This very valuable resource can be quite extensive and may even contain the core repertoire of a notable composer. Access to these collections is a challenge to the researcher, given the personal relationship between the donor and the recipient. Scores and correspondence are not viewed by the owners of these materials as an historical artifact but, rather, as memorabilia. Sensitivity to this fact, however, can yield unexpected rewards.[22]

Brown's dissertation was the first full-scale perspective on Price's life and music and the first dissertation on Black music in the history of Yale's music department. Her dissertation was titled "Selected Orchestral Music of Florence B. Price (1888–1953) in the Context of Her Life and Work." The focus of Brown's dissertation was on Price's music, but Brown knew she had just begun to open the door to finding answers to her many questions: Who and what were the factors that allowed Price to succeed in Little Rock, Arkansas? What became of her parents and her husband? What was the New England Conservatory like for women at the turn of the century, and for those with African heritage? What was the cultural life of Chicago in the late 1920s for African Americans, when most information from the period deals with jazz? How much music did Price write? And most important, where is it? Again, for Rae Linda Brown, this was about reclaiming a part of African American history – which is to say, American history. Part of Price's music was lost, but now found. When edited, it could be performed, recorded, accessible: no longer hidden.

Brown's recovery of Price's music and the path toward understanding Price's life story became a lifelong commitment to this African American woman composer who deserved a place in the canon of American music. Brown was a meticulous researcher, trained as a musicologist by Claude Palisca (1921–2001), an internationally renowned American musicologist who was also head of the Yale University music department. Brown credited Palisca for her ability to "keep digging" for details on Price. Her goal was to revise her dissertation into a full biography of Price, and as she continued her research process Brown was able to track down a few of Price's friends and colleagues in Chicago who held some of her music and their memories. Brown realized that until she was able to find primary sources from Price herself, *oral history* would become central to her uncovering more of Price's life (on which more will be discussed later in this chapter).

Brown's quest for biographical information led her to confer with other musicologists, historians, and librarians at major collections of African American history. Important collections for Brown included the Moorland-Spingarn Collection at Howard University, where she found the first page of Price's Symphony No. 2 in G Minor; the Vivian G. Harsh Research Collection of Afro-American History and Literature at Chicago Public Library, where Brown and her assistants were able to pore over editions of the *Chicago Defender* and Chicago's weekly newspapers; the Detroit Public Library, which held the Michigan WPA Papers; the Chicago Historical Society, which shared with Brown the uncataloged papers of the Chicago Woman's Symphony Orchestra; the Library of Congress, where Brown had unprecedented access to uncataloged materials; and the Arkansas State Library, which supplied Brown with census records, land documents, wills, probate records, and the like, in an age before websites such as Ancestry.com.

Further assisting Brown along the way were historians at the University of Arkansas, who provided Brown with a wealth of information with the necessary cultural and historical context of Arkansas in the late 1800s and early 1900s; Chester W. Williams, dean emeritus and librarian of the New England Conservatory of Music, who found the original handwritten 3x5 index cards from 1906 with Florence Price's three-year course of study, which Brown transcribed because it was in shorthand; Samuel A. Floyd, Jr., at the Center for Black Music Research, a constant source of support to Brown throughout her academic career; and several other Black music centers, such as the Schomburg Center for Research in Black Culture and the E. Azalia Hackley Collection of Negro Music in the Detroit Public Library.[23]

As her research developed, Brown was invited to include articles on Price in *American Music*, *Black Music Research Journal*, *Black Music in the Harlem Renaissance: A Collection of Essays*, the *International Dictionary of Black Composers*, and the *New Grove Dictionary of Music*. She was also the music editor of the five-volume *Encyclopedia of African American History and Culture* and contributed the piece on Price.

In the decades that followed, Brown also focused on editing, publishing, and supporting artists' and ensembles' access to Price's scores. Important to the telling of her story, Brown pushed to have Price's music performed and recorded. This was essential in honoring the legacy and showcasing the gift of Price as a composer. Brown edited several of Price's scores – piano music, art songs, arrangements of spirituals, and a string quartet. Her first published edition was a Price art song, "My Dream," with Hildegard

Publishing. Other editions included Price's vocal music, "The Heart of a Woman," *Five Art Songs*, "I'm Goin' to Lay Down My Heavy Load," and "The Glory of the Day Was in Her Face," all published by Classical Vocal Reprints.

Some of Brown's editions were not published but were offered to professional artists for recording. For example, Price's vocal pieces "Hold Fast to Dreams" and "Sympathy" were recorded by opera singer Louise Toppin in 2000. Classical pianist Althea Waites was the first artist to record Price's piano music – namely, the Sonata in E Minor – in 1987. In addition, Waites's album *Black Diamonds* in 1993 included CD liner notes by Brown. The professional and personal relationship of Waites and Brown was mutually beneficial and impactful in promoting Price's music.

To further advance Price's music into the mainstream, in 1994 Brown wrote to the senior editor of G. Schirmer, Inc., the American classical music publishing company, for their consideration of the Price piano score. Brown wrote:

There is an exceptional amount of interest in Price's award-winning Sonata for Piano in E Minor, written in 1932. This is due, in part, to my edition of the score, now making it accessible for the first time, and in part, the interest has come from the recording of the sonata by pianist Althea Waites. . . . I can assure you that the sonata would do well in your catalog of music by women composers, African American composers, and American composers of piano music.

The response Brown received from William J. Holab, November 22, 1994, stated:

Dear Ms. Brown, Thank you for your letter of November 14, 1994. We are not familiar with Florence Price's work, but would be interested in investigating this further. Could you please send us a score and recording of the Sonata for Piano in E minor. . . . I look forward to hearing from you and to hearing a "new" composer's work.

G. Schirmer Music published Brown's edition of the Piano Sonata in E Minor in 1997. Within the same time frame, Brown began working on the Symphony in E Minor and approached A-R Editions with a proposal for publication of the score. A-R Editions is the publishing vehicle for the American Musicological Society (AMS), which produces a national series of scholarly writings on American music-making titled *Music of the United States of America* (MUSA). In Brown's proposal she informed the editors that while Price was successful in having her vocal music and teaching pieces for organ and piano published, none of her large-scale works (symphonies, concerti, orchestral suites) were published. There was much interest in these latter works, and there were performances by chamber and symphony orchestras in the US. However, no published performing editions (i.e., conductor scores and full parts) existed.

To create these MUSA editions, Brown collaborated with Wayne Shirley, a reference librarian, music specialist, and editor in the Music Division at the Library of Congress in Washington, DC, whom she had met while working on her master's thesis on the James Weldon Johnson Collection. The MUSA/A-R Editions of Florence Price's Symphony No. 1 in E Minor and Symphony No. 3 in C Minor were published in 2008.[24] Brown and Shirley worked from scores written in ink by Price. In addition, Brown wrote the historical preface to the symphonies, a monograph titled *From Behind the Veil: The Music of Florence B. Price* that offered a synopsis of the research Brown had collected on Price, as well as an analysis of each symphony. Brown pursued any avenue available to present the work of Florence B. Price. Whether through academic publications or before a concert hall prior to a performance of a Price work, Brown honored Price whenever and however she could.

So, what did it take for Brown to uncover the hidden figure of Price – and why did it matter to her? As context for Brown's study of Price, one must acknowledge the risk involved in her early scholarship: While Gail Woldu, the first Black woman to achieve a music PhD at Yale, chose a relatively safe topic in Gabriel Fauré, Brown took a much greater chance by studying Price. She had to convince a committee of known scholars in European music history that Price's work was worthy of the time and attention involved in putting a magnifying glass to her compositions. Given the boldness of writing on Price to begin with – an unknown, Black, woman, American composer – there was a "quiet revolution" undertaken within Brown's work (in reference to Samuel Floyd's depiction of Southern as a "quiet revolutionary"). Brown's methods were traditional *and* avant-garde, moving Black historiography forward while building on what came before.

Brown named Southern as a beloved mentor in her book acknowledgments, but even without this direct mention Southern's work is evident in Brown's.[25] Their approaches to their respective academic projects had a great deal of overlap: While Southern got her start specializing in early music, Brown's Yale advisor, Claude Palisca, was also an early music specialist. Early music's dealings with fragments make it a natural complement to the study of Black musics, a notion to which Floyd alludes in his essay on Southern (whose formal training was in Renaissance music) and which Guthrie P. Ramsey, Jr., spells out more clearly in his foreword to Brown's *The Heart of a Woman*.

The rigorous training and tools for studying music of the Renaissance, in Floyd's estimation, enabled Southern's field-defining contribution, *The Music of Black Americans*. According to Floyd, this work, intended as a textbook for a Black music course, came to be when, "encountering a paucity of information in secondary sources, [Southern] was nearly able to skip the preliminary stage of familiarizing herself with secondary material and proceed directly to the research of primary sources."[26] In a similar vein, Ramsey writes that from Palisca Brown "received support and the tools to hear through the silences of history," leading her to "apply the same rigorous standards to Price that Palisca had to his own groundbreaking studies on early music."[27]

Both Brown and Southern applied the traditional methods of Western historical musicology to include Black art as well. Southern and Brown, to be sure, were both revolutionary by the nature of their work. From the 1970s through the 1990s, even among the shifts happening in historical musicology, breaking open the canon to make room for Black excellence in art music was itself revolutionary. Incorporating Floyd's language for Southern thus places Brown within the context of Black music historiography. Southern launched the field of modern Black music studies. She mentored Floyd, and both Southern and Floyd brought Brown into the fold. Brown, in turn, mentored countless scholars like Ramsey and Bill Banfield; and each of those scholars honored this by lifting as they climbed.

To understand Brown's work, one must bear in mind her crucial position within the second wave of Black music scholars. Additionally, one must also understand Brown's own personal context – the "productive bias," to use Guthrie P. Ramsey's phrase,[28] of lived experience that enabled her to see Price more clearly and to gain the trust of Price's community more easily. As the first woman in her family to attend college, as well as the first to complete a PhD, Brown worked for excellence all her life. She was recognized early as a very bright student and reached performance levels in organ and piano. She was, however, often the first and only Black woman to enter each of her professional spaces in academia. To meet that challenge, Brown built up a community of scholars – starting with Black graduate students at Yale Divinity School and Yale's African American Studies department – to help her withstand the intense pressures and difficulties of being a Black woman in academia. However, in many spaces, she stood alone. This isolation as a Black woman in a white, male-dominated field was an important axis on which Brown could connect with Florence Price.

Like Price, Brown received a high caliber of training in her craft, higher than that of many of her peers. And, like Price, Brown had to fight to establish her own legitimacy and worth despite a culture that falsely suggests Black women's lack of worth.

Establishing the discipline of Black music studies was Southern's revolution, and Brown followed in her footsteps, turning on its head perceived notions of what scholarship means. In the work of these luminaries of Black music studies, it becomes clear that robust scholarship comes not just from extensive time in the archives, but retrieval work akin to that of early music studies. In addition, for Black music studies (let alone academic work as a whole), human relationships prove indispensable. The hidden figures of Black art music may or may not have traces in academic archives; however, their presence remains within Black communities. It is only by gaining trust within those communities that one may successfully write Black music histories.

Even within document-based archives, human relationships and communities sometimes leave evidence. One example within Brown's papers is a manila envelope, with numbers and descriptions written in small script in the corner. Those numbers and descriptions correspond with photographs inside the envelope – including film negatives. Those descriptions specified the subjects: one photograph showed Florence Price's daughter and her friends headed for a school dance; another showed Price's smiling preschool-aged grandson. The photographs came from Marion Ross, a family friend of Florence Price – one who was remarkably generous with her memories of the Price family. Ross's name is the final one in Brown's list of Price's loved ones who had spent extended time with her, giving an oral history of Price's life.[29]

As noted earlier, this oral history was indispensable given the absence of physical documentation remaining from Price. Brown writes in the "Sources" section of *The Heart of a Woman*, "The necessary evidence required to write a detailed biography of Florence Price is surprisingly scant. .... Since Price was a devoted single mother who also had a commanding career, she probably had precious little time to sort through and organize her scores, file press clippings, and the like."[30] It is not surprising that people who knew and loved Price would be happy to talk at length with Price's would-be biographer. However, the willingness to give that biographer the originals of those photographs, rather than prints, seems well beyond the granting of interviews: it constitutes material evidence of an unusual level of trust.

Brown also had an unprecedented relationship with Price's living descendants. In the early years of her research, within her letters, Brown and her correspondents lament the difficulty of reaching Price's descendants. Without responses from living descendants, who held the rights to Price's music until 2018, distribution of Price's music would have broken copyright laws, leaving the musicologists and artists who wished to promote her work in a bind.

Later in her correspondence, however, a clear shift happened: Brown had made contact with Price's grandson (the same pictured in Ross's photographs) and went from referring to him formally as Lawrence Robinson to informally as Larry. This shift came with the news that Brown had secured distribution rights for Price's music.[31] This was a significant gift for Brown.

Both the photographs and the copyright permissions indicate the degree of trust that made Brown's work on Price possible. She induced some information from publicly available records: for example, the biographical detail of Price's abusive first marriage has a clear paper trail within Brown's papers. But the visual information about the people and places discussed would have been absent from the book without the trust from Marion Ross and Larry Robinson.

Reflecting on the gifts of trust and rapport with interviewees that allowed her to capture these oral histories, Brown stated in one of her talks:

This rich source for the investigation of Price's music, of which oral history is an integral factor, had been virtually untapped until this study. . . . Many of these folks have since passed on and I want to express my appreciation to them. They gave me personal photographs. They gave me her music – one page at a time. They shared their stories – all personal, some bone-chilling, for they lived and worked in the early 20th c. [sic] segregated America. They were all musicians. Family. And there was information from Lawrence Robinson (Price's grandson), who shared some stories of his own; and Vicki Taylor Hammond and Timothy Taylor (also grandchildren), who gave their blessing to my project. . . . Family.[32]

Price and Brown had in common personal and professional histories (divorced, single parents; support from their communities of friends and colleagues; and prolific, strong work ethics), to the extent that Brown once stated that Price's identity "had intertwined with mine." Both women's lives were cut short before reaching an important pinnacle of success: Price passed away at sixty-five before her first professional trip to Europe to hear a commissioned work; Brown's life ended at sixty-three before her biography on Price was to be published. The threads that have brought Price's music to the forefront of American music, played internationally by renowned orchestras of the world, necessitated primarily an African American perspective and tools to "keep digging" to gain access to the sources and resources of a "hidden" past.

Closing

Before her death, Brown asked me [Carlene] to have her book published and to ask one of her closest friends, music professor and historian Guthrie P. Ramsey, Jr., to edit the book. In essence, Brown trusted that her work, the story of Florence Price, would be handled with care. Ramsey and I understood whose legacies needed to be carried forward, both Florence B. Price and Rae Linda Brown, and the importance of telling their stories. The responsibility of telling these stories well led to my hiring C. E. Aaron as a research assistant to catalog Brown's papers, to make her scholarship accessible to those who would carry forward Brown's work on Price. Together, we [Carlene and Aaron] have worked to help ensure that Rae Linda Brown and her scholarship will not be hidden.

This is how Black women's work is not to be forgotten, hidden, or dismissed. Gifting the stories, the work of Black women to those who will listen, honor, and create new canons that represent Black excellence in the music, must be considered essential to American music history. Price's music is now heard around the world, from solo artists to internationally acclaimed symphony orchestras. Her life story has been published. As we record, perform, and celebrate Price's music, it is time to ask: Who else have we yet to uncover?

Notes

1. Rae Linda Brown, *The Heart of a Woman: The Life and Music of Florence B. Price*, (Urbana: University of Illinois Press, 2020), 186.
2. Arionne Nettles, "Florence Price was one of the greatest composers of the 20th Century. Until recently, she was overlooked," *WBEZ Chicago*, July 21, 2022, www.wbez.org/curious-city/2022/07/21/who-was-florence-price.
3. Shirley Graham, "Spirituals to Symphonies," *Etude* 54, no. 5 (1936): 691–692, 723, 736. The byline appears as Shirley Graham, since she published this article prior to her marriage to W. E. B. Du Bois.

4. Alain Locke, *The Negro and His Music*, Afro-American Culture Series (New York: Arno Press and New York Times, 1936), 1.
5. Maud Cuney-Hare, *Negro Musicians and Their Music*, 1st ed. (1936; repr., New York: Da Capo Press, 1974), 262.
6. Brown, *The Heart of a Woman*, 47.
7. Hare, *Negro Musicians and Their Music*, v.
8. Leo Treitler, *Music and the Historical Imagination* (Cambridge, MA: Harvard University Press, 1989), 89.
9. Guthrie P. Ramsey, Jr., "Cosmopolitan or Provincial? Ideology in Early Black Music Historiography, 1867–1940," *Black Music Research Journal* 16, no. 1 (1996): 24.
10. Ramsey, "Cosmopolitan or Provincial?," 26.
11. Hare, *Negro Musicians and Their Music*, vi and 23.
12. Alain Locke (ed.), *The New Negro: An Interpretation* (New York: Simon & Schuster, 1925), 1, 2, 4–5, 114–115.
13. Brown, *The Heart of a Woman*, 136.
14. Graham, "Spirituals to Symphonies," 691–692.
15. Brown, *The Heart of a Woman*, x.
16. Mildred Denby Green, *Black Women Composers* (Boston, MA: Twayne, 1983), 15–29.
17. Eileen Southern, *The Music of Black Americans: A History*, 2nd ed. (New York: W. W. Norton, 1983), xv, xvi, 44–45, xv.
18. Green, preface to *Black Women Composers*.
19. Rae Linda Brown, *Music, Printed and Manuscript, in the James Weldon Johnson Memorial Collection of Negro Arts and Letters: An Annotated Catalog* (New York: Garland, 1982).
20. University of Arkansas, "New Recording Features First Major Female African-American Composer," *Arkansas News*, January 18, 2018, https://tinyurl.com/294y6k72.
21. Rae Linda Brown, "Selected Orchestral Music of Florence B. Price (1888–1953) in the Context of Her Life and Work" (PhD diss., Yale University, 1987), 5–6.
22. Brown, "Selected Orchestral Music of Florence B. Price," 6.
23. Ibid., 8.
24. Rae Linda Brown and Wayne Shirley, eds., *Florence Price: Symphonies Nos. 1 and 3* (Middleton, WI: A-R Editions, 2008), 19.
25. Brown, *The Heart of a Woman*, xvii.
26. Samuel A. Floyd, "Eileen Jackson Southern: Quiet Revolutionary," in *New Perspectives on Music: Essays in Honor of Eileen Southern*, edited by Josephine Wright and Samuel A. Floyd, Detroit Monographs in Musicology/Studies in Music 11 (Warren, MI: Harmonie Park Press, 1992), 7.
27. Guthrie P. Ramsey, Jr., "Keep Digging: Florence Price, Rae Linda Brown, and the Art of a Woman," in Brown, *The Heart of a Woman*, xi.

28. Guthrie P. Ramsey, Jr., "Who Hears Here? Black Music, Critical Bias, and the Musicological Skin Trade," *Musical Quarterly* 85, no. 1 (2001): 1–52.
29. Rae Linda Brown papers, Stuart A. Rose Manuscript, Archives, and Rare Book Library, Emory University, https://search.libraries.emory.edu/catalog/9937229717402486.
30. Brown, *The Heart of a Woman*, xxi.
31. Rae Linda Brown papers, Emory University.
32. This transcript draws directly on the notes Brown prepared for the talk.

3 | Price and the Black Concert Tradition in the United States

LOUISE TOPPIN

To begin with Matilda Sissieretta Joyner Jones (ca. 1868–1933) – the greatest Black concert artist of her time – may seem an unlikely beginning for exploring the cultural landscape of Florence Beatrice Price. As a child in Little Rock, Price may have been unaware of the significance of this vocalist's career for her own future as a professional musician. Jones, who was reportedly the highest paid African American musician of her time, made her New York debut in Steinway Hall in 1888, the year Price was born. Jones concertized throughout the world, performing at the White House for presidents (Benjamin Harrison, Grover Cleveland, William McKinley, and Theodore Roosevelt), and European royalty. And in keeping with the operatic tradition of sobriquets – bestowing special nicknames on singers that refer to other famous people and places – Jones was frequently referred to as "the Black Patti," a reference to the superstar Italian soprano, Adelina Patti (1843–1919).

Musicologist Eileen Southern points out that "by the mid-1890s the black prima donna had almost disappeared from the nation's concert halls because of a lack of public interest."[1] The rise of segregationist laws in the early twentieth century further restricted opportunities. In order to sustain her concert career, Jones worked with her managers Rudolph Voelckel and John Nolan and her husband David Jones to form the Black Patti's Troubadours in 1896. Fortunately, the arrival of Jones's group coincided with the rise of vaudeville shows and touring ensembles. It is significant to note that within this artistic landscape the Black Patti's Troubadours' concert music and art song sets helped concretize African Americans as professional concert performers by the turn of the twentieth century.

While there is no evidence that Jones and Price ever met, elements of their biographies do align. Their educational successes (both studied at the New England Conservatory), personal struggles, and career triumphs connect them to the burgeoning Black concert tradition. Jones's work in education, performance, and entrepreneurship provided a possible model for Price and her peers to visualize a successful career in classical music as African American women. In the face of overwhelming prejudice and the adversity of Jim Crow laws, Jones and Price showed resilience and demonstrated pride in their race as they produced high-quality art.

Their stories – and those of so many Black American concert artists – are a part of an overlooked narrative in American and classical music history. While documented evidence of composers of African descent reaches as far back as the early sixth century, documentation of Black concert composers harkens to the sixteenth century.[2] Composers such as Vincente Lusitano (ca. 1520–1561), Ignatius Sancho (ca. 1729–1780), Joseph Bologne, Chevalier de Saint Georges (1745–1799), and José Maurício Nunes Garcia (1767–1830) worked successfully in Europe and South America, laying a foundation for future generations. Although a broader story remains to be told, this chapter focuses on the Black concert tradition in the United States of the nineteenth and twentieth centuries. As will be shown, the intersection of Emancipation, establishment of colleges and universities for the formerly enslaved, Jim Crow laws, the institutionalization of music education, and the rise of a Black professional class laid the foundation for the development and cultivation of a community of Black composers, performers, teachers, and patrons – a community that Price actively participated in and contributed to.

Classical Music, Minstrelsy, and the Rise of the Spiritual

For the more than two centuries of chattel slavery in the United States, enslaved African Americans would have been exposed to Western classical music through concerts, opera performances (particularly in New Orleans), churches, and social gatherings. Although relegated to balconies in most settings, those working in plantation homes during social events would have opportunities to hear and perform European music. This exposure allowed musicians to consider European musical styles in their own practice. There are many accounts of enslaved African Americans being recognized for their skills as musicians, primarily singers and violinists.[3] The most skilled could command a sizable fee for their plantation owners, and they were hired out temporarily to provide entertainment for social events, bar rooms, and parties.

Although enslaved musicians were rarely able to reap any financial benefit, some were able to hone their craft and reach "star" status. One of the earliest and most successful was soprano Elizabeth Taylor Greenfield (1809–1876), who was born into slavery and classically trained. She was later freed by her owner's family and performed widely in the United States and Europe, singing repertoire by Handel, Donizetti, Bellini, and early American composers.

Another example is the blind pianist Thomas "Blind Tom" Greene Wiggins (1849–1908). Because of his visual impairment, he was unable to work and was allowed to move freely about the plantation. It was discovered that he was a musical prodigy when, upon hearing the piano music his owner's daughter played, he was able to replicate it flawlessly. His owner encouraged him to develop his skills as a pianist and composer. He was hired out continuously to perform concerts throughout the United States. His extreme talent produced tremendous sums of money for his owner, who legally petitioned to remain his "guardian" post-Emancipation, a ruling Wiggins's mother fought for decades.

African Americans in the north also forged careers as professional musicians; however, their free status did not guarantee an easier existence. In *African American Music: An Introduction*, Josephine Wright writes, "American audiences of the late eighteenth and early nineteenth centuries viewed professional musicians largely as purveyors of entertainment (i.e., as a servant class), rather than elevated cultural leaders in society, and race proved less of an inhibiting factor for the Black composer-musician at this time than it would in the post-Reconstruction era when judicial segregation of the races became the law of the land."[4] However, free African Americans also had to remain vigilant for unscrupulous people who tried to kidnap them and sell them south into slavery. Such was the case with violinist Solomon Northup (1808–1863) from New York. Although Northup had the papers to prove he was a free man, he was kidnapped and sold illegally into slavery for twelve years before regaining his freedom. He would later record his experience in his memoir, *Twelve Years a Slave*, published in 1853.[5]

In the musical sphere, African Americans who aspired to be professional musicians also had to contend with the popular music of their time – minstrelsy. Minstrelsy was a musical theater form built on the mocking depiction of enslaved people by white entertainers wearing blackface; its origins are often credited to Thomas Dartmouth Rice (1808–1860), a New York musician and dancer who created the character Jim Crow in 1828. Inspired by an enslaved man Rice saw singing and jumping in Kentucky, Jim Crow was one of many stock characters developed for minstrel shows. Built upon racist stereotypes and derogatory characterizations, minstrelsy shaped perceptions about the African American community that resonate to this day. Jim Crow even became the moniker to describe the restrictive racial laws that began to appear in 1865 and continued until the *Brown* v. *Board of Education* desegregation ruling in 1954 and the passage of the 1964 Civil Rights Act.

As early as 1865, African Americans created their own blackface minstrel shows. Organizers worked to tailor shows to suit African American performers and included religious music, comic songs, spirituals, and operatic arias. While satirizing enslaved people, these performances offered African American entertainers employment, narrative and interpretive control (to a limited degree), and a route to concert music and musical theater.[6] The economic power of minstrelsy is evident in the career of James Bland (1854–1911). Born free and educated at Howard University, Bland wrote for Tin Pan Alley but also composed the popular minstrel tunes "Oh Dem Golden Slippers" and "Carry Me Back to Old Virginny." The latter was originally believed to be written by Stephen Foster and would serve as the Virginia state song from 1940 to 1997.

While minstrelsy continued to dominate as the most popular American musical form after slavery, spirituals (formerly called "sorrow songs" during enslavement) began to find new life in the concert hall. Although singing spirituals was life-sustaining during enslavement, some African Americans were less interested in continuing the tradition post-enslavement, viewing the repertoire as relics of the past. Fortunately for future generations of Americans, many of the songs were notated during the Civil War by three abolitionists – William Allen (1830–1899), Charles Ware (1840–1921), and Lucy McKim Garrison (1842–1877) – and published as *Slave Songs of the United States* in 1867. In the foreword the authors outline their reasoning and process of collecting more than 600 songs on several trips to South Carolina in 1861: "The musical capacity of the Negro race has been recognized for so many years that it is hard to explain why no systematic effort has hitherto been made to collect and preserve their melodies."[7] Their work brought these vernacular songs into the written tradition, facilitating access for future generations of composers and enabling them to create new works from this source material.

In 1871, the validity of a Black concert tradition based on spirituals was proven by the Fisk Jubilee Singers. After only five years in existence, the Historically Black Fisk University experienced financial trouble. The college administration consented to send the Fisk Jubilee Singers, conducted by George White, on a tour of the United States to raise funds for the university. The repertoire they presented featured Western classics, consistent with the musical training received by students at Fisk and other institutions established post-Emancipation to educate African Americans. Although audiences were intrigued by the novelty of Black singers presenting European repertoire, fundraising efforts garnered only modest gains. The choice to add spirituals to their program turned a mediocre fundraising effort into a robust, financially successful campaign. Their performances of African American melodies combined with Western classical music structure was groundbreaking. They established a model for other universities (especially the Historically Black Hampton Institute, founded in 1868) to create touring ensembles for the dual purpose of displaying the talent of their students and raising funds for their universities. These ensembles were the vehicles for disseminating these newly formed spirituals throughout the world.[8]

The Fisk Jubilee Singers performed before prestigious audiences and royalty. On one such tour in Europe, the African-British composer and violinist Samuel Coleridge Taylor (1875–1912), who was pivotal in the development of the Black concert tradition, first heard the ensemble. Captivated by the beauty and sincerity of the melodies, he was convinced that spirituals should be used as source material by Black composers. His own catalog of works consisted of many pieces derived from spirituals, including his best-known piano suite, *Twenty-Four Negro Melodies*. His contemporary, the Czech composer Antonín Dvořák (1841–1904), head of the National Conservatory in New York, challenged American composers to acknowledge that spirituals should be the foundation for the American musical tradition and stated that "a great and noble school of American classical music would be founded upon America's negro melodies."[9]

An article published by the *Cleveland Gazette*, a Black newspaper, on June 3, 1893, set the stage for the opinions expressed by African American writers. The article praises Black music, connects it to slavery, and notes that this repertoire had achieved popularity in Europe and America because of touring choirs like the Fisk Jubilee Singers. The unnamed writer takes Black music out of the fields and puts it into the European concert halls, where he asserts it was "the secret of [the Jubilee choirs'] success abroad. The prediction that the American school of music is to be built upon what are commonly referred to as Negro melodies seems to be a bitter pill indeed for many prejudiced musicians (white) to swallow."[10]

Composers such as Price and Henry "Harry" Thacker Burleigh (1866–1949) would make significant contributions to the genre that we now know as concert spirituals. Developed from Fisk Jubilee Singer Ella Sheppard's spiritual arrangements and codified by Burleigh, concert spirituals are settings of spirituals for voice and piano that draw upon the style and form of art song and would have been familiar to both Price and Burleigh since childhood. For analyses of Price's concert spirituals, please consult Chapter 6 of this volume.

As American music shifted away from German Romanticism and toward an American nationalism, African Americans were vocal about the inclusion of their music in education, concert programming, and publishing. In 1915, composer-conductor R. Nathaniel Dett was surprised to find within the publisher G. Schirmer strong prejudice against the higher development of Black music. "As for me," he contended, "I cannot see why the same principles making English folk music a success should not do so for Negro music. Folk music is folk music and development is development."[11] Although there was a concerted effort, clearly America was not ready to accept a musical framework based on the folk music of the formerly enslaved. Nor would it allow access to performance venues for African American musicians who were highly trained and just as capable of performing European classical music as their white peers.

Paving the Way: HBCUs and Legislation

The end of the American Civil War in 1865 marked not only the end of more than two hundred years of slavery; it allowed the formerly enslaved to visualize new possibilities for their lives. However, a lack of employment opportunities, available housing, medical care, and an educational foundation posed challenges for the four million newly freed people. In the years immediately following the Civil War, assistance was provided by individuals from the north and, most importantly, from the United States Congress. One of the first actions by Congress was the establishment of the Freedmen's Bureau in 1865 for the purpose of providing basic services (e.g., food and medical attention) while beginning to address the need for education and workplace protection.

Price was among those born after the Civil War to benefit from these political actions. Beyond the primary goal of the Freedmen's Bureau to provide basic reading, writing, and math skills, the agency expanded the educational possibilities for African Americans, such as learning trades and skills for teaching and other professions. Education was seen as a clear step towards equality and survival in the new post–Civil War landscape.

Prior to the establishment of the Freedmen's Bureau, African Americans could access higher education in a few colleges and universities founded in the north as early as 1837, the first being Cheney University in Pennsylvania. The Freedmen's Bureau therefore built on the existing model and opened more schools, primarily in the southern states. The earliest of these schools are still renowned today, commonly referred to as Historically Black Colleges and Universities (HBCUs): Clark University in Atlanta (1865); Fisk University in Nashville (1866); and Howard University in Washington, DC (1867). Others were established in northern and western states, such as Delaware State University (1891), Wilberforce University (1856) and Central State University (1887) in Ohio, and, more recently, Charles Drew University of Medicine and Science (1966) in California and the University of the Virgin Islands (1962). This legacy of HBCUs continues into the present. According to the National Center for Educational Statistics, there are currently 101 HBCUs in the United States, with the majority in, Alabama, Arkansas, DC, Florida, Georgia, Kentucky, Louisiana, Maryland, Mississippi, Missouri, Oklahoma, South Carolina, Tennessee, Texas, Virginia, and West Virginia.

A blueprint of how an equal society could function began to emerge in the next few years of the Reconstruction period. Often cited as the period from 1865 until 1877, Reconstruction hosted the rebuilding of the country and determination of the civil rights of the newly freed slaves. During this era, several important pieces of legislation became law. The Thirteenth Amendment (1865) abolished slavery and established the Freedmen's Bureau (1865). The Fourteenth Amendment (1868) granted citizenship and equal civil and legal rights to African Americans and emancipated slaves and "all persons born or naturalized in the United States." The Civil Rights Act of 1875 guaranteed African Americans equal treatment in public transportation, accommodations, and service on juries under federal law; and the Reconstruction Acts (1867–1868) determined how the southern states would be admitted back into the Union. Although white supremacy was particularly pervasive in southern states, as evidenced by Black Codes – laws passed as early as 1865 restricting the movements of Blacks within a state – the Reconstruction laws added a level of protection that helped African American citizens to begin exerting themselves as freed persons in the country.

Even with the new laws and educational opportunities, employment was still a challenge. Those employed in domestic work and sharecropping found little improvement in their financial circumstances. Other African Americans, both born free and the newly freed, utilized their leadership skills and business acumen to work as ministers, abolitionists, teachers, farmers, and business owners. Middle- and upper-middle-class African Americans, seduced by the legal protections of Reconstruction (which reframed southern cities once hostile to African Americans as favorable locations for future prosperity), relocated their families to the Deep South. These new Southerners brought with them notions of new professional employment options for Black Americans. Price's parents, Dr. James Smith and Mrs. Florence Gulliver Smith, were both born free in northern cities and exemplified for their children and Arkansas community the vocational possibilities that could be procured through education. Dr. Smith was a dentist, while Mrs. Smith was a successful businesswoman and music teacher. Reconstruction also saw the rise of thousands of African American politicians, who worked to use their oratory talents on the local, state, and national levels to govern as representatives, senators, and even state lieutenant governors.

The progression from enslaved musicians to classically trained professional musicians is plausible when considering the integral role of music and music-making within African societies.[12] Slave owners, dealers, and transporters attempted to systematically erase African cultural elements as a means of dehumanizing the enslaved. Once Africans arrived in North American colonies, music was simultaneously restricted, for fear of insurrection via instrumental coded messages, and encouraged, as there was a presupposition that enslaved people were happy and harmless when singing. The unsuccessful erasure became especially apparent with the creation of new cultural practices that remain foundational in current American culture.

Performing and Teaching Opportunities

The narrowing of educational and professional access precipitated by Jim Crow legislation led to widespread entrepreneurship in Black communities. Some performers, pedagogues, intellectuals, and composers were concerned that success in vaudeville and musical theater was not enough to show white society that African Americans were their musical equals. Thoroughly steeped in Western classical music through their training at conservatories and HBCUs, African American musicians wanted access to the growing roster of classical performance venues – venues they were routinely barred from due to their race. The most accessible avenues for performance were often college campuses (primarily HBCUs), churches, and concert spaces created to cater to Black performers and audiences.

The years 1870–1900 saw coast-to-coast opportunities blossom to address the need for suitable creative outlets. The Colored American Opera Company in Washington, DC, presented light opera and gave opportunities for African Americans to display their talents onstage from 1873 to 1876. The Hyers family from California organized a touring company and, in 1876, sisters Anna (ca. 1855–1929) and Emma (ca. 1857–1901) added a new genre to their act: musical dramas. Their first production, *Out of Bondage*, also titled *Out of the Wilderness*, written by Joseph Bradford and produced by the Hyers family and journalist-music philosopher Pauline Hopkins, is considered to be the first known musical produced in the United States.[13] Through their musical dramas, the Hyers family staged comedies about slavery that did not resort to the tropes of minstrelsy; theirs was an essential creative voice in the development of African American musical theater until the 1920s.

A Trip to Coontown (1898) by Bob Cole (1868–1911) and James P. Johnson (1873–1954) was the first African American musical to appear on Broadway. J. Rosamond Johnson (1873–1954), his brother James Weldon Johnson (1871–1938), Will Marion Cook (1869–1944), and others found success working in musical theater composition and production in New York City. Their contemporary, opera impresario and baritone Theodore Drury (1867–1945), created another opportunity. In 1900, Drury presented the inaugural production by the Theodore Drury Grand Opera Company in New York City. According to Lucy Caplan in her article "The Improbable Rise of the First African American Opera Impresario":

Theodore Drury founded an opera company that presented operas from the standard repertory performed by largely African American casts. The company represented virtually the only opportunity for Black singers to perform full operatic roles. Working within the context of pervasive Jim Crow segregation, Drury became an unparalleled advocate for the performance of grand opera by and for African Americans, creating opportunities for Black singers at the turn of the 20th century when mainstream venues and audiences remained hostile to their participation. . . . By all accounts, it [*Carmen*] was the first performance of grand opera in which not only the cast, but also the entire creative team, including Harry T. Burleigh as the conductor, and much of the audience, were African American.[14]

Although Drury's company was in existence for only seven years, it laid an important foundation for African American participation and success in opera. A successor to Drury was Harry Lawrence Freeman (1869–1954), who wrote and produced twenty-four operas in New York City that reflected African American themes, such as *The Tryst* (1911), *Voodoo* (1928), and *Zululand* (1941–44). In 1933, when soprano Catarina Jarboro (1898–1986) performed with a major, predominantly white American opera company at the New York Hippodrome, this began a twenty-year shift in attitudes toward the acceptance of African Americans in major opera companies. It was not until 1955 that Marian Anderson (1897–1993) made her historic debut that led to integration in the country's most important opera house, the Metropolitan Opera.

Other artists chose to establish newspapers, concert series, festivals, and schools/training programs. E. Azalia Hackley (1867–1922), an influential singer, teacher, and patron of some of the most prominent musicians of the twentieth century, established the Vocal Normal Institute. Hackley could count Florence Talbot, Roland Hayes, Marian Anderson, Clarence Cameron White, Carl Diton, and R. Nathaniel Dett as former students, mentees, and/or benefactors of her philanthropy. Hackley's generation took seriously their obligation to nurture the next generation of performers by providing scholarships and pushing back on performances in segregated spaces.[15] They were determined to change the system that had diminished their own performance opportunities.

The founding of the National Association of Negro Musicians (NANM) fostered a supportive professional environment for classical musicians. Dett and White had called for the establishment of such an organization as early as 1914, but it was delayed by the start of World War I. It was formally established in 1919 in Chicago by Nora Holt and Henry L. Grant, with Holt's Chicago Music Association becoming the first NANM branch. The goals of this organization – to preserve "Negro spirituals" and promote African American excellence – paralleled those of New Negro leadership: "stimulating progress, to discover and foster talent, to mold taste, to promote fellowship, and to advocate racial expression."[16] Throughout her career, Florence Price was an active member of NANM. The organization afforded her opportunities for performance as a pianist, organist, and composer; gender equality at the administrative level; and media coverage. NANM provided a vital community for Price's professional success, in addition to highlighting the importance of performing, studying, and advocating for Black classical repertoire.

Toward a Black Music Pedagogy

Prior to Emancipation, one of the few colleges that admitted students regardless of race and sex was Oberlin College and Conservatory. Boston Conservatory, New England Conservatory, and Cincinnati Conservatory, all founded in 1867, either distributed funds to help educate African American music students or, in the case of New England and Boston, admitted students regardless of race or sex. A long list of well-known African Americans, including Joseph Douglass, Nellie Brown Mitchell, and Louis Vaughn Jones, matriculated through these institutions. Along with the earliest HBCU music schools, these schools became important centers for the solidification of a Black concert tradition and the codification of a burgeoning Black musical pedagogy.

According to Kira Thurman, one mission for many HBCUs was to create a conservatory of music modeled after music schools like New England Conservatory or Oberlin, in order to offer African American music students rigorous training.[17] Initially, many HBCU professors were white European immigrants from Germanic or Eastern European countries, bringing with them a curriculum that emphasized Bach, Beethoven, and Brahms. The curriculum of these earliest universities, based on the repertoires and styles of Germanic composers, continues to dominate American musical education to this day.[18]

For students at the elementary- and secondary-school level, the influx of pedagogues, musicians, and composers who were not deterred by race but dedicated to the talent of their students facilitated access to high-quality music instruction. Part of the mass movement to educate African Americans between the 1870s and 1918 was the understanding that music education promised to cultivate new generations of politically minded, culturally sophisticated, and socially aware citizens, who would in turn advance their rights in a nation that still refused to recognize them.[19] As early as 1899, many Black Americans moved to Europe to pursue performance opportunities not available to them in America. But for those who stayed, they used the arts to show equality with whites during the Harlem and Black Chicago Renaissances.

With the support of her parents and a musically rich environment at home and in her community, it is no surprise that Price would enroll at the prestigious New England Conservatory in 1903. This was the same conservatory that graduated Sissieretta Jones in the 1880s and J. Rosamond Johnson and Maud Cuney-Hare in the 1890s. New England's Boston location would have provided Price with a thriving musical community. She would have heard the Boston Symphony Orchestra, the Handel and Haydn Society, chamber and solo concerts at Boston Conservatory and Harvard, and performances by outstanding artists of all ethnicities throughout the city.

Upon her graduation in 1906 with her organ performance degree and piano pedagogy diploma, Price took a job at Shorter College, which was founded in 1886 by the African Methodist Episcopal Church in Little Rock, and there she served as head of the music department from 1906 to 1910. As Shorter was a Christian school, it is possible that Price played for daily chapel along with her teaching responsibilities (probably courses in music education and instrumental music). It is also probable that she accompanied piano and organ concerts for the campus and community.[20] Price's time at Shorter was marred by the untimely death of her father in 1910 and her mother's choice to leave Little Rock for Indianapolis and pass for white. This was a double blow for Price, who ostensibly lost both of her parents at the age of twenty-one.[21]

Soon after her father's death, Price moved to Atlanta and joined the faculty of Clark University as head of the music department. As she had at Shorter, Price participated as pianist and organist for the faculty and students. In her assigned courses, she taught European and African American composers. This infusion of cultural information was presented for the purpose of teaching her students about their cultural heritage and instilling racial pride.[22] Price also used her academic position to expose her students to a range of artists, as her parents had used their home to host a range of musical and political figures. Visitors included singers E. Azalia Hackley and Florence Cole Talbert, violinists Joseph Douglass and Clarence Cameron White, and pianists Carl Diton and Hazel Harrison. The guest artists and students benefited equally from these visits: the artists were performing and mentoring the students, and the students were exposed to artistically mature, critically successful African American performers. Under Price's direction, the students developed their talents and cultural awareness, which extended into their communities.[23]

Although her time in the academy was relatively short, Price's work was impactful in the establishment of a model for a Black music pedagogy that situates African American musical ideals within a Western curricular framework. Following a model that has been passed down for centuries – learning foundational technique and knowledge of Western music from master teachers – Price's work deviated from that standard model by coupling music pedagogy with Black nationalistic ideas in the teaching of history, theory, and performance. Black nationalism in this context references the post-Reconstruction period in which Blacks developed separate communities to advance ideals of racial pride and economic advancement.

Price's students learned two integrated musical cultures: a combined African American and European curriculum. This transformed the curriculum into a dynamic pedagogy that allowed African American students to see themselves reflected in the performances and scholarship that was written about, for, and by them. Price created culturally relevant teaching pieces for her piano and organ students and utilized musical examples from her peers in the Black concert tradition for her theory and history courses. In the music she created for her students, she reflected her experiences as a Black woman from the south in her use of descriptive titles and representative musical gestures. She supported the curriculum she taught by bringing in the most important African American composers, performers, and thinkers of the day to inspire, reinforce, and elevate her students. She did not shy away from her identity; she amplified it!

Although Black music pedagogy developed tentatively, it continued to expand in some pockets of the country. Particular examples include composer and professor Undine Smith Moore's Black Music Center at Virginia State University, and African American music courses taught at both predominantly white and HBCU campuses. The Black music pedagogy that Price actively participated in fostered our current flourishing Black concert tradition. The diligent work of earlier generations laid the foundation for performers such as myself and countless others to envision a career performing the concert works of Black composers worldwide in our most venerated halls. We have firmly established that there *is* a viable Black concert and opera tradition worthy of consideration. We have been able to perform to sold-out halls, commercially record concert works, receive GRAMMY nominations and awards, teach masterclasses on Black repertoire, establish competitions such as the George Shirley Vocal Competition, regularly teach classes on Black composers, publish the scores of Black composers, and assume leadership roles in helping Black composers find a place in our musical canon.

Conclusion

Florence Price came of age as a professional musician in an era that was fraught with contradiction: Legislation designed to improve equality was in place, yet she had to navigate limited access to opportunities that would have provided stability for her career and her family. She contributed to a new way of thinking about music education and pedagogy by enhancing her teaching curricula with culturally relevant material, sensitive performances, and academic opportunities. Price was a unique voice in the American musical landscape and unapologetically used spirituals, juba, and Black popular music as source material in her compositions. Though her music was performed by well-known artists such as Marian Anderson, Price, like so many of her generation, had to work entrepreneurially to function as a professional musician. Her bravery, resilience, and struggle provided a foundation for those who are part of and define the Black concert tradition in our time.

Notes

1. Eileen Southern, *The Music of Black Americans: A History*, 2nd ed. (New York: W. W. Norton, 1983), 244.
2. Jon Silpayamanant, "Early Black Musicians, Composers, and Music Scholars (505–1505 CE)," *Mae Mai* (blog), February 17, 2021, updated June 12, 2023, https://silpayamanant.wordpress.com/bmc_505-1505/.
3. Dena J. Epstein, *Sinful Tunes and Spirituals: Black Folk Music to the Civil War* ([1977] Urbana: University of Illinois Press, 2003); Christopher J. Smith, *The Creolization of American Culture: William Sidney Mount and the Roots of Blackface Minstrelsy* (Urbana: University of Illinois Press, 2013).
4. Josephine Wright, "Art/Classical Music," in *African American Music: An Introduction*, edited by Mellonee V. Burnim and Portia K. Maultsby (New York: Routledge, 2006), 139.
5. Solomon Northup, *Twelve Years a Slave* ([1853] New York: Penguin Random House, 2016).
6. Southern, *The Music of Black Americans*, 234.
7. William Allen, Charles Ware, and Lucy Garrison, *Slave Songs of the United States* (Bedford, MA: Applewood Books, 1867), 1.
8. Southern, *The Music of Black Americans*, 227–228.
9. Joseph Horowitz, *Dvořák's Prophecy: And the Vexed State of Black Classical Music* (New York: W. W. Norton), xvi.
10. Horace J. Maxile, Jr., and Kristen M. Turner, *Race and Gender in the Western Music Survey* (New York: Routledge, 2022), 110.
11. Georgia A. Ryder, "Harlem Renaissance Ideals in the Music of Nathaniel Dett," in *Black Music in the Harlem Renaissance*, edited by Samuel A. Floyd, Jr. (New York: Greenwood Press, 1990), 59.
12. Mary Caton Lingold, *African Musicians in the Atlantic World: Legacies of Sound and Slavery* (Charlottesville: University of Virginia Press, 2023).
13. Sandra Jean Graham, *Spirituals and the Birth of the Black Entertainment Industry* (Urbana: University of Illinois Press, 2018).
14. Lucy Caplan, "The Improbable Rise of the First African American Impresario," *San Francisco Classical Voice*, February 6, 2017, https://tinyurl.com/3s9bfjpx.
15. Southern, *The Music of Black Americans*, 397.
16. Maude Cuney-Hare, *Negro Musicians and Their Music* (New York: Da Capo Press, 1974), 242.

17. Kira Thurman, *Singing Like Germans: Black Musicians in the Land of Bach, Beethoven, and Brahms* (New York: Cornell University Press, 2021), 33.
18. Thurman, *Singing Like Germans*, 38.
19. Ibid., 23.
20. Brown, *The Heart of a Woman*, 60.
21. Ibid., 61.
22. Ibid., 64.
23. Ibid., 67.

PART II
———

Genre and Style

If I am getting to the specifics of Florence Price's language that we learned more as we [performed], I think I would maybe classify them in two categories . . .
 The rhythmical aspect, dare I say, the "dance" aspect of it. . . . I think once we allow ourselves to feel the music a little bit more rhythmically, I think we get closer to the spirit of her language, even in slow movements.
 And another one. . . . There is a prayer in pretty much all of her works. . . . A prayer that is very much heartfelt.
 —Yannick Nézet-Séguin, music and artistic director of the Philadelphia Orchestra

4 | New Analytical Approaches for Florence Price Scholarship

JANE FORNER AND ELLIE M. HISAMA

What would it mean to hear and analyze Florence Price's music intersectionally?[1] How can we be attuned to her compositions with feminist ears? And how can collaborative analyses lead us to an inclusive music theory? These questions arise from our personal meditations on how we have approached Price's music thus far. My (Jane Forner's) experience of playing Price's songs, piano pieces, and organ music, and engaging with these works as a scholar and teacher, has reflected a process of acknowledging not only the systemic gaps but also the decades of restorative work done by women – performers, educators, academics, librarians, and others – who have kept the flame of Price's music burning, who sought out opportunities to uplift and promote her work and other neglected Black women in music, past and present.

At the same time, lacking many commercial recordings and analytical literature on most of her oeuvre, teaching Price's music, even in the past few years in the wake of increased and sustained mainstream interest in her work, has felt like a "do-it-yourself" process. To analyze the songs with my students has meant reading the poetry aloud, playing and singing for them in class; until a critical mass of analytical literature exists, much of our work on Price and other composers kept at best at the margins of textbooks will happen in these DIY spaces. However, that is something we can encourage: to listen and sing and play as a form of collaborative analysis that takes place in our classrooms and practice rooms – and that for music-theoretical work has as much importance as traditional venues.

Such mainstream venues have, historically, been the site of an (un) conscious "boycott" of Black women composers. This terminology stems from Jacqueline Thompson's talk at the First National Congress on Women in Music, which was held at New York University in 1981 and formed part of a session titled "Black Women in American Music." Therein she spoke of "the problem of the unconscious boycott" of music by women and Black Americans (though we might, less generously, observe that this has often been quite conscious). And it remains that more and more analytical work is needed to rectify the gaps in our shelves, playlists, concert programs, and curricula to counter this (un)conscious "boycott," while recognizing and weaving into the new (hi)stories we write that they will be built, after Saidiya Hartmann, on the violence that these gaps signify.[2]

When I (Ellie Hisama) first became aware of the absence of women composers as an undergraduate student in the 1980s, from music I played in my private violin lessons, chamber music ensembles, and orchestras to music I studied in my history and theory classes, I pored through libraries in New York City, seeking traces of those whose presence I sensed and unfurling long lists of many women I had never heard of, and whom my teachers had never heard of, either. The special "Women and Music" issue of *Heresies: A Feminist Publication of Art and Politics* (1980), with J. K. Thompson's contribution on Florence Price, was a delightful find.[3] There were disappointingly few resources in the libraries I could access during my student years that did not primarily or exclusively focus on the music by white composers. I was excited to learn of Rae Linda Brown's 1987 dissertation at Yale on Price's orchestral music, but it was not easily available in the predigital days of the early 1990s.[4] As Samantha Ege wrote in 2018, Price "simply did not exist" in Western music history as it was written and taught for many decades.[5]

One recording I was thrilled to find was pianist Althea Waites's 1993 CD *Black Diamonds*, which contained Margaret Bonds's brilliant "Troubled Water" for solo piano, a work that caught my ear and one that I include in teaching chromatic harmony.[6] When asked to contribute examples to the volume *Music by Women for Study and Analysis* (a collection of score excerpts designed as an accompaniment to Aldwell and Schachter's *Harmony and Voice Leading*, which then dominated the field of undergraduate music theory textbooks), I added two works by Black composers, Bonds's "Troubled Water" and Price's "Hold Fast to Dreams." I felt it imperative that, in addressing the severe gender imbalance in music theory, the anthology should not focus exclusively on music by composers who were white and European.

A traditional endeavor in music theory is to provide close readings of musical structure, largely leaving aside considerations of social, political, or historical issues, which in North America have been considered to be under the purview of musicology. Music theory is the last of the music subfields to accept and act upon the necessity of anti-racist and feminist work and to acknowledge that a composer's lived experience may be relevant in analytical explorations of their music. After the plenary session at the Society for Music Theory's 2019 annual meeting, which caused a seismic shift in the field, music theory is at the incipient stages of forging new research paradigms and pedagogies in working towards gender and racial equity, with recent PhDs and students at the forefront of these key activities.[7] The field is being inexorably altered through innovative research and teaching, impactful engagements with nonacademic communities, and sustained attention to issues of diversity, equity, inclusion, and belonging – all of which may inform exciting new directions in Price scholarship.

In her study of the impact of gentrification in Washington, DC, on an urban sound world, Alison Martin observes that "taking an intersectional approach to listening fosters a way to analyze the lives and experiences of Black people and to audibly gauge pasts, presents, and the speculative sonic future on multiple axes, such as race, class, and gender. Intersectional listening enables us to interrogate music, sound, and noise, as well as what lies in between these distinctions in their relation to broad understandings of space and place."[8] Although the material discussed in our chapter (i.e., songs by Price) differs in kind from the subject of Martin's study (i.e., the sounds of a city and its inhabitants during gentrification), her formulation of intersectional listening has significant implications for an inclusive music theory, one that pays attention to how experiences impact artistic creation and the ways listeners can apprehend that art.

The intersection of musical language, class, race, gender, and sexuality must not be cast aside as irrelevant by those who wish only to bathe in the brilliance of Price's music. It is our fervent hope that Price's music will be performed, programmed, reflected upon, and written about through this posture of intersectional listening, with an understanding of how Price's experiences as a Black woman profoundly affected her creative life and career. An introduction to Price's music instead would include discussion of individual works, reflections on the discrimination she faced, an examination of the relationship of her music to twentieth-century tonality, inclusion of African American vernacular elements, and twenty-first century performance practices.

In this chapter, we advocate for analytical approaches to Price's music that foreground *both* the importance of assessing her compositions with serious analytical nuance *and* hearing music through and with the person. We do so with the caveat of wishing to avoid two traps: one, animating an old false binary between that which is "in" the music and that which is extrinsic; and two, reinscribing notions of serious music analysis as focused purely on "the notes." The richness of Price's oeuvre can be analyzed in modes wherein questions of technique, harmony, form, and other properties are neither divorced from the multiple cultural realities (then/now) in which the music is embedded and through which it is produced, nor beholden to music-theoretical techniques that were developed by men and for men.

Analytical writings by Samantha Ege, Horace J. Maxile, Jr., and Elektra V. Carter among others, provide a strong foundation for additional work on Price's compositions.[9] Samantha Ege's exploration of Price's compositions and reflections on the presence of Black musical idioms in some of her music, and what she identifies as its "actantial and expressive capacity," are critical contributions to our thinking about Price's work.[10] Ege's insights about Price's vernacular influences, such as dance rhythms, in her music light a path of thinking about the "layers of significance and signification" that the vernacular holds.[11]

In his analysis of Price's Piano Sonata No. 1 in E Minor, Horace J. Maxile, Jr., elaborates on what has become the prevailing conception of her music: the consistent presence of "African American vernacular elements" alongside formal and stylistic elements of the late nineteenth- and early twentieth-century European classical tradition, which he classes as "two musical impulses, the Black folk and the neo-Romantic."[12] Specific examples of the former that Maxile identifies include a predilection for half-diminished chords and "pendular thirds" (an often repeated rocking back-and-forth between two notes normally a minor third apart[13]); an emphasis on backbeats and syncopation (especially with octave doublings);[14] and a "proclivity for linear chromatic chord progressions."[15] Paying attention to these vernacular "emblems" offers a method of analysis for Price that draws out her connections to African American musical heritage and how these are interwoven with her deep training in the European classical tradition, which Maxile achieves in his assessment of the piano sonata.

To hear Price's music with feminist ears is to be attuned to these interweavings, but also to the rich biographical, cultural, and historical contexts that not only informed her practice as a musician, composer, and teacher but seeped into the corners of all her music. These are threads at which we may pull and uncover, not as separate, "extra-musical" scraps of information that offer colorful background context, but elements as equally fundamental as notes on the page.

In building on the decades of feminist music scholarship that has sought to hear and understand music in these ways, we aim to offer pathways for students, scholars, and performers alike to negotiate their own way through the work of Price. We maintain that weaving these threads together – of identity, biography, history – is imperative and enables individuals to pursue different forms of understanding the music of Price and other composers. While this chapter focuses on a selection of Price's songs, we hope that others will take up the work of studying the significant body of Price's instrumental works in relation to intersectional listening and collaborative analysis.

Analyzing the Art Songs

Price's many art songs offer models for such potential approaches. Virtually all of Price's song settings fit within the stylistic formula that Maxile identifies. Beyond this overarching generalization, however, there are several features that appear across many of the songs and which exemplify the analytical approach we suggest here, where attention to formal and localized details – in this case, matters of harmony, voice-leading, text-setting – intersect with personal and cultural aspects that encourage a richer hearing and understanding of Price's compositions.

Existing preliminary literature on the songs has offered a grounding in musical and poetic analysis on which we aim to build here, some of which demonstrates valuable models for the intersectional analytical approaches we advocate. Elektra V. Carter's excellent analysis of Price's setting of Otto Leland Bohanan's "The Washerwoman," for example, situates the song's harmonic experimentation within a history of Black feminist thought and, of specific relevance to "The Washerwoman," the topics of education, domestic service, and social mobility. Their approach blends this rich and vital context into a focused analysis of the music, considering how "the themes of entrapment, futility, and labor are recurrent themes in black poetry and music centered on women."[16] They argue, specifically, that Price's "harmonic treatment serves as a mechanism to dramatize or re-read the narrative material at hand,"[17] offering a vivid interpretation of how Price's deployment of C Phrygian and loosely associated harmonies epitomizes her rendering of Bohanan's protagonist. What such an approach provides for interpreters of Price is a path to listen to how these histories can be felt through the music, without adhering to a single, unified analysis. We might hear, for instance, resonances with other musical or literary pieces that reflect the racialized social politics of laundry in post-Reconstruction America, such as Zora Neale Hurston's short story *Sweat* (1926), where the working lives of Black women in the early twentieth century are evoked through themes of survival, strength, marital unhappiness, and misogyny, and Ruth Crawford's song "Chinaman, Laundryman" (1932), with text by H. T. Tsiang, a Chinese dissident whose words powerfully illuminate the exploitative working conditions of a Chinese laundry worker in the US in the early twentieth century.[18]

In this chapter, the following group of songs are discussed, in light of some shared stylistic tendencies, with the goal of presenting a set of analytical snapshots that contribute to a catalogue of Price's style.

1. "Song of the Open Road," no. 4 of *Four Encore Songs*, text by Ogden Nash
2. "Bewilderment," text by Langston Hughes
3. "Beside the Sea," text by Paul Laurence Dunbar
4. "Sympathy," text by Paul Laurence Dunbar
5. "Hold Fast to Dreams," text by Langston Hughes
6. "Songs to the Dark Virgin," text by Langston Hughes

The discussion of "Songs to the Dark Virgin" draws together and brings into conversation different interpretations by a number of analysts, providing an example of a collaborative analytical discussion that might reflect a class or study group's exploration of a piece in which contrasting readings may emerge.

Harmonic Adventures and Poetic Interpretations

Price's writing at climactic and cadential moments in the songs is especially important, featuring surprising twists and turns, often avoiding, delaying, and replaying a perfect authentic cadence (PAC), and featuring more unusual chords and harmonic progressions. Much of these more unexpected harmonic "calling cards" are palpable especially in the piano part, principally concerning three main harmonic ideas: half-diminished chords; chords built on stacked seconds, (0246), (0248), and (02468); and extended seventh and ninth chords and chords comprising stacked fourths and/or fifths. (The use of [02] and so on indicates unordered pitch classes forming triads, tetrachords, etc.; for instance, if C is 0, (024) is C,D,E.)[19] A note on terminology: There are other ways to read the harmonic functionality of these chords, and language from set theory is used as a shorthand to indicate certain harmonic sonorities that recur frequently in Price's music. While this is an efficient way to describe such occurrences, it is neither the only nor the most necessary way to analyze the songs.

Sometimes Price's avoidance of perfect cadences occurs through typical means – such as resolving stepwise chromatically (reflecting the penchant for linear chromatic progressions that Maxile noted, for example) or using plagal or interrupted cadences – but it is also common to find here more far-flung sonorities. Many of her songs follow an approximate pattern of beginning with a relatively simple vocal melody (often featuring her idiomatic use of pendular thirds and pentatonic-inflected lines) and accompaniment pattern (e.g., broken chords), which both become increasingly more erratic, unpredictable, and fragmentary in the latter part of the song. In both strophic and through-composed songs, it is in these processes of disintegration that approaches to cadences at important structural junctures – ends of poetic verses and ends of songs – are disrupted through, especially, chords that are variations and extensions on (024). In essence, Price tends to introduce these more complex sonorities as pre-cadential harmonies, very often followed by a final cadence that avoids perfect resolution, instead ending frequently with vigorous statements of the tonic in the piano. In other words, only very occasionally is a final tonic chord absent, but it is often simply affirmed rather than reached via conventional cadential processes.

We see an example of this, for instance, in the conclusion of the third movement of Price's Suite No. 1 for Organ ("Air"), which is already full of extended harmonies, repeatedly leaning into "blue notes." In the final fifteen measures or so, a coda of sorts consisting of highly chromatic chords in sequence follows a strong final V–I cadence in the tonic (E♭ major) at measures 32–33. In measures 35–38, we find the presence again of (0248), major ninth chords, and diminished harmonies in alternation. Especially noteworthy are three chords in measures 37–38: The first and second hexachords together contain all twelve pitches, each (02468). The pentachord at measure 38 (which sounds as a major ninth chord) is (02469). Linear chromatic descent in the bassline occurs through measures 40–44, landing on the tonic.

To what extent are these patterns idiomatic features of Price's overall compositional voice, and to what extent do they represent individual musical responses to each poem? I suggest that she has certain compositional tendencies, and when we identify them in the songs we can make our own interpretations as to a poetic-musical analysis. The short, eight-measure "Song of the Open Road" (the last of the *Four Encore Songs*), for example, a mildly absurd and humorous setting of a poem by Ogden Nash, contains four instances of variations of seconds-based chords (Ex. 4.1).

In this case, the presence of these chords tells us more about their prevalence in Price's harmonic toolkit than reflecting a particular poetic mood, though perhaps their unusual sonorities contribute to the song's

Example 4.1 Extensions of (024) chords in Price, "Song of the Open Road" from *Four Encore Songs*; piano part shown in m. 2, m. 4, m. 5, and m. 6.

whimsical function. In other songs, locating these variations on or extensions of (024) chords as "harmonic disruptors" helps to map her longer-range circuitous routes to (and avoidance of) conventional tonal closure – patterns and moments that call our attention to Price's musical rendering of poetry.

In two settings of poems by Langston Hughes and Paul Laurence Dunbar, we find exemplary instances of a song format where a relatively straightforward first half, featuring repeated melodic figures and four-measure phrase structures, yields to increasing chromaticism and meandering accompanimental figures, reaching pre-cadential extended harmonies based on (024) chords. In "Bewilderment," Price's setting of Hughes's "Prayer" (1927), the first two couplets feature a lightly pentatonic vocal melody accompanied by a rocking, dirge-like ostinato piano figure that insists on the tonic D minor (often with an added minor seventh), a pattern which breaks down by the end of the third couplet, "Which crown to put upon my hair." The piano reaches a point of chromatic intensification toward the final line, "Lord God, I do not know," with the arpeggiation of (02468) in the right hand at measure 51 (Ex. 4.2), essentially an extension of a B♭ dominant seventh chord, followed by two subversions of a PAC that weaken tonal closure despite the eventual V–i motion in the left hand from measure 54 beat 3 to measure 55 beat 1. The German augmented sixth chord at measure 52 beat 4 continues the implied motion leading from VI to V (B♭ to A), which *strengthens* the sense of chromatic voice-leading toward the dominant, landing on V6/4 in measure 53. Yet this never resolves to a dominant chord proper, the F♮ persisting and the dominant seventh chord at measure 54 beat 1 further undermined by lacking the fifth. As a result, the following dominant–tonic motion lacks the strength of a PAC and is undercut again by the persistent G♯ in the right-hand arpeggiated chord in measure 55. In the

Example 4.2 Price, "Bewilderment," m. 51–end.

concluding cadenza-like piano flourish, the insistence on the tonic, with five statements of the tonic in open octaves, rings hollow.[20]

From the song's opening dirge-like piano ostinato and pentatonic vocal melody to these chromatically frustrated cadences, the sentiments of struggle and paralysis encapsulated in Hughes's poetry are enhanced: "I ask you this/Which way to go; I ask you this/Which sin to bear." There is no progression or resolution of these feelings: They break down toward the final plea of uncertainty, just as the mechanisms of tonal certainty come undone.

A very similar process occurs in "Beside the Sea," a setting of Paul Laurence Dunbar's poem "Longing" (published in 1913), which follows a relatively strophic pattern for verses 1 to 3, modulating from the tonic F major to the dominant and mediant before returning to the tonic. As shown in Example 4.3, from measure 30, multiple consecutive seventh chords assist in destabilizing a secure key area, while the melodic lines unravel away from the established predictable two-measure phrases and continuous sixteenth-note accompaniment. The final four measures begin with a full measure of (02468) chords, restated in three octaves, followed by three measures of the tonic F major stated as emphatic triads and arpeggiated

Example 4.3 Price, "Beside the Sea," m. 30–end.

chords. Price's idiomatic approach to chromatic voice-leading – more widely, to be sure, a hallmark of late Romantic harmony – is evidenced here in the striking replacement of the dominant at the climax of the song. The presence of the C at the root of the three chords in measure 33, and its continuous sounding in the vocal line, appears as a dominant anchor whose function and stability is undermined by the harmonies – although there is a keen logic in the pentachord's resolution, as each note in measure 33 falls or rises by semitone to one of the notes in the tonic triad. Price's musical treatment reflects the poem's core themes of loss, longing, and absence in the context of a romantic relationship filtered through naturalistic imagery ("the ocean's moan") – we also hear poetic parallels here with Dunbar's poem "The Wind and the Sea" (published in the same year, 1913): the "cry of the wanton sea/And the moan of the wailing wind." Note also the textural and gestural similarities between these two endings in addition to the absence of traditional tonal closure: multi-octave piano chords followed by sixteenth-note arpeggios; strategic use of piano rests; and the vocal line ending in long, held notes.

Price's setting of Dunbar's 1899 poem "Sympathy" similarly begins with a relatively simple, squarely tonal melody that gives way to harmonic disintegration as the poetic imagery – of the "caged bird" that sings – becomes increasingly violent. A stable tonic drops away in favor of a weighty chromaticism, absent (024) chords but featuring sequences of extended half-diminished, seventh, ninth, and augmented chords underpinned by a chromatically descending bassline. After the opening melody returns, again Price concludes the song with grandiose statements of the tonic and piano flourishes, arriving through a powerful plagal cadence that symbolises the penultimate line, "that upward to Heaven he flings," a prayer that is both hopeful and defiant.

"Hold Fast to Dreams," setting Hughes's "Dreams" (1922), also places harmonic intrigue at the center of the song, featuring two instances of (0248) in measure 10 and measure 11, occurring between the two verses. Price chooses to disintegrate and fragment the flowing, unbroken arpeggiated piano accompaniment that she had established from the beginning for the line "Life is a broken wing that cannot fly," her moments of harmonic ambiguity – chords that do not *go* anywhere specific or point in any particular direction – mirroring the stalling of optimism in the text. The song once again features roiling piano flourishes at the end, but its most remarkable feature is that it modulates and concludes, with a measure of frenzy, in the tonic minor, bitterly enunciating the final lines: "Life is a barren field/frozen with snow." Hughes's poetry is full of dreams of all kinds: "Bring me all of your dreams/You dreamers/Bring me all of your/Heart melodies" ("Dream Keeper" [1932]); in "I Continue to Dream," *Montage of a Dream Deferred* (1951), "each relationship, each moment of life is poisoned by the exclusion of black people from the American Dream. What grows as one reads is the 'boogie-woogie rumble' of the dream deferred, the rumble of all of these black voices rising in frustration and rage."[21] The hope of the dream which must be held fast is always seized, in Price's setting, by that frustration and rage, by the agony which explodes on the high A of "frozen" and the piano's insistent D minor displays.

In all these examples, Price's music tends to follow broad patterns of passages of relative harmonic, rhythmic, and melodic stability, which are *either* interrupted by bursts of unstable harmonic and melodic activity that subsequently return to stability *or* gradually disintegrated until the end. In the latter case, abrupt tonic flourishes in the final measure often follow avoided cadences and/or unstable melodic and key areas, exaggerated tonic statements that seem to insist too much. We might hear these final moments as encapsulating the duality of resignation and hope that suffuses many of the songs (and poems). There is a hollowness in the sudden, not-quite-prepared and overstated arrival of the tonic that communicates cynicism, a recognition of futility, but it is a sonic gesture that simultaneously brims with sudden optimism.

We can hear, through repeated listening and playing, how brief moments of instability in the middle of the songs tend to anticipate the higher level of emotional intensity at its conclusion. In this context, the presence of those seconds-stacked chords signifies beyond the immediate – a harbinger, perhaps, but also a reflective stepping-out that invites individual reflection and interpretation by the listener, singer, or pianist. In isolation, these unusual moments might pass by as mere harmonic color, but their affective functions are an integral part of Price's musical signifying through shared imagery across multiple songs. When the (024)-based sonorities occur in these pre-cadential and interstitial spaces, whether leading to the final measures of the song or appearing as a halting interruption, multiple unravelings emerge: of texture, of familiar harmonic progressions, of melodic lines, but also evident is a veil lifting, a moment where we sense a perpetual tightrope of hope and resignation. In these moments Price is self-consciously articulating a musical response to the poetry in its cycles of hope/struggle/optimism/pessimism.

The curated artifice of art song itself is subjected, by Price, to scrutiny; she lays out often predictable melodic and rhythmic patterns only to fragment them as the poetry concludes, then inserting, very often, what almost feels sometimes like a *forced* ending, a triumphant flourish that overstates the tonic (often without "normal" cadential preparation) in a gesture that sometimes reads as hollow, sometimes hopeful, sometimes as a bursting of affect. It is a burst of hope that is aware of its own failure, yet which still hangs onto a glimpse of a promise of a better future and an overcoming of the present.

Listening "in Our Various Ways" to "Songs to the Dark Virgin": A Mosaic of Analytical Voices

A jewel in Price's songbook, "Songs to the Dark Virgin" (1941) presents an exquisite setting of a poem by Langston Hughes (Ex. 4.4).[22] Mildred Denby Green characterizes the words as "very sensuous," and Rae Linda Brown writes that "Price has captured the passion [of the text] vividly."[23] The title and the text, set forth in three verses, each is introduced by the subjunctive ("Would that I were a jewel / Would that I were a garment / Would that I were a flame"), raise the central issue of the identities of the speaker and the "dark virgin" who is being addressed.

Example 4.4 Price, "Songs to the Dark Virgin," mm. 19–24.

"Songs to the Dark Virgin" has received analytical attention from several scholars. The mosaic of analytical voices presented here responds to the multivalent song in tune with Barbara Christian's exhortation that we should analyze works "in our various ways" rather than invent a theory that prescribes how one should read the works, and further, should "share … our practice, as much as possible since … our work *is* a collective endeavor."[24]

Bethany Jo Smith interprets the narrator as a male addressing a female and the virgin as the Black Madonna.[25] Penelope Peters proposes two readings: The first interpretation corresponds with Smith's, understanding the protagonist to be male and the dark virgin as female; in her second interpretation, the speaker is also the dark virgin who is addressing herself.[26] Meng-Chieh [Mavis] Hsieh finds Peters's second interpretation more convincing, agreeing that "the loathing of [the dark virgin's] skin and race comes from a cruel and segregated society."[27] Noting the source of Hughes's poem in the volume *The Weary Blues*, which presents a "unitary first-person voice," Michael Lively posits that the narrator is "apparently a Black male," while noting the uncertainty of specific meanings in Hughes's poetics.[28] In Elizabeth Durrant's Black feminist analysis of the song, the protagonist is a Black woman who is addressing her lover, "the Black virgin whose gender identity and sexual orientation are ambiguous." Durrant emphasizes that we need not assume the protagonist is a straight man and the dark virgin a woman.[29] In a queer reading consonant with an understanding of Hughes's poetics, the song can also be heard as a Black male speaker addressing a male "dark virgin," with both the lyrical and musical layers enfolding a gender-expansive reading.[30]

The song proffers several of Price's striking musical signatures: harmonic and linear sevenths and ninths, which are a defining feature of the song; a piquant use of nonharmonic tones and chromatic inflection; an avoidance of perfect cadence rather than a typical cadential progression decisively leading to a closing tonic harmony; and the concluding piano flourish present in other songs as discussed above, including in "Beside the Sea" and "Bewilderment."

The F minor that opens the song is thrown off-kilter in the very first beat by the E♭ octave that answers the right hand's F minor triad; the steady sixteenth-note groups in the piano keep listeners on unsteady ground as they try to find their harmonic bearings. Durrant observes that the "atmosphere ... not easily confined to a single tonality, [reflects] the complex multiplicity of the singer's identity as she serenades her lover."[31] "Songs to the Dark Virgin" is structurally similar to other songs set by Price in that it features an interior section where the harmonies destabilize before returning to the opening melody for the final verse. However, while the song employs a "thwarted" tonality through the use of ever-present sevenths, other settings by Price discussed in this chapter (for example, "Hold Fast to Dreams" and "Beside the Sea") often sit very squarely in the tonic to begin with, almost over-simplistically so, and then present moments of striking chromatic contrast.

The presence of an unsettling seventh is a touchstone in "Songs to the Dark Virgin." The piano's lush sixteenth notes played *andante con moto* and *pianissimo*, which Brown describes as "dark and murky,"[32] introduce an F minor opening tinged by an E♭ seventh in measure 1, a sound that persists throughout the first four measures and later in the song. Each verse also gains in intensity, moving from *pp* and *mp* of verse 1 in measures 1–2, to *mp* of verse 2 in measure 7, to *mf* of verse 3 in measure 19. Brown describes the opening text as follows: "the darkness of the body is set against the light of the jewels ("Would that I were a jewel ... that all my shining brilliants might fall at thy feet"), much the same way that the accompaniment begins to rise out of its darkness only to fall again in reflection of the text."[33]

The E♭ clouding the F minor lifts at measure 5 with the E♭ ninth sonority capping the verse with a half cadence. In measure 6, the dissonant F does not disappear into an E♭ with a move to an A♭ major tonality, but is retained as a common tone in yet another F minor triad with an added E♭ seventh, now with F at the top of the piano texture and the root of the triad that resumes the sixteenth-note flow of verse 2. The expected PAC is thus undercut and the A♭ tonality denied.

The vocal line is marked by prominent motion by a major or minor seventh, such as the minor seventh, E♭ to D♭ in measures 3–4 ("that" to "all"); the major seventh D♭–F–A♭–C outlined in measure 5; the E♭ to D♭ in measures 22–23 ("to anni-[hilate]"); and another major seventh from D♭ moving up by thirds to C in measures 25–26 ("Thou dark"), which in measure 27 supplies the optional ninth, E♭, as the singer's final pitch. The F is a central actor in the song, as the root of the F minor triad with added sixth that pervades the song, and which gives way to F♭ in measure 14 in both the voice's and the piano's G♭ ninth harmony on the crucial word "hide." Its disappearance is only brief, as it emerges in measure 15 in the B♭ minor seventh that leads to an E♭ dominant seventh at measure 18. The expected A♭ harmony is thwarted by the familiar F minor plus E♭ in the cascading sixteenth notes that resume in measure 19.

The turn from "shimmering silken garment" (mm. 8–9) whose folds "wrap and absorb thy body" (mm. 10–12) to the imperative "Hold and hide thy body" (mm. 13–14) has been read in contrasting ways in the literature.[34] Peters characterizes verse 2's "hide" and verse 3's "annihilate" as "disturbing verbs," with the second interpretation of the poem suggesting that the phrase "annihilate thy body" indicates the narrator's destruction from self-loathing of her "dark flesh," which cannot be disguised.[35] Smith likewise reads this verse as representative of "collective shame in the narrator's race and his body" and adds that the flame of annihilation can serve as a euphemism for lynching.[36] Lively muses that Price may have layered an "additional level of meaning" that conceals the concept of hiding, carrying forward Peters's argument that "a sense of despair" is concealed from "an alien society," through Henry Louis Gates's concept of an author's "signifyin(g)" of experiences – a practice that may be familiar to African Americans but not necessarily apparent to white readers.[37]

Durrant, in contrast, asserts that "hide" does *not* suggest shame, but rather is part of a "protective instinct" that is meant to "shield them [the speaker and her lover] from the violence of the outside world."[38] She hears the word "annihilate" in measures 22–23 over the E♭ leap of a major seventh up to D♭ as "set in a way that sounds exciting rather than intimidating," noting that the emphasis and elongation of the phrase "to annihilate thy body" sounds nonthreatening. She further hears measure 23's E♭ leap up to D♭ on "[to an]-ni-hi" as Price's "bold reclamation of these fears [of racial violence] and a "reimagining ... as a celebration of sexual pleasure," with Price's setting of the word "annihilate" as a representation of such pleasure.[39]

A queer hearing of verses 2 and 3 and of this particular passage savors the exuberant, playful, and sensuous pleasure of the shimmer, the enfolding, the absorption, and the annihilation. Brown's beautiful words about the song leave room for such a hearing:

In verse two, the "I" and the "body" are enveloped one with the other ("Would that I were a garment ... that all my folds might wrap about thy body"). Musically, the piano accompaniment encircles the voice, at times above it, at times they are in unison (sostenuto markings highlight the duet). The rapture is made complete in the final verse.[40]

Her remarks about the relationship of piano and voice, in their separation, encircling, and unison sounding, also bring to the surface the mutual pleasure of the I and the Thou.[41]

The F♮ that went briefly into hiding in measure 14, camouflaged as F♭, prominently reemerges in measure 16 beat 4 in a B♭ minor seventh; and in measure 21 to the words "one sharp" describing the flame of annihilation.[42] The F's absence in measure 23 is again brief, with the F emerging as a pedal in measure 24; F once again as part of an outlined D♭ major seventh triad, measures 25–26; and the F minor triad again clouding the stable A♭ tonic triad until the last three beats of the song when F finally no longer sounds, affirmed rather than reached, as discussed in the earlier section "Harmonic Adventures and Poetic Interpretations." An A♭ major or F minor tonality as the secure home for "Songs for the Dark Virgin" is never really established in the piece, thus maintaining the song's askew quality throughout.

Conclusion

The loving work of Carlene J. Brown and Guthrie P. Ramsey, Jr., thankfully has brought Rae Linda Brown's biography of Price, *The Heart of a Woman*, to posthumous publication.[43] As a community, we must safeguard this previous research and remain vigilant about those who would minimize or overlook this foundational body of work. The necessary revisioning of music history and music theory with Price as an agent will take root despite the clamor of voices that continue to deny the significance of composers outside the Western canon and that work to leave white supremacist patriarchy in place.[44] We hope that this study of Price's compositional practices will contribute to more extended explorations of the music and careers of composers and musicians who have long been excluded and marginalized.

As Ege observes, "When we highlight only a few figures, we isolate them from their communities. That kind of exceptionalism is not helpful; it continues to perpetuate this idea that there aren't Black classical musicians or composers, that there's only one or two great ones who come around once in a blue moon, but that's not true at all."[45] Price is but one example of a composer whose music should be more widely known. We should listen to, study, program, and bring her compositions into studies of music history, music theory, and twentieth-century arts and letters more broadly, as well as avoid exceptionalist narratives that promote only a handful of composers and musicians who achieved success "despite" their gender and/or race. In the words of Alexandra Kori Hill: "It is imperative that methodologies of Black composers, performers, and pedagogues are understood as part of ... [Western classical music] history, in addition to acknowledging the systemic barriers and setbacks those individuals and organizations faced in the past and in the present."[46]

Michele Moody-Adams remarks on the importance of "a genuinely dialogic engagement with the thought of those ... agents who make progress happen" and the "tireless exertion and passionate concern of dedicated individuals," quoting a speech delivered by Dr. Martin Luther King, Jr., in 1959.[47] That is, an individual's success is part of a cloth stitched by many who are often unsung and invisible. Future analytical approaches to Price's music might think through her work in the context of the community of women – friends, family, pupils, colleagues – that surrounded her compositional activity, recalling how Vanessa Blais-Tremblay has articulated the enmeshment of motherhood, caregiving, composition, and performance in the work of women jazz musicians.[48] Marc Edward Hannaford has recently applied this framework to a rich analysis of Mary Lou Williams, conceiving of her music theory "as a site of abstract, speculative work in service of Black creativity and life," where musical primary sources are read and heard through the community Williams created around her.[49] A feminist intersectional listening to Price should not extract her music from the communities from which it emerged, but ensure that it is understood as part of a collective endeavor of voices, marked by both struggle and success, which deserve a place in history.

Notes

1. A note about this essay: The authors cowrote the introduction and the conclusion; the sole-authored portions of the introduction are indicated. Jane Forner is primary author of the sections "Analyzing the Art Songs" and "Harmonic Adventures and Poetic Interpretations," and Ellie Hisama is primary author of the section "Listening 'in Our Various Ways' to 'Songs to the Dark Virgin': A Mosaic of Analytical Voices."
2. Saidiya Hartmann, "Venus in Two Acts," *Small Axe: A Caribbean Journal of Criticism* 12, no. 2 (2008): 1–14.
3. J. K. Thompson, "Florence Price," in "Women and Music," *Heresies: A Feminist Publication of Art and Politics* 10, 3, no. 2 (1980): 31, https://archive.org/details/heresies_10.
4. Rae Linda Brown, "Selected Orchestral Music of Florence B. Price (1888–1953) in the Context of Her Life and Work" (PhD diss., Yale University, 1987).
5. Samantha Ege, "Florence Price and the Politics of Her Existence," *Kapralova Society Journal: A Journal of Women in Music* 16, no. 1 (Spring 2018): 9.
6. I include a sample student response to an assignment focused on "Troubled Water" in Ellie M. Hisama, "Considering Race and Ethnicity in the Music Theory Classroom," in *Norton Guide to Teaching Music Theory*, edited by Rachel Lumsden and Jeff Swinkin (New York: W. W. Norton, 2018), 255–257.
7. The four papers presented at the plenary session – by Yayoi Uno Everett, Philip Ewell, Ellie M. Hisama, and Joseph N. Straus – were published, with an introduction by session chair Elizabeth West Marvin, in *Music Theory Spectrum* 43, no. 2 (Fall 2021): 320–363. The impact of graduate students is evident in the three open letters sent to the American Musicological Society, the Society for Music Theory, and the Society for Ethnomusicology in 2020 by the graduate-student-led advocacy group Project Spectrum: www.projectspectrummusic.com/publications.
8. Alison Martin, "Plainly Audible: Listening Intersectionally to the Amplified Noise Act in Washington, DC," *Journal of Popular Music Studies* 33, no. 4 (2021): 108.
9. Samantha Hannah Oboakorevue Ege, "The Aesthetics of Florence Price: Negotiating the Dissonances of a New World Nationalism" (PhD diss., University of York, 2020); Horace J. Maxile Jr., "Culture and Craft in Florence Price's Piano Sonata in E Minor (First Movement)," in *Analytical Essays on Music by Women Composers: Concert Music, 1900–1960*, edited by Laurel Parsons and Brenda Ravenscroft (New York: Oxford University Press, 2022), 137–163; Elektra V. Carter [formerly known as Marquese Carter], "The Poet and Her Songs: Analyzing the Art Songs of Florence B. Price" (DMA diss., Indiana University, 2018).
10. Ege, "Aesthetics of Florence Price," 74.

11. Ibid., 76.
12. Maxile, "Culture and Craft," 139–40.
13. Olly Wilson, "Black Music as an Art Form," in *The Jazz Cadence of American Culture*, edited by Robert G. O'Meally (New York: Columbia University Press, 1998), 93.
14. Maxile, "Culture and Craft," 140.
15. Ibid., 146.
16. Carter, "The Poet and Her Songs," 24.
17. Ibid., 27.
18. An analysis of Crawford's "Chinaman, Laundryman" is included in Ellie M. Hisama, "The Politics of Contour in Crawford's 'Chinaman, Laundryman,'" in *Gendering Musical Modernism: The Music of Ruth Crawford, Marion Bauer, and Miriam Gideon* (Cambridge: Cambridge University Press, 2001), 60–98.
19. Megan Lavengood and Brian Moseley provide a useful introduction to set theory, including identification of pitch-class sets, in the free online resource Open Music Theory, version 2, https://tinyurl.com/bdhz66kn.
20. In measure 55, there are four extra sixteenth notes without grouping indicated in the original score, a relatively common Price touch that indicates a freer, cadenza-style measure for the pianist.
21. Monica Michlin, "Langston Hughes's Blues," in *Temples for Tomorrow: Looking Back at the Harlem Renaissance*, edited by Geneviève Fabre and Michael Feith (Bloomington: Indiana University Press, 2001), 245.
22. Hughes's "Songs to the Dark Virgin" (1926) is available at https://poets.org/poem/songs-dark-virgin.
23. Mildred Denby Green, "A Study of the Lives and Works of Five Black Women Composers in America" (DME diss., University of Oklahoma, 1975), 124; Rae Linda Brown, *The Heart of a Woman: The Life and Music of Florence B. Price* (Urbana: University of Illinois Press, 2020), 225.
24. Barbara Christian, "The Race for Theory," *Cultural Critique* 6 (Spring 1987): 53.
25. Bethany Jo Smith, "'Song to the Dark Virgin': Race and Gender in Five Art Songs of Florence B. Price" (MM thesis, University of Cincinnati, 2007), 90.
26. Penelope Peters, "Deep Rivers: Selected Songs of Florence Price and Margaret Bonds," *Canadian University Music Review/Revue de musique des universités canadiennes* 16, no. 1 (1995): 80.
27. Meng-Chieh [Mavis] Hsieh, "A Stylistic and Comparative Analysis of Selected Art Songs by Florence Price and Margaret Bonds" (DMA thesis, Hartt School, 2019), 41.
28. Michael Lively, "Multi-Linear Continuity and 'Songs to the Dark Virgin' by Florence Price [1888–1953]," *College Music Symposium* 63, no. 1 (2023), 23 https://tinyurl.com/kacx486j.
29. Elizabeth Durrant, "Chicago Renaissance Women: Black Feminism in the Careers and Songs of Florence Price and Margaret Bonds" (MA thesis, University of North Texas, 2021), 21, 25.

30. For a discussion of Hughes in the context of a flourishing of queer cabaret culture, see Shane Vogel, "Closing Time: Langston Hughes and the Queer Poetics of Harlem Nightlife," *Criticism* 48, no. 3 (2006): 397–425.
31. Durrant, "Chicago Renaissance Women," 21.
32. Brown, *The Heart of a Woman*, 225.
33. Ibid.
34. Green notes the "intricate, folding line" of the accompaniment in measures 10–11; see Green, "Study of the Lives and Works," 125.
35. Peters, "Deep Rivers," 80.
36. Smith, "'Song to the Dark Virgin,'" 90.
37. Lively, "Multi-Linear Continuity," 26, 34, n.26, 21.
38. Durrant, "Chicago Renaissance Women," 23.
39. Ibid., 24–25.
40. Brown, *The Heart of a Woman*, 225–226.
41. Ibid. Brown notes that the "annihilate" provides a dramatic climax in the song.
42. Durrant refers to the presence of the F in measure 29 as a "harmonic disruption." See Durrant, "Chicago Renaissance Women," 25.
43. Brown, *The Heart of a Woman*, 226.
44. An important recent volume that illuminates the work of Afrodiasporic composers is *Composing While Black: Afrodiasporic New Music Today/ Afrodiasporische Neue Musik Heute*, edited by Harald Kisiedu and George E. Lewis, translated by Harald Kisiedu, Jessie Cox, and George E. Lewis (Hofheim: Wolke Verlag, 2023).
45. Stephen Raskauskas, "How Women of the Chicago Black Renaissance Changed Classical Music around the World," *WFMT*, April 10, 2018, https://tinyurl.com/4umtkfvd.
46. Alexandra Kori Hill, "Make the Familiar New: New Negro Modernism in the Concertos of Florence B. Price" (PhD diss., University of North Carolina at Chapel Hill, 2022), 161.
47. Michele Moody-Adams, "Repairing the Raft and Staying Afloat: Philosophy, Race, and Gender," unpublished manuscript, 2020; Martin Luther King, Jr., "Address at the Thirty-Fourth Annual Convention of the National Bar Association, Milwaukee, Wis., August 1959," in *The Papers of Martin Luther King, Jr.*, vol. V: *Threshold*, edited by Martin Luther King, Clayborne Carson, Ralph Luker, and Penny A. Russell (Berkeley: University of California Press, 1992), 267. Ellie Hisama thanks Professor Moody-Adams for sharing this manuscript.
48. Vanessa Blais-Tremblay, "'Where You Are Accepted, You Blossom': Toward Care Ethics in Jazz Historiography," *Jazz and Culture* 2 (2019): 59–83.
49. Marc Edward Hannaford, abstract of "Mary Lou Williams's Apartment: Sites of a Speculative Music Theory," paper presented at the Joint Annual Meeting of the American Musicological Society and the Society for Music Theory, November 11, 2023, Denver.

5 | Reflections of Price in the Mirror of Her Art Songs

MINNITA DANIEL-COX

A song is but a little thing,
And yet what joy it is to sing!
In hours of toil it gives me zest,
And when at eve I long for rest;
When cows come home along the bars,
And in the fold I hear the bell,
As Night, the shepherd, herds his stars,
I sing my song, and all is well.
—Paul Laurence Dunbar, "The Poet and His Song" (1895)

Published in 1940, Florence Price's setting of Paul Laurence Dunbar's "The Poet and His Song" conveys the spiritual sustenance of a song: Through days of toil, the joy of singing is a reminder that "all is well." Price understood the effectiveness of the written word and the manner in which songs use text to harness the transcendent communicative ability of the human voice, impacting the creator, performer, and listener.

As a result, her vocal works represent multiple layers of compositional choices through which she communicates a range of narratives, including those which stemmed from her innermost self. Within the works of Price, her values, hope, life experiences, and identity are revealed. Her choice of poets, sources, performers, themes, musical style, and linguistic style is made specifically to reflect herself, a Black woman, there between the "lines and dots."[1]

Price chose to represent her African American heritage unapologetically in her life and her compositions. She could have followed the practice of racial passing that was not uncommon for those of her time with a lighter complexion and ambiguous phenotype. Yet, she embraced her Black identity. Similarly, Price also could have composed under only a pen name or under her husband's name, hiding her sex, which was, again, not uncommon for women competing within the male-dominated classical sphere. Yet, she chose to reflect her womanhood in her music as well. Price's first, and most revolutionary, compositional choice was to acknowledge her own identity in the mirror of her works, and she encouraged other African

American women composers to do the same, as evident in her correspondence with Irene Britton Smith.

Her art songs were one of the most pertinent ways in which she represented herself. To do so effectively, Price chose poets from all spheres of society, setting those with great literary acclaim, local poets, and anonymous texts. Seen repeatedly in her art song texts are texts from women poets. including settings of Mary Rolofson Gamble's "The Moon Bridge," "Summer Clouds," and "Love-in-a-Mist," as well as a significant inclusion of African American women, such as settings of Georgia Douglas Johnson's "Lethe," "My Little Dreams," and "The Heart of a Woman" and Louise C. Wallace's "I Remember" and "The Crescent Moon." Another African American woman poet seen repeatedly in her songs is Price herself. However, of the diverse list of poets represented in Price's vocal oeuvre, Paul Laurence Dunbar (1872–1906) and Langston Hughes (1901–1967) appear most often. These writers were vital to the establishment and development of the African American Renaissance – a term that I use to best reflect the national scope of the Harlem Renaissance.

Price chose not only the words of Dunbar and Hughes but also their personas as representatives for her voice. In their works and lives they advocated for equality, celebrated Black culture, and highlighted the perspectives of Black women. That Price set them both regularly is evidence of the ways in which she saw her compositional voice as being in dialogue with Dunbar's and Hughes's own artistic and intellectual outlooks.

The Poets

Paul Laurence Dunbar, a native of Dayton, Ohio, was the first African American poet to make his "living by his pen."[2] Born in 1872, Dunbar was a household name by the time Price was born and was proclaimed the poet laureate of the Negro Race by Mary Church Terrell. His works were seminal in the establishment of the African American Renaissance, and throughout his tragic and short life he wrote diligently about the future and uplift of African Americans.

At seventeen, Dunbar published *The Tattler*, a newspaper for Dayton's African American community. His output of published poetry, essays, short stories, plays, musicals, and an operetta laid a foundation of influence for the African American literary voice. Dunbar's works are particularly noteworthy in that they offer historical snapshots of African American life at the turn of the twentieth century. His works set African American life as a celebrated centerpiece and include political views, current events, fashion, dances, cuisine, and other cultural elements.

During his lifetime he penned a libretto for Samuel Coleridge Taylor's operetta *Dream Lovers* and song lyrics to Broadway musicals with Will Marion Cook – works that are some of the earliest examples of contemporary American musical theater. Two such productions, *In Dahomey* and *Clorindy or The Origin of the Cake Walk*, were also some of the first examples of all-Black casts to play on Broadway. Since Dunbar's death in 1906, at the age of thirty-three, he has been the subject of several operas, including *The Mask in the Mirror* (2012) by Richard Thompson, *Paul Laurence Dunbar: Common Ground* (1995) by Adolphus Hailstork, *The Dunbar Operas* by Steven M. Allen (2016), and *The Mask* (2017) by Jeff Arwady.

Dunbar's influence within the African American literary tradition is so great that it is often taken for granted. His works influenced the titans of African American literature, including Langston Hughes (discussed more later), Maya Angelou, Nikki Giovanni, James Weldon Johnson, Claude McKay, and Margaret Walker. Paul Laurence Dunbar is your favorite poet's favorite poet. In fact, Angelou was so impacted by Dunbar's works that she used the phrase "I know why the caged bird sings" as title to both a poem and her autobiography. This line is extracted from Dunbar's poem "Sympathy":

When his wing is bruised and his bosom sore,—
When he beats his bars and he would be free;
It is not a carol of joy or glee,
But a prayer that he sends from his heart's deep core,
But a plea, that upward to Heaven he flings—
I know why the caged bird sings!

Price's affinity for Dunbar came with good reason, and she was not alone. His poetry has consistently been set by composers since his lifetime; they include, among others, H. Leslie Adams, Steven Allen, Carrie Jacobs Bond, B. E. Boykin, Harry T. Burleigh, John Carpenter, William Dawson, R. Nathaniel Dett, Reginald Evans, Marques L. A. Garrett, Adolphus Hailstork, Jake Heggie, Sylvia Hollifield, Ulysses Kay, Betty Jackson King, Lena McLin, Robert Owens, Zenobia Powell Perry, Simon Sargon, Irene Britton Smith, William Grant Still, Howard Swanson, Richard Thompson, George Walker, and Khyle B. Wooten. Price's settings of Dunbar include "Beside the Sea," "Dat's My Gal," "Easy-Goin'," "Dreamin' Town," "Forever," "Goo'-Bye, Jinks," "I Grew a Rose," "Life," "Love Song," "Lover's Lane," "My Neighbor," "Nightfall," "The Poet and His Song," "The Sum," "Summah

Night," "Sympathy," "Wadin' in de Creek," "Wen I Gits Home," "What's the Use?," and "The Wind and the Sea."

"What's the Use?," composed in 1937, is an example of Price's "crossover" composing. The dialect paired with the nonchalant nature of this song harken to early jazz, complete with a turnaround before the last tag. Here, Price juxtaposes a highly syncopated accompaniment with a patter-like melody. This melody, in a modified strophic form, is tuneful and mostly diatonic, with mode mixtures of the seventh and third scale degrees common in the African American musical tradition.

What's the use o' folks a-frownin'
When the way's a little rough?
Frowns lay out the road fur smilin'
You'll be wrinkled soon enough.
What's the use?
What's the use o' folks a-sighin'?
It's an awful waste o' breath,
An' a body can't stand wastin'
What he needs so bad in death.
What's the use?
What's the use o' even weepin'?
Might as well go 'long an' smile.
Life, our longest, strongest arrow,
Only lasts a little while.
What's the use?

The rapid succession of eighth-note arpeggiations in the vocal line mimic laughter, bouncing along playfully and challenging the performer to maintain vocal buoyancy and flexibility to support the levity of the text and give life to the varied tagline "What's the use?" (Ex. 5.1). The charm of the song lies in the vivid imagery and folk wisdom; life is too brief and valuable to frown, sigh, weep, or wallow. Seemingly shallow, this short, accessible song reflects a tenet found in the prayer of serenity – to accept the things you cannot change. The unchangeable certainty of the end of life is reason enough to enjoy it in the meantime. It is our gift or our "longest, strongest arrow." The profound humor of Dunbar's dialect poetry, the elegant excellence of his standard English poetry, and the celebrated Blackness in it all would time and again attract Price's compositional interest.

Dunbar gave the development of African American literature a good start but left much work to be done. That was continued by a poet born in Joplin, Missouri, 1901: James Mercer Langston Hughes. Hughes was

Example 5.1 "What's the Use?," mm. 23–28.

heavily influenced by the works of Dunbar. While a college education was denied Dunbar, Hughes attended Columbia University and completed his education at Lincoln University in Pennsylvania. He won the Harmon gold medal for literature in 1930 for *Not Without Laughter*, his very first novel. As a columnist for the *Chicago Defender*, he discussed African American contemporary concerns. In Hughes, the Black excellence of Dunbar continued. Descended from Dunbar's world of spirituals, minstrel music, parlor and work songs, Hughes lived in a world of gospel, stride, blues, swing, and jazz. Hughes is credited with having written the first jazz poem, "The Weary Blues", and with it he established the jazz poetry genre – a fusion of jazz rhythms and spoken poetic texts. With Countee Cullen, Zora Neale Hurston, and Claude McKay as literary peers, Hughes would empower new generations of Black writers. The roots of the African American Renaissance would continue to bear fruit in the material of

Sonia Sanchez, Yusef Komunyaaka, Jane Cortez, and Amiri Baraka as Black art edified Black art.

While both Dunbar and Hughes were forced to work menial jobs due to lack of opportunity, Hughes was able to leverage these jobs to see the world and traveled as Dunbar did not. Hughes traveled to Benin, Cameroon, Côte d'Ivoire, England, France, Ghana, Italy, Nigeria, Russia, Senegal, Spain, and Togo, sampling cultures around the world – yet struggle continued. Hughes is the source of the inspiration for Lorraine Hansberry's *A Raisin in the Sun*, debuted on Broadway in 1959, and Martin Luther King's "I Have a Dream" speech delivered in 1963. The sentiments of Dunbar's "We Wear the Mask," published in 1895, reverberate in Hughes's "Minstrel Man," published in 1925 thirty years later. The influence of Dunbar and Hughes is incalculable.

As with Dunbar, many composers have been drawn to Hughes's texts. They include H. Leslie Adams, William Bolcom, Margaret Bonds, Uzee Brown, Dave Brubeck, John Alden Carpenter, Cecil Cohen, Ricky Ian Gordon, Sylvia Hollifield, Hall Johnson, Dorothy Rudd Moore, John Musto, Robert Owens, Ned Rorem, Erik Santos, Elie Siegmeister, William Grant Still, Howard Swanson, Richard Thompson, George Walker, and many more. Price and Hughes were contemporaries at a time when thriving networks of African American artists were well connected. Price might have met Hughes through Estella and Margaret Bonds; Margaret's rich collaboration with Hughes marked a defining point in her career. Whatever the circumstances of Price's introduction to Hughes, she set his texts repeatedly. Price's settings of Hughes include "Ardella," "Bewilderment," "Dream Ships," "Fantasy in Purple," "Feet o' Jesus," "Hold Fast to Dreams," "Judgement Day," "Monologue for the Working Class," "My Dream," "Songs to the Dark Virgin," and "We Have Tomorrow."

"Songs to the Dark Virgin," one of Price's most celebrated art songs, was made famous by Marian Anderson on her second American tour. It has been performed and recorded repeatedly in the century since its composition. Complex in nature, this poetry could be viewed in a variety of ways. Price chose to interpret the text metaphorically, producing a romantic setting in which the poet offers their complete being in exchange for that of the "dark one."

This art song is written in the tradition of German lied, with the piano accompaniment embodying powerful musical moments and poetic concepts, uniting text and music into one. In the African American answer to Franz Schubert's "Gretchen am Spinnrade," the introduction begins with surging arpeggiations through both hands in the piano. This gently pulsating figure supports the beginning of each strophe, like a throbbing heartbeat, and melts helplessly into the stillness that punctuates the refrain "Thou dark one." Each of the three stanzas is set with great attention to linguistic rhythm. The singing tradition of African Americans is not lost in Price's works, and a memorable, singable melody like the one in this song is her hallmark. This gently rising melody is modified in each strophe through rhythmic augmentation and melodic variation, with each variance broadening beyond the last. This evolving melody is accompanied by new harmonies and varying harmonic rhythms, elongating the lines and creating growing intensity. This stretching emphasizes the contrast between the movement and stillness of the piece and creates a vastly different musical context for the repetition of the refrain. A masterful composer for the voice, Price set the stage for the skilled performer to employ timbral variety and communicative presentation to complete a stunning art song.

The result is a work that rushes forward only to hesitate as the lovesick are wont to do. Evidence of Price's masterful fusion of music and text is exhibited by the fourth measure. The established arpeggiated pattern in the piano shifts from bass to treble clef, mirroring the melody and descending with the text "shining brilliants might fall." Another especially effective moment of text painting occurs in the harmonic hug of a major chord shifting to diminished under the text "hold and hide." This sensitivity to text is prevalent throughout Price's song output. She set text, whether in dialect or standard English, with clarity and ardor. Price wrote lieder with seasoning!

Cultural elements of marginalized communities are often safeguarded underground or outside of the mainstream. Both Dunbar and Hughes created a literary African American *verismo* through their use of realistic contexts and dialectical tendencies that intersected with two popular genres of their time: minstrelsy and jazz. Dunbar's collaborations with Will Marion Cook represent the earliest days of contemporary American musical theater and are a part of the minstrel tradition. This controversial art form used blackface, racial slurs, and stereotypes for comedic entertainment. Intersecting with dimensions of the minstrel tradition, jazz was vilified and called the "devil's music."

Both minstrel music and jazz created unfiltered platforms where the "inappropriate" could reside. Problematic linguistic and thematic considerations aside, minstrelsy and its descendants (jazz, blues, hip hop, rock, country, and house) are places of frank anger, lust, rebellion, hope, and celebration – all influencing each other and evolving without the filter of "polite" society. Minstrel music and jazz archived unfiltered cultural elements and created arenas for furtherance of rebellious Black thought. While tropes and stereotypes abound within these realms, they are, in part, distractions, hiding the real messages; "Every Niggah (Dahkey) is a King" from Dunbar and Cook's *In Dahomey* in 1903 evolves into "Every Nigger is a Star" from Boris Gardiner's album of the same name in 1973 to "Wesley's Theory" from Kendrick Lamar's *To Pimp a Butterfly* released in 2015.

The horrifically beautiful developmental journey of spirituals, minstrelsy, and jazz mirrors that of African Americans as a whole. Whether caused by discomfort with this journey or intellectual racism, the prioritization of the Western European classical tradition in North American academia has created an extreme lack of pedagogical and academic research regarding the musical linkages between minstrelsy, jazz, rock, hip hop, and house music and their impact on American culture. These genres propagated styles that have impacted music globally, appearing both in their original forms, influencing other musical styles, and creating new genres like contemporary country, reggae, R&B, pop, and hip hop. The impact of hip hop, fruit of the minstrelsy tree, is an excellent example and brings to mind the highlife of Ghana, the ska of Jamaica, the Chicano rap of Mexico, the Brit-hop of the United Kingdom, and rap in Russia, where it maintains its political voice and is used to "fight the powers that be."[3] The nine elements of hip hop – B-boyin, Emceein, Graffiti Art, Deejayin, Beatboxin, Street Fashion, Street Language, Street Knowledge, and Street Entrepreneurialism – have affected culture on a worldwide scale. This is simply one extension of the legacy of Dunbar and Hughes.

These rebellious, dialect-wielding poets would connect with the edgiest music of their time, helping to inspire numerous other artists in various genres and media. And their intent is not lost. Indeed, N.W.A.'s "Fuck tha Police," released in 1988, both reflected the historic violence of slave patrols and gave prophesy to a renewed civil rights movement that would begin with the murder of George Floyd on May 5, 2020. The exclusion of a scholarly focus that puts these genres into conversation with each other has drawn a metaphorical line in the sand between music of the classical European tradition and the music of the African American tradition.

Within the confines of her era, Florence Price was edgy in her own way and regularly traversed this line musically, carefully merging styles or simply eliminating stylistic lines completely when desired. She composed music for the concert stage, advertisements, and Chicago's "Black Belt" movie theaters, using the pen name Vee Jay for times when she desired anonymity. Whether she moved between concert and contemporary music due to financial need or personal desire, she did it with fluency and excellence. Dunbar, Hughes, and Price all understood the racial coding of "appropriate" art and the need to step outside the privilege of formality to connect with and represent African Americans of all classes and walks of life.

Dialect

Dunbar's and Hughes's musical influences are natural byproducts of their revolutionary literary work. Both used their linguistic skills to create works that depicted African American culture not only through relevant topics, traditions, experiences, and perspectives, but dialect as well.

Dunbar came of age in the era of the plantation literature tradition, where authors used stock characters to portray whitewashed and idyllic antebellum scenes from the days of yore. The push to "make America great again" has been the reaction to each progressive movement within the United States since its inception, and Dunbar's time was no different.

Uninterested in looking back, newly freed African Americans looked forward and sought to establish and reclaim their representation in American culture. The deceptively simple question "No longer enslaved, who do we want to be now?" led to the question of separation versus integration. This was more than a decision regarding physical proximity to whites; it was one of assimilation into white culture. Should African Americans prove their equality by conforming to white cultural standards or should they, already so excluded, remain removed? This conundrum would filter into the artistic language of this time. Could not African Americans speak as eloquently as whites? Some would attempt to prove their equality in this way and distance themselves from dialect, as it was seen by some as a continuation of the minstrel and plantation tradition legacy.

The challenge of dialect comprehension by whites also created a sublanguage for African Americans, highlighting cultural differences all the more. It should be noted that the dialect of minstrel shows intended harm, but that does not negate its value to the relevant communities. Though complex and exact, African American dialect was, and still is, considered "unprofessional" and/or "inappropriate." Nonetheless, Dunbar used dialect and stock characters to deliver scathing social commentary and to depict honestly and accurately the familial lives of African Americans, as in "When They 'Listed Colored Soldiers."

Hughes's "I, Too" continues in this tradition, but his bold advocacy contrasts with Dunbar's necessarily more understated approach. No longer are messages of discontent shrouded in dialect, stock characters, and analogies; nor are sexual implications filtered through Victorian values. The "New Negro" turns inward, and third person becomes first. The dialectical approach had evolved, but the goal remained the same: to give dignity to the Black experience. As Hughes said in his essay "The Negro Artist and the Racial Mountain": "We younger Negro artists who create now intend to express our individual dark-skinned selves without fear or shame. If white people are pleased, we are glad. If they are not, it doesn't matter. We know we are beautiful. And ugly too."[4]

Price's choice to use dialect in her songs speaks volumes. She saw herself reflected there as well and returned to it time and again throughout her vocal works. It is because of this that her dialect compositions should be performed and studied in the scrupulous manner of any foreign language repertoire, with attention to diction and style. The racial dynamic in the United States has created a sensitivity regarding the performance of spirituals and songs in dialect. With a history of musical appropriation and racism, some hesitation is to be expected. All that is required for the successful performance of these works is respect for the genre, ability to communicate vocally, and understanding of one's audience. Hall Johnson describes the most important consideration as "the right mental attitude on the part of the singer." The right attitude will create a genuine connection to the song and avoid a "minstrel show" with caricatures that would cause embarrassment for performer and audience.

Because the dialect in Price's songs is born of the African American experience, they are at their core about race and, as such, their cultural elements should be fully embraced. Tools like the *Dunbar Dialect Glossary* housed at the University of Dayton and Felicia Raphael Marie Barber's *A New Perspective for the Use of Dialect in African American Spirituals: History, Context, and Linguistics*, as well as forewords to collections including *The Books of American Negro Spirituals* by James Weldon and J. Rosamond Johnson (plus other writings by them) and *Thirty Spirituals Arranged for Piano and Voice* by Hall Johnson, are all very helpful for preliminary study. Additional coaching with specialists regarding delivery and style is imperative, as is listening. Numerous resources of recorded dialect song literature exist and they should be noted for their style. Recorded performers of this repertoire include Marian Anderson, Kathleen Battle, Harry Belafonte, Angela Brown, H. T. Burleigh, the Fisk Jubilee Singers, Roland Hayes, Mahalia Jackson, Robert McFerrin, Jessye Norman, Odetta, Leontyne Price, Florence Quivar, Derek Lee Ragin, Paul Robeson, George Shirley, Darryl Taylor, and Louise Toppin.

Example 5.2 "Don't You Tell Me No," mm. 26–33.

In Her Own Words

Based on her known works, Price is one of the most popular poetic sources for her songs. It seems that sometimes someone else's words simply would not do. By writing her own texts, Price archives her lived experiences. In addition to the texts for "Resignation," "Spring," and "Trouble Done Come My Way," Price penned "Don't You Tell Me No" sometime after her move to Chicago. Composed between 1931 and 1934, this Tin Pan Alley style song features the melodramatic style and trendy vernacular common for the genre.

The song is in AABA form with an introductory verse. Above an accompaniment influenced by cakewalk and ragtime, the syncopated entrance of the chorus croons with a descent and rise on the text "O mama," toggling playfully between a raised and flatted third (Ex. 5.2). Continuing with chromatic ascent, the melody rises and falls, matching the pleading of the text. The syllabically set B section begins with "Don't scold me, just hold me" on repeated notes, pleading further. The sassy and playful character of this song requires facility with vernacular and large intervallic leaps. The performance practices of parlor and Tin Pan Alley style songs, with occasional glissandos and a more straight tone, are acceptable and expected. This work harkens to the 1899 hit "Hello, My Baby," but boasts a more elegant melody and sophisticated harmonies.

Themes, Sources, and Styles

Price regularly chose themes that celebrate common human experiences. But it is the consistent elevation of, and advocacy for, the Black female perspective that makes her work revolutionary. To take the African American woman, whom Malcom X described as "the most disrespected person in America," and celebrate her worth and value, in the face of rejected suffrage and Jim Crow was, and still is, revolutionary. Price brings to the table a compositional dexterity made possible by her experiences, education, and naturally prodigious gifts. By including universal themes within the beautifully diverse spectrum of Black feminine experience, she both contextualizes that experience and highlights its humanity. As Rae Linda Brown noted: "Marginalized in her occupation, by her gender, and by her race, Price's story is not one of defeat but one of triumph specific to African American women." Price's reflection in her songs is present in the literal representation of both the Black and the feminine at a time when issues of race often superseded those of gender. Phrases such as "Thou dark one" and "A great swart cheek" adorn songs that directly depict the Black woman. "Brown Arms," "Songs to the Dark Virgin," and "The Washerwoman" are all examples of works that reflect Black womanhood.

Price's texts for the voice draw from a variety of sources and topics, from the sacred and profound to the secular and humorous. "The Glory of the Day Was in Her Face," a song of stately grandeur; "The Flea and the Fly," a song of wry humor; "We Have Tomorrow," a song of hope; and "The Heart of a Woman," a song of longing, are just a sampling of the wide spectrum of topics and moods within her songs. Of her sacred vocal works, texts are most often drawn from spirituals (as Elektra V. Carter explores in Chapter 6). Her sacred text settings can be seen as representative of personal beliefs; her Presbyterian upbringing exposed her not only to a Christian faith that would sustain her throughout her life, but also to hymnody and sacred works commonly performed in the conservative church style of worship to which she was accustomed.

Her numerous sacred works mirror the faith of her personal life, with "Death's Gwineter Lay His Cold Icy Hand on Me," "Go Down, Moses,"

"Heav'n Bound Soldier," "I Am Bound for the Kingdom," "I Couldn't Hear Nobody Pray," "I'm Goin' to Lay Down My Heavy Load," "I'm Workin' on My Buildin'," "Joshua Fit the Battle of Jericho," "My Little Soul's Goin' to Shine," "My Soul's Been Anchored in de Lord," "Nobody Knows the Trouble I've Seen," "Peter Go Ring dem Bells," "Rise Mourner," "Save Me Lord, Save Me," "Some o' These Days," "Weary Traveler," "Were You There When They Crucified My Lord?," and "You Won't Find a Man Like Jesus," all serving as examples.

In addition to her mastery of more traditional classical styles, Price wrote contemporary music of her time and has a significant output of popular songs, often composed under the pen name Vee Jay. These songs include ballad, dance music, and vaudeville styles and appeared in advertisements and musicals. She often used Chicagoan poets for these works, and she collaborated with poet LeRoy Gregory often. Her skill with improvisational styles of the contemporary music of her time made her a sought-after composer in the genre. Some of these compositions include "If I Didn't Love You," "Just to Be Near You," "Let's Give Love Another Try," and "You're in My Heart to Stay." These songs evidence the ways in which Price leaps easily from classical to popular with skill made possible only by existing within multiple intersections. "Don't You Tell Me No" and "What's the Use?" are examples of this effective and accessible music as well.

Musical Autobiography

Price's songs are not just a reflection of who she was, but of her life journey also. Through her works Price shows us not just any African American feminine experience, but her own specifically. Price experienced racial and political struggle: two marriages, one ending in divorce and the other in separation; the birth of three children; the death of a child; single motherhood; ill health; and a myriad of other dishes from the buffet of life. As compositional responses to these events, these songs are the most direct reflection of Price.

A general autobiographical assumption can be made regarding her move to Chicago, her divorce, and her compositional output. Once settled in Chicago, Price continued her musical education and submitted numerous compositions to the 1931 and 1932 Wanamaker competitions. More than simply writing to pay the bills or teach, Price thrived in Chicago and her song output reflects this, with most of them composed after 1934 (i.e., after she achieved national acclaim). The high artistic quality and variety of her songs from this period, intermingled with an output of varied instrumentation and style, signaled a compositional maturation. Whether bolstered by her divorce, her relocation, her furthered education, or her participation in a thriving arts community (most likely a bit of all four), it is clear that this new life proved fertile compositional soil.

While her biographical songs may not align chronologically with Price's major life events, many of her songs reflect her responses to her lived experiences. Several of her songs are dedicated to her daughters. To daughter Edith, her dedications include "God Gives Me You," (for her 1943 wedding) and "Easy Goin'." Price's namesake, Florence Louise, is the dedicatee of "Child Asleep," (written for her fifteenth birthday), "Songs to the Dark Virgin," and "Sympathy." It was she who proved pivotal in promoting her mother's compositions and is responsible for submitting Price's papers to the University of Arkansas, where they are housed. Price also gave birth to a son in 1914, Thomas Jr., who died in early childhood and whose memory Price kept alive with the undated art song "To My Little Son" (based on the eponymous poem by Julia Johnson Davis). Its first four lines open, poignantly:

In your face I sometimes see
Shadowings of the man to be,
And eager, dream of what my son
Shall be in twenty years and one.

It was not until twenty years after her mother broke ties with the African American side of her family and moved to Indiana that Price composed "Brown Arms." This heartbreaking composition, with text by Price, is dedicated "To Mother." The solemn song provides insight into Price's feelings about the abandonment of her mother. Much like the loss of her son, this event was life-changing for her. She submitted this profoundly personal song to the Wanamaker competition but lost to her student and friend Margaret Bonds that year.

Listen, oh brown kind mother,
I am weary and I would rest.
Put your old warm arms about me,
Let me lie on your withered breast.

I am very sick of cities,
Of faces cold and strange;
I long for your sun-washed spaces,
Blue skies and windswept range.

Example 5.3 "Brown Arms," mm. 13–17.

I am sick of huddled houses
And the selfish hearts of men.
Put your warm kind arms about me,
Let me lie on your heart again.

The accompaniment for this song begins with a pedal open fifth in the left hand of the piano accented with drum-like, pentatonic, parallel chords in the right hand, possibly indicating influence of the Indianist movement of the late nineteenth and early twentieth centuries (Samuel Coleridge Taylor's *The Song of Hiawatha* is another reflection of this popular movement). The use of the pentatonic scale is well documented in spirituals as well, and both may have drawn Price to set the emotional work in this manner. The strength established by the rhythmic opening chordal motive expands into chromaticism as the emotions of the text build (Ex. 5.3), only to return and be overcome with emotion again in the final section.

Example 5.4 "Brown Arms," mm. 20–26.

Within the accompaniment is felt the determination to share profound emotion and the spilling over that comes with that sharing. The rhythmic repetition in the accompaniment sets the tone and repeats, creating a pattern that establishes a haunting atmosphere and over which the melody lies exposed. The irregular melody outlines a minor pentatonic scale, shifting with the accompaniment through the chromatic sections. The melody is through-composed; chant-like moments contrast with sections of soaring lyricism. In one such lyric moment, Price uses the accompaniment to describe the "wind swept range" of a mother's love, with a glissando that flows up and down, then ascends above the staff and sweeps down across the staves landing in the left hand (Ex. 5.4). This sweeping motion continues through the following interlude with upward sweeping eighth-note chords in the right hand.

The song ends in a world of emotional vulnerability. With the motive abandoned and shifting into the relative major, the final melodic line extends upward, sobbing up a perfect fifth – pleading. The final note floats above the staff, not quite resolving satisfactorily, on the third scale degree.

The Dedications

Dedications and songs written for specific performers offer another incredible glimpse into Price's heart. In a subtle but telling gesture, Price's song dedications regularly paid tribute to Black women. Price not only reflected the African American feminine perspective in her works, but those songs – those mirrors – are then gifted to those she wanted to honor.

One such revealing dedication heads Price's *Two Traditional Negro Spirituals*. Composed in 1930 and published in 1939, the dedication reads, "as sung by the slave grandmother of Fannie Carter Woods, Chicago, Illinois." Woods's grandmother, Malinda Carter, sang these melodies to Price for her to notate and preserve. In his *Florence Price: Two Negro Spirituals*, John Michael Cooper states that "the main autograph shows that Price originally notated the melodies as they were already known to her, but then altered them – adding some notes, changing others, making an annotation about performance style ('a pitch between F and F sharp') in order to reflect Fannie Carter Woods's renditions." Price's zeal to accurately preserve this music by putting the singer's knowledge above her own reflects her unwavering commitment to honor the voices of African American women. Price's *Two Traditional Negro Spirituals* also show her commitment to embrace her diasporic legacy. These were her spirituals too.

At the time of her death, Marian Anderson, the world-famous contralto, had compositions from numerous composers in her collection. Many of them were by women, and over fifty of those compositions were sent to her by Florence B. Price. Price chose the voice of a pioneering African American woman and advocate for civil rights to perform her works, and she eagerly collaborated with the singer to arrange the works specifically for Anderson's voice and preferences. This choice was not a difficult one, as Anderson's fame lent credibility to any composer whose music she performed. By performing Price's "My Soul's Been Anchored in de Lord" on the steps of the Lincoln Memorial in 1939 and including Price's "Songs to the Dark Virgin" on her second American tour, Anderson cemented their successful relationship. Letters between Price and composer John Alden Carpenter provide evidence of the effectiveness of this collaboration. After having to request Carpenter's sponsorship for her induction into the American Society of Composers, Authors, and Publishers (ASCAP) at the outset of her career, Price could, and did, return the favor by granting Carpenter access to Anderson.

Born in Philadelphia in 1897, Anderson became the first African American singer to perform at the New York Metropolitan Opera in 1955. Due to career limitations and overt racism in the United States, Anderson established her career as a concert and recital artist rather than on the operatic stage. She worked as a delegate to the United Nations Human Rights Committee, a goodwill ambassador for the United States Department of State. An important voice for the civil rights movement, she sang at the March on Washington for Jobs and Freedom in 1963. That same year she was the recipient of the first Presidential Medal of Freedom, followed by the Congressional Gold Medal in 1977, Kennedy Center Honors in 1978, the National Medal of Arts in 1986, and a GRAMMY Lifetime Achievement Award in 1991.

Anderson's background contrasts with Price's, as her family lacked means for her formal music training. Instead, she found support in her musical pursuits through her church and community. Despite their differing origins, their collaboration became a force for equal rights as Anderson championed Price's music. Alisha Lola Jones describes how Price met Anderson in the 1930s: "both women became deeply entrenched in a network of black women artisans. They found refuge, exposure, and collaborative partners in black musician's guilds such as the NANM [National Association of Negro Musicians]."[54] Elizabeth Durrant explores this further in Chapter 12.

Price's relationship with Anderson was inspirational and career-changing, each amplifying the excellence of the other. Price chose Anderson as her voice more than any other singer. Their connection was one of friendship and warmth, as indicated in a letter from Price in 1944 beginning with greetings to her "Dear Friend" and concluding with well wishes from her daughters and herself. In Anderson, Price found a performing voice that mirrored her own compositional one and that understood her "in-betweenness," to borrow a phrase from Naomi André. Price, as a composer, mirrored this dual artistic, racial, and political consciousness. In Anderson, Price seemed to see herself. She had chosen one of the most powerful voices of her era to sound for her. In turn, Anderson was able to program repertoire of the highest caliber that reflected and celebrated her own Black femininity.

Conclusion

Florence B. Price amplified the voices of Black women while modeling the excellence and equality celebrated by the African American Renaissance. She portrayed Black women in her works not only as brilliant, capable, and strong, but also weak, abused, forgotten, and resigned. She chose themes that gave voice to African American culture, women, and spiritual tradition; and she chose a diverse array of poets and returned regularly to poets and performers whose activist goals matched her own. From the joys of motherhood and love to the ongoing pain of racist and sexist oppression to the sustenance of faith, Price is reflected in her vocal works, filtered through the rich complexity unique to an intersectional life. The mirrored facets of each song reflect a freedom of expression that Price did not experience in her physical life. These songs reflect who she was, her journey, and who she hoped to be: a Florence bold enough to make demands and advocate without reservation or apology. Restricted by racism and sexism, we can only know what Florence Price was capable of accomplishing, *in spite of*. The celebration of her triumphs must always be tempered with the sober realization that there could have been so much more.

Regardless of what could have been, Price reflected herself in every facet of her compositional process from sources, topics, and themes to poets, dedicatees, and performers. In them she saw reflections of herself, and she utilized the chronological collaboration between poet, composer, and performer to integrate that reflection into every layer of her compositions, intensifying the Black feminine intent. Price understood the infinite value of her representation and knew that in celebrating herself in her songs she celebrated all Black women. This revolutionary act created the American voice for which composers of her time were so desperately searching. The charge to take up the mantle of her songs and celebrate her identity with her belongs to every singer.

Notes

1. "Lines and dots" pays homage to Paul Lawrence Dunbar's poem "When Malindy Sings" (1895), in which he writes "Easy 'nough fu' folks to hollah, / Lookin' at de lines an' dots." In summary, Dunbar is talking about the prescriptive nature of sheet music's lines (i.e., the stave) and dots (i.e., the notes). As a Black woman, Price expresses herself in between and far beyond classical music's prescriptive methods. Paul Laurence Dunbar, "When Malindy Sings,"

in *Majors and Minors: Poems by Paul Laurence Dunbar* (Toledo, OH: Hadley & Hadley, 1895), 139.
2. Thomas Morgan, "I Know Why the Caged Bird Sings," preperformance lecture at University of Dayton, February 25, 2012.
3. This line comes from Public Enemy's song "Fight the Power," which was released on the album *Fear of a Black Planet* in 1990.
4. Langston Hughes, "The Negro Artist and the Racial Mountain," *The Nation*, June 23, 1926, 692–693.
5. Alisha Lola Jones, "Lift Every Voice: Marian Anderson, Florence B. Price and the Sound of Black Sisterhood," NPR, August 30, 2019, https://tinyurl.com/3y7metwt.

6 | The Concert Spirituals: Price as Griot-Composer

ELEKTRA V. CARTER

Marian Anderson's famous 1939 recital upon the steps of the Lincoln Memorial has been cemented in social memory as a significant step in the movement for racial equality. Anderson began with "My Country 'Tis of Thee" – an ironic nod of patriotism in the face of Jim Crow segregationist policies that barred her from Constitution Hall – and ended with Florence Price's rousing "My Soul's Been Anchored in the Lord" (Price uses "de Lord" in her monograph copy). The latter, a spiritual that has become psychosocially associated with the steadfast ethos of nonviolent resistance, still stands as a vital piece of concert spiritual repertoire. The minor pentatonic melody and the call-and-response refrain "my soul's been anchored in the Lord" fall under what Amiri Baraka termed "Afrological" expressive tools.[1] On the other hand, the operatic range and melodic sweep, the Tchaikovskian piano accompaniment, and the use of developmental gestures preceding the final refrain hearken to Eurological tools learned through her classical training. "My Soul's Been Anchored in the Lord" is also an example of a speakerly text – in this case, a folk text that has taken on multiple levels of meaning ranging from a devotional outcry to a political rallying cry.[2]

In this way, Price becomes part of the griot tradition in a modernistic context. Like Robert Schumann transmitting personal narrative through German lieder, Price passes along both personal and political narratives of Black resilience through faith in the Negro spiritual genre. She is a keeper of the oral tradition in the same way the djeli class of the Mande people transmit their oral history through the kora song repertoire.[3] These two aesthetics (i.e., the Eurological and Afrological) do not overshadow the other, but rather create a unique expressive framework greater than the sum of these stylistic parts.

In this chapter I explore the evolving ethic of the concert spiritual and venture a working definition of this genre through Price's own oeuvre. To achieve this, I contextualize the concert spiritual as a vital part of Price's career, offer analyses of musical style and signifyin(g)[4] gestures in her published and unpublished spirituals, and explore a unique addition to the vocal genre – what I have come to call pseudo-spirituals.

The Development of the Concert Spiritual

The genesis of the concert spiritual was the result of generations of oral transmission and intercultural exchange between white and Black musicians. Their prevalence was preceded by the folk spiritual repertoire. Eileen Southern wonderfully summarizes the emergence of the folk spiritual genre in *The Music of Black Americans*:

> It is not known precisely when the term *spiritual* was first used in print to apply to the religious folksongs of the black American. Obviously, the term points back to the three species of sacred song early set up in the history of Protestantism – psalms, hymns, and spirituals – which, in turn, points to the Scriptures, Col. 3:16. . . . Over the years black men and women would have had ample freedom to develop a repertory of religious songs away from the surveillance of the whites, in the independent black churches, segregated camp and bush meetings, and "invisible churches" on the plantations.[5]

The folk spiritual takes on a new identity in the hands of Black arrangers at land-grant institutions around the turn of the twentieth century. The works of Ella Sheppard and the successful tours of the Fisk Jubilee Singers helped to catapult the Negro spiritual to the status of an emergent commercial genre. While the choral and commercial spirituals experienced a rise in popularity, Harry T. Burleigh began to codify a musical language for spirituals to be used in classical concert settings. Eileen Southern later discusses the importance of the emergence of the concert spiritual and Burleigh's compositions:

> As an arranger of spirituals for the solo voice Burleigh made a unique contribution to the history of American music. Before he published his "Jubilee Songs of the United States of America in 1916," spirituals were performed on the concert stage only in ensemble or choral arrangements. Burleigh's achievement made available to concert singers for the first time Negro spirituals set in the manner of art songs.[6]

Burleigh and his collaboration with Dvořák have consistently been credited with helping to open the door to the proliferation of the spiritual as a concert genre. The economic advantage of music notation versus the oral tradition was that this powerfully affective genre could now enter the hallowed halls revered by "respectable" white society. Concurrently with the racial uplift of the New Negro Renaissance, there arose a tension amongst Black composers and historiographers tied to aesthetic representation. Guthrie P. Ramsey, Jr., notes:

A most striking quality of early Black music historiography ideology is how writers ... particularly African-American ones ... negotiated the generally accepted "divide" between Euro-based and Afro-based aesthetic perspectives ... writers in the cosmopolitan school took their creative and intellectual direction from Europe, extending Old World practices, attitudes, and hegemony. The provincial group, on the other hand, "involved those who resisted, or reinterpreted, or, most likely, failed to receive: the pan-European musical model promoted by the cosmopolitan school."[7]

Although Ramsey, in his description of the cosmopolitan vs. provincial dichotomy proposed by Richard Crawford, references trends among historiographers of the eighteenth century, it is not difficult to see similar trends among composers of Price's time.[8] As noted previously, Price subverted these dichotomous expectations in a highly individual style. By the middle of the twentieth century, the inclusion of concert spirituals for voice and other instruments in classical recital programs had become a standard practice by Black performers. Even in the present day, the National Association of Negro Musicians (NANM) requires the inclusion of spiritual arrangements for their vocal competitions. One Black concertgoer captured how ubiquitous the concert Negro spiritual had become by the 1960s:

Attending a recital of a Negro singer in Orchestra Hall, recently, I was amazed, disappointed and hurt, to note that she did not include in her program any Negro spirituals.... Millions of Negroes will never make it, unless our greats remember to "lift as we climb."[9]

This dictum "lift as we climb" embodies the uplift ethos of the New Negro. Implicit in this statement is the responsibility of those Black folk who had distinguished themselves and the race to help others to reach their achieved status. Price honored this call in her own way by always including the spiritual topic even as she achieved wider acclaim.

The importance of the social fabric of Black Chicago concert life cannot be underestimated, given that this was the city in which Price established her renown. Concert artists such as Chicago native Abbie Mitchell made it their mission to promote new works by Black composers. Mitchell included works by Price in recitals at the Chicago Civic Theatre (1931) and at the Chicago Woman's Club (1935).[10] Exploring the rich concert music culture of 1890–1930s Chicago, Ellistine Perkins Holly writes, "Black concert life in early twentieth-century Chicago was an interesting mix of church Lyceum and Sunday Clubs, jubilee troupes, dramatic and music concert companies, choral clubs, and occasionally, theater concerts and recitals."[11] The proliferation of the spirituals are a sterling example of this network's efficiency.

Marian Anderson advanced wider cultural appreciation of the concert spiritual not only through her 1939 performance of "My Soul's Been Anchored in the Lord" but also through her commercial recording of the work and the programming of concert spiritual sets in her recitals.[12] This lifelong sense of sisterhood between Anderson and Price contributed to the long-term canonization of this particular concert spiritual through numerous appearances on future commercial recordings, such as Leontyne Price's *Leontyne Price Sings Spirituals* (1961) and Roberta Alexander's *Songs My Mother Taught Me* (1999). However, it is only by diving into more examples of Price's spirituals and pseudo-spirituals that one can understand the diversity of expression, topical play, and signifyin(g) gestures that are hallmarks of Price's approach to spiritual arrangements.

Classification of Spirituals

Shirley Graham's 1936 article "Spirituals to Symphonies" offers a vital historical perspective on the classification of Negro spirituals. In this article for the widely read *Etude* music journal, Graham celebrates the Black composer's monumental climb from the music of the spirituals to one of the most highly regarded of classical genres – the symphony. Graham ventures beyond a cataloging of significant works, though, and instead grants present-day readers a glance into the complex politics of the Negro spiritual during the Black Renaissance years. Commenting on the bourgeois politics of respectability surrounding the performance of spirituals, she notes, "There should be stress on the fact that it is the 'Africanisms' of these spirituals which our composers are endeavoring to develop to-day."

Graham then ventures to describe "three classes of spirituals":

1. The oldest and nearest related to the African chant. This type of song is that which began by a "leader" (in Africa the medicine man, voodoo man or priest) and calls forth a choral response. These melodies fall into a scale closely related to the pentatonic and can be easily imagined as being sung over the accompaniment of beating tom-toms.
2. Melodies of a slightly later period find the addition of tones from the European scale, a greater spontaneity of group singing and the lessening of the strong drum beat.

3. To the third group belong those harmonious, rich musings of united spirits which move with all the dignity of men who, through suffering have come into a deeper realization of their relation with powers outside themselves.[13]

This classification system foregrounds what I would describe as "Africanisms" while accounting for European influences. However, this classification system does not account for the textual themes of spirituals and relies on the idea of a linear developmental timeline that journeys uninterrupted from less European influence to more. This thereby puts the Eurological influences on a pedestal without fully acknowledging the depth of meaning found in the Afrological imprint. For this reason, I incline towards Randye Jones's classification system of the concert spiritual:

A number of American and European composers did take up the challenge [from Dvořák] of using the Negro spiritual in their compositions for various instrumental and vocal forces. They integrated the spiritual into Western art song form, and their works were often influenced by contemporary popular music styles – such as blues, gospel, and jazz – of the era.[14]

She describes the classification that informs this chapter as follows:

1. Call-and-response: A "leader begins a line, which is then followed by a choral response; often sung to a fast, rhythmic tempo ("Ain't That Good News," "Swing Low, Sweet Chariot," "Go Down, Moses").
2. Slow and melodic: Songs with a sustained, expressive phrasing, generally slower in tempo ("Deep River," "Balm in Gilead," "Calvary").
3. Fast and rhythmic: Songs that often tell a story in a faster, syncopated rhythm ("Witness," "Ev'ry Time I Feel the Spirit," "Elijah Rock," "Joshua Fit the Battle of Jericho").[15]

Jones's system foregrounds the Afrological expressive materials and the importance of storytelling through song. Moreover, her focus on rhythm and the spectrum of lyricism allows for a more nuanced exploration of how the expressive layer of musical meaning interlocks with the unique narrative impulse of each spiritual. She builds upon the work of Hall Johnson, R. Nathaniel Dett, Eva Jessye, and others who made it their career goal to preserve the place of the spiritual in the concert hall. This post-Reconstruction generation of composers not only arranged spirituals for public performance but left behind indexes of spiritual melodies that would have otherwise been lost in the historical record.

The importance of affect and expression is a recurring theme in these indexes, perhaps due to the important psychological impact of spirituals for

Black people in the United States. Arthur C. Jones discusses this impact saying, "Perhaps the most important of these functions, from a psychological standpoint, was the use of the songs for coping with and transcending emotional and physical trauma."[16] However, rather than aesthetically apologize for the tragic legacy of the enslaved Black folks of generations past, Price sought to alchemize this deeply traumatic sound legacy toward a New Negro aesthetic that incorporates blues and jazz alongside the concert spiritual and Europeanized genres. Alain Locke, author of *The New Negro* and major philosopher of the Black Renaissance, shows his deference for the folk song (Negro spirituals in this case) in his concept of the renaissance. This statement, coupled with the "race woman" rhetoric of the time, placed limits on the expressive capabilities of composers like Price who sought to create synthesis while preserving the Africanisms that Shirley Graham praised.

My contribution to this classification system accounts for the spiritual topic, and Price's contribution to the repertoire, the pseudo-spiritual. I introduce the concept of the spiritual topic in my dissertation, "The Poet and Her Songs: Analyzing the Spirituals of Florence B. Price."[17] Therein, I describe the spiritual/supernatural topic as "identified by its shared musical characteristics with the Negro spiritual. The use of pentatonicism, the flatted sixth and seventh scale degrees, and the primacy of expression in delivery are central." Unlike the folk or concert spiritual, pseudo-spirituals set a contemporary poetic text while still foregrounding the spiritual topic. In Price's case, she writes these texts or sources them from existing media. For example, she sources "Words for a Spiritual" from a text by a poet with the pen name "Capricorn" that originally appeared in the "Line o' Type or Two" section of the *Chicago Daily Tribune*. Through the inventive genre of the concert spiritual Price was able to tap into the pathos of the spiritual while addressing her personal and political concerns. My approach to classifying the spirituals allows one to identify idiomatic trends while leaving space for stylistic variance. Moreover, it moves the scholarly conversation from relative African-ness or European-ness to nuanced narrative interpretations.

Jones's classification system resembles Hall Johnson's system for describing his own concert spirituals. Hall Johnson organized the spirituals into categories entitled "moderate and rhythmic," "slow but rhythmic," "slow and quiet," and "fast and bright." It is worth noting that several of Price's spirituals would more accurately be described as moderate and rhythmic. In my analysis, I attribute this to Price's intentional reimagining of spirituals that are typically fast and bright, like "Some o' These Days."[18]

Table 6.1 categorizes Price's known spirituals according to Jones's system. The reader will notice that most of Price's spirituals could be described

Table 6.1 Price's concert spirituals and pseudo-spirituals using Randye Jones's categories of Negro spirituals.

Call-and-response	Slow and melodic[1]	Fast and rhythmic
I Am Going to Lay Down My Heavy Load (1926)	Feet o' Jesus (1944)	Heav'n Bound Soldier (SSA) (1949)
Great Camp Meetin' (choral unison) (n.d.)	Resignation (SATB) (n.d.)	I Am Bound for the Kingdom (1940)
In My Heart (choral unison) (n.d.)	Resignation (n.d.)[2]	I'm Workin' on My Buildin' (1940)
Swing Low, Sweet Chariot (SATB) (n.d.)	Words for a Spiritual (ca. 1948)	Joshua Fit de Battle of Jericho (n.d.)
You Won't Find a Man Like Jesus (1939)	City Called Heaven (n.d.)	King Jesus Is a-Listenin' (4 voices) (n.d.)
	Death's Gwineter Lay His Cold Icy Hand on Me (n.d.)	My Little Soul's Goin' to Shine (n.d.)
	Go Down, Moses (n.d.)	Rise Mourner (n.d.)
	Peter Ring Dem Bells (n.d.)	Roll, Jordan, Roll (4 voices) (n.d.)
	Save Me, Lord, Save Me (n.d.)	Some o' These Days (n.d.)
	Were You There (n.d.)	Study War No More (4 voices) (n.d.)
		Weary Traveler (1951)

[1] "Feet o' Jesus," "Resignation," and "Words for a Spiritual" are pseudo-spirituals, as opposed to adaptations of preexisting spirituals.

[2] "Resignation" exists in two versions, one for the traditional concert spiritual combination of voice and piano and the other for four voices unaccompanied.

as either "slow and melodic" or "fast and rhythmic"; the latter category is often marked "moderato" or "andantino," leaning against more traditional practices in tunes like "Some o' These Days." Price privileges the choral setting of call-and-response tunes, showing preference for a choral treatment of textual antiphony. Price composed more than thirty-two extant spirituals during her active years of composition; however, there remain unfinished manuscripts, sketches, and more scores lost to the historical record. What place of significance did these works have in Price's prolific compositions? Though "My Soul's Been Anchored in the Lord" has become a repertoire staple of Black concert singers, what of the remaining thirty-one spirituals? Through engaging with the following three case studies, it becomes clear that Price arranged a variety of spiritual types in her repertoire, displaying a refined mode of storytelling.

The Spiritual Topic: "Peter Go Ring dem Bells"

The first of these case studies is the recently published "Peter Go Ring dem Bells." In this spiritual, Price's skill at invoking the spiritual topic is on full display. Like "Feet o' Jesus," "Peter Go Ring dem Bells" conjures up imagery of church bells, heavenly realms, and the transcendent connection of the oppressed subject to the Divine. Unlike "Feet o' Jesus," this is a preexisting spiritual melody from the plantation oral tradition.

John Michael Cooper discusses the provenance of this spiritual in his preface to the recent edition of the score from Wise Music Classical:

> [I]ts earliest documented appearance occurs in connection with The Hampton Institute (now Hampton University, Virginia).... [B]y 1874 its success merited the publication of a book authored by two of its teachers [Thomas P. Fenner and J. M. Waddy], with an added section titled "Cabin and Plantation Songs, as Sung by the Hampton Students," arranged by the Institute's music director, Thomas P. Fenner. This appendix included (p. 174) a four-part harmonized setting of "Peter, Go Ring dem Bells" – a setting whose melody is identical to Price's, and whose words and harmonies are similar.[19]

Cabin and Plantation Songs as Sung by Hampton Students documents how J. M. Waddy credits this tune to an enslaved blacksmith named Thomas Vess, who would sing it at secret prayer meetings. Waddy noted, and Fenner was sure to include in the subscript to his arrangement, that "it seemed like a prayer meeting did not go on well without him."[20] "Peter Go Ring dem Bells" aligns well with the well-documented use of spirituals as part of religious services. Moreover, the text can be interpreted as a fervent prayer for divine intervention.

The text of "Peter Go Ring dem Bells," as with most spirituals, lends itself to innumerable layers of interpretation and is shown below. For example, Peter may represent the Biblical keeper of heaven's gates, a conductor on the Underground Railroad, or even the concept of salvation itself. "Hearing from heaven" could either represent prayers or manifestations answered or the more literal hearing that this is the night to escape the plantation.

Peter, go ring dem bells,
I heard from heav'n today.
Oh Peter, go ring dem bells,
I heard from heav'n today.

I wonder where my mother is gone;
I heard from heav'n today.

I thank God an' I thank you, too,
I heard from heav'n today.

I wonder where sister Mary is gone;
I heard from heav'n today.
I thank God an' I thank you, too,
I heard from heav'n today.

Oh, Peter, go ring dem bells,
I heard from heav'n today.

—Text of Price's "Peter Go Ring dem Bells"

Price chooses a ternary ||: A:|| ||: A':|| BA as the form for her arrangement. She shows a preference for ternary and sonata form principles in her vocal works. This is likely due to how well sonata form lends itself to developmental techniques that support narrative and rhetorical approaches to composition. The A' section is melodically identical while introducing new text. Her setting highlights a mournful and transcendent lens – one that belies a desire for escape from the trials of life as a Black woman in a white man's world.

She begins with a particularly colorful quartal bell tone motive to welcome the bells of freedom. The missing thirds and leading tones offer an ethereal and pleading tone to the speaker's request to "ring dem bells." In measure 10, Price's signature pentatonic melody appears as a "sigh" figure highlighting the second repetition of the plea to ring the bells. At this point in the spiritual, the sparse accompaniment conveys the intimacy of this prayer. The listeners' function as voyeurs of a profoundly personal utterance is another characteristic of the spiritual topic. Price closes the A section with a satisfying perfect authentic cadence in measures 11–12, which settles the uncertainty of the bell tones. Paired with the sigh figure falling "from heaven," it is clear the Divine is listening.

The A' section is marked by more stable diatonic harmonies as the subject wonders aloud where their mother and "sister Mary gone." The countermelody in the right hand of the piano in measures 13–15 functions as a call-and-response with the women in question (Ex. 6.1). Again, the spiritual topic easily increases the pathos of this moment while sustaining a static melody.[21]

The return of the A section brings back the original bell tones to round out the subject's prayer. As a sign that the subject has found peace, Price finally resolves the quartal harmonies of the beginning in measures 38–40.

Example 6.1 Price, "Peter Go Ring dem Bells," mm. 13–15.

In a mere three pages, Price guides the listener into a profoundly personal moment of reflection, while conjuring the healing ethos of the spiritual topic that Arthur C. Jones referenced. "Peter Go Ring dem Bells" exemplifies Price's mastery of the spiritual topic as pathos and ethos. The concert spiritual offers a liminal space where both spiritual and psychological processing can occur in a public forum. This and other signifyin(g) gestures appear throughout Price's concert spirituals.

Signifyin(g) Gestures in "Words for a Spiritual"

A notable feature of Price's vocal works is her ability to signify on preexisting texts – both musical and otherwise. Signifyin(g) as a musical practice has been explored by a number of historians, literary scholars, and musicologists as a mode of expression keenly employed by historically oppressed peoples.[22] As I have written elsewhere on the power of signifyin(g), "The relationship between the sign of the original narrative or musical narrative, the new composition, and the griot subverts traditional notions of signification." And as it relates to Black expressive cultures in the United States, "The genius of signifyin(g) is in the signifier's ability to exert power over the oppressive Eurocentric structures that surround them by deconstructing the oppressor's narratives."[23] This is the tradition with which many of Price's vocal works align and is present in some of her instrumental music, as will be addressed in Chapter 9. Price's gestures of signification are most apparent in her pseudo-spirituals. These works are usually signifyin(g) on the tropes of the spiritual, but use new poetry instead of Biblical or folk texts. For example, in my dissertation analysis of "Words for a Spiritual" I discuss how Price transformed a text written in heavy dialect in the style of minstrel portrayals and translated it into an effective spiritual for the present times. The full text of "Words for a Spiritual" is shown below:

Slow me down, Lawd. Ah's a-goin' too fast;
Ah can't see mah brother when he's walkin's past.
Ah miss a lot o' good things day by day;
Ah don't know a blessin' when it comes mah way.

Slow me down, Lawd. Ah wants to see
More o' the things that's good for me;
A little less o' me an' a little more o' You,
Ah wants the heavenly atmosphere to trickle thru.

Let me help a brother when the goin's rough;
When folks work together it ain't so tough.
Slow me down, Lawd, so I can talk
With some o' Your angels, Slow me down to a walk.[24]

Price rarely utilized dialect in her concert spirituals. This is due to the politics of respectability and uplift latent in the Black Renaissance. The ethos of the New Negro called for a sharp turn away from the racialized stereotypes portrayed in blackface minstrelsy in favor of cultivated artistic products that reflected the dignity of Black people. Composers like R. Nathaniel Dett balanced their desire for stylistic integrity and respectable presentation by prescribing pronunciation rules for what linguists now term African American English (AAE). Others like Price were less prescriptive, preferring to alter the spelling for key words like "Lawd" for "Lord."[25] However, "Words for a Spiritual" offers opportunities to communicate with more vernacular music styles, like the use of blue notes in the melody and harmony.

In Price's score, these blues inflections appear alongside the now common use of quartal harmonies within a mostly A minor pentatonic soundscape. The flexibility of the concert spiritual genre allows Price to experiment with musical intertextuality and fusion. She marries experimental harmonies with the spiritual topic whilst signifyin(g) on a dialect text. In so doing, she signifies on the oral tradition of the work song by flipping the narrative from a plea for collective strength to a prayer to be "slowed down." Price is signifyin(g) on the spiritual itself, whilst composing a new spiritual for the trials of the modern day. Price similarly signifies on tropes of the work song and the sorrow song in "Resignation." Her text unfolds below:

My life is a pathway of sorrow;
I've struggled and toiled in the sun
with hope that the dawn of tomorrow
would break on a work that is done.

My Master has pointed the way,
he taught me in prayer to say:
"Lord, give us this day and our daily bread."
I hunger, yet I shall be fed.

My feet, they are wounded and dragging;
My body is tortured with pain;
My heart, it is shattered and flagging,
What matter, if, Heaven I gain.

Of happiness once I have tasted;
'Twas only an instant it paused
tho' brief was the hour that I wasted
Forever the woe that it caused
I'm tired and want to go home.

My mother and sister are there;
They're waiting for me to come
Where mansions are bright and fair.

—Text of Price's "Resignation," by the composer

Price's text belies a latent concern with sorrow and pain as she toils. The biographical references are potent but could also apply more broadly to the issues of domestic work and trials of Black womanhood; Price would also explore labor issues in her orchestrated song "Monologue for the Working Class."[26] Price also invokes the spiritual topic here using pentatonic melodies. The work has resonance with her unpublished "City Called Heaven" both in textual content and in musical material.

Verse: I am a po' pilgrim of sorrow
I'm tossed in dis wide worl' alone
No hope have I for tomorrow
I've started to make Heav'n my home.

Refrain: Sometimes I am tossted an' driven Lord.
Sometime I don't know where to roam
I heard of a city called Heaven
I've started to make it my home.

Verse: My mother has reached pure glory
My father's still walkin' in sin
My brothers an' sisters won't own me
Because I am try'n to get in. (Repeat refrain)

Example 6.2 Pentatonic opening statement of Price's "City Called Heaven," mm. 1–8.

When comparing "Resignation" and "City Called Heaven," Price's text syllabification is nearly identical; both melodies are minor pentatonic figures, and the opening of "City Called Heaven" bears resemblance to the metrical text setting of "Resignation" (Ex. 6.2).[27]

Perhaps "Resignation" was Price's experiment at reinventing "City Called Heaven" to reflect her current struggles as a single parent and freelance musician.

Harmonic Invention in "Going to Lay Down My Heavy Load"

One of Price's most signature characteristics is her inventive use of harmony to suit narrative functions in the spirituals. Price's contemporaneous harmonic references included George Chadwick, Protestant hymnody, and the works of her contemporary and professional acquaintance William Grant Still, to name a few. She expertly code-switches from the formalized mores of Western classical harmony to the more circuitous routes of the blues and jazz. The resultant sound can often lead to moments of "harmonic discontinuity" – moments of harmonic breakdown often representing the fracturing of masking gestures in the art songs.[28] Though less dramatic, there are similar moments in Price's unpublished spiritual setting "I'm Going to Lay Down My Heavy Load."[29] This rousing jubilee spiritual – one that explores the joyful aspects of the Protestant theology of Christ's triumphant Second Coming – combines Price's love of Black folk dances like the juba and her interest in harmonic play. Since this is an arrangement of a preexisting folk spiritual from the Black oral tradition, it falls under the category of concert spiritual. The play between conventionally highbrow and lowbrow styles speaks to Price's Afrological aesthetic as expressed in her letter to Frederick Schwass, in which she wrote that "it seems to me to be no more impossible to conceive of Negroid music devoid of the spiritualistic theme on the one hand than the strongly syncopated rhythms of the Juba on the other."[30]

This spiritual is of the call-and-response variety with "I'm going to lay down my heavy load" as the persistent refrain. The speakerly text looks forward to a time in which the labors of life will cease. At the same time, the preacher-like speaker warns listeners to get their house in order, since the Second Coming (the day of Jubilee) waits for no one, as shown in the following text.[31]

RESPONSE: I'm going to lay down my heavy load
CALL 1: O! by and by, by and by
RESPONSE: I'm going to lay down my heavy load
CALL 2: The river of Jordan ain't got no bounds
RESPONSE: I'm going to lay down my heavy load
CALL 3: If you ain't got Jesus you'll surely drown
RESPONSE: I'm going to lay down my heavy load
CALL 4: Some o' these mornings bright and fair
RESPONSE: I'm going to lay down my heavy load
CALL 5: Going to put on my wings and try the air
RESPONSE: I'm going to lay down my heavy load

At the outset of the piece, Price foregrounds a cakewalk rhythm in the piano accompaniment. Cakewalks were plantation dances performed around holidays for the entertainment of slave owners. A former slave was quoted in an article entitled "Before 'De War" as saying, "Us slaves watched white folks' parties where the guests danced a minuet and then paraded in a grand march, while the ladies and gentlemen going different ways and then meeting again, arm in arm, and marching down the center together. Then we'd do it too, but we used to mock 'em, every step."[32]

For the enslaved, the cakewalk offered a chance to mock the lavish celebrations and mannerisms of their owners, including donning costumes, and signifyin(g) on the genteel bourgeois European dances popular

Example 6.3 Price, "I'm Going to Lay Down My Heavy Load," mm. 8–12.

in nineteenth century southern society. This led to a syncopated take on the foxtrot rhythm, which later became a precursor to the march-like rhythms of ragtime. Scholar Megan Pugh identifies the cakewalk as America's first national dance, tracing its origins as a plantation folk idiom to its nascent popularity in early American musical theatre. This is a vital resource for further exploration of cakewalk's influence on later genres like ragtime.[33] This folk rhythm is accompanied by a stride piano texture (another ragtime characteristic) that arrives in measures 8–12 and transports the listener to the sound world of the antebellum plantation (Ex. 6.3).

Price also introduces a pentatonic countermelody in the right hand of the piano. This layering effect at each reiteration of the refrain pervades the piece and embraces the signature heterophony of Black vernacular music. The accompaniment takes on a sequential character akin to organ improvisation before settling harmonically in measures 18–20. Herein, Price introduces secondary dominant extension chords that obscure the tonic key before landing squarely in F major at the end of the A section. The first jarring moment of harmonic discontinuity arrives in the B section.

In measures 23–24, Price leads the singer through a direct modulation to A major, the mediant neighbor to the home key. While this harmonic surprise adds intrigue to the next iterations of the refrain, it does create a heavy load for the composer, who must now navigate back to the home key in little time. Price navigates these choppy waters by way of a retransition using the now blue note C♮ as a pivot back to F major in measures 29–32. The harmony speaks directly to the narrative focused on the escape from the trials of life to the joys of the time of Jubilee.

In terms of timbre, Price leads the subject from light through the darkness and confusion of the B section, safely home to the Promised

Example 6.4 Price, "I'm Going to Lay Down My Heavy Load," mm. 37–39.

Land of the A section. To solidify the point further, Price accompanies "try the air" with a bright fantasia-like section in measures 37–39 (Ex. 6.4). As the piano line ascends to its melodic zenith, the image of the subject taking flight is palpable. To seal in the sublimity of the final refrain statement, the piano line echoes the dotted "heavy load" motive in the highest range yet. It is as if the Divine sings back in confirmation of the release of life's heavy load.

"I'm Going to Lay Down My Heavy Load" exemplifies Price's ability to code-switch harmonically while creating a new more integrated aesthetic for Black vocal writing. Rather than an arrangement of a spiritual in the spirit of Burleigh's more sparse settings, Price "interprets the text." She takes on the role of the griot-composer, marrying text to music with the facility of the great lieder composers. Surely, this harmonic language sets Price apart as an experimentalist in the art form of the concert spiritual.

Conclusion: Price's Spirituals Today

This brief exploration of Price's concert spirituals reveals that Price was saying something with her works. This "something" was at times deeply embedded in the vernacular tradition, while at other times was a deeply personal exploration. The concert spiritual undoubtedly served a number of sociopolitical roles in the period of uplift. Though the Negro Renaissance had three self-proclaimed male exponents in the form of Alain Locke, W. E. B. Du Bois, and Booker T. Washington, Price made her mark by resisting the pressure to stand squarely in the sorrow song camp. Rather, she sought a synthesis of expression that crossed both temporal and class boundaries. It is for this reason these spirituals remain timely today. For as all speakerly texts do, the ethos of Price's concert spirituals evolve as the struggle of Black Americans evolves. My hope is that even as interest in Price's symphonic works rises among American orchestras, these works, which constitute both miniature dramatizations and intimate portraits of early Black American life, are also preserved for the historical record and in the concert hall.

Notes

1. Amiri Baraka, *Digging: The Afro-American Soul of American Classical Music* (Los Angeles: University of California Press, 2009).
2. Henry Louis Gates, Jr., *The Signifying Monkey: A Theory of African-American Literary Criticism* (New York: Oxford University Press, 1988).
3. Roderic C. Knight, "Kora," *Grove Music Online*, 2001.
4. The "g" in parentheses derives from Henry Louis Gates's landmark work *The Signifying Monkey*, in which he writes: "The bracketed or aurally erased *g*, like the discourse of black English and dialect poetry generally, stands as the trace of black difference in a remarkably sophisticated and fascinating (re)naming ritual graphically in evidence here." Gates, *The Signifying Monkey*, 51.
5. Eileen Southern, *The Music of Black Americans: A History*, 3rd ed. (New York: W. W. Norton, 1997), 180–181. Emphasis in original.
6. Ibid., 271.
7. Guthrie P. Ramsey, "Cosmopolitan or Provincial?: Ideology in Early Black Music Historiography, 1867–1940," *Black Music Research Journal* 16, no. 1 (1996): 14.
8. Richard Crawford, *The American Musical Landscape* (Berkeley: University of California Press, 1993).
9. Ruth Smith McGowan, "Reader Disappointed When Singer Omits Negro Spirituals," *Chicago Defender*, February 6, 1965, 9.
10. Maude Roberts George, "Abbie Mitchell Wins High Praise in Song Recital Here," *Chicago Defender*, November 1931, 10; "Abbie Mitchell in Recital at Woman's Club," *Chicago Defender*, March 1935, 5.
11. Ellistine Perkins Holly, "Black Concert Music in Chicago, 1890 to the 1930s," *Black Music Research Journal* 10, no. 1 (1990): 141.
12. Alisha Lola Jones, "Lift Every Voice: Marian Anderson, Florence B. Price and The Sound of Black Sisterhood," NPR, August 30, 2019, https://tinyurl.com/3y7metwt.
13. Shirley Graham, "Spirituals to Symphonies," *Etude* 54, no. 5 (1936): 692.
14. Randye Jones, *So You Want to Sing Spirituals: A Guide for Performers* (Lanham, MD: Rowman & Littlefield, 2019), 39.

15. Jones, *So You Want to Sing Spirituals*, 5.
16. Arthur C. Jones, "The Foundational Influence of Spirituals in African-American Culture: A Psychological Perspective," *Black Music Research Journal* 24, no. 2 (2004): 257.
17. Elektra V. Carter [formerly known as Marquese Carter], "The Poet and Her Songs: Analyzing the Art Songs of Florence B. Price" (DMA diss., Indiana University, 2018), https://scholarworks.iu.edu/dspace/handle/2022/22585.
18. Hall Johnson, *Thirty Spirituals for High Voice and Piano* (New York: G. Schirmer, 2007).
19. Florence B. Price, "Editor's Programme Note," in *Peter Go Ring dem Bells*, edited by John Michael Cooper (G. Schirmer/AMP, n.d.), www.wisemusicclassical.com/work/60621/Peter-Go-Ring-dem-Bells–Florence-Price/.
20. Thomas P. Fenner, Frederic Rathbun, and Bessie Cleaveland, *Cabin and Plantation Songs*, 3rd ed. (New York, Knickerbocker Press, 1901), 3.
21. All examples engraved by Alex Ostergard; Florence B. Price, "*Peter Go Ring dem Bells*," piano–vocal score, series 2, box 13, folder 16, Florence Beatrice Price Smith Papers Addendum (MC 988a), Special Collections, University of Arkansas Libraries, Fayetteville.
22. Gates, *The Signifying Monkey*; Samuel A. Floyd, *The Power of Black Music: Interpreting Its History from Africa to the United States* (New York: Oxford University Press, 1995); Christopher Small, "Africans, Europeans, and the Making of Music," in *Signifyin(g), Sanctifyin', and Slam Dunking*, edited by Gena Dagel Caponi (Amherst: University of Massachusetts Press, 1999).
23. Carter, "The Poet and Her Songs," 45.
24. Quoted in Capricorn, "A Line o' Type or Two: Words for a Spiritual," *Chicago Daily Tribune*, August 20, 1948.
25. Felicia Raphael Marie Barber, *A New Perspective for the Use of Dialect in African American Spirituals: History, Context, and Linguistics* (Lanham, MD: Rowman & Littlefield, 2021).
26. Carter, "The Poet and Her Songs."
27. Florence B. Price, "City Called Heaven," piano–vocal score, Florence Beatrice Price Smith Papers Addendum (MC 988a), Special Collections, University of Arkansas Libraries, Fayetteville.
28. Carter, "The Poet and Her Songs."
29. Florence B. Price, "I'm Going to Lay Down My Heavy Load," piano–vocal score, series 2, box 12, folder 29, Florence Beatrice Price Smith Papers Addendum (MC 988a), Special Collections, University of Arkansas Libraries, Fayetteville.
30. Florence Price to Frederick L. Schwass, October 22, 1940, box 1, folder 1, correspondence, Florence Beatrice Price Smith Papers (MC 988), Special Collections, University of Arkansas Libraries, Fayetteville.

31. Engraved by Alex Ostergard from Price, "I'm Going to Lay Down My Heavy Load."
32. "Before 'De War," *Detroit Free Press*, November 30, 1902.
33. Megan Pugh, *American Dancing: From the Cakewalk to the Moonwalk* (New Haven, CT: Yale University Press, 2015).

7 | The Solo Keyboard Works

GWYNNE KUHNER BROWN AND JOE WILLIAMS

Of the many genres in which Florence B. Price composed, her pieces for solo organ and piano are uniquely revealing of her remarkable range and distinctive artistic voice. One reason these compositions stand apart is that she was a virtuosic performer of both organ and piano. From the time she arrived at the New England Conservatory of Music in 1903 aged fifteen, she was a standout. She was repeatedly featured as an organist in the conservatory's concerts, playing large-scale works by European Romantic composers and by her teacher, Henry M. Dunham.[1] Throughout her career she performed publicly as an organist and pianist, including stints as a silent film accompanist and appearances as soloist in her own Concerto in One Movement.[2] As Maria Cizmic writes, "hours of practice transform the piano into an intimately known entity. ... Pianists stop thinking of their instrument as a mechanism with action, hammers, dampers, strings, and soundboard and instead perceive the piano as an integrated part of their own musically expressive bodies."[3] Price's intimate relationship with the piano and organ makes her works for solo keyboard a very direct expression of her compositional voice.

A second reason that these pieces offer deep insight into Price's musical mind is that as a composer of solo keyboard music she did not have to swim against the cultural current that she referred to in her July 5, 1943, letter to conductor Serge Koussevitzky as "two handicaps – those of sex and race."[4] Keyboard performance and composition aligned with the cultural expectations for Black, middle-class women in the late nineteenth and early twentieth centuries. While Price's efforts and success as a symphonist were unprecedented for a Black woman, there was solid precedent for her virtuosity at the keyboard and her ambition as a composer of works for solo organ and piano.[5]

Third, Price's solo keyboard compositions faced few barriers to performance. Her nonvirtuosic pieces were appropriate for students, and many of her pedagogical compositions were published during her lifetime, allowing them to be played widely. Her own prowess as a performer, and her relationships with other virtuosos such as Margaret Bonds and T. Theodore Taylor, meant that her more demanding works could be brought to life without first requiring a persistent campaign for publication or performance, such as those she mounted unsuccessfully with the Arthur P. Schmidt Company or with Koussevitzky.[6]

As critics and scholars have recently begun to pay more attention to Price's music, many have emphasized her use of African American vernacular idioms while treating the European classical elements as relatively uninteresting.[7] Organist Nicole Keller describes as "dogged" Price's "use of traditional form and structure, especially in the organ works," and writes that the composer "does not break new ground in harmonic expression ... as we see in the works of her contemporaries such as Charles Ives."[8] Rae Linda Brown writes that Price's "compositions fuse Euro-American structures with elements from her own American cultural heritage, which creates an art music that, while utilizing European forms, affirms its integrity as an African American mode of expression. The musical synthesis she creates demonstrates how the African American composer could transcend received musical forms in articulating a unique American artistic and cultural self." Brown rightly celebrates Price's creation of a distinctive, hybrid musical language, but unfortunately separates the European elements from Price's "own American cultural heritage," casting the former as something to "transcend."[9]

In fact, European classical music was part of Price's life from the beginning. She took piano lessons from her mother at the age of three and wrote, in her words, "little tunes" that she shared on one occasion with the African American piano virtuoso John William "Blind" Boone.[10] Recalling her time at the New England Conservatory as a teenager, she cited her piano teachers as her strongest influences:

Edwin Klahre, [my] first piano teacher at N.E.C.[,] insisted upon mechanical perfection in technical practice and performance, laying less stress upon expression. ... Next I studied with J. Albert Jeffrey – the exact counterfact of Klahre. He lay the greatest emphasis upon expression. The two opposites gave me the inestimable advantage of strict discipline in both expression and technic – a happy combination.[11]

Although Price doubtless felt the weight of being a rare African American student there, she was not an outsider when it came to the classical tradition. It was as much a part of her as spirituals.

Some writers' disinclination to focus on the European elements of Price's music may stem from attitudes regarding her class. As a middle-class Black woman, Price's adherence to nineteenth-century European conventions can be interpreted as taking part in strategies of respectability and uplift that place her outside of a cultural Blackness understood by many music critics and scholars as rooted in vernacular traditions. Discussing novels by middle-class Black women, Ann duCille has sought to challenge "the implicit definition of what 'genuine,' 'authentic' African American art is," underscoring "the problems that arise when African American expressive culture is viewed through the lens of vernacular theories of cultural production and the master narrative of the blues as sexual signifier." She continues:

> [S]uch evaluations often erase the contexts and complexities of a wide range of African American historical experiences and replace them with a single, monolithic, if valorized, construction: authentic blacks are southern, rural, and sexually uninhibited. Middle-class, when applied to black artists and their subjects, becomes a pejorative, a sign of having mortgaged one's black aesthetic to the alien conventions of the dominant culture.[12]

In a similar vein, the presence of the European classical tradition in Price's music risks being seen as unimaginative, inauthentic, or even opportunistic – a kind of musical "passing" akin to what her mother may have urged upon her at the New England Conservatory.[13]

The relevance of duCille's argument goes deeper still: Just as sexuality is no less present in the middle-class novels of Jessie Fauset and Nella Larsen than in the working-class blues of Bessie Smith and Ma Rainey, pleasure is no less present in Price's counterpoint or arpeggiated accompaniments than in her syncopations and harmonies that evoke ragtime and jazz. Her virtuosic enjoyment of the physical experience of keyboard playing is unmistakable in numerous pieces that implicitly or explicitly evoke European and African diasporic dances such as the waltz, cakewalk, juba, and tarantella. In an era when Black women's bodies were conditioned to be of service, Price reclaimed her selfhood at the keyboard. Her scores show her boldly taking up space: her fingers on the keys, her feet on the pedals, her body seated in front of the organ or piano.

Price fully embraced the pleasure afforded to her as a player of and composer for keyboard instruments. She embodied the race pride, confidence, and joy of her own creations. Furthermore, her scores offer other keyboardists the distinct pleasure of playing her music. Still, "What is absent from conversations on black experiences in classical music," writes Kira Thurman, "is classical music's shocking power of aesthetic pleasure."[14] Therefore, in the discussion that follows, we endeavor to highlight the presence of pleasure: embodied, aesthetic, intellectual, and expressive. At the keyboard Price took and shared pleasure in a uniquely personal way, reflecting each of the musical identities she fully owned.

Short Works

Of Price's twenty extant pieces for organ, only three were published during her lifetime, all in 1951: *Adoration*, *Offertory*, and *In Quiet Mood*. These nonvirtuosic, ternary-form pieces show Price crafting appealing music for those who might play or hear it in a church setting, while also following her own sonic bliss. *Adoration*, the simplest of the three, has been arranged for various instruments, and violinist Randall Goosby has recorded two moving performances. The secret this piece conceals in plain sight (or hearing) is its similarity to popular music. It is easy to imagine sentimental lyrics that would suit the A section's singable melody, which occupies four-measure phrases and is accompanied by harmony never more adventurous than the occasional borrowed chord. The cakewalk rhythm (short–long–short) of the middle G major section (mm. 25–40) would be obvious at a faster tempo. The title *Adoration* evokes religious devotion when played slowly on the organ, but would also suit romantic devotion if this piece were arranged and performed like a popular song. The work is a remarkable demonstration of the fine line between sacred and secular music, and of Price's subtle use of resources from both sides of the line.

Offertory is a peaceful work with a few quirky touches. Although every phrase is four measures long, the A section (mm. 1–20) consists of five phrases, the outer pairs of which feature a similar, gently rocking melody over a mostly diatonic D major accompaniment. The contrasting middle phrase (mm. 9–12) shifts to linear whole-tone harmony, while the melody resembles the cry ("Oh!") in the middle of the spiritual "Were You There" (Ex. 7.1).

The piece's B section (mm. 21–36), in the key of ♭VI (B♭), again wanders into unusual harmonic territory. Price draws from jazz with her agile reharmonizations of repeated melodic ideas, and with sequential, chromatic chord progressions (e.g., mm. 31–34). The placid closing A section is capped off with a tangy whole-tone coda.

Composed in 1941 and first titled *Evening* and then *Impromptu for Organ*, *In Quiet Mood* lulls the listener with soft dynamics, an almost constant eighth-note ostinato, a slow-moving pedal part, and a languorous melody. At the same time, the piece is testament to the principle that if one plays softly enough, one can get some remarkably eccentric music through the church door. Many phrases stretch out over five measures, using the fifth to provide a sense of breath and relaxation. Most striking is how the piece's consistently

Example 7.1 Price, *Offertory*, mm.10–11.

dense, undulating texture supports a modernist harmonic journey: After two phrases in E♭ major, increasingly fraught chromaticism leads to a middle section (mm. 30–41) that alternates between the A♭ whole-tone collection and linear, atonal chromatic chords. Sunny E♭ major returns in measure 42, and much of the first section's material returns. A reharmonization of the melody in measure 59 ushers in a final section that reintroduces the unsettled whole-tone and chromatic harmonies from before, this time with parallel thirds and rhythmic gestures that make the piece's debt to Claude Debussy unmistakable, before the final satisfying resolution to E♭ major.

Like her shorter compositions for organ, many of Price's pedagogical pieces for piano found publication during her lifetime.[15] In these works, she extends opportunities for pleasure even to her youngest students, tapping into children's imaginations to convey core technical and musical concepts. "Criss Cross" is noteworthy for introducing hand-crossing at the beginner's level. "The Froggie and the Rabbit" primes the young pianist's ears with two tonal centers: Froggie sings in F major, while Rabbit sings in C major. Two late-intermediate pieces that also rely on animal imagery, "The Goblin and the Mosquito" and "Dragon Flies," both cleverly exploit alternating hand patterns.

Culinary metaphors serve as tasty motivation for students to practice at the keyboard. Price's "Pop Corn" – a staple snack of the American South – ingeniously challenges the young pianist to "pop" left-hand wrist staccato chords amidst buttery two-note slurs in the right, all over the course of three striking key changes. Through the imagery of a tasty snack, this piece addresses pianistic concepts such as articulation, hand distribution, chromatic-scale fingering, and grace-note coordination. Similarly, "Tip-Toe to the Cookie Jar, or Caught in the Jam (Strawberry)" invites students to picture themselves as staccato critters sneaking across the staff to obtain some irresistible finger legato jam. Perhaps once a student mastered each of these pieces, Price would award the respective delicacy!

Only two of Price's sets of character pieces found publishers in her time: *In the Land o' Cotton* (G. Schirmer, 1928) and *Dances in the Canebrakes* (Affiliated Musicians/Mills Music, 1953).[16] These are versatile and effective works, substantial enough to include on a recital program yet approachable enough to serve as teaching pieces for more advanced students. Left unpublished until long after Price passed in 1953, however, was the most fascinating of her character suites, *Thumbnail Sketches of a Day in the Life of a Washerwoman*.

Avoiding both literalistic depictions of manual labor and predictable tragic or humorous affects, the *Washerwoman* set consistently emphasizes its protagonist's complex and varied inner life. The first movement, "Morning," begins with rich chromatic harmonies that build over six measures from *pianissimo* to a *fortissimo* climax on a $G\flat^{13}$ chord spanning most of the keyboard. This dissonant, modernist opening immediately invites the listener to hear this set not as picturesque vignettes of a stereotypical "Mammy" figure, but as the composer's profound statement of solidarity and care across class lines.

"Morning" gets busy early with Price's multilayered signifyin(g). Her use of half notes for the first several measures, followed by an ostinato pattern with fluttering sixteenth notes, resembles "Prelude: Night," the first movement of R. Nathaniel Dett's well-known and oft-performed suite *In the Bottoms*. Dett describes his piano suite as program music "giving pictures of moods or scenes peculiar to Negro life in the river bottoms of the Southern sections of North America."[17] The beginning of Price's *Washerwoman* suite pays homage to Dett's remarkable piece, while also signaling her determination not to have her sketches misunderstood as generic caricatures. More abstractly, the opening of "Morning" can also be heard as a riff on the creation of the world evoked by such works as Ludwig van Beethoven's Symphony No. 9, Gustav Mahler's Symphony No. 1, and Richard Strauss's *Also sprach Zarathustra*. By expanding gradually from a low, soft, consonant chord to a thunderous sonority, Price depicts the beginning of the washerwoman's day of toil as sublime. Unlike the Beethoven, Mahler, and Strauss examples (in D minor, D major, and C major respectively), Price's "Morning" is in the distinctly "Black" key of $G\flat$ major. And while those European works' obscure (but unavoidably male) protagonists have time to spare, the washerwoman has to get on with it, spending only six measures on the creation of the world before proceeding with her day.

The second movement, "Dreaming at the Washtub," is strikingly volatile and compressed (especially compared to the gentle "Dreaming" movement from *In the Land o' Cotton*).[18] Although the middle section of "Dreaming at the Washtub" evokes labor, both it and the dreamier outer sections feature the cakewalk rhythm, suggesting that the washerwoman's spirit continues to dance throughout. The distinctive subjectivity of the protagonist is also suggested by idiosyncrasies of harmony and form: Both outer sections nod only briefly to diatonic lyricism and four-measure phrasing (their simplicity and tunefulness evoking some of Edvard Grieg's *Lyric Pieces*) before shifting to jazz-inflected chromaticism and two- or three-measure-long gestures. The harmony resolves conclusively only at the very end of each outer section, both times settling on one of Price's favorite sonorities, the major chord with an added sixth.

The third movement, "A Gay Moment," is a juba dance full of syncopation and short, motoric gestures. The tempo is not fast but Andantino con moto, and Price also marks it Tempo giusto, which can be understood as meaning either in strict time (no rubato) or at the correct tempo: whatever the washerwoman has energy for at this moment. Although it is the simplest of the movements harmonically, triads are outnumbered by added sixth and seventh chords. Creating a dynamic pull against the 2/4 meter, the lower bass note often falls not on the first but the second beat of the measure, and the syncopated main theme generally ends on the last eighth note of the measure. This brief movement shows the washerwoman enjoying a moment of pure, unshadowed happiness; at the same time, complex rhythm and knowing humor reflect her distinctive personality. Thus, Price avoids perpetuating two common misunderstandings of Black life: among some sympathetic whites, that it involves endless suffering, and among believers in racist stereotypes, that access to simple joy is characteristic of the race.

In the final movement, "Evening Shade," the suite's protagonist takes her rest without surrendering any of her inner complexity. Revisiting some rhythms and phrase contours from *Morning*, this movement forgoes obvious markers of African American style, featuring instead impressionistic parallelism, complex quartal and extended harmonies, and languid slippages from key to key. At three points (mm. 8, 13, and 27), a fermata calls the performer to extend a moment of mild tension; the sonority immediately following the fermata, which might be expected to resolve the tension, is invariably more dissonant. Despite the overall mood of relaxation, the washerwoman's mind is still busy. Happily, the gently dissonant phrase that follows the third fermata is a familiar refrain, and the piece soon comes to rest with a tranquil quartal sonority.

Suite No. 1 for Organ and *Fantasies Nègres*

Price premiered her Suite No. 1 for Organ in 1942 at Grace Episcopal Church in Chicago. There, the audience bore witness to her joy as she gave rein to the juiciest European organ licks and contrapuntal finger-twisters alongside jazz harmonies, juba rhythms, and sparkling wit. This is among her most distinctive and memorable compositions.

In the first movement, "Fantasy," a stentorian minor-key pronouncement alternates with passages of off-the-chain chromaticism. The contrast between the two is heightened by the use of triplets only during the chromatic flights. Although the pronouncement theme is diatonic and harmonically buttoned-up, it is at the same time gesturally ostentatious, featuring at various times a fermata over the precipitous leading tone that begins the piece, a sweeping scalar ascent (m. 2), and a pedal trill (m. 30). The organist is invited to unleash their ultimate inner diva at each statement of this theme, which concludes the movement with one final flourish and a thunderous C minor chord.

Although harmonically much wilder, the episodes in between these pronouncements are otherwise more reserved, featuring dense textures and sequences that favor stepwise motion. The performer, who has mastered the intricate legato passagework and can confidently navigate the chromatic labyrinth, has a very different experience from the first-time listener, who is likely to be disoriented in these chromatic sections until the return of the main theme provides a satisfying tonal reorientation. A particularly good example comes in measures 42–50, where converging chromatic lines lead to three cadences, separated by rests, which draw out the listener's suspense before the delightful arrival of the expected theme (see Ex. 7.2). There is plenty for an organist with a theatrical soul to work with here.

To summarize the remainder of the suite, the second movement, "Fughetta," is a lively, dancelike Allegretto in 6/8. This time the theme is pentatonic as the performer revels once again in bravura polyphony and careening chromaticism. The following movement, "Air," returns to the sunny key of E♭ major and indulges even more luxuriously in sensuous, even erotic, pleasure. Marked Andante cantabile, the movement floats smoothly along, never rising above *mezzo forte*. Polyphonic voices emerge and then gently blend again into the texture, creating a murmuring polyphonic conversation. Chromaticism creates interest but little tension. Price's embrace of jazz is heard in her use of syncopation, numerous

Example 7.2 Price, Suite for Organ No. 1, "Fantasy," mm. 42–50.

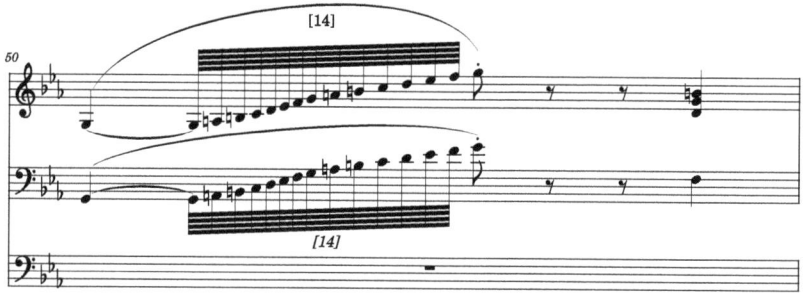

extended chords, linear voicings, an emphasized ♭7 in the main motive, and soulful lyricism. The movement concludes with gentle waves of resolution basking in the afterglow.

The final movement brings the rhythmic density and exuberance of the juba dance. In keeping with the emphasis on touch indicated by the title, "Toccata," the organist's fingers fly through gratifyingly impressive arpeggiated sequences and chromatic passagework.[19] In sum, the four short movements of Suite No. 1 show Price completely at home in organ composition and performance, experiencing and sharing pleasure by calling on the abundance of technical and theatrical resources at her command.

Price's four *Fantasies Nègres* for solo piano join the Suite No. 1 for Organ in being relatively large-scale works that are highly idiomatic for their instrument. Her *Fantasies Nègres* share several common features: stately introductions, pentatonic themes either based on or evoking spirituals, and lavish displays of pianistic technique. It is easy to hear in the *Fantasies* a foretaste of the Concerto in One Movement, which Price would premiere in 1934 – but in the *Fantasies* the pianist provides her own orchestra.

The first *Fantasie Nègre* is the best known of the four, having been published in 1992 as part of the anthology *Black Women Composers: A Century of Piano Music (1893–1990)*, edited by Helen Walker-Hill. Its main theme is a spiritual, "Sinner, Please Don't Let This Harvest Pass." This melody appears in full ten times, rendering the movement a theme and variations that is interrupted by a contrasting episode in G major. Aside from two forays into the relative major and a few chromatic passages, the piece remains rooted in E minor throughout. None of the three following *Fantasies* is as consistently dedicated to a single key or preexisting melody.

Rather than large-scale harmonic motion or thematic development, the pleasures of the *Fantasie Nègre* in E minor lie in its textural and stylistic variety. Beginning with the dedication "To my talented little friend, Margaret A. Bonds," this *Fantasie* calls the listener's attention equally to the composer's versatility and to the pianist's virtuosity. From the cadenza-like opening, which hints at the main theme, through the poignant lyricism of the contrasting Andante cantabile section (set up by a *lusingando* transition), to the thunderous closing pages, Price condenses the technical pyrotechnics and soul-caressing expressiveness of a piano concerto into a solo piece requiring fewer than ten minutes to perform.

The end of the piece emphasizes pianistic pleasure over harmonic progress. Two of the last three iterations of the theme (mm. 226–260) are accompanied by increasingly impressive ostinato patterns. Left-hand octaves leaping a fourth between the root and fifth of the tonic triad (mm. 226–231) expand to cover a sixth as they loop in the third of the chord (mm. 232–239), then whirl into a descending chromatic pattern (mm. 240–245) before returning to the root and fifth, but now thundering from E1 to E4 (mm. 246–257). Samantha Ege likens these "stomp-like octaves" and "circling countermelodies" to the ring shout, a liberatory collective ritual with roots in West African culture that was practiced during slavery. At the same time, these ostinato patterns also call to mind Frédéric Chopin's famous Polonaise in A♭ Major ("Heroic"), Op. 53, which also features ostentatiously virtuosic left-hand octaves. Unlike Chopin's, Price's octaves never modulate; more like the circular ring shout, the purpose is not to progress (harmonically) but

Example. 7.3 Price, *Fantasie Nègre* No. 2, in G minor, mm. 1–11.

to transcend (pianistically). For the player with the necessary technique, which Bonds clearly had at the age of fifteen, the first *Fantasie Nègre* puts European pianistic virtuosity to work in celebration of African American expressive culture.

The same can be said of the three later *Fantasies Nègres*, but each offers its own distinctive journey.[20] For example, in the introduction of the *Fantasie Nègre* No. 2, in G minor (see Ex. 7.3), majestic monophonic calls are answered by rising, keyboard-spanning arpeggios. The calls (mm. 1, 3, 5, and 7), which consist of three pitches (D, C, and A) and feature pendular thirds, clearly evoke African American folk music, while the arpeggios (mm. 2, 4, 6, and 8) come from European pianistic tradition.

The call-and-response structure, of course, is quintessentially African American. Although every pitch in the introduction comes from the D7 chord, the listener can easily hear D as the tonic and C♮ as the subtonic (♭7) rather than as the seventh of a dominant seventh chord. The last two measures of the introduction (mm. 9–10) deliberately downplay any sense of the D chord needing to resolve to G minor by omitting both F# (the leading tone) and C (the seventh of D7), instead ruminating on four notes of a D pentatonic scale (D–E–G–A). When the piece's key of G minor arrives at "Andante moderato" in measure 12, it feels logical but not inevitable; European functional harmony, like the European pianism represented by the arpeggios, is present but not dominant (so to speak).

European pianism is front and center in the *Fantasie Nègre* No. 4 in its many nods to Sergei Rachmaninoff. The combination of numerous cadenza-like passages (starting with the introduction), thickly voiced chords and abundant octaves, soaring melodies, and vertiginous chromatic sequences are present in abundance, calling to mind the Russian composer-pianist's concerti. The rhythm and contour of a prominent motive in the *Fantasie*'s introduction (F#–E–C#–C#, heard unaccompanied in measures 11 and 14) closely resembles a theme found in the middle of Rachmaninoff's Piano Concerto No. 3 (A–G–E–E, heard first in measure 2 of the Intermezzo section). Adding to the likelihood that the similarities are not merely coincidental is the fact that Rachmaninoff performed this concerto with the Chicago Symphony Orchestra on January 14 and 15, 1932, three months before Price composed her piece.[21] Whether Price attended this concert or not, she likely knew Vladimir Horowitz's extremely popular 1930 recording of the concerto with the London Symphony Orchestra.[22]

While indulging in Rachmaninoffian expansive expressiveness and virtuosity, this *Fantasie Nègre* revels equally in the characteristic pentatonic melodies, rhythmic drive and complexity, and stylistic omnivorousness that speak to Price's African American musical sensibility. As John Michael Cooper notes in his preface to the Schirmer edition, the composer revised *Fantasie Nègre* No. 4 several times, with four complete manuscript versions extant. He writes that "Price's evolving concept" shows the work being condensed and "the stylistic contrasts between its themes significantly enhanced in ways that focused on Price's African American heritage." He highlights in particular the replacement of the earlier "nocturne-like central F-sharp major episode," which he provides as part of Appendix B, with "the more compact, blues-influenced G-major episode given in measures 103–23 of the latest version."[23] The themes of the two episodes provide a striking contrast indeed: The "Allegretto cantabile" melody in F# major is expansively lyrical and in 6/8 time, while the later G-major "Andantino" theme is in a restless and syncopated 4/8. The earlier theme, however, is no less "focused on Price's African American heritage"; the phrase structure of its essentially pentatonic melody sings out in two-measure units whose musical grammar is derived from the spiritual. The "nocturnal" arpeggiated accompaniment amplifies the expressiveness of the melody, but does not water down its distinctively Black folk substance. The contrast between the two themes lies in the kind of Black song being evoked: the spiritual versus jazzy popular music.[24]

First Sonata for Organ and Piano Sonata in E Minor

Price was not the first African American to compose solo keyboard sonatas, but she seems to have been the first whose sonatas have escaped oblivion.[25] Her *First Sonata for Organ* was completed in 1927. (Despite the optimistic title, it was not followed by a second; the same is true of the Suite No. 1 for Organ.) Likely composed during her studies at the Chicago Musical College, it may be a "student piece," but the nearly forty-year-old Price was far from unformed as a composer.[26] In his descriptive analysis of the *First Sonata for Organ*, Calvert Johnson provides a detailed account of the elements that Price derived from Félix-Alexandre Guilmant's *First Sonata*, a piece she knew very well.[27] Johnson writes, "Not only are all three movements of both sonatas respectively in the same keys and tempos, but registrations, thematic relationships, structures and growth, and many details correspond in parallel fashion." He provides several examples of these parallels, particularly in the first movement, while also noting individualities, including Price's more elaborate development of themes and her more "adventuresome" key explorations.[28] Knowing about her European model makes Price's imaginative playfulness all the more apparent.

One sign of her free-spiritedness lies in the way Price deviates from Guilmant's fairly consistent four-measure phrasing. Price's first movement, which follows the model's format of French overture-style introduction followed by allegro pedal solo, switches things up: After a foursquare phrase structure in the introduction, she ushers in unpredictable, flexible phrase lengths that dance across expectations and become the rule rather than the exception for the rest of the movement. For example, the pedal solo (mm. 17–41) begins with a four-measure phrase followed by phrases of six, three, four, and seven measures in length.

Another intriguing difference between Price and Guilmant comes in their first movements' second themes, both in F major. Guilmant's style in measures 93–100 recalls Richard Wagner, featuring chromaticism in both melody and harmony and a romantic, lyrical sweep sustained across eight measures. When it returns in the recapitulation (starting at m. 260), the theme's Wagnerian character is even more pronounced, with rich pedal tones and fuller voicing of the chords. In striking contrast, Price's second theme (starting at m. 89, and later at m. 199) evokes a decorous Protestant hymn with its reserved, diatonic harmony, four-measure phrases (at first), and simple tunefulness that ranges only slightly too widely for the imaginary congregation. She tips her hat to Guilmant, though, a few measures into the second theme area (mm. 103–106) with an exact quotation of the French composer's melody (mm. 105–108).

Price's second movement also nods to her model without obscuring her own personality. The fugal opening resembles Guilmant's, but unlike his diatonic scalar theme, her first two measures are pentatonic, a characteristic nod to African American folk music. She uses the same key of A major, but enjoys thwarting the listener's expectations by following four measures of E7 (mm. 33–36) with a sudden, ten-measure digression in C major, whose parenthetical nature she highlights with a change of registration. Both second movements end tranquilly with several measures of tonic pedal (twelve out of Guilmant's last twenty-one measures, and seventeen of Price's last eighteen); while Guilmant gilds that note with several chromatic harmonies above, Price instead luxuriates in the pentatonic scale (A–B–C#–E–F#) that opened the movement, which she embellishes briefly with a neighboring $B^{\o 7}$ arpeggio.

As Johnson points out, the two sonatas' final movements share a time signature (2/4), key (D minor), fast tempo, and "sixteenth-note violinistic theme."[29] Price features a more syncopated accompaniment and slightly wilder harmonies in the development section. The most distinctive feature of her finale is the return at measure 106 of the hymnic secondary theme from her first movement, a cyclic gesture not found in Guilmant's sonata. This structural difference coincides with the striking stylistic similarity between the third movements' hymnic secondary themes. The contrast between the secondary themes in the sonatas' first movements turns out to have been a result of Price's cyclic scheme – in a sense, she was prefiguring Guilmant's hymnic theme (even though it was composed first). Price shouts out to her model by ending her sonata with the very same chord, a mighty eleven-note D major triad spanning five octaves.

Five years after composing the *First Sonata for Organ*, Price's Sonata in E Minor won first prize in the piano category of the 1932 Rodman Wanamaker competition. (Her *Fantasie Nègre* No. 4 received an honorable mention, and her Symphony No. 1 in E Minor took first prize in its category that same year.) Unpublished until Rae Linda Brown edited the G. Schirmer edition in 1997, the sonata is rivaled only by the first *Fantasie Nègre* (published by Hildegard in the 1990s) as Price's best-known work for piano. Unlike the organ sonata, the piano sonata does not use a singular European model. Instead, Price draws freely on a variety of inspirations both from canonic piano composers and from African American genres and practices to create her highly individual magnum opus for solo keyboard.

The sonata has been reasonably well represented in performance, with Althea Waites making the first professional recording in 1993. Although many pianists are equal to the sonata's length, difficulty, and seriousness, not all are equipped to fully appreciate and explore its idiosyncrasies.[30] One example is the lyrical second theme (Allegretto) of the first movement's exposition, a beautiful pentatonic melody that unfolds over a gently rocking chromatic accompaniment, which Ege connects to water imagery common in spirituals.[31] After the first time through, the eight-measure melody is repeated not once but twice more, notated almost identically each time.[32] However decorous and lovely it may be, the third iteration is well outside the bounds of conventional classical practice. Horace A. Maxile, Jr., reads the extra repetition as "particularly emblematic of African American musical culture" in that it is "suggestive of a circularity encountered in certain realizations of communal songs or choruses (a spiritual-like melody), fortifying the vernacular presence in the early moments of the movement."[33] The score's deadpan refusal to provide cues to the pianist about how to vary the thrice-heard melody evokes the composer silently raising her eyebrows as if to say: You know what to do, don't you? Any performer who dutifully plays it the same way three times should probably step away from Price's sonata.

Another quirky passage in the first movement begins at measure 87, where Price presents a new theme in G major. The arrival at the key of the relative major, combined with the wistful pentatonic melody and gentle cadential harmony, strongly suggests that this is the exposition's closing theme. As Maxile observes, Price playfully marks the moment with "a straight eighth-note accompaniment pattern that is reminiscent of Alberti bass – a pre-existing stylistic convention associated with piano music of the Classical and Romantic eras," which "sits in stark contrast to the culturally emblematic back-beat figures that characterize the accompaniments up to this point."[34] The placid resolution to G major in measure 89 promises to usher in the exposition's poignant close. Instead, Price spins off abruptly into a cadenza-like section that features chromatic sequences and the theatrical prolongation of a pedal D (measures 104–109 and 119–122). Over the course of this extroverted section there are nods both to George Gershwin's *Rhapsody in Blue* (measures 105–108 evoke that work's opening scale and the rhythm of its first theme) and to the spiritual "Nobody Knows the Trouble I've Seen."[35] It is not until measure 123 that the exposition resolves demurely to G major and presents the actual closing theme, which is teasingly similar, but not identical, to the false one back at measure 87. Not only is the cadenza section impressive and pleasurable from a pianistic standpoint; it also demonstrates Price's interest in breaking open the conventions of sonata form to make room for her whole musical self.[36]

In her discussion of the Andante second movement, Ege highlights that Price brings together Harry T. Burleigh's singularly influential transformation of spirituals into concert music with contrasting themes whose style imitates Chopin and Robert Schumann.[37] Ege connects the overt shifts between African American and European styles in this movement to code-switching, the strategic employment of different ways of speaking depending on context. As she notes, "Price positions the spiritual-inspired melody as the main theme as if … stating its authoritative position as a key compositional (re)source. She code-switches with ease into the Romantic languages of Chopin and Schumann as these languages inhere just as authentically within her own compositional voice."[38] Price's use of rondo form to highlight her heartfelt, undisguised, and expert inclusion of distinctive European pianistic styles makes this movement a poignant statement of her belonging in this tradition, and of its belonging to her.

The final movement – a scherzo movement and a rondo finale unexpectedly fused together – evinces how Price demands from the performer an engaged response to her compositional voice. In the contrasting episode of the scherzo (Cantabile maestoso, mm. 83–121), it is critical that the pianist indulge in the rubato called for by the score's lush Rachmaninoff-style lyricism and expansiveness; only a lack of understanding would lead them to continue the even eighth-notes appropriate to the previous section. In the transition back to the opening tarantella theme at measure 122, Price indicates an abrupt return to the original allegro and writes *forte* rather than the *mezzo forte* of the movement's opening. Performers who ignore these markings in order to smooth the transition – an understandable impulse – do Price a disservice by sonically implying that the simplistic tarantella theme is as heartfelt and graceful as the Rachmaninoff episode. Inflating the seriousness of this theme instead of amplifying its contrast risks leading listeners to hear the tarantella theme as a pedestrian idea masquerading as a profound one. Instead, as Ege writes, it is imperative that the performer "revel in the sharp twists and turns of the movement, rather than push a forced sense of continuity throughout."[39]

The second large section of the finale, which begins at measure 154, inaugurated by a shift from 6/8 to 4/8, another Allegro marking, and a spirited new theme, is a tour de force of different styles, moods, and ideas. Hurtling from antebellum Black dances to spiritual-evoking lyricism to European Romanticism, Price relies on the performer to know which ideas are meant to be caressed and which should be cavorted through. A sense of both large-scale flow and moment-to-moment comprehension is required if the pianist is to collaborate with the composer in telling a deeply satisfying story.

Conclusion

Price's compositions are performed best by those who recognize and honor their African Americanness – an honoring that requires a full comprehension of the weight of the spirituals, but also calls musicians at times to dance, to laugh, and to relax into pleasure. They are performed best, too, by those with the requisite technique for, and knowledge of, music in the European classical tradition. Her works invite imaginative co-creation and co-enjoyment. Her shorter and "easier" compositions offer an unrivaled training ground for the performance of her sonatas, Suite No. 1 for Organ, and *Fantasies Nègres*, not to mention the works of other African American composers of her generation and beyond. Price led the way, drawing freely on folk music, jazz, popular song, romanticism, impressionism, modernism—any source that offered the aesthetic, emotional, spiritual, and sensual experiences she craved for her performers, her listeners, and herself.

Notes

1. Rae Linda Brown, *The Heart of a Woman: The Life and Music of Florence B. Price* (Urbana: University of Illinois Press, 2020): 52–53.
2. Ibid., 99, 152–153, 197.

3. Maria Cizmic, "Embodied Experimentalism and Henry Cowell's *The Banshee*," *American Music* 28, no. 4 (Winter 2010): 439–440.
4. Florence Price to Serge Koussevitzky, July 5, 1943, box 50, folder 4, Serge Koussevitzky Archive, Music Division, Library of Congress, Washington, DC.
5. Josephine Wright identifies more than eighty African American women in Boston with careers in classical performance during the last three decades of the nineteenth century. Josephine Wright, "Black Women in Classical Music in Boston during the Late Nineteenth Century: Profiles of Leadership," in *New Perspectives on Music: Essays in Honor of Eileen Southern*, edited by Josephine Wright (Warren, MI: Harmonie Park Press, 1992), 377.
6. Brown, *The Heart of a Woman*, 74–75, 186–188.
7. As Horace J. Maxile, Jr. notes, this tendency can be traced all the way back to Alain Locke. Maxile writes, "While Price's music garnered approval from critics during the 1930s, there were some who thought her musical conservatism did not fully embrace or, perhaps, advance certain progressive ideologies of contemporary African American writers and thinkers." Horace J. Maxile, Jr., "Culture and Craft in Florence Price's Piano Sonata in E Minor (First Movement)," in *Analytical Essays on Music by Women Composers: Concert Music, 1900–1960*, edited by Laurel Parsons and Brenda Ravenscroft (New York: Oxford University Press, 2022), 139–140.
8. Nicole Keller, "The Organ Music of Florence Price: A Pedagogical Perspective," *American Organist* 56 (2022): 51.
9. Brown, *The Heart of a Woman*, 10.
10. Correspondence, 1929–1953, series I, box 1, folder 1, Florence Beatrice Smith Price Papers Addendum (MC 988a), Special Collections, University of Arkansas Libraries, Fayetteville.
11. Correspondence, 1929–1953.
12. Ann duCille, "Blues Notes on Black Sexuality: Sex and the Texts of Jessie Fauset and Nella Larsen," in *American Sexual Politics: Sex, Gender, and Race since the Civil War*, edited by John C. Fout and Maura Shaw Tantillo (Chicago: University of Chicago Press, 1993), 198.
13. Brown, *The Heart of a Woman*, 53–55. The complex effects on Price of "gendered racial identity" are incisively and insightfully discussed in Alexandra Kori Hill, "Make the Familiar New: New Negro Modernism in the Concertos of Florence B. Price" (PhD diss., University of North Carolina at Chapel Hill, 2022), 27–31.
14. Kira Thurman, "Singing against the Grain: Playing Beethoven in the #BlackLivesMatter Era," *The Point*, September 29, 2018, https://tinyurl.com/43p88es6.
15. Rae Linda Brown writes that Price "easily secured publishers, including G. Schirmer, McKinley, Theodore Presser, Gamble Hinged Music, Carl Fischer, and Clayton F. Summy" for her teaching pieces, mostly for piano.

Brown, *The Heart of a Woman*, 89. Brown's discussion of Price's efforts to publish her piano compositions can be found at 74–75 and 180–181.

16. "At the Cotton Gin," from *In the Land o' Cotton*, was first published by G. Schirmer in a method book in 1927.
17. R. Nathaniel Dett, *In the Bottoms: Characteristic Suite* (Chicago: Clayton F. Summy, 1913), 3.
18. In his preface to the G. Schirmer edition of the score, John Michael Cooper notes that "Dreaming at the Washtub" was the second movement in the "original version of the work," but is omitted from the final version. "Dreaming" is provided as an appendix in that edition, whereas Barbara Garvey Jackson's ClarNan Editions version includes all four movements in their original order.
19. In Calvert Johnson's edition, the movement is titled "Toccato." His preface includes "[sic]" to indicate that this title is from Price's manuscript. However, there do not seem to be any other pieces by Price whose conventional titles she deliberately tweaked, and the program for her premiere performance of the work in 1942 lists the movement as "Toccata." It seems most likely that the final "o" on the manuscript was a slip of the pen.
20. *Fantasie Nègre* No. 3 has been reconstructed and recorded by Samantha Ege, but as of this writing the score awaits publication, so it is not discussed in detail here. Ege, *Fantasie Nègre: The Piano Music of Florence Price* (Lorelt LNT144, 2021).
21. Frank Villella, "Sergei Rachmaninoff: 'There is nothing he cannot do at the keyboard,'" *Experience CSO*, April 17, 2023, https://tinyurl.com/4s74ecxa.
22. The recording extends across five 78 rpm records. The Intermezzo theme is all the more prominent because it is heard at the start of a side. *Rachmaninoff: Concerto No. 3, in D Minor for Piano & Orchestra*, Vladimir Horowitz and the London Symphony Orchestra (Victor DM-117, 1930).
23. Florence B. Price, *Fantasie Nègre No. 4 in B Minor*, edited by John Michael Cooper (G. Schirmer, 2020), v.
24. If the later revision was undertaken specifically for Marion Hall's 1937 performance at a Composers Forum concert under the auspices of the Works Progress Administration, it would have made sense for Price to make the piece peppier and more populist in style to suit the tastes of her Depression-era audience. See Ellistine Perkins Holly, "Black Concert Music in Chicago, 1890 to the 1930s," *Black Music Research Journal* 10, no. 1 (1990): 147. Cited in Price, *Fantasie Nègre No. 4 in B Minor*, iv.
25. According to Anne Key Simpson, R. Nathaniel Dett composed a piano sonata in E minor and one in F minor, both of which he performed in recital but never published. Anne Key Simpson, *Follow Me: The Life and Music of R. Nathaniel Dett* (Metuchen, NJ: Scarecrow Press, 1993), 383.
26. *Music of Florence Beatrice Price*, vol. 4: *First Sonata for Organ*, edited by Calvert Johnson (ClarNan Editions, 1993), ix.

27. In 1904, Price played Guilmant's sonata for an audience at New England Conservatory that included the composer. He was impressed, congratulating her on the performance. Johnson, *First Sonata for Organ*, ix; Brown, *The Heart of a Woman*, 52.
28. Johnson, *First Sonata for Organ*, ix, xiv.
29. Ibid., xiv.
30. The sonata may at times be less serious than one might expect; Ege notes that the Cantabile maestoso section of the third movement "blur[s] the lines of pastiche and parody" with its exaggerated Romantic gestures. Samantha Ege, "The Aesthetics of Florence Price: Negotiating the Dissonances of a New World Nationalism" (PhD diss., University of York, 2020), 106.
31. Ibid., 92–93.
32. There are two small differences in the phrase's third repetition: The last two measures are marked *mp* instead of *p*, and the final chord in measure 77 has an extra note.
33. Maxile, "Culture and Craft," 155–156.
34. Ibid., 150–151.
35. Maxile identifies the presence of the spiritual in measures 113–114. Ibid., 151–152.
36. The score calls for the exposition to be repeated. As the section takes up close to half of the movement even without being repeated, pianists can be forgiven for choosing to go straight to the second ending. Nonetheless, they should understand the indicated repeat as a reflection of Price's willingness to take up space.
37. Ege, "The Aesthetics of Florence Price," 93–103. In referring to the themes of the contrasting episodes as "Chopin Theme" and "Schumann Theme," Ege draws on Rae Linda Brown's preface to her edition of the sonata (G. Schirmer, 1997).
38. Ege, "The Aesthetics of Florence Price," 95–97.
39. Ibid., 105.

8 | Price and the Violin: Between Virtuosity and Vernacularity

KATHARINA UHDE AND R. LARRY TODD

A key figure in establishing a "Black musical idiom" and an American musical identity, pianist-composer Florence Price was groundbreaking in her efforts to create a compositional style that incorporated Black vernacular songs.[1] This chapter focuses on her violin works, including the two fantasies in G minor (1933) and F♯ minor (1949), and Violin Concerto No. 2 (1952). We also contextualize Price and the violin within a cultural network that included other Black violinists active during her life.

Price's violin works offer an astonishingly multilayered view of her instrumental practice. Her violin fantasies, especially No. 2 in F♯ minor, are suffused with Black vernacular thematic material, revealing her masterful ability to "transcend European influence" in an inherited Romantic national language.[2] Fantasy No. 1 in G minor uses newly composed tunes modeled on an African American idiom while showcasing the European fantasy genre.[3]

Her two violin concertos notably diverge from this path; each presents a different side of her versatile compositional persona. The first concerto references the genre's Romantic tradition by alluding openly to Tchaikovsky's Violin Concerto Op. 35 (1878), while Price's one-movement sectional second concerto reflects an American identity to an international audience (the work was composed before her planned European sojourn, which did not happen). Price's violin output confirms the breadth of her stylistic range and resists categorizing. There is one quality, however, that stands out and unites these works: Each highlights tunes and navigates virtuosity and vernacularity in its own way to create an individual, characteristic work.

Fantasy No. 1 (1933)

In a recent article we argued that Price's violin fantasies responded to her desire to discover what Ege called a "national musical idiom,"[4] which Price arguably captured more authentically than the Czech composer Dvořák, however worthy of acknowledgment his efforts were.[5] To judge by Fantasy

No. 1, elements of her American identity, including her African American cultural heritage, could be part of the work through the incorporation of folklike tunes. At the same time, references to classical genres and forms such as the fantasy, concerto, and sonata form were significant for Price. Had she envisioned the national musical idiom fully expressible in song, she would not have composed so many large orchestral and instrumental works, which afforded her a sufficient space to reimagine old, perhaps dusty, compositional models in inventive ways.[6]

In Price's Fantasy No. 1, references to bravura and virtuosity are manifest in "runs, flourishes, and improvisatory garlands in the violin part,"[7] as well as in Price's confident use of flying staccato, tremolo, and spiccato. Advanced violinists will find here opportunities for exhibiting the violin without betraying an "empty" virtuosity – to invoke Maiko Kawabata, a "true" vs. "empty" virtuosity paradigm.[8] "True" virtuosity, in Maiko Kawabata's interpretation, could be described as a type of virtuosity which, as the old French violinist Pierre Baillot wrote, "extend[s] the limits of execution ... not to bring astonishment by means of an increased number of difficulties conquered, but to offer increased means of eloquence or increased effects that influence the soul," whereas "empty" virtuosity, in Kawabata's view, could be read into pieces that imitate the acrobatic nature in some of Paganini's violin music, but do so in a manner which is "out of context," thereby disregarding its role in the context of an entire piece.[9]

What does "vernacularity" mean? One dictionary defines the adjective "vernacular" as "using a language or dialect native to a region or country rather than a literary, cultured, or foreign language."[10] Applied to Fantasy No. 1, when Price introduces the "Lento" theme in measure 38 with its "syncopation, lyrical 'vocal' thirds that would support a portamento-inflected manner of singing, a piano accompaniment emphasizing offbeats, and a symmetrical descending and ascending sequence of sixth chords," she injects vernacularity into the piece via markers of song, syncopation, offbeats and soulful portamento connections between notes. Price knew best how to write for the violin "as an extension of the voice," which could communicate, if not the words, then at least the musical gestures of a "language or dialect native to a region or country."[11]

Other passages within this fantasy diverge from projecting "vernacularity." In one instance she seems to evoke Dvořák's *New World* Symphony, which could be viewed as a "literary" or "cultured" language, given the symphony's established position in the canon in 1933, when she composed the fantasy. As we have shown elsewhere, a brief passage in Price's Fantasy No. 1 (with the pitches C–C–C–B♭–G–B♭ being repeated no fewer than three times) seems to quote from Dvořák's symphony (compare the second movement, mm. 39–41 with Price's Violin Fantasy No. 1, mm. 83–88).[12] However, another interpretation of this likely intended musical quotation is also possible: Perhaps Price is proposing classical music (as represented by Dvořák's *New World* Symphony) as her starting point from which she gradually expanded outward into vernacular and folkloric idioms (as represented in her manifestations of Black vernacular music). Thereby she showed the musical world that inventing a national idiom for America, indeed, did not require a Czech composer's input, but instead someone who knew how to bridge the divide between "cultured" and "vernacular."

Fantasy No. 2 (1949)

Violin Fantasy No. 2 in F♯ Minor (1949) is based upon the spiritual "I'm Workin' on My Buildin'." The tune seems to have been personally meaningful to the composer, given that on March 26, 1940, she arranged it as the second of two spirituals.[13] Shortly thereafter, she quickly dispatched Violin Fantasy No. 2, a textless, poignant rumination on the melody. In what follows, building on existing scholarship, we explore how Price here navigates "vernacularity," drawing also on her diary entries from 1946 to 1950.[14] As it happens, several entries in the diary directly relate to "I'm Workin' on my Buildin'" and arguably yield performative insights, that is, "implicit" knowledge that views music as an embodied experience of sound brought to life by performers, not just an abstract text irrespective of performative realities.

As we examine Price's diary, preserved in the University of Arkansas, we note that some entries circle around compositional activities, particularly around writing melodies. Many entries impress as little nuggets of wisdom gleaned from her lessons or acquired practice. Thus, on November 12, 1946, Price observes: "Try out intervals, playing 2 octaves apart. ... Generally speaking, in phrasing, a long note belongs to that which follows."[15] On Monday, November 25, she writes: "Action words should have special attention. Don't put [them] on two quick-moving notes. Rewrite some songs. Don't go up on word 'closes.'" On Sunday, November 17, 1946: "Dr. Harris will not be in city next week. Call him next Sun. a.m. In meantime, the assignment for next lesson is – Write many melodies for songs (to words) using no bar lines. Do at least one song a day. Phone him next Sun. morning."[16]

Evidently, she pondered questions of vocality, notation, bar lines, and how to transfer vernacularity into music, at a time when she was working with American composer Roy Harris (1898–1979). As we know, one of the autographs of the fantasy discloses that her version of "I'm Workin' on My Buildin'" was written "as sung to Fannie Carter Woods of Chicago by her grandmother Melinda Carter / a former slave from Memphis Tennessee."[17] In our recent article we operated under the assumption that this song was not documented anywhere other than on her manuscript.[18] But there are, in fact, several published and recorded collections of spirituals that have songs with similar titles (Table 8.1).[19]

Price's version is the only one we found that reads "I'm Workin' on *My* Buildin'"; other than that, it shares its chorus–verse–chorus structure with the other versions, in which the verses express a hypothesis ("If I was x, I tell you what I'd do, I'd do y, and work on the/my buildin' too."), while the choruses reflect a religious devotion to the Lord. Regarding the melody, the closest version of the tune to Price's that we could find was recorded in Arkansas in 1969, sung by Ollie Gilbert (Table 8.1, column 4).[20] As we listened to Gilbert's performance – vocal inflections; bent notes; and monophonic, emotionally gripping delivery and quality – we were confronted with the limits of our own hearing, which almost inevitably "others" qualities that sound different from ourselves. But we were also reminded of what Price wrote in her diary about bar lines and were curious to explore her words further. When she assigned herself the task of writing "at least one song a day" "using no bar lines," was she training herself to rehear vernacular music? Did she practice notating melodies in order not to lose in translation that freedom of the unmeasured mode, which relates to some research on the fantasy genre we have pursued in Eurocentric repertoires of Joachim and Mendelssohn?[21]

In order to learn to play Gilbert's melody, we first transcribed it, with limited success due to far more inflections and bent notes than we could readily accommodate with symbols. We continued listening to her song as "sound" versus "text," memorizing her inflections by ear. We tried out how it would sound if we played this version of "I'm Working" *within* Violin Fantasy No. 2 in F♯ Minor instead of Florence Price's tune, an experiment that occurred at the 2022 joint annual meeting of the American Musicological Society, the Society for Ethnomusicology, and the Society for Music Theory in New Orleans (Exx. 8.1 and 8.2).

Without claiming that we can know what Florence Price heard in Melinda Carter's version of the tune (even if we had a recording of Carter's version), we conducted this experiment in an effort to better

Table 8.1 "I'm Workin' on My Buildin'" in songbooks, recordings, and Price's *Two Traditional Negro Spirituals* (1940, published 1949).

Songbooks		Florence Price	Recordings	
Howard Washington Odum and Guy Benton Johnson, *The Negro and His Songs* (University of North Carolina Press, 1925), 77.	John W. Work, *American Negro Songs and Spirituals* (New York: Crown Publishers, 1940), 97.	Florence B. Price, *Two Traditional Negro Spirituals*, No. 2, "I'm Workin' on My Buildin'" [1940] (New York: G. Schirmer, 2020).	US-Wc, Cat. #1041 (MFH #724). As sung by Ollie Gilbert, Mountain View, Arkansas, on October 28, 1969.	US-Wc, Cat. #1212 (MFH #724). As sung by Mrs. Claudie Richardson, Mountain View, Arkansas, on August 31, 1971.
"Workin' on the Buildin'"	"Workin' on the Buildin'"	"I'm Workin' on My Buildin'"	"I'm Workin' on the Buildin'"	"Working on the Buildin'"
"The sinner may be a gambler or a dancer or a rogue or a drunkard. But each name has the same signification in the religious phraseology of the Negro song. There are various ways of repenting and of serving the Lord just as there are many ways of offending and sinning against him.		CHORUS I'm workin' on my buildin', workin' on my buildin', I'm a workin' on my buildin', all for my Lord.	CHORUS I'm workin' on the buildin' Workin' on the buildin' Workin' on the buildin' For my Lord, for my Lord.	VERSE 1 If I was a preacher, I'll tell you what I'd do, I'd keep on a preachin' And I'd work on the buildin' too. Date recorded: January 2, 1937 Contributor(s): Performer: Knox, Lillie; Performer: Wright, Martha; Recordist: Lomax, John A. Setting: At the home of

'Workin' on the Building' appeals to the average Negro."

VERSE 1
If I was a sinner man, I tell you what I'd do,
I'd lay down all my sinful ways an' work on the building too.

CHORUS
I'm workin' on the building fer my Lord,

Fer my Lord, fer my Lord,

VERSE 1
If I was a mourner, I tell you what I'd do,
I'd give my heart to Jesus and work on my buildin' too.

CHORUS
I'm workin' on my buildin', workin' on my buildin',
I'm a workin' on my buildin', all for my Lord.

VERSE 2
If I was a sinner, I tell you what I'd do,
I'd give my heart to Jesus

VERSE 1
If I were a preacher, Tell you what I would do,
I'd keep on preachin' And work on the buildin' too.

VERSE 2
Get the Holy Ghost childring,
Get the Holy Ghost childring,
Get the Holy Ghost childring,
An' work on the buildin' too.

VERSE 3
If I were a gambler, Tell you what I would do,
Quit my gamblin'

CHORUS
I'm workin' on the buildin', on my God's buildin',
I'm workin' on the buildin', all for my Lord,
All for my Lord.

VERSE 2
If I was a tinner,
I'll tell you what I'd do,
I'd quit my Tinnin'
And I'd work on the buildin' too.
I'm workin' on the buildin', on my God's buildin',
I'm workin' on the buildin', all for my Lord,
All for my Lord.

Genevieve W. Chandler
Location: Murrells Inlet, Georgetown County, South Carolina, United States

Table 8.1 (cont.)

Songbooks	Florence Price	Recordings	
I'm workin' on the building fer my Lord, **I'm workin on the building, too.**	and work on my buildin' too. CHORUS **I'm workin' on my buildin', workin' on my buildin', I'm a workin' on my buildin', all for my Lord.**	An' work on the buildin' too. The following verse is the same as Verse 3, with "drunkard" replacing "gambler."	**VERSE 3** If I was a printer, I'll tell you what I'd do, I'd quit my Printen' And I'd work on the buildin' too. **I'm workin' on the buildin', on my God's buildin', I'm workin' on the buildin', all for my Lord, All for my Lord.** **VERSE 4** If I was a liar, I'll tell you what I'd do, I'd quit my lyin' And I'd work on the buildin' too.

VERSE 2
If I wus a gamblin' man, I tell you what I'd do,
I'd lay down all my gamblin', an' work on the building, too.

VERSE 3
If I was a 'ho'-munger, I tell you what I'd do,
I'd lay down all my munglin' and work on the building, too.

And so on for the dancer and the drunkard and the 'cussin' man.

I'm workin' on the buildin', on my God's buildin'
I'm workin' on the buildin', all for my Lord,
All for my Lord.

VERSE 5
If I was a drunkard, I'll tell you what I'd do,
I'd quit my drinkin'
And I'd work on the buildin' too.

I'm workin' on the buildin', on my God's buildin'
I'm workin' on the buildin', all for my Lord,
All for my Lord.

Table 8.1 (cont.)

Songbooks	Florence Price	Recordings
		VERSE 6 If I was a liar, I'll tell you what I'd do, I'd quit my lyin' And I'd work on the buildin' too. **I'm workin' on the buildin', on my God's buildin'** **I'm workin' on the building, all for my Lord** **All for my Lord.**

Example 8.1 Florence Price, "I'm Workin' on My Buildin'" (No. 2 of *Two Traditional Negro Spirituals*).

Example 8.2 "I'm Workin' on the Buildin'" as sung by Ollie Gilbert on October 28, 1969 (US-Wc, Cat. #1041 [MFH #724]).

understand vocal elements in fantasies in general. The takeaway is that transferring the vocal idiom to the instrumental is indeed challenging.

As Emlyn Stam has observed, reenacting recordings from an older era may be a straightforward enough performance-based research method – and yet, as we record ourselves and listen to how we sound in comparison to Gilbert, we notice we are worlds apart.[22] But we also learn that the effort of searching for Florence Price via listening to a singer whom Price could have known, with a tune that Price also set, is still rewarding, for it makes us aware of *how* we listen, and *how* we perform Price.

Let us return to the diary. On February 17, 1949, Price writes: "To Carol Brice, ... printed copies of 'I'm Bound,' 'I'm Working,' & 'April Day.' 3 c enclosed for reply to my questions 'will you record either of these?'" "I'm Working" is an abbreviation for her song "I Am Workin' on My Buildin'." And who was Carol Brice (1918–1985), the woman Florence Price hoped would respond? She was an African American contralto, a concert singer, recording artist, and professor who broke many racial barriers for African American musicians. She won a Grammy Award for her solo work in *Porgy and Bess* in 1978. While we were not able to establish that Brice did record the spiritual, we did find a recording from 1947, which features Brice, two years before she received Price's letter.[23] In this recital, Brice performed a miscellany, including a Negro spiritual by Edward Boatner (1898–1981). Brice's voice is full and rich; her vibrato is rather small and fast; she connects ascending intervals (25:21) and uses blue notes (25:15) for expressive purposes. What would it have been like to hear Carol Brice perform "I'm Working on My Buildin'"? In search of expanding our own understanding of Price's vocality and vernacularity, we experiment with reenacting that narrow and slightly faster vibrato in Brice's recording.

What is it like for performer/scholars to experiment with their own sound after listening to singers such as Gilbert and Brice? For one, our interpretive imaginations become more open for Florence Price. In comparison to our first recording of Price's two fantasies,[24] we have deepened our understanding of vocal inflections, continuity of phrasing (as if playing without bar lines), bending blue notes, and fine-tuning the quality of the violin's vibrato, all of which brought us closer to Price's vernacularity. The experience of reenacting Gilbert's and Brice's recordings on the one hand mirrors our own musical identity and the culture in which we learned to play our instruments, and on the other hand reveals gaps in our knowledge and understanding of music from another time and culture.

Virtuosic Markers and Sound Imaginations around Florence Price: Clarence Cameron White

Searching for Florence Price's virtuosity and vernacularity also requires taking a closer look at her culture and at the role the violin played in it. Price's exposure to Chicago's rich musical scene brought her into contact with many fine violinists, both from Chicago and elsewhere. Price's musical network extended throughout the US. She corresponded with musicians, conductors, orchestras, and organizations. She was a member of the National Association of Negro Musicians (NANM) from 1920 and, after moving to Chicago in 1927, she was at various times a student at the Chicago Musical College and American Conservatory of Music; she was also a member of several musical clubs there. According to the Blythe Owen papers at Andrew University, which Marianne Kordas has investigated in several publications and conference presentations, Price was a member of the Chicago Musicians Club of Women, the Chicago Club of Women Musicians, the Women's Musical Club of Chicago, the Lake View Musical Society, the International Society for Contemporary Music, and the Chicago chapters of the Mu Phi Epsilon and Sigma Alpha Iota music sororities.[25]

To illustrate how one of her contemporaries, violinist Clarence Cameron White (1880–1960), wrote for the violin, we shall consider two of his pieces and their virtuosic markers that recall nineteenth-century traditions of the instrument. Alexandra Kori Hill, L. Moody Simms, and Eileen Southern have explored White's legacy as an influential musician for the formation of NANM and a virtuoso violinist and composer.[26] Trained at Oberlin and Howard University and privately in violin with Will Marion Cook (1892) and Joseph Douglass (1896–1901), White met Samuel Coleridge-Taylor (1875–1912) in 1904, who exerted a lasting influence on his work with Black folk material.[27] White twice travelled to London, where he studied with Mikhail Zacharewitsch, and to Paris once (1930–1932). White's Violin Concerto in G Minor, Op. 63 (1945) and Concertino in D Minor for Violin and Orchestra (1952) are among his larger orchestral works.

Known as one of the most "virtuosic performers" of his day with an "admirable technique" and an unusual breath of colors,[28] White may have benefited considerably from his studies with Mikhail Zacharewitsch during the second London sojourn (1908–1910). Zacharewitsch had trained under the Belgian violinist and composer Eugène Ysaÿe and left recordings of Schubert's "Ave Maria" and Sarasate's *Zigeunerweisen*, which White would likely have known.[29] Zacharewitsch's recording of "Ave Maria" features different types of portamento and vibrato; of the former, one type involves a glissando from one note to another, sometimes referred to as a "one-fingered slide."[30] A second type, known as the B-portamento,[31] is a slide executed by the finger that begins the slide, hence B-portamento, which is finished by another finger (Fig. 8.1, no. 41).

Many violinists occasionally used the L-portamento (Fig. 8.1, no. 42), even though it was associated with poor taste. We noticed that the most expressive passages in the "Ave Maria" featured one-finger and B-portamenti (as opposed to L-portamenti). Sometimes Zacharewitsch even used two consecutive slides, thereby breaking two rules, the "consecutive slide" rule and the rule to avoid downward slides.

Example 8.3 is a transcription, based on Zacharewitsch's "Ave Maria" recording, of the end of the first statement of the theme, a climactic passage

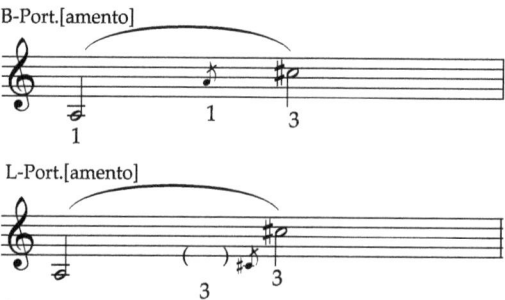

(In order to facilitate comprehension, we will call the portamento in connection with the Beginning note the B-Portamento, and that carried out by the Last finger the L-Portamento.)

Figure 8.1 Carl Flesch, *The Art of Violin Playing*, vol. 1, p. 30.

Example 8.3 Schubert, "Ave Maria," with Mikhail Zacharewitsch's B-portamenti (marked with a line above an x) and one-finger slides.

with several slides in each measure. Zacharewitsch's use of one-fingered slides and B-portamentos, together with the continuous vibrato, creates an intensely emotional sound.[32]

Let's compare Zacharewitsch's aesthetic with that of his student, Clarence Cameron White. Among White's own compositions is "Lament," Op. 12 No. 2, from *Bandanna Sketches*, which begins with a tune in C minor; the same theme is used in Samuel Coleridge-Taylor's *Symphonic Variations on an African Air* for orchestra.[33] Like Schubert's "Ave Maria," "Lament" is a slow showpiece opening with a soulful melody on the G string repeated later on in octaves. Our experiment entailed transferring Zacharewitsch's portamento and vibrato to White's "Lament," thereby augmenting the articulation instructions in White's piece. White's training with Zacharewitsch likely influenced the former's aesthetic and performance practice. Unlike "Ave Maria," "Lament" contains fingerings by the composer himself, which are revealing.[34] The fingerings are quite nuanced. White used one-finger slides in measures 1, 32, and 35; B-portamenti in measures 28, 33, 34, and 35; and in measures 33, 34, and 35 a specific type of B-portamento that proceeds from one note to the same note but exchanges fingers in doing so. We added additional portamenti as part of our experiment. We assumed that, as in the "Ave Maria" recording, White likely would have played the octave melody in measures 45 to 52 with portamenti, even though octaves are not marked with fingerings because the default options are to use the

Figure 8.2 Schubert, 'Ave Maria,' with a transcription of Mikhail Zacharewitsch's articulation

fingering 1–4 or 1–3. Based on White's fingerings in the beginning, he would likely have used slides to perform the octaves.[35]

As to the question of vibrato, Hill convincingly argues that, like Zacharewitsch, White was among those violinists who followed Eugene Ysaÿe, Fritz Kreisler, and others and relied upon continuous vibrato to transform the earlier "dry and austere" sound aesthetic into something warmer.[36] Hill writes: "From Cook, he was most likely exposed to aspects of the German violin school due to Cook's study at the Hochschule für Musik

Figure 8.3 Clarence Cameron White, Lament Op. 12 No. 2 from Bandanna Sketches (1918)

in Berlin."[37] Whether White adopted his vibrato from Cook or Zacharewitsch is unclear; we believe that most likely the latter inspired White's sound, given that Cook was trained in Berlin, where Joseph Joachim's school of playing offered a more reserved vibrato than was common among Ysaÿe's pupils, including Zacharewitsch. Overall, we imagine that the vocal elements that were likely part of White's performance aesthetic – including nuanced slides – would have rendered this music

Figure 8.3 (cont.)

poignantly and expressively, paying tribute to its roots in the tradition of the spirituals.

White's "Slave Song," Op. 12 No. 3, in F major (from *Bandanna Sketches*) is a short piece in ABA' form. While the piano's harmonic motion

Figure 8.3 (cont.)

oscillates between scale degree three and flat three, the violin intones a sweet melody arpeggiating down from scale degree five. The B section is marked by the piano's even offbeats against a mournful violin tune again in F major, repeated an octave higher and reaching F5. Syncopated gestures infuse the B section with a folklike quality. The return of the A section deserves special mention, for it features a Paganinian brand of virtuosity dominated by artificial harmonics. Thus, here we find an approach to the violin idiom, which brings together a melody with expressive leaps, a title

Figure 8.3 (cont.)

expressing White's ancestral heritage, and, lastly, a mastery of violin-technical idiomacy, which for listeners would have recalled the nineteenth-century European virtuoso tradition.

To offer one final example of White's aesthetic, his *Levee Dance*, Op. 26 No. 2 (1927), presents a folk tune with lively syncopations in the opening A section. The B section introduces the Negro spiritual "Go Down Moses," which spins into variations, first with arpeggiations, then double-stops. The return of A showcases effects for the bow, including ricochet and flying staccato. The left hand, too, encounters some demanding feats in the form of double-stops and wide registers spanning up to A6. Price may have modeled her own *Levee Dance* (1937, for piano) on White's composition.

White integrates the vernacular tunes in his violin music into a language of nineteenth-century Romanticism, bringing to mind similar acrobatic pieces by composers such as Fritz Kreisler. Harmonics and "showy" bow strokes are fun to watch because they produce unusually glassy (harmonics), percussive (ricochet), or whimsical (flying staccato) effects. Whether the sound or the appearance of such feats is more impressive is difficult to say. But, as we shall now explore in Florence Price's Violin Concerto No. 2, her virtuosity does not follow that of White, Fritz Kreisler, or other showpiece composers.

Florence Price's Violin Concerto No. 2 (1952)

The second violin concerto was premiered posthumously on November 2, 1953, at Curtiss Hall in Chicago's Fine Arts Building, just months after the composer's death. This concert is not mentioned frequently in the literature; in fact, a *New York Times* article from February 2018 claims: "[Concerto No. 2] was dedicated to the violinist Minnie Cedargreen Jernberg, who performed it, a decade after Price's death [November 24, 1964], at the dedication of an elementary school in Chicago named for Price."[38] The work falls into a sectional one-movement form (Table 8.2). Although interpreted as a strophic form with thematic variations[39] or double variation form,[40] the concerto may also be heard as a sectional fantasy with idiomatic displays for the violin.[41]

Price's fantasies, including her Violin Fantasy No. 1 (Table 8.3), are multi-sectional one-movement works, which typically begin with a "free" improvisatory section and send with a large finale, which was standard for the operatic fantasia genre.[42] Like the fantasies by European nineteenth-century violinist-composers, which often bring together a "loosely knit, sectional approach ... and are animated by an increasing energy that drives to the end," this concerto opens with an improvisatory section and proceeds through various keys and meter changes while gaining in tempo, energy, and virtuosity.

As in Price's Symphony No. 3, where she "no longer composed melodies and rhythms closely aligned with African American spirituals and Black

Table 8.2 Formal plan of Florence Price's Violin Concerto No. 2.

Tempo moderato	Rotation 1	Exposition Primary theme 1, D major	Two sharps	4/4	mm. 1–16
			Two sharps	4/4	mm. 17–43
		Primary theme 2, D major	Two sharps	4/4; 4/4	mm. 33–58
		Transition	Two sharps	2/4	mm. 59–82
		New theme in F major?	One flat	4/4	mm. 83–91
Andante cantabile		**Secondary theme in D♭ major**	Five flats	4/4	mm. 92–120
Allegretto	Rotation 2	Development	Two sharps	4/4	mm. 121–134
		Primary theme 1, and primary theme 2, tonally unstable, fragmented	Two sharps	4/4	mm. 135–169
Andante cantabile		**Secondary theme in G major**	One sharp	4/4	mm. 170–198
Tempo primo	Rotation 3	**Recapitulation with primary theme 1 in D major**	Two sharps	4/4	mm. 199–213
Vigoroso			Two sharps	4/4	mm. 214–220
Tempo moderato			Two sharps	12/8	mm. 221–223
		Primary theme 2 in E minor		4/4	mm. 224–237
Andante cantabile		**Secondary theme in B♭ major**	Two flats	4/4	mm. 238–265
Allegretto		**Primary theme 2 in A major**	Three sharps	4/4	mm. 266–276
Allegro	Rotation 4	**Coda with primary theme 1 in D major**	Two sharps	4/4	mm. 277–302
Andante con espressione		**Secondary theme in D major**	Two sharps	4/4	mm. 303–318
Allegro			Two sharps	4/4	mm. 319–328

Table 8.3 Formal plan of Price's Violin Fantasy No. 1.

Andante	Two flats	C	mm. 1–13
Allegro	Two flats	2/4	mm. 14–60
Andante	Two flats	4/4	mm. 61–93
Da capo	Two flats	2/4	mm. 14–27
Coda	Two flats	2/4	mm. 94–131

folk dance,"[43] the Violin Concerto No. 2 explores a new language, as Hill has shown. Price was preparing to tour Europe in the spring of 1953 when she unexpectedly passed away.[44] This concerto, among other works, exudes the enthusiasm and ambition of a composer ready to share her music with an international audience. Like many fantasies, the work references sonata form by featuring contrasting themes that appear in various harmonic relationships before sounding in the tonic (primary theme 1, m. 277; secondary theme, m. 303). Price maneuvered into her work one bold (P1), one elegant (P2), and one lyrical (S) theme, and placed them at structurally important points such as key or meter changes (see Table 8.3). All told, there are four rotations of her themes, the last of which dispenses with P2.

Price begins with a fanfare-like primary theme (P1), which juxtaposes a modal mixture of D major and F minor. The intensity of this opening yields to Debussian parallel chords and a whole-tone scale (mm. 10, 13), as in Symphony No. 3, where, as Brown writes, Price worked with C minor in alternation with its relative major, E♭ major, before leading the listener into more ambiguous tonal terrain, including whole-tone passages.[45]

The second primary theme now enters in the solo violin in measure 33. Eventually, the second theme appears in D♭ major, overflowing with warmth shared by the soloist (mm. 92–97) and orchestra (mm. 98–102). A freer development-like section ensues in measure 121, with its own rotation of all three themes, albeit in the "wrong" keys. The recapitulation appears in measure 199 with primary theme 1; primary theme 2 then follows in E minor, signaling yet another inventive surprise. In measure 238 one of the most remarkable passages follows – namely, another rendition of the secondary theme, this one recalled in B♭. While the orchestra plays the theme, the violin ornaments it in a manner reminiscent of the concerti of Beethoven, Brahms, and Joachim. A brief coda (m. 277) revives the opening and secondary theme, both now in the tonic key of D major (m. 303) to conclude this whirlwind of a concerto. Though we can discern four rotations in the formal plan, Price's harmonic choices, particularly in the "recapitulatory" rotation, are unusual, given that two of the three themes are not stated in D major, but in E minor, B♭ major, and A major.

As in her fantasies, Price thus asserted that structural freedom was more important to her than strictly following a model. The plan of her second violin concerto allowed her to situate virtuosic moments in transitional and developmental passages, where we encounter everything from fast spiccato runs (m. 127) to double-stops marked *martelé* (mm. 129–130), runs in slurred sixteenth-note sextuplets (mm. 139, 141), and fast runs in separate sixteenth-note sextuplets (mm. 146, 159). When she presents the secondary theme in B♭ major in the orchestra at measure 238 – which we have just compared to violin concerti of Beethoven, Brahms, and Joachim – she uses a type of virtuosity that can be described as ornamental virtuosity. Here, Price maintains a slower tempo that renders the sixteenth-note sextuplets at a moderate (and therefore not markedly virtuosic) speed and manner of performance, rather than invoking a *perpetuo mobile*.

Thus, though to be sure Price's violin part attains a high level of difficulty (mm. 29, 127, 129, 159, 222, 276, and 321), she avoided the type of Paganinian virtuosity that White had embraced and that some composers after Paganini had explored in harmonics, double harmonics, bouncing bow techniques, "noisy" bow strokes (*sautillé*, ricochet, flying staccato) and double-stops such as thirds, sixths, and octaves. Arguably, Price was keen to avoid "empty," ostentatious virtuosity that would perhaps have given quick satisfaction to an audience.

The "Presence" of Minnie Cedargreen Jernberg in Price's Violin Concerto No. 2

Although we know little about the interaction between Price and Minnie Cedargreen Jernberg (1888–1957), the dedicatee of Violin Concerto No. 2, the possibility remains that somehow the composition reflects the violinist's "presence." Karen Leistra-Jones has shown, for instance, that "Joachim's presence ... continues to be felt today" in Brahms's Violin Concerto, owing largely to Joachim's cadenza for the work. In contrast, traces of Cedargreen Jernberg's "presence" may be more subtle. We can assume that the violinist's sound was present in Price's imagination, that the two perhaps knew each other personally, and perhaps met with their respective instruments in hand. As Sally Macarthur writes, "bodies as producers and consumers necessarily mediate all experiences of art, and, to that extent, art exists not in the transcendental realm outside signification but, rather, in the physical, material world."[46]

How and where is this violinist present in this concerto? There must be traces of composer–performer collaboration, even if we cannot clearly discern them. A composition never exists just as "text"; it is mediated by bodies, in this case by Minnie Cedargreen Jernberg, who was sixty-five years old at the time of the premiere on November 2, 1953. She performed the concerto two more times, in 1955 and 1964, both times from the manuscript.[47] A member of a Swedish immigrant family that had settled in Des Moines, Iowa, she studied during her teens with Herbert Butler (1864–1946), one of Joseph Joachim's advanced pupils.[48] Among Jernberg's accolades were appearing as a soloist with the Chicago Symphony Orchestra; performing at Orchestra Hall and with the Thomas Orchestra in Chicago, as well as the Musicians' Club and the Lake View Musical Society; and winning a "Paganini Medal while studying at the American Conservatory in the 1920s."[49] Her teacher, Herbert Butler, dedicated a work to her.[50]

Like Clarence Cameron White and Will Marion Cook, Jernberg spent a year in Berlin, where she studied with Issay Barmas (1872–1946), another top Joachim student.[51] The performance practice of Barmas and Joachim may offer an interpretive lens through which to understand the meaning of virtuosity in Price's second concerto.[52] Traditionally, discussions of violin virtuosity inevitably recognize the nineteenth-century eminence of Paganini as one whose music appeared to transcend the limits of technical possibility and represent the *ne plus ultra* of showmanship. Typically associated with white male composers, virtuosity has crossed the gender divide, although the way in which virtuosos were sometimes "objectified" has differed for men and women. Despite the link of "showmanship" to virtuosity, Price appears not to have composed "showmanship" into her violin works. Why not? Could it be that, in light of the struggles she experienced throughout her life as a composer with a self-perceived dual handicap, composing visible virtuoso spectacles was not in her interest?[53] Could it be that as a Black composer-pianist she compensated in a way by protecting her body and/or those bodies for whom she composed the work? According to Tavia Amolo Ochieng' Nyongó, we cannot speak about embodying music – and, by analogy, about performing virtuosity – without acknowledging the politics of race and how the body, arms, hands, fingers, etc. of the performer configure themselves in certain ways to bring a piece to the stage.

Because of the complex physical demands that virtuoso music places on the performer, virtuosity displays a strong visual component. But sometimes the judgment of history has not tied the term to certain composers' music because of the derogatory connotations. "The music itself" – a nineteenth-century idea that claims that there is an autonomous music that expresses only itself in an "art for art's sake" manner – is sometimes viewed as the actual goal of music, allowing "virtuosity" to be detached from the music itself. As Nyongó writes, "The emphasis on music over performance hinges on a regrettable dualism between sound and vision."[54]

Be that as it may, the opening of Florence Price's Concerto No. 2, from the solo's entrance in measure 17 to the start of the solo's primary theme 2 in

Example 8.4 Price, Violin Concerto No. 2, mm. 17–32.

measure 33, is a case in point, demonstrating that what could be perceived as visually provocative or violinistic showmanship seems to be intentionally circumvented. As Example 8.4 shows, the solo violin presents itself with an opening phrase that features a rising, slurred, ornamented arpeggio of triplets (m. 18) and a responding elegant, rhythmic, dotted gesture, settling on the E6 before coming to a halt on a fermata, D5 (m. 20). The second part of the phrase consists of a descending line (mm. 21–24), again in eighth-note triplets, which yields another elegant, rhythmic, dotted – and now expanded – gesture (mm. 25–27) with a continuation in rising sixteenth-note sextuplets, all in legato slurs (m. 29), before the harmony settles on the dominant preparation for the upcoming primary theme 2. There may be many ways this opening could be described in terms of how the body must configure itself to execute all those ascending and descending slurs Price wrote.

We would like to point to a type of idiomatic writing that Joseph Joachim was known for. As Uhde has observed in one of Joachim's pieces that, like Price in her opening, also avoids consecutive down-and-up-bow motion:

To create a sense of ... simplicity, Joachim found it necessary to use violin-technical idioms diametrically opposed to those of the *Bravourstück* (the latter typically includes sautillé, ricochet, staccato, and passages requiring great physical investment ...), namely, smooth legato runs with few bow changes, which require the actions of the bow arm and body to be kept to a minimum.[55]

Perhaps it could be argued that Minnie Cedargreen Jernberg's "presence" is in this Joachimian way of choreographing a passage. Keeping visual markers and explicit showcasing at a minimum, Price chose an opening that nevertheless responds to traditional generic expectations of the first solo in a concerto – to feature the violin's entire register and to introduce the instrument via scales or arpeggios. Thus, Price's response to one of the problems of virtuosity – that "dualism between sound and vision" noted by Nyongó above – was to acknowledge, perhaps even unintentionally, an existing nineteenth-century style of virtuosity, possibly recalling Minnie Cedargreen Jernberg and her legacy.

Conclusion

We have explored how searching for Florence Price as performers can change the way we sound. We have entered a subjective realm in search of Price's performative identities, acknowledging that we are too removed in time and place to find definitive answers. But we have also seen that some questions she may have considered, such as how we hear with and without bar lines, are useful to the investigation. Furthermore, we found that there was considerable value in attempting to reenact historical recordings, so as to position the richness of Price's vernacularity within the European traditions of virtuosity and the nineteenth-century fantasy. Finally, we are grateful to have entered into a performative relationship with this composer's music, even now fully seventy years after her life, as it encourages new ways to do research, to perform, and to learn.

Notes

1. Samantha Ege, "The Aesthetics of Florence Price: Negotiating the Dissonances of a New World Nationalism" (PhD diss., University of York, 2020), 34; Horace J. Maxile, Jr., "*Fantasie nègre: The Piano Music of Florence Price*, by Samantha Ege: Lorelt LNT 144, 2021, CD," *Journal of the American Musicological Society* 75, no. 2 (2022): 405–409; Samantha Ege, *Fantasie Nègre: The Piano Music of Florence Price*, Lorelt LNT 144, 2021, CD.
2. Rae Linda Brown, "Selected Orchestral Music of Florence B. Price (1888–1953)" (PhD diss., Yale University, 1987), ii.

3. Katharina Uhde and R. Larry Todd, "'I'm Workin' on My Buildin': Freedom and Foundation-Building in Florence Price's Two Violin Fantasies," *Journal of the Society for American Music* 17, no. 3 (2023): 244.
4. Ege, "The Aesthetics of Florence Price," 34, cites Florence Price, "Class Essays, 1938," series I, box 1, folder 3, Florence Beatrice Smith Price Papers Addendum (MC 988a), Special Collections, University of Arkansas Libraries, Fayetteville.
5. Uhde and Todd, "'I'm Workin' on My Buildin'," 246.
6. We acknowledge that Minnita Daniel-Cox is offering an alternative reading (see Chapter 5 in this volume).
7. Uhde and Todd, "'I'm Workin' on My Buildin'," 253.
8. Maiko Kawabata, *Paganini: The "Demonic" Virtuoso* (Woodbridge, UK: Boydell Press, 2013), 110.
9. Kawabata, *Paganini*, 112. Kawabata quotes Pierre Baillot, *The Art of the Violin*, 12, trans. Louise Goldberg (Evanston, IL: Northwestern University Press, 1991).
10. "Vernacular," Merriam-Webster Dictionary, www.merriam-webster.com (accessed March 1, 2024).
11. Uhde and Todd, "'I'm Workin' on My Buildin'," 248 and 256.
12. See ibid., 248–249.
13. Florence Price, *Two Traditional Negro Spirituals*, edited by John Michael Cooper (New York: G. Schirmer, 2020), ii.
14. "Florence Price's Diary, 1947–1950," box 1, folder 7, item 1, Florence Beatrice Smith Price Papers Addendum (MC 988a), Special Collections, University of Arkansas Libraries, Fayetteville.
15. "Florence Price's Diary, 1947–1950," 10.
16. "Florence Price's Diary, 1947–1950," 17.
17. John Michael Cooper, preface to Florence Price, *Fantasy No. 2*, edited by John Michael Cooper (New York: G. Schirmer, 2020).
18. Uhde and Todd, "'I'm Workin' on My Buildin'," 243–260.
19. The following links lead to recorded performances of "I'm Workin' on My Buildin'" referenced in Table 8.1: US-Wc, Cat. #1041 (MFH #724), as sung by Ollie Gilbert, Mountain View, Arkansas on October 28, 1969, https://maxhunter.missouristate.edu/songinformation.aspx?ID=1041; US-Wc, Cat. #1212 (MFH #724), as sung by Mrs. Claudie Richardson, Mountain View, Arkansas on August 31, 1971, https://maxhunter.missouristate.edu/songinformation.aspx?ID=1212 and, for a 1937 recording, https://archive.culturalequity.org/field-work/spain-1952-1953/keep-workin-building.
20. "I'm Workin' on the Building," US-Wc, Cat. #1041 (MFH #724), as sung by Ollie Gilbert, Mountain View, Arkansas on October 28, 1969. https://maxhunter.missouristate.edu/songinformation.aspx?ID=1041.
21. See, for example, Katharina Uhde "Rediscovering Joseph Joachim's Fantasias (1850-52)," *Musical Times* (December 2017), 1–26; R. Larry Todd, *Mendelssohn: A Life in Music* (New York: Oxford University Press, 2003), 110, 388.

22. Interview with Katharina Uhde and Emlyn Stam, "Emlyn Stam: Being in Practice-Based Research," YouTube, February 14, 2023, www.youtube.com/watch?v=FRuGpVyfigc.
23. Carol Brice in concert, singing Edward H. Boatner's "On Ma Journey" (24:50–27:21), www.youtube.com/watch?v=UEtOyuxx0_g&t=1490s.
24. Uhde and Todd, Florence Price's Two Violin Fantasies Nos. 1 (www.youtube.com/watch?v=OdqRGJqqjiU) and 2 (www.youtube.com/watch?v=rZ0UXH_LWRs).
25. Marianne Kordas, "What We've Managed to Transcribe Thus Far: Lessons from the Blythe Owen Letter Transcription Project," *Music Reference Services Quarterly* 23 no. 3-4 (2020): 153–170.
26. L. Mood Simms, Jr., "Clarence Cameron White: Violinist, Composer, Teacher," *Negro History Bulletin* 43, no. 4 (1980): 95–96.
27. Mellonee V. Burnim and Portia K. Maultsby, eds., *African American Music: An Introduction*, 2nd ed. (New York: Routledge, 2015), 146.
28. L. Moody Simms Jr., "Clarence Cameron White," 96.
29. Mikhail Zacharewitsch, "'Ave Maria' by Franz Schubert, (1825)," www.youtube.com/watch?v=K2grl_fEaVg.
30. David Milsom, *Theory and Practice in Late Nineteenth-Century Violin Performance: An Examination of Style in Performance, 1850–1900* (Farnham, UK: Ashgate, 2003): 87.
31. Carl Flesch, *The Art of Violin Playing*, vol. 1 (New York: Carl Fischer, 1924), 30.
32. Readers curious about Mikhail Zacharewitsch's use of portamento are invited to listen to his "Ave Maria" at www.youtube.com/watch?v=K2grl_fEaVg and to follow the marked score at https://jmp.sh/GFukKknr. Due to the length of the example, the entire "Ave Maria" score could not be included.
33. The same theme is used in Samuel Coleridge-Taylor's *Symphonic Variations on an African Air* for orchestra. Simms, "Clarence Cameron White," 95.
34. See *Bandanna Sketches (Four Negro Spirituals) by Clarence Cameron White*, Op. 12, "No. 2. Lament (I'm troubled in Mind)" (New York: Carl Fischer, 1918).
35. Readers may consult the annotated score of White's "Lament" at https://jmp.sh/GFukKknr.
36. Alexandra Kori Hill, "Clarence Cameron White: Classical Violin Performance and Pedagogy in the African American Community" (MA thesis, West Virginia University, 2015), 30.
37. Hill, "Clarence Cameron White." 30.
38. Micaela Baranello, "Welcoming a Black Female Composer into the Canon. Finally," *New York Times*, February 9, 2018, https://tinyurl.com/4dhhyyj9.
39. Alexandra Kori Hill, "Make the Familiar New: New Negro Modernism in the Concertos of Florence B. Price" (PhD diss., University of North Carolina at Chapel Hill, 2022), 129.

40. Douglas Shadle, "Florence Price Violin Concerto No. 1, Violin Concerto No. 2," liner notes for Florence Price, Violin Concerto No. 2, Er-Gene Kahng and Janacek Philharmonic Orchestra, cond. Ryan Cockerham, recorded May 2–4, 2017, Albany Records, streaming audio, Naxos Music Library, 8.
41. Uhde and Todd, "'I'm Workin' on My Buildin'," 252.
42. William Drabkin, "[The Fantasy in the] 19th and 20th Centuries," in Christopher D. S. Field, E. Eugene Helm, and William Drabkin, "Fantasia," *Grove Music Online*, 2001.
43. Rae Linda Brown and Wayne Shirley, eds., *Florence Price, Symphonies Nos. 1 and 3* (Middleton, WI: A-R Editions, 2008), xlix.
44. Hill, "Make the Familiar New," 126.
45. Brown, "Selected Orchestral Music," 184.
46. Sally Macarthur, *Feminist Aesthetics in Music* (Westport, CT: Greenwood Press, 2002), 17.
47. Hill cites the program of the 1955 performance, which took place on February 21,1955, at the Musicians Club of Women Chicago, in Music Room 833 in the Fine Arts Building on 410 South Michigan Avenue in Chicago. Until contrary evidence emerges, we can assume that the 1955 and 1964 performances featured the violin part and a piano reduction versus an orchestra. Hill, "Make the Familiar New," 127.
48. Ernst Wilhelm Olson, *The Swedish Element in Illinois: Survey of the Past Seven Decades* (Chicago: Swedish-American Biographical Association Publishers, 1917), 257; biographical information on Herbert Butler: https://harmonicorde.com/Butler/Herbert%20Butler.html
49. "Tuesday Musical Treat," *Evening Times-Republican* [Marshalltown, Iowa], January 8, 1913, 8.
50. Obituary, "Mrs. C. Richard Jernberg," *Chicago Tribune*, March 14, 1967, 46.
51. Herbert Butler dedicated his Ballade, Op. 6, to Minnie Cedargreen Jernberg, *Evening Times-Republican* [Marshalltown, Iowa], January 8, 1913.
52. Issay Barmas was one of Joachim's students; see Robert Eshbach, "Joseph Joachim, Biography & Research," https://josephjoachim.com/2014/11/04/joachims-students/. Issay Barmas wrote the violin manual *Die Lösung des geigentechnischen Problems* (Berlin: Bote & Bock, 1913).
53. See, for example, letter of Florence Price to Serge Koussevitzky, July 5, 1943, box 50, folder 4, Serge Koussevitzky Archive, Music Division, Library of Congress, Washington, DC.
54. Tavia Amolo Ochieng' Nyongó, "Review of Rip It Up: The Black Experience in Rock 'n' Roll, and: Right to Rock: The Black Rock Coalition and the Cultural Politics of Race, and: Afropunk: The "Rock 'n' Roll Nigger" Experience," *TDR: The Drama Review* 50, no. 1 (2006): 184.
55. Katharina Uhde, "Joseph Joachim and the Violin Romance: Reforming the Playground of Virtuosos," *Nineteenth-Century Music Review* 22 (2025): 90.

9 | Concertos and Chamber Works: The African American Idiom in Texture and Form

ALEXANDRA KORI HILL

Prior to 2009, Florence Price's instrumental music was believed to be minimal. The instrumental works present in the papers donated by Price's eldest daughter, Florence Robinson, supported that conclusion: *The Deserted Garden* and *Elfentanz*, both for violin and piano; the first page of a violin II part for the Violin Concerto No. 2 (which suggests a Violin Concerto No. 1); and fragments from her *Five Folksongs in Counterpoint* for string quartet.[1] Barbara Garvey Jackson addressed this lacuna in her 1977 article on Price. But it was not until the 2009 recovery of Price's papers that the true scope of her contribution to instrumental music could be thoroughly considered.

As of 2025, there are now four Florence Price collections housed at the University of Arkansas in Fayetteville. The three most recent collections, acquired between 2010 and 2022, contain the bulk of Price's instrumental repertoire.[2] Several compositions, such as the Violin Concerto No. 1 in D Major (1939), the Violin Concerto No. 2 (1952), the Piano Quintet in A Minor (ca. 1935), and the *Five Folksongs in Counterpoint* (1951), have been taken up by artists and ensembles such as Er-Gene Kahng and the Janáček Philharmonic, the Apollo Chamber Players, Randall Goosby and the Philadelphia Orchestra, and the Catalyst Quartet. What has accompanied this surge in interest is not only excitement. There has been frustration, confusion, debate, and compromise, fueled by the acquisition of Price's copyright by G. Schirmer and the swift (re)publication of her works for the masses. It is important to note that G. Schirmer had not been unaware of Price or her music: the company published Price's art song "Songs to the Dark Virgin" in 1941 and Rae Linda Brown's edition of Price's Piano Sonata in E Minor in 1997.[3]

G. Schirmer is not the only company to have printed Price's works (for others, see ClarNan Editions, founded by Barbara Garvey Jackson; Hildegard Publishing; and the published editions by musicologist Helen Walker-Hill). However, as one of the most popular mainstream publishing companies, its publication of Price's materials communicates an assumed accuracy in the scores and parts. And yet the G. Schirmer editions of Price's music have been plagued with major errors – in some cases, the replication of old errors in addition to new ones.[4] Performers, scholars, and editors have been very vocal about this problem, which has exposed the complexity, rigor, knowledge, time, and manpower needed to produce clean, well-researched editions; the exorbitant prices practiced for renting and performing works by Black composers; and the question of which individuals, companies, and institutions truly benefit from such practices.

Several positions have developed around the Price editions published by G. Schirmer. The first position is that supply must meet demand despite a lack of manpower to adequately prepare the repertoire for publication. The second position is that such egregious errors reflect a systemic disrespect for the music of Black composers. The third position claims that errors in Price's manuscripts and parts indicate her lack of skill with orchestration and perhaps composition in general. There are several issues with each. First, twentieth-century classical musicians expect a certain level of thoroughly researched and edited music parts for a performance, particularly in works by historical composers. Because detailed knowledge of the history and traditions of Black composition is lacking in predominately white mainstream performance and academic spaces, Price's music is not only new but stylistically unfamiliar.[5] And while the last five years have witnessed an increase in scholars who specialize in Price and other Black composers, it is not at the size or of the age of scholarly communities specializing in the study of canonical figures.

Secondly, because of the accessibility of prepared editions (which are also not immune to mistakes), classical musicians rarely see or take part in the decades- and centuries-long process of manuscript comparison and correction that results in the types of critical editions many performers expect. This has also been exacerbated by G. Schirmer's hesitancy or unwillingness to collaborate with Price scholars and editors – and even to not always allow orchestral librarians access to the source material; lack of a systematic approach to checking, verifying, and correcting idiosyncratic elements of Price's musics; and the systemic lack of investment in Black women composers from music publishers.[6] Lastly, the assumption of Price's lack of knowledge of orchestration to explain manuscript errata, leading to corrections – and, in some cases, recompositions – indicates a lack of knowledge about her basic biography and the urgent need for more scholarly analysis of Price's aesthetic as expressed in instrumental works. It also highlights the ubiquitous, discriminatory assumption that a Black woman was not as skilled as her white peers and antecedents.

This latter position also fails to account for Price's lack of sustained time and resources to hire individuals to engrave, check accuracy, and create multiple collections of parts for more than one orchestra to perform the work. As noted by Margaret Bonds, neighbors from throughout Chicago's South Side were invited to help Price copy out parts for her first symphony; and as Philadelphia Orchestra principal librarian Nicole Jordan observed, Price was "her own copyist, librarian, her own everything."[7] Price was not the only composer who continued to work on their orchestration skills (see Johannes Brahms), nor did every canonical composer prepare clean copies of a work in time for a debut (see Wolfgang Amadeus Mozart and Ludwig van Beethoven). And Price is certainly not the first nor the last composer whose works will be misunderstood due to their unique (read, idiosyncratic) content and character, or whose works may be completed/altered following their death (see Béla Bartók's Viola Sonata). Price's violin concertos have been particularly affected by these latter issues, from mistakes in rental parts and Price's own manuscripts, to frustration and confusion over the work's narrative choices and harmonic content.

Due to these problems and the lack of extensive published analysis and contextualization of Price's instrumental music, this chapter will focus on three key formal elements – signifying, call-and-response, and juba dance – within the Concerto in One Movement (1934), String Quartet in A Minor (1935), Piano Quintet in A Minor (ca. 1935), Violin Concerto No. 1 in D Major (1939), *Negro Folksongs in Counterpoint* for string quartet (ca. 1949, 1951), and *Five Folksongs in Counterpoint* (1951). Since this companion contains separate studies of Price's keyboard works (Chapter 7), violin fantasies and second violin concerto (Chapter 8), and symphonies (Chapter 10), my use of "instrumental music" is very specific and slightly inconsistent. My use of the term refers to Price's chamber music and works for solo instrument with orchestra. The grouping of these two genres is not only a matter of convenience but a way to reflect the importance Price and her stylistic peers placed on genre.

Because of her embrace of genre and unique application of African American idioms in her chamber works and concertos, I, as do several of my colleagues in this volume, place Price within the ethos of the New Negro arts movement of the early twentieth century. I add to this categorization of Price and her peers the descriptor "New Negro modernists." For New Negro modernist composers, genre was not restrictive so much as necessary to the cultivation of a classical tradition rooted in Black cultural practices, in turn contributing to the discourse and expression of American culture. The significance was not solely a matter of proving one's mastery; it was one of several commentaries on America's place and contribution to the classical music tradition, requiring a substantial repertoire in the vein of the Germanic, French, and Italian schools. Price's instrumental music, written in a style that merged African American idioms and forms with Western classical genres, is a significant example of the ways Black artists of her time contributed to and defined the aesthetic thrust of New Negro arts movements like the Harlem Renaissance and Black Chicago Renaissance.

We are witnessing the development of a performance practice for Price's instrumental works. There will be multiple points in this chapter where I embrace the lack of clarity and the uncertainty within the archive. There will be multiple points where the idiosyncrasy of her style is embraced, where I lean into Jordan's remark, when commenting on Price's music in relation to African American religious music, that "dissonance" per the rules of Western harmony "is tonality" per the rules of Black American music. I situate my analysis of the above selections from Price's instrumental repertoire as one possible, though rigorously researched and considered, analysis. We are in the literal weeds of publication, interpretation, and conservation of Price's instrumental music; we cannot currently see the end of the path. But regardless of the mistakes and uncertainties, it is essential, as Jordan states, that we do not stop "respecting her voice and taking the time to understand who she is ... how she presents herself on paper and trying to embody that character before we make an assumption of her intention."[8]

Price's Instrumental Works: An Overview

There are currently twenty-two instrumental works by Florence Price classified as concertos or chamber works. Four of these are incomplete: a rhapsody for piano and orchestra, a fantasy for piano and orchestra, a second piano concerto, and a brass octet. Three were published in her lifetime, including an arrangement for band of her *Three Little Negro Dances* for solo piano. The remainder survive in manuscript form during her lifetime and after her death, with the majority published by G. Schirmer since its acquisition of Price's copyright (Table 9.1).

Scholarly and archival interventions in Price's chamber music and concertos for solo instrument and orchestra highlight the importance of studying, isolating, and clarifying the composer's creative process and the development of their style. It is the role of the scholar and archivist to make sense of the material left behind, through a combination of analytic study of the primary materials; application/development of an analytic frame to effectively contextualize said materials in their historical, cultural, and

Table 9.1 List of known and extant concertos and chamber works by Florence B. Price.

Title	Instrumentation	Composition year	Publication year	Publisher	Notes
Concerto in One Movement	Piano & orchestra	1934	2020	G. Schirmer, New York	Arranged by Trevor Weston in 2011 from the surviving two-piano version; orchestral manuscript recovered at auction in 2019
The Deserted Garden	Violin & piano	1937	1937, 2022	Theodore Presser, Philadelphia; G. Schirmer, New York	
Elfentanz	Violin & piano	N/A	2020	G. Schirmer, New York	
Fantasie for Piano and Orchestra	Piano & orchestra	N/A	N/A	Manuscript	Unfinished
Five Folksongs in Counterpoint for String Quartet	2 violins, viola, cello	1951	2021	G. Schirmer, New York	Originally titled *Five American Folksongs in Counterpoint* for string quartet
Mellow Twilight in Gems of Melody for Violin and Piano, Series 3	Violin & piano	1929	1930, 2020	McKinley Music, Chicago; G. Schirmer, New York	Arranged by Henry S. Sawyer; Price's original version for solo piano was published by McKinley in 1929; original republished by G. Schirmer in 2020
Moods for Flute, Clarinet, and Piano	Flute, clarinet, piano	1953		Manuscript	Dedicated to Lillian Poenisch, clarinetist and cofounder of the Woman's Symphony Orchestra
Negro Folksongs in Counterpoint	2 violins, viola, cello	1949, 1951	2022	G. Schirmer, New York	
Octet	3 trumpets, 2 horns, 2 trombones, tuba	N/A	N/A	Manuscript	Incomplete; different in instrumentation and melodic content from Suite for Brasses and Piano

Table 9.1 (cont.)

Title	Instrumentation	Composition year	Publication year	Publisher	Notes
Piano Concerto No. 2	Piano & orchestra	ca. 1938	N/A	Manuscript	Unfinished; one fragment misidentified as "Violin Concerto No. 2" in University of Arkansas Special Collections (MC 2618)
Piano Quintet No. 1 in A Minor	Violin I, violin II, viola, cello, piano	ca. 1935	2017, 2021	ClarNan, Fayetteville	Edited by Lia Jensen-Abbott; republished with revisions completed by Tomoko Kashiwagi
Piano Quintet No. 2 in E Minor	Violin I, violin II, viola, cello, piano	1936	2022	G. Schirmer, New York	Originally believed to be lost, a three-movement work
Rhapsody, Based on a Folk Tune for Piano and Orchestra	Piano & orchestra	N/A	N/A	Manuscript	Unfinished
Sea Gulls	Soprano I, soprano II, alto I, alto II, piano, violin, viola, cello, flute, clarinet	ca. 1951	N/A	Manuscript	Lyrics by Nora Holland
Spring Journey	Soprano I, soprano II, alto, piano, violin I, violin II viola I, viola II, cello I, cello II, double bass	1935	N/A	Manuscript	
String Quartet in A Minor	2 violins, viola, cello	1935	2019	G. Schirmer, New York	Edited by John Michael Cooper
String Quartet in G Major	2 violins, viola, cello	1929	2017	ClarNan, Fayetteville	Edited by Er-Gene Kahng

Title	Instrumentation	Date	Publisher	Notes
Suite for Brasses and Piano	2 A trumpets, 2 horns, 2 trombones, tuba, piano	1930	G. Schirmer, New York	2021	Also titled Octet for Brasses and Piano, published under this title by G. Schirmer
Three Negro Dances	C piccolo, D♭ piccolo, 2 flutes, 2 oboes, 2 bassoons, E♭ soprano clarinet, 3 B♭ soprano clarinets, 2 E♭ alto saxophones, B♭ tenor saxophone, E♭ baritone saxophone, 2 B♭ trumpets, 2 B♭ cornets, 4 F horns, 3 trombones, euphonium, tuba, timpani, percussion	1939	Theodore Presser, Philadelphia; G. Schirmer, New York	2021	Arranged by Eric W. G. Leidzén from Price's *Three Little Negro Dances* (1933) for solo piano, also published by Theodore Presser; original piano version published by G. Schirmer in 2021
Three Negro Spirituals	Violin, piano	ca. 1933	ClarNan, Fayetteville	2017	Edited by Barbara Garvey Jackson; first two arrangements are undated, third dated from 1933
Violin Concerto No. 1 in D Major	Violin & orchestra	1939	G. Schirmer, New York	2018, 2022	Orchestral version published in 2018; piano reduction and solo part published in 2022
Violin Concerto No. 2	Violin & orchestra	1952	G. Schirmer, New York	2019, 2022	See note for Piano Concerto No. 2

aesthetic contexts; and identification of the development of the work from sketches and first iteration to final iteration, a process which is not always so straightforward.

A case in point is Price's Suite for Brasses and Piano, which may either have begun as a work titled Octet or is one of two works for brass ensemble. Scored for seven brass instruments and piano, there are portions of the manuscript labeled "Octet," but with the same instrumentation as the Suite for Brasses and Piano. However, there are also copies of an unfinished manuscript labeled "Octet" that contains different instrumentation and different melodic content in the opening (see Table 9.1). This leads to several questions: (1) Was Price working on two different works for brass ensemble, finishing one (Suite) and not finishing the other (Octet)? (2) Did the Suite begin as an octet, with no piano, and then shift to include piano, reducing the three trumpets called for in the Octet to two trumpets in the Suite? (3) Did Price plan to write two octets, one all brass and one with brass and piano, finally landing on "Suite" for the latter? It is a series of questions that Rae Linda Brown sought to answer in relation to Price's counterpoint quartets. While we now have *Negro Folksongs in Counterpoint* (1949, 1951) and *Five Folksongs in Counterpoint* (1951), the latter was initially titled *Five Negro Folksongs*, requiring Brown to consider the possibility that these quartets were not two separate works, but the former being the seed that developed into the latter.[9] As will be discussed later in the next section, the different source material and number of movements suggest that Price was composing two separate works, initially planning a second set of Negro folksongs in counterpoint and changing the name as the source material moved beyond the scope of African American folk song.

Price and Signifying

When Er-Gene Kahng and the Janáček Philharmonic released the world premiere recording of Price's violin concertos on Albany Records in 2018, it was the culmination of a crowdsourcing endeavor that was part of Albany Records non-profit model and reflected the lack of mainstream attention and resources directed towards champions of Price's music. It marked the introduction of these works to violinists and scholars of Florence Price, American music, and Black composers; their narrative form was considered idiosyncratic at best and nonsensical at worst.

Listeners were thrown by the obvious Tchaikovsky quotations in the first violin concerto and the repetitious form of the second violin concerto, including yours truly. Although diversion from standard forms in concertos is nothing new, there was a specific urgency to make these concertos "make sense" within the precedents of previous, canonical works. But as I listened more and studied the scores, I realized I was trying to make this concerto fit within a specific, predetermined formal box. Philadelphia Orchestra music and artistic director Yannick Nézet-Séguin reached a similar conclusion as he prepared the work for the 2023 performance:

> The first concerto I found very, much more difficult to tackle and I would not advise people to start with this piece ... it really has helped to have done more of her works because it can appear disjointed, the first concerto. Actually, once you accept that it's not disjointed but more rhapsodic, and it goes more within an improvisation of the violin and then the orchestra brings it back, almost a stroll in a countryside, then I find it marvelous.[10]

What Nézet-Séguin expresses in the back-and-forth between soloist and ensemble is an articulation of Price's use of call-and-response as texture and form; and his later discussion of Price's reference and homage to Tchaikovsky and other canonical composers of D major violin concertos speaks to two key features in Price's music: call-and-response as form and signifying. Therefore, to understand Price's music is a matter not only of setting aside preconceived notions of form, but also of centering Black music forms and procedures that are not always referenced or understood with the specificity required in classical music spaces. Required are analytic frameworks from Black music studies and musicology, such as Samuel A. Floyd's music signifyin(g) theory.

Music signifyin(g) is a key feature of Floyd's Call–Response concept, applied in his study of African music retentions in African American music, *The Power of Black Music* (1995).[11] Floyd's music signifyin(g) builds on Henry Louis Gates's literary signifyin(g) theory, which in turn was inspired by Sterling Stuckley's theorization of the ring shout in African American musical practice during the enslavement period.[12] Whether used in literature, oratory, comedy, or music, signifying is a practice of purposeful quotation and transformation. It is a knowing wink to the listener, presenting them with something familiar and then ripping the rug out from under them through the familiar's (re)situation within a new, unfamiliar context.

As theorized by Floyd, music signifyin(g) is a compositional process that communicates the composer/performer/improvisor's knowledge of familiar content now presented in a new context. It can be a melody, a rhythmic pattern, a key area, or a riff on a particular genre or style (e.g., for Floyd, ragtime is a signifyin(g) genre on classical music). Music signifyin(g) is one of a multitude of musical features, rhythms, aesthetics, forms, and procedures within African American music-dance and cultural memory.

Building upon Floyd's work and diverging from my colleague Elektra V. Carter, I use the term "signifying" rather than "music signifyin(g)" in my discussion of Price's engagement with Tchaikovsky's Violin Concerto and American and Black folk music in her Counterpoint Quartets. I do this for the following reasons: to reflect the function of signifying as an intertextual, satirical process used and applied across creative disciplines; and to attempt a clear, specific definition of signifying within a musical context due to the immense importance of this strategy within Black cultural and social life writ large.

Extant materials indicate there is precedent for Price's signifying on Tchaikovsky thanks to a concert held on August 29, 1935. It was the final day of the annual National Association of Negro Musicians (NANM) conference, which took place in New York that year; Price was performing as soloist for her Concerto in One Movement at the Juilliard School of Music Auditorium (130 Claremont Avenue).[13] In addition to Price's concerto, the conference orchestra also performed Dvořák's *New World* Symphony (1893), Coleridge-Taylor's *Bamboula*, and Tchaikovsky's Concerto in D Major Op. 35 for Violin and Orchestra (1877). Four years later, Price completed her first violin concerto.

Of the three completed concertos, the Violin Concerto No. 1 in D Major is of unknown provenance; there are currently no existing writings by Price telling us or hinting at whether the work was a commission or not; whether it was performed in her lifetime; and whether it was written with a specific violinist in mind. At a time when studying the music "alone" has become more of an exception than the rule in musicology, Price's Violin Concerto No. 1 presents a conundrum, an uncomfortable middle ground, because all we have is the music.

But the music can still tell us about the composer: their sense of craft; what they prioritized (melody versus contrapuntal motion); what musical characteristics and idiosyncrasies found their way across their works, whether they intended them to or not. What the Violin Concerto No. 1 tells us about Price is that she was a keen student of compositional procedures across traditions, and of how some of those procedures (e.g., antiphony in classical music, or call-and-response in African American

Example 9.1 Price, Violin Concerto No. 1, 1st movement, motives 1 and 2, mm. 23–29.

musics) achieved a similar purpose within the context of the composition. Additionally, Price incorporated procedures from African American traditions that highlight the participatory nature of music-making in Black musical communities. This is done to not only communicate her knowledge and familiarity with the earlier work, but it is done also to transform the familiar into something new. Similarity does not equal synonymity: While signifying in African American musics is a process similar to allusion in classical music, its function is rooted in reference *and* transformation rather than reference as solely homage or stylistic codification.

The most salient signifying examples are present in the first movement, Tempo moderato. The opening line of the solo part — A to B♭, in a minor second interval — is a significant sonic reference to the Tchaikovsky. While her phrasing goal is similar to Tchaikovsky's (E6 in m. 24), Price diverges rhythmically by measure 25 (Ex. 9.1).[14]

By this point, Price is signifying not only on Tchaikovsky's melody, but on the directional and rhythmic content of the melody itself. Through a sixteenth-note sequence, Price moves to the dominant by measure 26 through a descending thirds sequence whose pitches are also used by Tchaikovsky in his descent to the dominant: B♮, C#, and A♮. Price's use of rhythmic diminution in measures 23 through 26 allows her to provide the soloist with a direction that emulates an improvisatory arc, indicative of melody as development.

By measure 28, Price signifies on Tchaikovsky's syncopated eighth-, sixteenth-, and thirty-second-note figure followed by chromatic triplets. Her third signifying motive appears at the boundary between the cadenza and recapitulation in measure 189 (Ex. 9.2).

Example 9.2 Price, Violin Concerto No. 1, cadenza II to recapitulation, m. 189.

Example 9.3 Tchaikovsky, Violin Concerto, cadenza to recapitulation, mm. 212–219.

Here, the rhythmic diminution is a Prician method of tension building and signifying process: Tchaikovsky also used rhythmic diminution leading up to the cadenza-recapitulation elision in measures 212–219 (Ex. 9.3).

The trilled half note and whole note, like the A–B♭ opening of the soloist's introduction, are a clear sonic calling card of Price's engagement with the older concerto. Price's fourth signifying motive begins the exciting drive to the movement's conclusion, similar to Tchaikovsky's use of the same motive. Price uses a small alteration in the first half of the sextuplet before launching into a direct quotation of the Tchaikovsky motive. Another salient example of Price's melodic signifying takes us once again to her play with phrase direction and octave variation. Price's main theme is distinctly hers, reflecting the pastoral lyricism that defined her large-scale works.

But rather than unspooling the melody as Tchaikovsky does, Price demarcates where the antecedent ends and the consequent begins. This leads to a four-measure opening phrase that is still not symmetrical in the Western classical sense, eliding with the beginnings of the next phrase on the "and" of beat four in measure 33. Tchaikovsky also elides the primary theme phrase with the second complete phrase in measure 31, taking off not on a downbeat but on the "and" of beat 3.

When Price brings back the main theme in measure 47, it is an octave lower with double-stops; when Tchaikovsky brings back the main theme in measure 41, it is an octave higher with chords and double-stops. These minutiae indicate Price's close study of the Tchaikovsky concerto's structure and precedents, as well as the tiny kernels of possibility that signifying provides. This was not a "copy and paste" process, but a purposeful reference to an older work still growing in popularity and cultural significance in Price's era. It is an example of her deft musical knowledge through her mapping of African American music processes with Western classical music forms.

While often categorized as arrangements due to her use of preexisting material, Price's *Negro Folksongs in Counterpoint* and *Five Folksongs in Counterpoint* may also be understood as examples of signifying at the level of form. Price's use of "counterpoint" versus "variations" or "arrangements" speaks to her identification of contrapuntal motion as a tool to achieve something similar to signifying: She sets something familiar in a unique context to create something new.

In the manuscript folder for *Five Folksongs in Counterpoint*, Price wrote in ink the details of the five-movement string quartet – details that tell us what folksong each movement is based on, to a degree. "No. 1 is based upon the Negro spiritual 'Calvary.' Southern USA." After No. 2, Price writes: "'Clementine' a ballad which Became [sic] a favorite during the Reconstruction period. It was popular in San Franciso [sic] Calif. near the end of the 19th century and is often sung now-a-days by college and community groups." For movement three, Price writes: "DRINK TO ME ONLY WITH THINE EYES was sung by settlers on the Eastern coast of America before the days of the American Revolution. The origin of the Tune cannot be traced back beyond about 1770. The poem was written by Ben Jonson in 1616." The fourth movement she leaves obscure, only writing "Several folksongs." over another marking in faint pencil that is barely perceptible. With movement number five she resumes her annotating, though not as detailed as the previous examples: "SWING LOW SWEET CHARIOT, Well-Known and one of the best-loved of American Negro folk tunes."

Though older than *Five Folksongs* by a few years, *Negro Folksongs in Counterpoint* only recently reentered the public sphere, performed as part of Louisville Public Media's "The Unheard" recital series in 2017.[15] An example of Price's interest in the craft of orchestration – of the relatedness and impact of individual parts on each other – is her utilization of fugal textures for the final movements of each quartet. In the *Negro Folksongs*, the fourth movement, "Joshua Fit de Battle of Jericho," is a fugue: The first violin enters on the tonic; the second violin on the dominant eight measures later (m. 9); the violist on the tonic eight measures after that (m. 17); and the cello three measures after (m. 20). This interlocking of independent but related parts takes on further significance when Price abandons the fugal texture for the first instance of rhythmic alignment in measure 60. This shift from polyphony to heterophony, first in sets of two and then between all four voices, is Price's tool to signal the arrival to the coda, enhanced by the più mosso marking to pick up the tempo and the accelerando in measure 64.

"Swing Low, Sweet Chariot," the fifth movement of the *Five Folksongs*, is more adventurous in its fugal writing. The cello introduces the theme, and when the viola starts its fugal entrance in measure 8, it is joined one measure later by a countermelody in the second violin and another melody from the first violin in measure 10. This results in a texture reminiscent of Gregorian chant, where the melody is placed in the tenor voice, typically the third or second to last staff in the notation system, which in this case is the same position as the viola. The main theme moves to the second violin at the end of measure 16, taken up by the first violin in the pickup to measure 25. Price does not use heterophony to demarcate the coda; instead, she uses a shift in rhythm and move to homophony, letting the first violin drive the group. It is not until the last six measures that the heterophony returns, along with Price's penchant for repetitive, accented half notes to denote the thrilling conclusion, which she uses in her piano concerto and second violin concerto.

Price's use of counterpoint to transform material beyond the typical theme and variation model is a strong indicator of her identification and embracement of related but distinct musical processes in classical and African American practice. This is also clear in her use of call-and-response as texture *and* form in her Concerto in One Movement.

Call-and-Response as Form

Call-and-response is a foundational component of African American music and culture. It can function as texture or form (sometimes at the same time) and is present in most African American music genres (although not every one of them). Call-and-response has two popular manifestations: (1) restatement of a motive and (2) completion of an unfinished motivic idea. Price uses both in her Concerto in One

Example 9.4 Price, Concerto in One Movement, two-piano reduction, mm. 1–9.

Movement, with the second type functioning as a texture and form in the opening of the "Moderato." The primary theme – the call – returns in different iterations in measures 1, 3, and 5, with the response appearing in measures 2 and 4. In measures 6–8, Price uses rhythmic augmentation to make clear the sequential function of call-and-response (Ex. 9.4).

Whereas the call of measure 1 begins on D (tonic) an octave plus one whole step above middle C, moving in a stepwise motion before landing on A (dominant), the call of measure 3 is a descending figure. Starting on G, moving to F♮ then D, Price moves from the dominant to the tonic on the third beats of measures 1 and 3, respectively. The call in measure 5 returns the harmony to the dominant, allowing for the augmentation of the response portion of the primary theme to be extended, preparing the half cadence in measure 9 that immediately precedes the entrance of the soloist.

The responses of measures 2 and 4 may not mirror the call in exact shape, but they do in terms of goals: Measure 2 ends with the dominant in the upper voice, whereas measure 4 ends with the tonic in the upper voice. Moving from A to E on the downbeats of measures 6, and 7, respectively, takes us closer to the harmonic arena of A major, emphasized by the tonic–dominant relationship between A and E and the cadential motion of the G♯ on the fourth beat of measure 8 to the dominant triad in measure 9.

Price utilized call-and-response in her String Quartet in A Minor (1935) as well. There, the timbral similarities between the violins enhance the rhythmic and phrasal interlocking unique to this texture. In the third movement, "Juba," this is apparent in the first violin's call and the response from the second violin. When listening to a recording or performance of this work without the score to reference, it is easy to mistakenly hear both the call-and-response portions as one instrumental part. This movement also features Price's use of call-and-response as a sequential model, most effective when passing motives around the quartet. Like her Concerto in One Movement, Price uses call-and-response as texture and form. This time within the da capo aria form instead of sonata-ritornello form, call-and-response enhances the other features in this movement Price draws upon to evoke the African American dance form: compound meter; syncopated rhythms; and use of modal rather than tonal harmony, allowing her to use the melody to drive the development, indicative of her incorporation of not only improvisational techniques but also African American harmony predominated by modal and non-Western harmonic systems. In addition to call-and-response, the "Juba" movements of Price's A minor quartet and A minor piano quintet illustrate her engagement with a practice centuries old by her era: the use of dance forms in classical genres.

Juba in the Chamber Works

It is not uncommon to draw upon dance forms in classical music. What was not as common, even in Price's time, however, was to explicitly utilize a Black dance form for movements traditionally inspired by or built upon white European dance. Composers like Franz Joseph Haydn, who chose to draw upon minuets for the form and character of the third movements of their chamber works and symphonies, set a precedent that was maintained even with the shift in the early nineteenth century to the less formal scherzo's lightness of character, triple meter, ABA/ABA' form. It was within this practice that Price introduced another traditional dance that, in the context of a Western classical genre, became an innovative choice: juba.

Price was not the first composer to draw upon juba: her contemporary R. Nathaniel Dett did so for his piano suite, *In the Bottoms*. Nor was she the first to incorporate Afrodiasporic materials: see Louis Moreau Gottschalk's *Bamboula* or Samuel Coleridge-Taylor's *24 Negro Melodies*. But Price is arguably the first to use juba with the purpose of incorporating Black expressive forms and adhering to stylistic precedents within large-scale genres. Her A minor string quartet and A minor piano quintet – along with her three completed symphonies (to be discussed in Chapter 10) – each have a third movement labelled "juba."[16] Price scholar Rae Linda Brown identified instances of juba rhythms in the symphonies in her dissertation; this section builds upon that important work.

Price's use of juba rhythms, pentatonicism, juba as title, and compound meter to better adapt the polymetric roots of the music-dance form is the culmination of aesthetic work that enacts New Negro modernist tenets. While working within the parameters of a classical tradition, Price adapts not only African American melody and modality – two of the most common manifestations of classical works impacted by Black music traditions – but African American style, rhythm, and character. And though her choice of juba has been primarily understood as a look back to antebellum-era sources, it is essential to note that by the mid twentieth century, juba rhythms and its sister dance form, the satirical cakewalk, had moved from the musical communities of the enslaved to the mainstream stage through the minstrel show. Ragtime, a stylistic cousin and successor to the musical cakewalks, also reflected this very American of processes: Black creative acts moving from the edges to center, even though its progenitors were either declined a seat on the pop culture train or, more often, restricted to the segregated train cars.

Sixteenth note–eighth note–sixteenth note is the rhythmic pattern Price uses routinely across her juba movements. It is a ubiquitous rhythm in rags, minstrel tunes, and cakewalks, such as Claude Debussy's popular and derogatory "Golliwog's Cakewalk" from his *Children's Corner Suite* (1913). But Price's pointed referencing of juba and more subtle nods to the cakewalk and ragtime create a pastoralism more tongue-in-cheek than naïve. In the case of the A minor quartet and A minor quintet, a subtle quotation of a song whose murky history connects it to the repertoire of coon song, and to an offensive parody turned children's folk song, reinforce this reading of Price's use of juba as not only an enactment of New Negro modernist ideals but an example of her perceptive, cutting humor: her rhythmic and modal signifying of "Shortnin' Bread."

After the C major opening section of the A minor string quartet's juba movement, "Shortnin' Bread" emerges in the middle, Allegretto section set in E major. The motive to the words "Mammy's lil baby loves" is given to the cello, an eighth-note set built upon an ascending major sixth on the first beat followed by a major second. The viola and second violin provide syncopated emphasis, the viola with the sixteenth(rest)–eighth–sixteenth figure on the first beat and the second violin providing a sixteenth(rest)–dotted eighth. These motives function as the rhythmic drive and foundation for the original melody in the first violin, lasting from measures 45 to 54. Of note is Price's use of ♭VI (C major triad) in measure 53, a chord substitution that would be mirrored in the A minor quintet, where "Shortnin' Bread" again makes an appearance.

Price again quotes "Shortnin' Bread" in the second section of the A minor quintet's juba movement, starting in measure 17. But instead of setting the familiar motive in one part, Price utilizes the ascending major sixth–major second figure and straight, cadential eighth notes as the melody, passed to the second violin, first violin, piano, and back. Price then allows the melody to develop a new direction, highlighting her original melody's relationship to the "Shortnin' Bread" theme through her use of the descending minor third as the main motivic thrust. She also continues use of idiosyncratic modulations; the first section with this theme is set in F major, whereas the second "Shortnin' Bread" section is in D♭ major, the ♭VI in F major.

Understood within this context, Price's use of juba is not only part of a movement amongst Black composers to incorporate Black music styles within classical genres – the "older" styles of Negro spirituals and juba, specifically. It is also a window into the reality of American music: of music that offends and perpetuates subjugation eventually removed of its teeth; of music adapted and transfigured via its new context; and of the importance of signifying to Price's compositional process, as Elektra V. Carter finds within Price's concert spirituals. These chamber works reflect a woman who recognized the structural and conceptual benefits of pointed quotation, especially of repertoire rooted in offense, mimicking and obscuring the layers of meaning, tradition, and signification of the Black music-dance traditions on which they were (allegedly) based.

Conclusion

Through her piano concerto, first violin concerto, and chamber music, Price illustrates how integral African American folk processes are to the character and form of these works. She maintains core elements of the genres in which she is composing while also incorporating African American musical features and processes. Sometimes those processes are overt (e.g., melody, modal harmony); sometimes they are more subtle, legible only to listeners familiar with African American music procedures (e.g., call-and-response, signifying). Regardless, they became her tools in articulating a soundscape that, to paraphrase Jordan and Nézet-Seguin, contains a "dance" and "spiritual" essence that is uniquely, sometimes confoundingly, hers.

This chapter offers an analytic snapshot of what we may discern and uncover from the instrumental music of Florence Price: a woman deeply familiar with the tradition in which she had grown, developed, and contributed to; a woman who did not have all the resources at her disposal to make composing her sole mode of income, an issue even modern-day composers are still facing. And yet she wrote, and we have now reached the point where we can debate, complain, and obsess over repertoire that we could not hold in our hands until 2009. What a blessing!

Notes

1. Florence Beatrice Smith Price Collection (MC 988), Special Collections, University of Arkansas Libraries, Fayetteville.
2. Florence Beatrice Smith Price Papers Addendum (MC 988a), Special Collections, University of Arkansas Libraries, Fayetteville; Florence Beatrice Smith Price Papers Second Addendum (MC 988b), Special Collections, University of Arkansas Libraries, Fayetteville; Florence Price Collection (MC 2618), Special Collections, University of Arkansas Libraries, Fayetteville.
3. Interview with Nicole Jordan, librarian for the Philadelphia Orchestra, July 24, 2023.
4. James Bennett II, "Pianist Sharon Su Found Errors in Sheet Music She Loved. So, She Fixed it," GBH, April 25, 2024, https://tinyurl.com/bdbf4s4a.
5. Interview with Nicole Jordan.
6. Sharon Su, "The Price is Wrong: How Error-Riddled Scores Get in the Way of Promoting Music of Marginalized Composers," *VAN Magazine*, February 15, 2024, https://van-magazine.com/mag/florence-price-schirmer-errors/; interview with Nicole Jordan.
7. Helen Walker-Hill, *From Spirituals to Symphonies: African-American Women Composers and Their Music* (Urbana: University of Illinois Press, 2007), 147; interview with Nicole Jordan.
8. Interview with Nicole Jordan.
9. Brown, *The Heart of a Woman*, 231–232.
10. Interview with Yannick Nézet-Séguin, October 22, 2023.
11. Samuel A. Floyd, Jr., *The Power of Black Music* (New York: Oxford University Press, 1995).
12. Henry Louis Gates, Jr., *The Signifying Monkey: A Theory of African-American Literary Criticism, 25th Anniversary Edition* (New York: Oxford University Press, 1988); Sterling Stuckey, *Slave Culture: Nationalist Theory and the Foundations of Black America, 25th Anniversary Edition* (New York: Oxford University Press, 1987).
13. "NANM Convention Program, 1935," folder 73, NANM Collection III 2, Center for Black Music Research.

14. All engravings of musical examples in this chapter are from Alexandra Kori Hill, "Make the Familiar New: New Negro Modernism in the Concertos of Florence B. Price" (PhD diss., University of North Carolina at Chapel Hill, 2022).
15. "The Unheard: Florence Price's Lost String Quartet," WUOL, Louisville Public Media, July 6, 2017, www.lpm.org/classical/2017-07-06/the-unheard-florence-prices-lost-string-quartet.
16. Her two works that do not are the G major string quartet (which has two movements) and the E minor piano quintet (where the third movement is an Allegretto).

10 | Symphonies to Tone Poems

DOUGLAS W. SHADLE

On April 25, 1953, Florence B. Price wrote a letter to Robert Whitney, conductor of the Louisville Orchestra, to gauge his interest in her music. Two weeks earlier, the national press had reported that Whitney and his orchestra, under the auspices of the Rockefeller Foundation, would receive $400,000 to commission, perform, and record forty-six new works over the next four years – a historic infusion of cash for new orchestral music in the United States. Critic Seymour Raven of the *Chicago Tribune* enthused, "Student composers as well as professionals will be compensated, foreign as well as American. Man alive!"[1] Naturally, Price was intrigued:

> I have recently decided to give more time to the writing of the kind of music which lies closest to my heart and already have been fortunate enough to win a number of composition contests and hear manuscripts performed, among which was the T.V. performance a few weeks ago of a group of pieces of mine performed by the Chicago Symphony Chamber Orchestra on their program of American music.... It is now my purpose to seek information as to how I might go about trying to be included among composers commissioned for scores in connection with the Rockefeller Foundation.[2]

Here, aged sixty-five, Price envisioned embarking on a new phase of her career refocused on the music she loved – music for orchestra. In fact, beyond the Chicago Symphony Orchestra (CSO) broadcast earlier that year, she had recently completed her second violin concerto and, as she explained to Whitney, planned to travel to Europe in a month to promote and attend performances of her music there. Unfortunately, Price fell deeply ill only two days before she was set to depart and suffered a brain hemorrhage that ultimately caused her death in early June.[3]

The turbulent context of this letter crystallizes the flow of Price's nearly twenty-five-year career as an orchestral music composer. (See Table 10.1.) Her first two works in this medium – a tone poem and a symphony – catapulted her into the national spotlight after they won prizes in a 1932 competition. Frederick Stock and the CSO debuted the new symphony to critical acclaim the following year.[4] Buoyed by these successes, Price penned an orchestral suite, three more symphonies, and a concert overture in rapid

Table 10.1 Florence B. Price, orchestral works.

Title	Instrumentation	Premiere (in Price's lifetime)
Ethiopia's Shadow in America	2+picc.2.2.2 – 4.2.3.1 – timp.perc(4) – cel – strings	N/A
Symphony in E Minor	2+2picc.2.2.2 – 4.2.3.1 – timp.perc(3) – strings	June 15, 1933, Chicago Symphony Orchestra
Mississippi River	3+picc.2+ca.2+bcl.2+cbn – 4.3.3.1 – timp.perc(4) – hp – strings	N/A
Symphony in G Minor	3+picc.2+ca.2+bcl.2+cbn – 4.3.3+btbn – timp.perc(?) – hp – strings	N/A
Symphony in C Minor	3+picc.2+ca.2+bcl.2 – 4.3.3.1 – timp.perc(5) – hp – strings	November 6, 1940, Michigan WPA Symphony
Symphony in D Minor	3+picc.2+ca.2+bcl.2 – 4.3.2+btbn.1 –timp.perc(2) – cel.hp – strings	N/A
Concert Overture No. 1	3.2.2.2 – 4.3.3.1 – timp.perc(4) – strings	June 16, 1939, American Concert Orchestra (Chicago)
The Oak	3+picc.2+ca.2+bcl.2 – 4.3.3.1 – timp.perc(4) – hp – strings	N/A
Songs of the Oak	3+picc.2+ca.2+bcl.2+cbn – 4.3.3+btn.1 – timp.perc(6) – cel[=org].hp – strings	N/A
Concert Overture No. 2	3+picc.2+ca.2+bcl.2 – 4.3.3.1 – timp.perc(4)	N/A

succession (to say nothing of the piano and violin concertos written during the same period). But, hindered by a local and national orchestral infrastructure strained by the lingering economic depression, she was able to secure only two more performances of orchestral music by the end of the decade.

The US entry into World War II in December 1941 rejuvenated the economy and, along with it, moral support for American composers. Sensing an opportunity to reinsert herself into the national orchestral landscape, Price wrote three new pieces in 1943 – a concert overture and two tone poems – but was unsuccessful in her calculated attempts to obtain performances as conductors declined to offer assistance. By 1953, she had begun to feel a fresh urge to follow an orchestral path after turning her attention elsewhere for nearly ten years. Robert Whitney, a fixture on Chicago's classical music scene in the 1930s, was as likely as anyone to lend a sympathetic ear. And, with the Rockefeller funds at his disposal, his orchestra was more than able to offer support. This time, though, nature had other plans.

The chronologically uneven development of Price's orchestral catalog presents challenges for stylistic analysis and contextualization. On the one hand, she was consistently invested in constructing a uniquely American aesthetic through creative engagement with the spirituals – a compositional project intersecting with that of several of her African American contemporaries, including William Grant Still, William Dawson, Margaret Bonds, and Irene Britton Smith. On the other hand, Price had to weigh a desire for stylistic distinction against the public's (or a conductor's) changing tastes and likely appetite for adventurousness – a hurdle facing every composer in a programming landscape awash with canonical music from previous eras. Ranging from colorfully melodious to thorny and abstract, Price's unique orchestral style fully manifests her efforts to create, as she once wrote, a "very beautiful and very American" musical language arising "from the melting pot just as the nation itself has done."[5]

The Wanamaker Prize Works

Price's career as an orchestral composer could hardly have begun more auspiciously. Shortly before she moved to Chicago in 1927, Rodman Wanamaker, heir to the Philadelphia department store fortune and a devoted arts philanthropist, announced that he would award $1,000 in prizes, raised by the Black employees of his stores, for the best pieces written by African American composers.[6] Over each of the next five years, musicians around the country eagerly awaited the announcement of winners at the National Association of Negro Musicians annual convention. During the contest's fourth run, in 1931, the organizers deferred the orchestral music category by a year to help applicants submit their best possible work while a fifth round of funding for smaller pieces would proceed apace.[7] Price, meanwhile, had broken her foot, which, as she recounted later, gave her time to focus on her entries.[8] When all the remaining winners had been decided, newspapers reported that Price would take home four separate awards: $500 for her Symphony in E Minor, $250 for a piano sonata in the same key, and two honorable mentions – one for her tone poem *Ethiopia's Shadow in America* and the other for a virtuosic piece for solo piano, *Fantasie Nègre* No. 4 in B minor.[9]

Black musicians generally held the Wanamaker contest in high esteem for its cultivation of creative talent, but composers themselves still faced substantial obstacles to publication and performance. Wellington Adams, a composer active in Washington, DC, and one of the contest's inaugural winners, observed in 1930, "They win prizes, but that's the end. Why not open the door of opportunity to our Wanamaker prize-winning composers, then give the public a chance to view their splendid work?"[10] He proposed a "Wanamaker Art Series of Negro Compositions" that would publish prize winners alongside "other race composers who, perchance, are unknown as such." Yet even this ambitious plan would offer little support to orchestral composers, who required access to an orchestra – an enormously expensive proposition – for performance. In September 1932, when Price's awards were announced, she had no immediate concert prospects for either winning piece.

Despite these obstacles, Price had begun to reinvent her compositional career in the mid 1920s by selectively entering contests, such as the Casper Holstein competition sponsored by *Opportunity* magazine, and spending two summers studying advanced harmony and orchestration at the Chicago Musical College. As Price biographer Rae Linda Brown has noted, this work expanded her creative palette and laid the professional groundwork for her eventual permanent relocation to Chicago in 1927.[11] Notably, her orchestration studies with Wesley La Violette culminated in the composition of a symphony, giving her ample practice for her eventual submissions for the Wanamaker prize, and she continued studying orchestration on scholarship at the American Conservatory of Music in 1929.[12]

Ethiopia's Shadow in America

The exact origins of *Ethiopia's Shadow in America* remain mysterious. One of the surviving manuscript scores is marked with the date 1929, indicating that Price did not write it expressly for the competition but was probably working on it during her conservatory studies. In fact, the contest went on hiatus that year as the organizers regrouped after Wanamaker's death; orchestral pieces would not be solicited again until the round that Price eventually won. It is possible that she wrote the piece with a group called the Ferrell Symphony Orchestra in mind, perhaps during her advanced orchestration studies. Founded in 1921 by the distinguished young violinist and linguist Harrison Ferrell, this all-Black orchestra was a South Side fixture for just over a decade and made special efforts to program music by Black composers.[13]

Ethiopia's Shadow is most appropriately classed as a tone poem because it fits squarely into the tradition of narrative and picturesque writing associated with that genre. Yet it deviates slightly from the genre's single-movement (or at least uninterrupted) norm with a three-movement structure. (It is also Price's only tone poem with clear movement designations.) Why she chose this formal scheme is unclear, though an announcement for the extension of the orchestral branch of the Wanamaker contest noted that entries must be "a suite of not fewer than three numbers."[14] Therefore, even if Price had not written the work exclusively for entry into the contest, by 1932 she had ensured that it would fit all the required parameters.

In any case, *Ethiopia's Shadow* is also distinctive in Price's orchestral output for its inclusion of an explanation of its narrative and pictorial elements. The title page of an extant manuscript dated 1929 reads:

"Ethiopia's Shadow in America" is intended to portray:

I. The arrival of the Negro in America when first brought here as a slave (Introduction and Allegretto);
II. His resignation and Faith__(Andante)
III. His Adaptation (Allegro)_A fusion of his native and acquired impulses[15]

As it follows enslaved Africans across the Middle Passage into plantation life and eventually to freedom, Price's triptych narrates a specific perspective on Afrodiasporic history that suffused theatrical revues in Harlem throughout the 1920s and, as musicologist Mark Tucker has shown, would later inform Duke Ellington's *Black, Brown and Beige*.[16] These artistic renditions of Black history, of course, projected broader interest in the subject generated by figures like Carter G. Woodson, who helped establish the Negro History Week in 1926 under the auspices of the Association for the Study of Negro Life and History.

Divided into two sections, the first movement opens with slow, bold gestures for brass, strings, and percussion reflecting the emotional intensity of arriving in a strange and imposing new land after a perilous – and at times deadly – journey across a vast ocean. This sense of awe fades in the Allegretto section of the movement, which juxtaposes the monotonous inexorability of hard plantation labor (signaled by a rhythmic motive in the percussion) with the secret joys of clandestine dancing in private. The second movement evokes the broad lyricism of the spirituals in a duet for solo violin and solo cello with lush string accompaniment. The final movement is characterized by what might be termed "timbral counterpoint" or "gestural counterpoint," in the sense that musical sounds and characters from earlier in the piece – the driving wood block, for example – recur in dialogue with one another in various combinations before the awe-filled intensity of the opening returns to finish the piece.

Symphony in E Minor

At the time of the Wanamaker prize announcement in September 1932, the entire city of Chicago buzzed with activity as it prepared for the Century of

Progress Exposition, a world's fair set to open the following spring. In December, fifty of the city's leading cultural lights, including Frederick Stock and Jane Addams, announced the formation of a group called the Chicago Friends of Music. Its immediate charge was to raise $100,000 for a new building to host music at the fair, but the organizing committee hoped that offering memberships at the low rate of one dollar – a necessity in the depressed economy – would spur a citywide groundswell of support for musical performances. By March, the group had failed to raise enough money to complete the project in time for the fair's opening, leading them to abandon the plan.[17]

While promising to refund membership payments to anyone who only wanted to support the hall, the Friends of Music quickly decided to redirect all remaining funds toward subsidizing a series of CSO concerts and other musical activities at the fair.[18] The revised plan required enlisting the logistical help of several musical organizations. These groups included the local chapter of the National Association of Negro Musicians, known more formally as the Chicago Music Association (CMA). In fact, prominent Black musicians had participated in the Friends of Music's grassroots efforts from the beginning. By the time the initial fundraising drive failed, the CMA reported a 100 percent participation rate through the efforts of music critic Maude Roberts George (president of the CMA), pianist Estella Bonds, and others.[19]

As the new plan took shape, George and Bonds continued to play key roles organizing the series by developing a "Negro Night" program for the CSO, designed to highlight African American artistry from compositional and performance angles.[20] In late April, for example, George revealed in her weekly column that Price was busy extracting parts for the symphony "preparatory to its public presentation in the near future," suggesting that they anticipated its premiere as part of the series.[21] A few weeks later, George reviewed a recital given by pianist Margaret Bonds, Estella's twenty-year-old daughter, in which she played John Alden Carpenter's Concertino. "It is hoped," George observed, "that [Carpenter] will have the opportunity of hearing Miss Bonds play his Concertino, for she displayed such rare understanding that we feel sure the composer would have been as thrilled as was the audience."[22] Carpenter's wife, Ellen Waller, chaired the Friends of Music, ensuring that they would both attend.

When the series was finally announced in May, its scope surprised everyone. Over two weeks, an augmented CSO would perform six different programs at the expansive Auditorium Theatre, each featuring a distinguished soloist, all for bargain prices. The second week promised to be a blockbuster: George Gershwin would appear as piano soloist in his own works, and the renowned African American tenor Roland Hayes would perform with the orchestra for the first time– in a program that also included the world premiere of Price's symphony and Margaret Bonds soloing in Carpenter's Concertino.[23] Maude Roberts George herself underwrote the costs for the Hayes concert beyond what the Friends of Music fund had provided.[24]

The Symphony in E Minor is unique in Price's orchestral catalog in that a lengthy theoretical analysis, probably written by Price herself, can be found among a set of notecards hastily copied by her daughter, Florence Louise Price Robinson, in the late 1960s. She observes that the first movement is in a relatively tight sonata form, displaying "counterpoint, imitation, canon, inversion, reversion, expansion, and contraction" in the development section. The second movement, in contrast, presents alternating timbral blocks occasionally punctuated by "cathedral bells." The third movement, the cards explain, is:

A juba (key of C) 2/4 decidedly syncopated, joyous in feeling, distinct and apart from jazz, however, in that the "noisemakers," such as cow bells, tin pans, squeals, etc., which are the outstanding features of jazz, are in this juba either entirely absent or minimized. Written in the key of C, it has four themes, modulating into A minor and E major, which are here and there interwoven contrapuntally yet easily spontaneously without any cautious effort at development or labored intent.[25]

Save for the description of the fourth movement, which is a rollicking perpetuum mobile finale in 6/8 in the home key of E minor, the analysis captures the symphony's fundamental features. Price's penchant for colorful orchestration is evident throughout the score.

Unlike *Ethiopia's Shadow*, which would not premiere until nearly sixty years after Price's death, the Symphony in E Minor received a wide hearing – the premiere was broadcast over the NBC Red Network – which led to extensive reviews in the press. Eugene Stinson, longtime critic of the *Chicago Daily News*, described it as a "faultless work cast in something less than modernist mode" and a "work that speaks its own message with restraint and yet with passion." It was, as he put it, "worthy of a place in the regular symphonic repertoire."[26] Other critics concurred that the symphony was a high-quality example of a fresh national spirit that had come to define the contemporary American orchestral landscape, and their only disagreement concerned which movement they enjoyed the most.

Price and the Federal Music Project

While Price's orchestral debut was an unqualified success, the CSO itself ran into severe financial difficulties as the lingering economic depression cut into ticket sales during the next concert season. In January 1934, the orchestra's management launched a campaign to cover a large projected deficit – the first such effort in nearly thirty years.[27] The fundraiser culminated in a playful gala event that featured musical gimmicks, such as a movement from a Beethoven symphony played by "four white garbed cooks upon plates and skillets and various other kitchenware."[28] A hugely popular series held during the second summer of the Century of Progress Exposition bolstered widespread community support for the orchestra, enabling it to sustain its regular schedule for the next several seasons.

The country's musical infrastructure began a radical reorganization in August 1935, when the federal government announced a work-relief program for unemployed musicians, called the Federal Music Project, under the management of conductor Nikolai Sokoloff. The inaugural Chicago project administrator, Joel Lay, envisioned a core of signature ensembles – an orchestra, a concert band, and a military band – as well as smaller dance and choral groups stationed around the city.[29] Although the plan to build a solid orchestra got off to a rocky start, the city had mustered three by the summer of 1936: a full-size professional group called the Federal Music Project Symphony Orchestra, a smaller group of about thirty-five musicians called the American Concert Orchestra, and an all-Black orchestra of similar size called the Colored Concert Orchestra – a reflection of the city's deeply segregated classical music landscape.[30]

Price remained fiendishly active in the months after her CSO compositional debut as she completed two more major works – a piano concerto and a violin concerto – directed a choral group called the Treble Clef Club, and, in June 1934, served as soloist at the piano concerto's premiere.[31] And while the Federal Music Project mainly focused on providing work for performing musicians, it also gave ample attention to supporting American composers, motivating Price even more. In Chicago, for example, the administration established a composers forum series that would feature new chamber music, and orchestras were charged with performing "worthwhile music of new composers who are not on relief rolls."[32] Local critic Edward Barry remarked that "the most alluring prospect of any of those offered the young composer is that of having an orchestral effort performed by the Federal Symphony orchestra."[33] The prospect was certainly alluring for Price, who wrote three more symphonies, an orchestral suite, and a concert overture by the end of the decade.

Mississippi River

Finished in 1934, and therefore just prior to the Works Progress Administration (WPA) period, the orchestral suite *Mississippi River* most appropriately belongs, with the piano concerto and violin concerto, in a chronological grouping of works that Price completed in the flurry of activity she experienced in the months after the successful premiere of the Symphony in E Minor.[34] Evidence strongly suggests that, of these three pieces, only the piano concerto was performed during her lifetime. Even so, the suite marked a significant stylistic departure from the First Symphony as Price abandoned sonata principles in favor of exploring the orchestra's dramatic and expressive possibilities with sweeping, almost cinematic gestures.

Designed to convey a journey down the Mississippi River from its head in Minnesota to the delta in Louisiana, the expansive piece defies neat genre categorization (though the narrative concept aligns with that of Bedrich Smetana's portrait of the Moldau in *Má Vlast*). On the one hand, Price's work contains several quotations of preexisting music, suggestive of a suite. On the other, certain extant manuscript sources contain the following inscription: "Symphonic Poem, The river, and the songs of those residing upon its banks." With a performance time of nearly thirty minutes, the piece's scale compares to well-known works like Richard Strauss's epic tone poem *Also Sprach Zarathustra*, as well as William Grant Still's roughly contemporaneous *Africa* (1930).

Brass chorales and birdsongs open the downriver journey and soon give way to soft drumbeats indicating entry into Indigenous lands. A distant quotation of the spiritual "Nobody Knows the Trouble I've Seen" opens a new section as harder rapids speed up the journey. The sounds of riverboat dancing eventually enter the scene, but the frivolity is broken by a lengthy rumination on three more spirituals – "Stand Still Jordan," "Deep River," and "Go Down, Moses." Short excerpts from "Lalotte" (a Creole tune from Louisiana) and "Steamboat Bill" (a song from the 1928 cartoon "Steamboat Willie") seemingly foreshadow a happy ending, but a return of "Nobody Knows" and a kaleidoscopic churning of the score remind us of the river's place as an unrelenting vehicle of Black migration, voluntary and otherwise. In this way, the piece captures the cosmic sense of history that Price also attempted to convey in *Ethiopia's Shadow*.

Symphony No. 2 in G Minor

The questions surrounding *Mississippi River* are mysterious enough, but few dimensions of Price research are more vexing than the fact that only a few pages of her Symphony No. 2 in G Minor survive. A document in the Federal Music Project collection held by the Library of Congress, dating from 1939, indicates that Price had completed the symphony in 1937 and revised it two years later. The principal extant source of the work is now a thirteen-page autograph held by the Special Collections division of the Mullins Library at the University of Arkansas in Fayetteville, where most of Price's manuscripts can be found. Marked "Allegro moderato," the first movement opens with a strident two-measure motive that becomes the seed for further melodic and rhythmic elaboration over the next several pages. The final page of the score is in pencil and ends with an incomplete measure, leaving many questions about not only the direction of the music itself, but where other versions (complete or incomplete) might be today.

Concert Overture No. 1

Supporting the larger national organization's efforts to encourage American composers, the Illinois Federal Music Project's signature classical ensemble, the Illinois Symphony Orchestra (ISO), programmed a wide range of pieces by locals, or at least musicians with local ties. Between 1937 and 1942, in fact, the orchestra's concerts featured music by several women and composers of color, but never Florence Price. The omission is especially striking given her prominence on a 1937 Composers Forum program that she shared with Clarence Cameron White. Regardless of the reason for her lack of engagement with the ISO, Price made her next Chicago orchestral debut on June 16, 1939 – nearly six years to the day after the Symphony in E Minor premiere – in a performance by the American Concert Orchestra (ACO) under the direction of conductor Ralph Cissne.

While the ISO functioned as a government-sponsored rival to the Chicago Symphony Orchestra in terms of its musical caliber and breadth of repertoire, the ACO performed a community outreach role by staging educational concerts for families, as well as concerts that featured local youths as soloists. Price's Concert Overture No. 1 (then called *Concert Overture on a Spiritual*) closed this second type of program following a suite from Rameau's opera *Dardanus*, Haydn's Symphony No. 64 in

A Major, Beethoven's Fourth Piano Concerto, arias by Mozart and Flotow, and the elegy and waltz from Tchaikovsky's Serenade for Strings.

A holograph manuscript held at the University of Arkansas indicates that Price wrote the concert overture between November and December of 1937. Unlike Price's other orchestral music written up to that point, this piece engages heavily with a spiritual, "Sinner, Please Don't Let This Harvest Pass," including with extensive direct quotation. For nearly a decade, Price had been exploring the compositional potential of the spirituals in new arrangements for voice and piano, as well as in larger works like *Fantasie Nègre* No. 1 in E minor, which is based on the same tune and rivals the overture's dramatic sweep. Perhaps arguing her own case, she wrote in a class essay in summer 1938 that "[Americans] are beginning to believe in the possibility of establishing a national musical idiom. We are waking up to the fact pregnant with possibilities that we <u>already</u> have a folk music in the Negro spirituals – music, which is potent, poignant, compelling. It is simple heart music and therefore powerful."[35]

Using the spiritual as a melodic foundation, the score displays Price's penchant for kaleidoscopic reorchestration and motivic transformation, both of which function as tools for shaping a larger emotional trajectory. The work's shape falls loosely into a theme and variations form, with several colorful and agitated presentations of the spiritual melody interrupted by episodes of deeply contrasting material where echoes of thematic fragments cut through the texture. Occasional polyphonic treatments also dot the landscape before the work reaches a magnificent climax with a restatement of the tune's opening motive in the brass. While most overtures tend to open orchestral concerts, this one likely would have caused tremendous audience applause to close the program on which it premiered.

Symphony No. 3 in C Minor

While the Illinois Federal Music Project infrastructure provided Price with opportunities for orchestral performances with relatively compact audiences, a different state – Michigan – would host her next major orchestral debut. In the summer of 1939, just after the premiere of her overture, the major publishing firm Theodore Presser released a new edition of a solo piano work, *Three Little Negro Dances*, arranged for wind band by Erik Leidzén, a specialist in the idiom. The arrangement was an instant hit on the Chicago shoreline as Glenn Bainum, the noted band director and music professor at Northwestern University, programmed it frequently. The US

Marine Band performed it at least once that August in Washington, DC. And the piece was so popular that it caught the ear of the Detroit-based orchestra conductor Walter Poole.

On September 16, 1940, Poole wrote Price a letter with an exciting request. "My Dear Miss Price," he began,

> The policy of the Michigan Symphony Orchestra in presenting the most interesting work of the modern American Composer has led me to become very interested in your Orchestral Works. I am quite anxious to do something from your pen. Could you give me information regarding "The Levee Dance," or "The Three Little Negro Dances for Orchestra"?[36]

Perhaps for the first time, a conductor was reaching out to Price, rather than the other way around. Yet Price had bigger plans. By late October, when she received a letter asking for a program note for the performance, Price had convinced Poole to give the world premiere of her next major work, the Symphony No. 3 in C Minor, rather than the short arrangements he had requested. More than that, she would also appear as soloist with his orchestra in her piano concerto. Brought about in part by Price's business savvy and in part by Poole's openness to the idea, this change marked a major turning point in her career.

The request to provide a program note for the concert audience also gave Price an opportunity to reflect on and express her aesthetic values. In her response, she explained that the symphony was "intended to be Negroid in character and expression." She continued:

> In it no attempt, however, has been made to project Negro music solely in the purely traditional manner. None of the themes are adaptations or derivations of folks songs. The intention behind the writing of this work was a not too deliberate attempt to picture a cross-section of present-day Negro life and thought with its heritage of that which is past, paralleled or influenced by contacts of the present day.[37]

"The other two movements," she went on, meaning the first and last, "were meant to follow conventional lines of form and development."

Price's invocation of Black history – a theme that had heavily informed her earlier pictorial pieces – seems to address a specific critique of her work that had arisen after the 1933 premiere of the Symphony in E Minor. Reflecting on an extraordinary series of symphonic premieres by Black composers – William Grant Still's in 1931, Price's in 1933, and William Dawson's in 1934 – the distinguished Harlem Renaissance philosopher and cultural critic Alain Locke observed: "In the straight classical idiom and form, Mrs. Price's work [in contrast to Still's and Dawson's] vindicates the Negro composer's right, at choice, to go up Parnassus by the broad road of classicism rather than the narrower, more hazardous, but often more rewarding path of racialism."[38] His implication was that Price's First Symphony was not overtly "racialist" enough. In her thoughts on the Third Symphony, however, she explained that her aesthetic goal was to be "Negroid in character and expression" – that is, authentic – without resorting to overly obvious sonic signifiers of racial identity, such as spirituals or jazz.

Threading this stylistic needle was no easy task, though if the criticism of the symphony's November premiere gives any indication, she had succeeded. Critic J. D. Callaghan of the *Detroit Free Press* observed that Price "spoke in the musical idiom of her own people, and spoke with authority. There was inherent in both works all the emotional warmth of the American Negro." Describing the work itself, he continued,

In the symphony there was a slow second movement of majestic beauty, a third in which the rhythmic preference of the Negro found scope in a series of dance forms, and a finale which swept forward with great vigor. . . . Beautiful and emotionally satisfying the whole work was, and there were moments in which true greatness seemed within the grasp of the writer. . . . The symphony is particularly appealing to Americans in that it is made up of the music which is native to us.[39]

Whereas Locke had claimed that "classicism" and "racialism" could ultimately converge into a "universal" music transcending race and nation, Callaghan felt that Price's music gave unique voice to the American experience specifically through its incorporation of Afrodiasporic signifiers – a view that resonated, and would continue to resonate, with Price's own beliefs.

Symphony No. 4 in D Minor

Price's final complete symphony –Symphony No. 4 in D Minor – resembles No. 3 in its breadth of conception while continuing the four-movement pattern established in the Symphony in E Minor. That is, a sonata form first movement leads to a lyrical second, a juba dance third, and a fast-moving fourth. In this case, however, brief quotations of the opening melodic motive from the spiritual "Wade in the Water" appearing throughout the first movement place this symphony outside the abstract aesthetic found in the others. The second movement evinces a similarly personal quality with substantial melodic solos for a variety of instruments, including the oboe, violin, and trumpet. The juba is arguably her most experimental among the movements in her catalog with this title, for the sly chromaticism found in the trio section of the Third Symphony's juba here appears throughout the movement, giving the uniquely percussive dance a few unexpected melodic twists and turns. Though Price would eventually contact Artur Rodzínski with a request to premiere this piece with the Cleveland Orchestra, he ultimately declined to review the manuscript, and it lay dormant until its 2018 world premiere in Fort Smith, Arkansas, Price's home state.

A Fresh Start

Just as Price's reputation as a talented orchestral composer grew, vast audiences were becoming acquainted with her solo vocal works through the efforts of renowned contralto Marian Anderson. Beginning in 1935, Anderson championed Price's music in recital at venues around the United States and abroad, including on several occasions at New York's Carnegie Hall. While Anderson's early performances often featured Price's spiritual arrangements, in 1939 she introduced an original art song with a text by Langston Hughes, "Songs to the Dark Virgin," which instantly became an audience favorite. With her confidence boosted by this additional wave of success, Price sought a new star champion for her expanding orchestral catalog: famed Boston Symphony Orchestra (BSO) conductor Serge Koussevitzky. "Having read that you are particularly interested in American music," she wrote in September 1941, "I am hoping you will give something of mine a trial."

Standing alongside Frederick Stock, Leopold Stokowski, and Arturo Toscanini as one of the country's most accomplished conductors, Koussevitzky had made national headlines earlier in the year for becoming a US citizen. With direct social ties to victims of Russian Communists and German Nazis alike, he mused in an interview on the day of his naturalization ceremony, "Is it strange that I consider this country the stronghold of freedom?"[40] Later, at the BSO's annual summer residency at the Berkshires, Koussevitzky affirmed his belief that American ensembles ought to program without regard to "racial or geographic boundaries." In a speech to a gathering of conductors there, he emphasized that "even if a manuscript, which is twelve or fifteen minutes long, has only twenty bars of worthwhile music, [a conductor] must play it."[41] Price's letter, penned only a few weeks later, took him up on the offer.

Koussevitzky tacitly declined Price's query, but she tried again on July 5, 1943, with a new letter. The conductor had once again made headlines only a few weeks earlier by writing a fiery missive to the *New York Times* arguing for redoubled efforts to support American composers during and after the war:

America, the leading country of the Western Hemisphere, is holding high the torch of future hopes and ideals. The war of destruction is not affecting her pioneering tradition bequeathed by the daring spirit of her forefathers. On the contrary, America is fully conscious of the mission to restore the rights of men, to protect the intellectual, creative and cultural forces from the deadly grip of Teutonic strangulation. An appeal on behalf of the composer is in line with deep-rooted American tradition. It manifests the true cultural standing and crystallizes the spirit of the nation: for only a country of surging aspirations can at a time of a world cataclysm proclaim ideals of enlightenment and justice. This is a challenge to the war of destruction. ... We musicians must be first to stand by the composer because we owe him most.[42]

Although we may never be certain that Price read the piece directly, her letter seemed to respond to the spirit of his remarks. "My dear Dr. Koussevitzky," it opens:

To begin with I have two handicaps – those of sex and race. I am a woman; and a I have some Negro blood in my veins. Knowing the worst, then, would you be good enough to hold in check the possible inclination to regard a woman's composition as long on emotionalism but short on virility and thought content; – until you shall have examined some of my work? As to the handicap of race, may I relieve you by saying that I neither expect nor ask any concession on that score. I should like to be judged on merit alone – the great trouble having been to get conductors, who know nothing of my work (I am practically unknown in the East, except perhaps as the composer of two songs, one or the other of which Marian Anderson includes on most of her programs) to even consent to examine a score.

Of course, one of those conductors had been Koussevitzky himself! After a months-long back-and-forth, he again declined to program Price's music. Even so, she had continued to prepare for an eventual performance so that she would be ready if the right moment should strike.

The Oak and *Songs of the Oak*

Both composed (or at least completed) in 1943, the pair of tone poems called *The Oak* and *Songs of the Oak* are easy to conflate but are entirely distinct works. Manuscripts held at the University of Arkansas indicate that

Price extracted *The Oak* almost wholesale from the first movement of an in-progress Symphony No. 5 in A minor that she evidently never completed or fully orchestrated. Remarkably, the work's style departs dramatically from her previous symphonic first movements in character and structure, perhaps reflecting a shift toward organic forms that would also manifest in her final works, particularly the second violin concerto. Almost entirely missing are the pentatonic melodies and dance rhythms found in her earlier orchestral music.

The Oak opens with a descending line in the basses and cellos, which serves as a head motive for later melodic elaboration. The slow, brooding, almost Wagnerian character generated as the strings unfurl a long, chromatic gesture permeates the work, though it is occasionally overtaken by longer episodes of emotional agitation, signaled with tremolo strings, and of placid reflection, created by soft strings and sturdy brass chorales. The seriousness of the opening returns with a slow march-like codetta, which the conductor can choose to end with a loud bang or with a diminuendo – the latter given in manuscript sources as the composer's preference. The symphonic draft indicates clearly, though, that the first movement was designed to end with the loud percussion hit, indicating that it should end quietly when performed as a standalone piece.

While *Songs of the Oak* shares in the *The Oak*'s seriousness, this substantially longer piece is easily one of Price's most evocative and picturesque, with gestures fitting for a film drama. Long brass chorales suggesting the wisdom and solidity of an ancient oak tree create structural pillars around which episodes of flitting birds, a summer thunderstorm, and other ineffable natural wonders appear in succession. A coda featuring an organ, another brass chorale, and slowly punctuated chimes seems to apotheosize the old oak tree in its wizened slumber as the ensemble fades to nothing.

Concert Overture No. 2

Completed early in 1943 (according to the surviving manuscripts), Concert Overture No. 2 continues where its predecessor left off: with a rhapsodic treatment of three traditional spirituals, "Go Down, Moses," "Nobody Knows the Trouble I've Seen," and "Ev'ry Time I Feel the Spirit." The first half of the overture captures the underlying character of each of the three spirituals in turn. The second half places these various characters in a mosaic-like combination, where recognizable melodic fragments from the earlier collection leap out of the texture, at times in their original character while at others substantially transformed – with rhythmic augmentation or significant reorchestration, for example, as in the development sections of Price's symphonic sonata-form movements. Like the two tone poems from this period, there is no direct evidence that this piece was performed during Price's lifetime.

Orchestral Music Afterlives

While the ebbs and flows of Price's activity as an orchestral composer were pronounced enough during her lifetime, global interest in her orchestral repertoire exploded in late 2018, when publisher G. Schirmer – an imprint of Wise Music Group – acquired the rights to her catalog and quickly began making these works available for performance. Price soon became one of the most frequently performed American composers of her generation and, within five years, had appeared on the programs of practically every major orchestra in the United States. The Third Symphony made a triumphant CSO debut under the baton of Riccardo Muti in May 2022, mere weeks after the Philadelphia Orchestra and Yannick Nézet-Séguin won a GRAMMY for their recording of the First and Third Symphonies on the Deutsche Grammophon label. The confluence of a major orchestra, a foreign conductor, and a recording on an international label is precisely what Price had sought when she contacted Serge Koussevitzky for the first time in 1941. Yet, as with the premiere of her First Symphony in 1933, individuals working quietly behind the scenes created the conditions for this monumental success.

In cosmic serendipity, two musicologists – Barbara Garvey Jackson and Rae Linda Brown – stumbled across Price and her music at roughly the same time in the mid 1970s. Jackson, a professor at the University of Arkansas, engaged in correspondence with Price's daughter, Florence Louise Robinson, in the months before Robinson's death in 1975, while Brown, a graduate student at Yale University, cataloged the musical contents of the storied James Weldon Johnson Memorial Collection held at the Beinecke Library there. Jackson eventually convinced Robinson to send the University of Arkansas a few of her mother's manuscripts, including materials for the Symphony in E Minor, while Brown unearthed a manuscript copy of the score for Symphony No. 3 in C Minor. Following Jackson's publication of a groundbreaking biographical article in 1977, the two began collaborating on performances of these pieces in venues around the country, with Brown continuing in this work until her passing in 2017. The explosion of interest in Price's music that occurred over this forty-year period would not have been possible without their pioneering efforts.

The Philadelphia Orchestra's award-winning recording – as well as a partner recording of the Fourth Symphony and William Dawson's *Negro Folk Symphony* – likewise benefited from meticulous behind-the-scenes scholarly work in partnership with eager performers. In November 2020, a moment when most orchestras were concertizing over livestreams because of pandemic-related restrictions, the Philadelphia Orchestra performed the First Symphony under the baton of Yannick Nézet-Seguin, who had come to love Price's music after leading a single movement the previous season. The orchestra's principal librarian, Nicole Jordan, and Lina Gonzalez-Granados, then a conducting fellow, seized the opportunity to scrutinize all available source materials for the symphony to create a score and instrumental parts of an editorial quality matching what a world-class ensemble expects from composers whose music has undergone generations of editorial revision and perfection – an experience that had not been afforded to Price during her lifetime.

Jordan suggested to Nézet-Seguin that the orchestra could make a lasting contribution to classical music culture by undertaking the same process with all of Price's large works – the three extant symphonies and the three concertos – and recording them. He was taken by the idea. "We didn't record it with the intention of winning a GRAMMY," she said in a 2023 interview. "We recorded it because it was the right thing to do."[43] Nézet-Séguin embraced his role as the most visible face of the orchestra, while championing Price's music with a vigor that had eluded her during her lifetime. "Getting to know a composer's language from a performer's perspective," he explained in an interview, "comes from playing, and replaying, and playing again."[44] For him, the editing and recording processes have helped give Price and her orchestral music the care and the accessibility they deserve. "The best chance of bringing this repertoire is to put the best resources in the world in its service: this orchestra and our wonderful librarian." Indeed, the musicological work of orchestra librarians is not always visible but is certainly audible. In Jordan's case, it is both: "For me in my role, I'm the first Black man or woman holding the title doing what I do. There are eyes on me for many reasons. How I choose this role is to be an advocate, where there is none. A librarian in an institution is an undervalued resource. We're the ones touching the music the most."[45]

Jordan, then, stands alongside Price and her South Side companions who, as Margaret Bonds once explained, helped the composer get her orchestral music ready for performances, as well as Barbara Garvey Jackson and Rae Linda Brown, in a lineage of musical women who have enabled Price's voice to resonate ever more powerfully in orchestra halls around the world.[46]

Notes

1. Seymour Raven, "Music News Booms Out in Major $ Key," *Chicago Tribune*, April 9, 1953.
2. Louisville Orchestra Records, Archives & Special Collections, University of Louisville.
3. Rae Linda Brown, *The Heart of a Woman: The Life and Music of Florence B. Price* (Urbana: University of Illinois Press, 2020), 232–236.
4. See Brown, *The Heart of a Woman*, 104–5.
5. Serge Koussevitzky Archive, Library of Congress.
6. "Wanamaker Prizes for Composers," *Pittsburgh Courier*, February 19, 1927.
7. J. Harold Brown, "Musicians at Hampton Confab Hear Results," *Norfolk New Journal and Guide*, August 29, 1931.
8. Brown, *The Heart of a Woman*, 101.
9. "Negroes Get Music Awards," *New York Herald-Tribune*, September 27, 1932.
10. "Adams to Organize Music Contest Winners," *New York Age*, September 6, 1930.
11. Brown, *The Heart of a Woman*, 74–75.
12. Roger Didier, "Critics Acclaim Symphony Written by Florence Price," *Kansas City Call*, June 23, 1933; "Awards," *Opportunity: Journal of Negro Life* 10 (1932): 391.
13. See Maude Roberts George, "News of the Music World," *Chicago Defender*, September 30, 1933.
14. Brown, "Musicians at Hampton Confab Hear Results."
15. Florence Beatrice Smith Price Papers Addendum, Special Collections, Mullins Library, University of Arkansas.
16. See Mark Tucker, "The Genesis of *Black, Brown and Beige*," *Black Music Research Journal* 13 (1993): 69–71.
17. "Reveal Plans for Lake Front Music Temple," *Chicago Tribune*, December 10, 1932; Edward Moore, "Abandon Plan to Build Music Temple at Fair," *Chicago Tribune*, March 2, 1933.
18. Edward Moore, "Friends of Music Plan Concerts," *Chicago Tribune*, May 14, 1933.
19. Maude Roberts George, "News of the Music World," *Chicago Defender*, January 21, 1933; Maude Roberts George, "News of the Music World," *Chicago Defender*, March 4, 1933.

20. Maude Roberts George, "News of the Music World," *Chicago Defender*, May 6, 1933.
21. Maude Roberts George, "News of the Music World," *Chicago Defender*, April 22, 1933.
22. Maude Roberts George, "News of the Music World," *Chicago Defender*, May 13, 1933.
23. Edward Moore, "Hand of Science Aids Production of *Pagliacci*," *Chicago Daily Tribune*, May 28, 1933.
24. See Samantha Ege, "Composing a Symphonist: Florence Price and the Hand of Black Women's Fellowship," *Women & Music: A Journal of Gender and Culture* 24 (2020): 25.
25. Florence Beatrice Smith Price Collection, Special Collections, University of Arkansas.
26. Eugene Stinson, "Music Views," *Chicago Daily News*, June 16, 1933.
27. "Symphony Group Plans Campaign to Obtain Funds," *Chicago Daily Tribune*, February 1, 1934.
28. Edward Moore, "Mad Burlesque," *Chicago Daily Tribune*, April 10, 1934.
29. "Bach or Berlin, It's All Same to WPA's Song Project Chief," *Chicago Daily Tribune*, November 18, 1935.
30. Edward Berry, "WPA Orchestra Boondoggles a Good Symphony," *Chicago Daily Tribune*, February 6, 1936; Edward Berry, "Plays Italian's Sonata First Time in US," *Chicago Daily Tribune*, May 11, 1936; "Concert Orchestra at Symphony Shell," *Chicago Defender*, July 4, 1936.
31. See Brown, *The Heart of a Woman*, 151–153.
32. "18,000 Musicians to Get Jobs in Federal Arts Relief Program," *New York Times*, August 4, 1935.
33. Edward Barry, "Bach Passion is Presented by Symphony," *Chicago Daily Tribune*, April 8, 1936.
34. See Chapter 9 on these concertos.
35. Florence Beatrice Smith Price First Addendum, Special Collections, Mullins Library, University of Arkansas.
36. Florence Beatrice Smith Price First Addendum, Special Collections, Mullins Library, University of Arkansas.
37. Florence Beatrice Smith Price Collection, Special Collections, Mullins Library, University of Arkansas.
38. Alain Locke, *The Negro and His Music* (Washington, DC: The Associates in Negro Folk Education, 1936), 115.
39. J. D. Callaghan, "Symphony by Negro Writer Acclaimed at Institute Debut," *Detroit Free Press*, November 7, 1940.
40. "Koussevitzky a Citizen," *New York Times*, February 20, 1941.
41. John Selby, "Teuton Music is Featured in Berkshires," *Richmond Times-Dispatch*, August 8, 1941; Howard Taubman, "Koussevitzky Asks Wide Aid for Music," *New York Times*, August 9, 1941.

42. Serge Koussevitzky, "Justice to Composers," *New York Times*, May 16, 1943.
43. Samantha Ege and Alexandra Kori Hill interview with Nicole Jordan, July 24, 2023.
44. Samantha Ege and Alexandra Kori Hill interview with Yannick Nézet-Séguin, October 22, 2023.
45. Samantha Ege and Alexandra Kori Hill interview with Nicole Jordan, July 24, 2023.
46. On Bonds, see Brown, *The Heart of a Woman*, 111.

PART III
———

Community and Reception

It all starts from loving the music, believing in it, believing that this is something for us.
—Yannick Nézet-Séguin, music and artistic director of the Philadelphia Orchestra

11 | The Influence of Harry T. Burleigh

RAE LINDA BROWN

In 1927, Florence Price and her family moved from Little Rock to Chicago. By now, she had already gained some success as a composer. She was writing piano music, particularly teaching pieces for children, organ music, and songs (i.e., art songs and arrangements of spirituals). Once established in Chicago, she quickly became one of the composers of choice for many of the city's singers and instrumentalists. Much of her music was heard during the Sunday musicales at Black churches throughout the city, and she was among a select group of Black composers whose music was in the repertoire of local white soloists and ensembles as well.

Personally, though, Price's life was shattering. Her husband's law practice was not doing well, and, from the late 1920s to the early 1930s, he – Thomas J. Price – went for long stretches without working. The financial strain of a home with no primary wage earner pushed Thomas and Florence to their limits. It was not long before the Price family plunged into serious financial difficulty. Her marriage ended in divorce in January 1931, which was the same month that she began working on her prize-winning Symphony in E minor. The work was premiered in June 1933 by the Chicago Symphony at the Century of Progress Exposition, a World's Fair which spanned two years.

Riding the waves of her success, which were born out of a hugely strenuous period, Price's prolificacy as a composer and performer far from diminished. In addition to the completion of the Symphony in E minor, she wrote several large-scale piano works, including her Piano Sonata in E minor, the *Fantasie Nègre* set for solo piano, and *Dances in the Canebrakes* (three dances based on "authentic Negro rhythms"). She also composed choral music, art songs, and chamber music, which were performed all over Chicago by both Black and white musicians.

During this highly fruitful period, Price completed her Concerto in One Movement, which was premiered in June 1934 at the commencement exercises of the Chicago Musical College, where she was taking graduate courses in composition and orchestration. The concerto was played twice more during the summer but received national attention when it was performed by the Woman's Symphony Orchestra of Chicago in October of that year. The concerto was performed several times during 1934. In all performances but the premiere, when Price played the solo part, Margaret Bonds, her friend and former student, was the soloist. One particular performance took place on August 25, 1934, at the largest of the Century of Progress Exposition's Negro pageants, "O, Sing a New Song," an extravaganza "presented by the Negroes of America at Soldier Field."[1] It is likely that Price met Harry T. Burleigh at this pageant.

Crossing Paths at a Century of Progress

African American pageants were like plays with precomposed, unrelated pieces of music that were drawn together into a narrative of racial pride and uplift. As was common practice, the pageant was conceived as a retrospective of the transformation of the African to the African American. The narrative of the three-part "O, Sing a New Song" began with life as a free people in Africa and continued through the dark days of enslavement (for example, Act I, titled "Africa," ends with a scene called "Ghost Ship: The Voyage"). After Emancipation, the African American emerges as a spirit-filled people, determined and hopeful, as told across Act II, "Plantation Life," and Act III, "America." The pageant was, in particular, a celebration of Black music, dance, and drama in its continuum of African origins through the 1920s. Furthermore, many of Chicago's talented African American artists were featured, including, alongside Price and Bonds, the pioneering choreographer Katherine Dunham and celebrated soprano Abbie Mitchell.

Pageants often drew from popular and vernacular styles (e.g., the blues, jazz, vaudeville, tap dance, and spirituals). However, "O, Sing a New Song" was different in that it also included the participation of many of the nation's most prominent Black classical composers and performers. Although classical music was virtually absent across the three acts, the musical "Prologue" that opened the pageant was given over entirely to large-scale concert music by Black composers. Its lengthy prologue was comprised of orchestral music in which four composer-performers conducted the orchestra each for their own work. Bookending the prologue was N. Clark Smith, a winner of the 1930 Rodman Wanamaker composition competition, who conducted the ensemble in the first two movements of his *Negro Choral Symphony* for orchestra and chorus; and Price's Concerto in One Movement, which, as the program suggests, she may have conducted herself. (This is the only documented occasion of her conducting her own work.) For this performance, Margaret Bonds played the solo part. Abbie Mitchell then concluded the prologue with an unidentified song.

Placed in between Smith and Price was Harry T. Burleigh, who offered an "Ode to Ethiopia." This work is almost assuredly the composer's "Ethiopia Saluting the Colors," originally an art song written for solo voice and piano (1915) and later orchestrated. It is doubtful that Burleigh both sang and conducted his own piece; it is more likely that N. Clark Smith, already on the podium and a seasoned conductor, led the orchestra in this dramatic song. Burleigh's setting both salutes the colors of the Ethiopian flag – yellow, red, and green – and gives a dramatic interpretation of Walt Whitman's 1915 poetic narrative describing a one-hundred-year-old Black slave woman, "Ethiopia," being watched by a Union soldier as she curtsies while observing General Sherman's army regiment pass in review.

Who are you, dusky woman, so ancient, hardly human,
With your woolly-white and turban'd head, and bare bony feet?
Why, rising by the roadside here, do you the colors greet?

'Tis while our army lines Carolina's sand and pines,
Forth from thy hovel door, thou, Ethiopia, com'st to me,
As, under doughty Sherman, I march toward the sea.

Me, master, years a hundred, since from my parents sunder'd,
A little child, they caught me as the savage beast is caught;
Then hither me, across the sea, the cruel slaver brought.

No further does she say, but lingering all the day,
Her high-borne turban'd head she wags, and rolls her darkling eye,
And curtseys to the regiments, the guidons moving by.

What is it, fateful woman – so blear, hardly human?
Why wag your head, with turban bound – yellow, red and green?
Are the things so strange and marvelous, you see or have seen?[2]
—"Ethiopia Saluting the Colors" by Walt Whitman

Although the poem unfolds from the soldier's perspective, Burleigh's setting reinforces Black dignity and pride. In fact, Burleigh's musical dramatization of the work and compelling use of a Black musical idiom deeply inspired new generations of African American composers. Margaret Bonds, for example, was introduced to Burleigh's "Ethiopia Saluting the Colors" in her late teens while studying art songs with Abbie Mitchell.

From Mitchell, Bonds revealed, "I learned the importance of the marriage between words and music, which is demanded if one is to have a song of any consequence."[3] Bonds, like Price and Mitchell before her, were drawn to Burleigh's distinct flair for Black art song composition.

How Burleigh Inspired Price's Songs

After writing two symphonies, a piano concerto, and several orchestra suites during the 1930s, Price turned to writing mostly chamber works, art songs, and arrangements of spirituals. The concentration on smaller compositional genres is easy to explain. During the Depression and in the war years it was much more difficult for most composers without a commission or the support of the Federal Music Project of the WPA to get large-scale works performed. Price's network of professional musicians in Chicago and those who performed in national and international venues made the choice to write songs, in particular, a logical one. She wrote about one hundred songs in all: about seventy-five art songs, thirteen popular/commercial songs, and fourteen arrangements of spirituals.

Most of Price's art songs are serious-minded and reveal a rather intense glimpse of her inner self. Price chose her texts from a wide variety of poets, many of whom were African American. By far, her favorite poets were Langston Hughes and Paul Laurence Dunbar. In addition to the nine settings of Hughes's poems, there are nineteen poems by Dunbar represented. She also set texts by James Weldon Johnson and Georgia Douglas Johnson (one poem each). These songs are intelligent and thoughtful, capturing some of the most passionate poetry written during the Harlem and Chicago Renaissance periods.

Harry T. Burleigh was very supportive of Price's career. In addition to singing her music, Burleigh tried to help promote Price's music through his own publisher, G. Ricordi & Co., for whom he was a music editor from 1911 to 1946. In the fall of 1943 Price sent Burleigh some of her music for his examination. He wrote the following reply, dated October 14, 1943:

823 E. 166th St., NY

My dear Mrs. Price –

Thank you so much for sending me your delightful songs; and the beautiful photograph – which I shall cherish <u>always</u>. I looked over the songs with genuine interest, and felt that you would like a music publisher to see them; so, I passed them on to the Editors at G. Ricordi and Co, Inc., who have published my compositions over a period of years. I knew that they would give your songs careful attention and every possible consideration.

They commented <u>very</u> favorably on your work; regretting that at this time the market for songs is not one that warrants such publications, and this plus the shortage of paper and engravers has caused a temporary retardation of all publishing.

I sincerely hope you will not feel that I took too much liberty in submitting your manuscripts to Ricordi. One of their music Editors is Ruggero Vené – a pupil of Respighi, whose ideas and opinions in music composition I value very highly. Personally, I consider the third song "I know why the caged bird sings" ["Sympathy," text by Paul Laurence Dunbar] a great setting of those words and melodically effective and dramatic and only in one or two spots does it appear too chromatic (perhaps the second verse– and even there it is in the look of the accidentals, rather than the sound).

Oct. 21

Do pardon and overlook the length of time it has taken me to finish this letter and to ask whether you wish me to return the MSS to you? or whether I may keep them? Kindly let me know.

New York has gone "all out" over Paul Robeson as Othello! He, in Ricordi & Co., cannot sell any songs at all. Octavo things are constantly being used.

Sincerely,
H. Burleigh[4]

One can appreciate Burleigh's excitement about Robeson. Robeson performed in *Othello* at the peak of his dramatic career internationally. He first performed the role in the 1930s in London. When the play opened on Broadway in 1942, it broke all records for Shakespearean productions, with 296 performances. Robeson toured in the play for ten months across the US with the exception of the South, where he refused to perform for segregated audiences.

Price's setting of Paul Laurence Dunbar's "Sympathy," to which Burleigh refers in his letter, is one of her most powerful songs. Dunbar's text, although published in 1895, speaks to the restlessness and determination of many African Americans to overcome hardship and struggle. Its descriptive language is so wrought with emotion that poet Maya Angelou used one of its lines as the title of her best-selling autobiography, *I Know Why the Caged Bird Sings* (1970).[5]

Since Price usually shared her newest works with colleagues and friends, "Sympathy" probably dates from mid 1943, when she sent the music to Burleigh for his perusal. Price's setting is in a modified ABA form. In verse one, the lyrical vocal line is gently underscored by an arpeggiated accompaniment. In this verse the poet seeks to establish a feeling of oneness with the "caged bird," who can only appreciate the warmth and beauty of nature from its prison. In the closing phrase, the voice soars upward with an octave leap on "I know" to dramatize the solidarity of the poet and the caged bird.

The second verse (B) is delivered in quasi-recitative; the several changes in meter allow for the rapid-fire delivery of the caustic text. The accompaniment is more sparse in this verse. At times, it is closely aligned with the voice; at other moments, chords punctuate the most cryptic words, "cruel," "pain," "scars," and "sting." It is this verse that bothered Burleigh visually with all of its accidentals. (Perhaps it bothered publishers as well, which could explain why this song was never published). This section is not so much dissonant, however, as it is harmonically unstable. The text, describing the agitation of the trapped bird trying to escape while the pain of old pulses within his body anew, is thus set in bold relief. As in Price's setting of Georgia Douglas Johnson's "The Heart of a Woman," the poet evokes the analogy of the obstructed bird and the suffocating self.

At the beginning of verse three, the text continues to depict the entrapped bird desperately trying to escape "when his wing is bruised and his bosom sore." Musically, there is a return to the A section (a simple melody accompanied by broken arpeggios on the tonic). However, the second and third verses are elided (the last line of the second verse is set to the A section of music that begins verse three) so that the text and the music are totally at odds here. It is not until the final lines of the poem, when the bird prays for the release of his soul, that the voice and accompaniment are conjoined.

Burleigh's art songs are characterized by a careful wedding of the text and music. His sophisticated harmonic vocabulary includes tonal ambiguity created by altered chords in the accompaniment and chromatic tones in the vocal lines. Further, most of Burleigh's art songs show little trace of ethnic influence, as he preferred to write in the post-Romantic traditions of the early twentieth century. This differs from the spiritual arrangements and art songs that embraced African American cultural histories, in which he more readily used a Black musical idiom.

One of Price's most provocative art songs, in which one can hear Burleigh's music as models, is a setting of Georgia Douglas Johnson's title poem from her collection *The Heart of a Woman*. In it, a woman's heart is metaphorically compared to a lone bird that wings "forth with the dawn" over "life's turrets and vales." It then "falls back with the night / And enters some alien cage in its plight / And tries to forget it has dreamed of the stars / While it breaks, breaks, breaks on the sheltering bars."[6] Published in 1918, Johnson's poem is strikingly feminist in its sensibility. Showing her awareness of how far women still had to come before they were completely "emancipated," Douglas's poem speaks of the "oppressiveness and pain of the traditional female lot."[7]

Price set the two-verse poem in a modified strophic form. In the opening lines, as the heart/bird wings "restlessly on," so does the music. In the entire twenty-five-measure song in E♭, the tonic is only briefly alluded to. The harmony and the vocal line seem to wander aimlessly, although nowhere is this song really dissonant. The fluid piano accompaniment and the several meter and tempo changes propel the music forward seamlessly. It is Price's utter intimacy with the poem that qualifies one of her most powerful settings.

Price's song is all the more poignant because it is her only setting by a Black woman poet. The feelings of a "caged bird," pained in its trapped existence, and the confession of broken, shattered dreams are vividly portrayed. Could this be the veiled autobiographical revelation of the composer herself, echoing that of the despairing poet? This inference might give the reader pause to consider that Price's childhood ambition was to become a doctor, following in her father's footsteps. And although she was far more successful in her career as a performer, teacher, and composer than even she anticipated, there were professional aspirations that went unfulfilled, and as a single mother she lived in aloneness.

Most of Price's spiritual arrangements are very straightforward. Here, too, one can hear the influence of Burleigh's successful arrangements for voice and piano. Starting with his "Deep River," published in 1916, and continuing in a rich series of arrangements published from 1917 on, Burleigh established the tradition of the concert spiritual. Like Burleigh, Price is careful to set the texts in bold relief. The accompaniment is never so elaborate, either harmonically or texturally, as to obscure the simplicity of the original folk tune and the directness of the text. The balance between the vocal line and the piano is carefully preserved.

Price's "I am Bound for the Kingdom" and "I'm Workin' on My Buildin'" were published together by Handy Bros. in 1949 under the title *Two Traditional Negro Spirituals*. These tunes were sung to Price by Malinda Carter, a former slave who was owned by a Squire Carter of Rutherford County, Tennessee. Price met Mrs. Carter through her granddaughter, Fannie Carter Woods, a Chicago resident and concert singer who premiered many of Price's songs.

Both of these arrangements readily show Burleigh's musical influence on Price. These settings are fairly short (perhaps the reason for issuing them together in publication) and both use the standard ABA (refrain-verse-refrain) structure common in spiritual arrangements. "I Am Bound for the Kingdom," recorded by Marian Anderson for Victor Records, begins with a threefold repetition of the title phrase and it concludes with the tag "Glory in my soul." The verse of the spiritual reads:

If you get there before I do,
Glory in my soul,
Look out for me I'm comin' too –
Glory in my soul.

The reader will readily recognize a similarity to one of the many verses of "Swing Low, Sweet Chariot," one of the most familiar of all slave songs:

If you get there before I do,
Comin' for to carry me home,
Tell all my friends I'm comin' too.
Comin' for to carry me home.

The tunes of the two spirituals are remarkably similar as well (save for the addition of the expressive flat seventh in "I Am Bound," leading this writer to believe that "I Am Bound" is, in fact, an amalgam of the two spirituals, "I Am Bound for the Kingdom" and "Swing Low, Sweet Chariot").

The publication's companion piece, "I'm Workin' on My Buildin'," is quite different in character. The refrain begins with the oscillating minor third that characterizes many of the more plaintive spirituals – for example, "City Called Heaven" ("I am a poor pilgrim of sorrow") and "Sometimes I Feel Like a Motherless Child." The verse, on the other hand, is fairly declamatory. This spiritual appears to have had numerous verses, each singer adapting the text to fit their individual situation and needs. Mrs. Carter, who may have been a bit more pious than some of her fellow slaves, chose this text: "If I was a mourner [verse 2 reads 'sinner'] / I'd tell you what I'd do, / I'd give my heart to Jesus / and work on my buildin' too." An alternative text for this tune, sung by less God-fearing individuals, expressed their repentance this way: "If I was a gambler / I tell you what I would do, / I'd throw away my gamblin' dice / an' work on the buildin' too."[8]

Burleigh's musical stamp is found, also, in Price's accompaniments. In both spirituals the accompaniment is chordal, with altered chords or substitutions used for expressive purposes. Most of the accompaniments in Burleigh's slower spiritual arrangements use rich, colorful chords that complement the vocal line. One only need listen to "Swing Low, Sweet Chariot," "My Lord, What a Mornin'," or "Give Me Jesus," to name just a few. Where Burleigh and Price differ is in the treatment of the vocal line. In Burleigh's accompaniments the vocal line is often doubled by the piano's upper note. This means that Burleigh's accompaniments can stand alone since the melody is in the upper voice of the vocal part. In Price's accompaniments, on the other hand, there is no doubling of the vocal line. Thus, the piano part exists to complete the vocal score, one mutually dependent upon the other.

Price's most frequently performed spiritual arrangement, "My Soul's Been Anchored in de Lord," is a notable exception to the simplicity of most of her spiritual arrangements. Arranged for opera singer Marian Anderson and made famous by her, the accompaniment, fully independent of the vocal line, is equal in importance to it. The expansive piano part, featuring large block chords that span the keyboard and punctuate the text, is reminiscent of the role of the orchestra in Romantic opera. Burleigh, before her, wrote only a few arrangements in this style. "Oh, Wasn't Dat a Wide Ribber?" and "You May Bury Me in de Eas'" are two examples.

"My Soul's Been Anchored" was written in 1937 and published by Gamble Hinged Music the same year. Price also arranged the spiritual for solo voice and orchestra and for SATB chorus and piano. The solo arrangement was recorded by Marian Anderson, Ellabelle Davis, and Leontyne Price. Florence Price's arrangement received national recognition when Anderson closed her historic concert at the Lincoln Memorial on Easter Sunday, April 9, 1939, with this song. Anderson sang it before 75,000 gathered on the Washington, DC, mall and millions more who were listening on the radio. "My Soul's Been Anchored in de Lord" became one of Miss Anderson's signature pieces, and she went on to sing it over one hundred times in concerts around the world.

Conclusion

Harry T. Burleigh and Florence Price were not close friends but, for certain, Burleigh, twenty-one years Price's senior, admired her work and was supportive of her career. Although Price did not ask Burleigh to assist her in securing Ricordi as a publisher for "Sympathy," she was probably grateful to him for initiating that dialogue. Price's unconquerable shyness hindered her from promoting her music more widely, and it inhibited her from asking her friends for professional support. In Burleigh, Price found a mentor and an advocate for her compositions. His decisive influence on her is apparent in many of the over 100 songs she composed during her career.

Notes

This chapter comes from Rae Linda Brown's unpublished and unpresented 2003 paper "Harry T. Burleigh's Influence." Its presence in this volume stems from the generosity of Brown herself, who granted permission for musicologist Jean Snyder (author of *Harry T. Burleigh: From the Spiritual to the Harlem Renaissance*) to share this work with Samantha Ege in April 2017, months before Brown passed away on August 20, 2017. Brown's original paper opened with a biographical overview of Price; it encompassed her Little Rock origins to her Chicago migration. However, this chapter purposefully omits the pre-Chicago narrative that Brown offers in order to avoid repetition. Instead, it dives straight into Brown's commentary on the composer's Chicago arrival. This then leads to the moment when Price's and Burleigh's professional paths crossed.

Additions to Brown's 2003 text include subheadings, further footnotes, poetic texts, and a parsing of points. One instance of the latter is where Brown talks about the "ethnic influence" in Burleigh's art songs; the sentence ending that paragraph has been added to clarify more of Brown's argument. Also introduced is an anecdote (that would have been known to Brown) in which Margaret Bonds discusses how she came across Burleigh's art songs. In the rare instances where such clarifications have been added, Brown's own musicological language has guided us in their formulation.

Through this re-presentation of Brown's 2003 work, which includes details from the author that were not published in *The Heart of a Woman: The Life and Music of Florence B. Price*, Brown continues to contribute fresh insights to the world of Price scholarship.

1. "Other Papers Say – The Negro Pageant," *Chicago Defender*, August 11, 1934, 14.

2. Walt Whitman, "Ethiopia Saluting the Colors (A Reminiscence of 1864)," in *Leaves of Grass* (Washington, 1872), 357–358.
3. Margaret Bonds, "A Reminiscence," in *The Negro in Music and Art*, edited by Lindsay Patterson (New York: Publishers Company, 1967), 191.
4. Harry T. Burleigh (New York, NY) to Florence Price, October 14, 1943. Correspondence, box 1, folder 1, item 29, Florence Beatrice Smith Price Collection (MC 988), Special Collections, University of Arkansas Libraries, Fayetteville. A footnote in *The Heart of a Woman* states: "It is not clear from the context of this letter to what Burleigh is referring with reference to Paul Robeson's relationship with Ricordi & Co." Rae Linda Brown, *The Heart of a Woman: The Life and Music of Florence B. Price* (Urbana: University of Illinois Press, 2020), 263.
5. Maya Angelou, *I Know Why the Caged Bird Sings* (New York: Random House, 1970).
6. Georgia Douglas Johnson, *The Heart of a Woman and Other Poems* (Boston, MA: Cornhill Company, 1918), 1.
7. Gloria T. Hull (also known as Akasha T. Hull), *Color, Sex, and Poetry* (Bloomington: Indiana University Press, 1987), 156–159.
8. John Lovell, Jr., *Black Song: The Forge and the Flame* (New York: Macmillan, 1972), 251.

12 | Black Feminist Bonds between Florence Price, Marian Anderson, and Margaret Bonds

ELIZABETH DURRANT

The women of the Black Chicago Renaissance had a mission: They fought to make a way out of no way by creating opportunities for Black women to succeed as classical musicians. They affirmed their allegiance to this cause while living amid the violence of Reconstruction and the debilitating restrictions of Jim Crow, in addition to facing the relentless scrutiny that attempted to constrain Black womanhood. Yet, despite social strictures that sought to narrow their influence and diminish their worth, these women proceeded to forge paths that not only granted them access to spaces that facilitated their growth as leaders but also allowed others to follow in their footsteps. Black women became the architects of thriving communities that nurtured the creativity and careers of many artists. Their successes presented further challenges to systems that strived to maintain the exclusionary status quo. These women's actions offered a direct refusal to accepting their own marginalization. Instead, they built paths to success and recognition that did not exist before their interventions. Through these efforts, they resisted the barriers that society set against them and taught their successors to do the same.

In this chapter, I utilize the careers of musicians Florence Price, Marian Anderson, and Margaret Bonds to exemplify the successful results of Black-women-run systems of resistance that sustained the Black Chicago Renaissance. Building upon the work of Patricia Hill Collins, I argue that the women of this time period incorporated methods of defying oppression that align with several principles of Black feminism. Specifically, by discussing examples of Black feminist concepts like creating "safe spaces," fostering community, and sharing survival knowledge and strategies, I demonstrate how Black women's efforts facilitated the achievements of Bonds, Price, and Anderson within the field of classical music.[1] In addition to individual benefits, I maintain that Black feminist thought helped all three of these women form connections with one another and significantly impacted their professional and personal lives. These alliances and the Black feminist networks that nurtured them also taught Price, Anderson, and Bonds how to use these tactics to support future generations of Black women musicians. As a result, the effects of Black women's collective care and labor have stretched far beyond the confines of their individual lifetimes to establish legacies that resonate within the broader history of music in the United States.

Black Women Building "Safe Spaces" in the Black Chicago Renaissance

In her landmark text *Black Feminist Thought* (1990), Patricia Hill Collins defines Black feminism as a movement that examines Black women's experiences with racism, sexism, classism, heterosexism, and other forms of discrimination as valuable survival knowledge. Awareness of these oppressions and their role in suppressing marginalized communities is an essential part of Black feminist thought and resistance.[2] As Collins explains, throughout history Black women have established ways to defy these systems, uplift one another, and encourage self-definition in spite of debilitating circumstances. Within artistic circles, many Black women have created and managed specific organizations to enable Black artistry in spite of intersectional oppression. These groups often align with Collins's definition of Black feminist "safe spaces" – that is, locations that circumvent the imposed limitations of the dominant culture by fostering leadership, creativity, networking, and community among Black women. These "safe spaces" not only challenge oppression, but also support Black art and artists in ways that have substantially impacted US cultural history.[3] By creating organizations to support Black musicians and hosting salons in their homes, as this chapter explores, Black women paved the way to facilitate each other's successes throughout and beyond the Black Chicago Renaissance.

As an artistic movement spanning the first half of the twentieth century, the Black Chicago Renaissance highlighted the city's status as a thriving cultural center that attracted writers, musicians, dancers, and artists. Although the Black Chicago Renaissance often receives less attention than the Harlem Renaissance (ca. 1917–1935), it is no less significant than its counterpart. Indeed, several artists (such as Nora Holt and Langston Hughes) were central figures within both artistic movements – a fact that demonstrates how the impacts of these eras exceed their designated timelines. Consequently, Chicago's music scene boasted some of the biggest names in blues, jazz, gospel, and classical music before its renaissance officially began. The mother of the blues, Ma Rainey, jazz legend Louis Armstrong, gospel pioneer Thomas A. Dorsey, and classical composer Scott Joplin are all part of the city's rich musical history. For many Black leaders, the purpose of these Renaissances was to serve the goals of racial uplift – a concept that proposed a system for Black people to prove their humanity, depth, and worth through higher education and grand artistic achievements. In addition to emulating white middle- and upper-class ideals, this ideology valued proficiency in Western art music as both a symbol of success and a tool for teaching future generations. Although this concept was designed as a survival strategy to help Black citizens navigate oppressive systems of dehumanization, it often perpetuated colorism, classism, and stigmas by marginalizing people with darker skin, chastising members of lower classes, and devaluing popular genres of music.[4] Nevertheless, those who believed in the power of racial uplift often dedicated their lives to serving its purpose. Women like Nora Holt (whose influence Lucy Caplan examines in Chapter 13) and Estella Bonds exemplify the many Black women who used their influence to support Black classical musicians. Their efforts created a solid foundation of "safe spaces" that would expand the legacies of Black feminist collaboration among classical musicians.[5]

The National Association of Negro Musicians (NANM)

Through her role as a music critic and a founding member of the National Association of Negro Musicians (NANM, no longer pronounced letter by letter but as "Nam"), Nora Holt celebrated Black women's artistic achievements while nurturing their careers. In 1917, Holt became the first music editor at the *Chicago Defender* – the nation's premiere African American newspaper – and the first woman on its regular writing staff. Lawrence Schenbeck describes the lasting influence that Holt's work had on the newspaper as a whole: "Her pioneering music journalism combined reviews, encouragement of young artists, educational outreach, and coverage of both local and national events of interest to Chicago's black classical musicians. Her column was the first to cover classical music on a regular basis for a black newspaper ... She set the tone for classical-music coverage in the *Defender* for years to come."[6] By occupying this position, Holt expanded the possibilities for recognizing Black classical musicians' work and set a precedent of women occupying important positions at this newspaper. As a result, her work fostered multiple "safe spaces" to support Black women's creativity.[7]

Holt continued this work by creating organizations that were dedicated to advancing Black classical musicians. In 1918, she formed the Chicago Music Association (CMA) to foster support for local Black artists. The next year, she used her journalistic voice to express the need for a national organization to assist Black musicians by publishing a column titled "Musicianal [sic] Unity" in the *Defender*.[8] She also sent letters to several people to organize a salon at her home to discuss the matter further. Afterwards, members of the Holt salon coordinated with other interested parties to set up a convention in Chicago[9] that officially established NANM – the CMA became its first local branch. Building this organization expanded Holt's ability to serve Black classical musicians, a process that yielded immediate results and had a palpable impact on classical music culture.

Through NANM and the CMA, Holt played a direct role in financing Marian Anderson's influential career as one of the most renowned singers of all time. Anderson was the first person to receive a NANM award for her performance at the inaugural convention in 1919. Cheryl A. Wall explains how Holt's published account, "A Chronological History of NANM," reminisced about Anderson's stunning performance and the subsequent show of financial support that Holt initiated when it ended.[10]

After listing the names of local and visiting artists, [Holt] concluded, "each participant was a star and each star an artist." But one star shone brighter than the rest, a young contralto from Philadelphia, Marian Anderson, who brought the audience to its feet with her performance of the aria "Adieu, forêts" from Tchaikovsky's Jeanne d'Arc. Holt recorded the response eloquently: "Every one [sic] stood and acclaimed her with cries of bravo and *bis*, while tears of joy were in the eyes of many musicians who felt that the dawn of a new era in music had arisen for our people." The crowd was so moved that a collection, begun with Holt's pledge of $50, was taken up to establish the first NANM scholarship, which was awarded to Anderson. Anderson would remain associated with NANM for the rest of her life and served as the honorary chairperson of the "Jubilee" convention in 1969.[11]

As the woman who cofounded NANM and the first contributor to the collection for the organization's initial scholarship, Holt was intimately involved in supporting Anderson's career. As Rae Linda Brown reveals, Holt's creation of the CMA further displays the depths of this connection because the CMA financed Anderson's attendance at the original NANM conference, when the singer was still in high school.[12] Therefore, Holt's actions lay claim to the very foundations of Marian Anderson's long and legendary career. In 1922, the CMA continued to subsidize Anderson's professional goals when it granted her the institution's first scholarship. Although Holt ended her leadership tenures at NANM and the CMA that same year, her labor in establishing both groups makes her inseparable from the resources that supported the young singer. By garnering financial support and performance opportunities to assist Anderson, Holt activated the systems that she put into place to enable Black women musicians to thrive within the field of classical music.

NANM's legacy of fostering Black women's success continued through the dedication of members like Florence Price, who actively served as a community leader through this organization. As Samantha Ege notes, Price is one of the women who benefited from the connections and opportunities that this institution afforded her, and she took her involvement in its workings rather seriously.[13] The composer was part of both the CMA and the R. Nathaniel Dett Club of Music and Allied Arts, another Chicago branch of NANM, named after composer Robert Nathaniel Dett. Rae Linda Brown discusses how Price's involvement in two of the most prominent branches of NANM shaped the majority of her artistic activity in Chicago:

> Price became one of the most active members of the R. Nathaniel Dett Club; she joined the club April 2, 1928, shortly after her arrival in the city. Although she was an official member of the Dett Club, holding various offices including chair of the composition committee, she was equally active in and became more visible through her activities in the Chicago Music Association. It was through this branch of the NANM that Price met the most distinguished members of the black community, including Maude Roberts George, Estella Bonds, and concert singer Anita Patti Brown. Price was present at nearly every meeting of the Chicago Music Association. She gave talks on "current events," accompanied members of the club in performance on the piano or organ, demonstrated and lectured on rare keyboard instruments at local museums, composed music for members of the club, performed her own organ and piano compositions, and represented the branch at national meetings of NANM. Indeed, during the 1930s, rarely a week went by without some mention in the *Chicago Defender* of Price's activities.[14]

NANM offered Price an array of opportunities to support her fellow Black classical musicians. In addition, through their positions as writers at the *Defender*, Holt and her successor Maude Roberts George magnified Price's efforts, which supported their goal of highlighting Black women's achievements in public spaces. Of course, Price was not the only woman who served as a leader within this organization. Ege further describes how Holt's efforts to found NANM set a precedent of Black women occupying important positions within its ranks. The author states, "During and after Holt's tenure, many more women (including [Estella] Bonds, [Maude Roberts] George, and Price) occupied leadership roles across NANM and its various branches. This increase extended the site of black women's fellowship to positions of greater institutional power."[15] The steady presence of Black women leaders not only sustained NANM's mission but also inspired younger generations to embrace their agency as members of a Black feminist collective.

The initiative that Margaret Bonds showed as a young participant in NANM demonstrates the aforementioned influence of operating within a group that centered Black women musicians. Given her mother Estella's status as one of the original NANM members, Margaret played an active role in this organization from an early age. In fact, when she was still in high school, she helped create a Junior Music Association branch that allowed young musicians like herself to participate in the organization's efforts. Founding this branch was just the beginning of Bonds's lifelong membership in NANM. It also reflects a small portion of the substantial impact that Estella Bonds's role as a community leader had on her daughter's career, as the former cultivated the heart of an artistic movement.[16]

The Bonds Salon

By establishing the Bonds household as a "safe space" for artists to gather, Estella created a stronghold that allowed the Black Chicago Renaissance to flourish.[17] She hosted a salon in her household that served as a creative outlet and a refuge for friends in need. Authors Langston Hughes and Countee Cullen, singers Roland Hayes and Abbie Mitchell, and composers Florence Price, William Dawson, and Will Marion Cook were all part of the Bonds salon.[18] Given Price's participation and Margaret Bonds's status as the host's daughter, this particular "safe space" had a significant impact on the lives and careers of both women.[19]

Young Margaret was absorbed into a vast collaborative network of artists whose guidance nurtured her professional growth. She studied composition with composer William Dawson, and singer Abbie Mitchell mentored her in exploring art song – a genre that would eventually become an important part of Bonds's legacy as a composer.[20] Her mother's salon also initiated Bonds's relationship with her piano performance and composition teacher, Florence Price.[21] As the two women worked together, they developed a bond that proved beneficial for both women's careers. Bonds earned recognition as a frequent performer and excellent interpreter of Price's music, and the two women often collaborated on performances of the older woman's pieces.[22] The Bonds household not only enabled Margaret to receive instruction and guidance from established musicians, but also normalized the experience of receiving mentorship from creative Black women whose influences shaped her career.

The relationship between the Bonds and Price families stretched beyond the artistic to encompass personal care when Estella sheltered Price and her daughters during their time of need, further exemplifying the powerful effects of Black women's fellowship.[23] Samantha Ege discusses Price's time living in the Bonds's home as an example of how Black women's networks played an essential role as sources of support for their members. Ege writes, "[W]hen Price's abusive marriage ended in divorce, financial woes, and no place to live, she knew that she could depend upon the wider family that formed her Chicago." Ege further describes how the timing of Price's stay coincided with preparing to submit her Symphony No. 1 to the 1932 Wanamaker competition – a contest designed to counteract the lack of recognition for African American composers by honoring their music. Price won first prize with her composition, and its subsequent premiere on June 15, 1933, by the Chicago Symphony Orchestra, under the direction of Frederick Stock at the Chicago World's Fair, made her the first African American woman to have a major American orchestra premiere her work. By tracing the timeline of this symphony's creation, Ege connects the historic event to Estella Bonds's efforts to foster care, community, and creativity in her home.[24] Margaret Bonds confirmed that the people who frequented their household embodied the deep roots of Chicago's Black artistic community by sharing an anecdote about how they came together to help Price achieve her goals.

During the cold winter nights in Chicago, we used to sit around a large table in our kitchen – manuscript paper strewn around, Florence and I extracting parts for some contest deadline. We were a God-loving people, and, when we were pushed for time every brown-skinned musician in Chicago who could write a note, would "jump-to" and help Florence meet her deadline.[25]

Price was a clear beneficiary of Black women's fellowship and care, which nurtured her personal well-being while also enabling professional success.

Ultimately, the women of the Black Chicago Renaissance carefully curated spaces that produced opportunities for musicians like Bonds, Price, and Anderson to collaborate and develop their craft.[26] The foundations of this influence helped to launch each woman's career while setting the stage for their interactions with one another as professional musicians.

The Concerto Collaborations of Florence Price and Margaret Bonds

In addition to their student–teacher relationship, Price and Bonds often shared the spotlight in musical performances.[27] Price's Concerto in One Movement is a particularly poignant example of how their collaborations provided each woman with multiple opportunities to display their artistry in different ways. For instance, Alexandra Kori Hill explains that on August 25, 1934, during the Century of Progress Exhibition program "O Sing a New Song," dedicated to honoring African American music's history, Price conducted the concerto while Bonds performed as the soloist.[28] This granted Price the opportunity to take on an authoritative role concerning the interpretation of her music and highlighted Bonds's skills as an excellent pianist, which supplemented her work as a composer. The successful combination of Bonds and Price as a creative team benefited both women by simultaneously advertising their accomplishments and granting them access to new opportunities to demonstrate the significance of Black women's artistry.

The performance of Price's Concerto in One Movement with the Woman's Symphony Orchestra of Chicago, conducted by Ebba Sundstrom on October 12, 1934, again with Bonds as the soloist, disrupted barriers within white women's organizations. Often, these organizations claimed to support women artists while denying Black women access to opportunities and resources.[29] As Brown explains, the Woman's Symphony Orchestra of Chicago was "a well-respected ensemble in the city" and its mission was to address "[t]he lack of serious opportunities for the orchestral music of American composers and women composers" through programming music by these marginalized composers in public concerts – with specific emphasis on local composers from Chicago.[30] The group's work was largely well received, and the concert that featured Price's concerto also boasted the attendance of famed composers Carrie Jacobs-Bond[31] and Amy Beach, both of whom "were honored at a luncheon" during the event.[32] Although on the surface this organization presents admirable intentions, it also conceals a layer of racial discrimination. Much like several women's organizations at the time, its focus claimed to serve all women, but there was an implied understanding that their benefits only applied to white women. The "white" focus in women's organizations was usually silent, but its overwhelming presence was often palpable considering the women they admitted and the works they chose to showcase. This unspoken discrimination was a large part of what necessitated Black women organizing groups like NANM and household salons to counteract exclusions from Black men's spaces and white women's spaces alike.

Consequently, the entry of Price and Bonds into a white-woman-run organization's event confronted the status quo. Through their creativity, these women forged a path that was largely inaccessible to Black women and set a new precedent of acknowledging Black women's artistry within this organization. Brown confirms this fact by relating the benefits that Price's work reaped from this performance. The author explains that "[t]he Woman's Symphony was an important institution in bringing Price's music to the fore. Her music won critical acclaim and, most important, wide-spread recognition."[33] Brown further states that "the performance of Price's *Concerto in One Movement* marked the beginning of a long and fruitful association between the orchestra and the composer."[34] Price and Bonds used their artistry to enter what was largely a segregated space, and through their efforts they not only showcased their success but also expanded the possibilities for other Black women musicians to follow the path that their Black feminist collaboration created.

The Artistic Alliances of Marian Anderson and Florence Price

Marian Anderson's Lincoln Memorial Concert on April 9, 1939, is another famous example of a Black woman's defiance of racist discrimination. By this time, Anderson was an internationally famous singer and, to honor her renowned status, Howard University specifically invited her to perform a concert in Washington, DC. Yet, despite Anderson's prominence and First Lady Eleanor Roosevelt's endorsement, the Daughters of the American Revolution (from which Roosevelt, once a member, would soon resign) steadfastly refused to host a Black woman's concert at their venue, Constitution Hall. As a result, Anderson's promoters made arrangements for her to sing an outdoor concert at the Lincoln Memorial. In the end, she performed for an integrated crowd of 75,000 people, who gathered to witness this historic event.[35] Anderson sang a mixture of patriotic songs, classical repertoire, and spirituals arranged by African American composers. The final piece she sang was Price's arrangement of the spiritual "My Soul's Been Anchored in the Lord." As Alisha Lola Jones explains, this decision exemplifies "a longstanding legacy of black women amplifying black women's perspectives through the politics of concert performance."[36] In her programming, Anderson created a historic moment that challenged Black women's oppression and cemented the artistic bond between Anderson and Price.

Her selection of Price's piece displays Anderson's dedication to supporting her fellow Black woman musician, while also revealing a strategy of Black feminist resistance to systems of marginalization that were often imposed on Black voices. Kira Thurman describes how the white, European audiences who praised Anderson often did so with careful attention to policing the putative differences between white and Black sounds:

Across decades, listeners tuned their ears for inaudible social cues and drew on racial discourses to make aesthetic judgments on performances of Schubert or Brahms. Their sonic observations were never benign or objective. Rather, they produced and maintained racial difference. For example, in the 1920s listeners praised Black classical musicians such as Marian Anderson and Roland Hayes as "Negroes with white souls," which suggested that through their dedication to classical music they had overcome their Blackness and the limitations it posed.[37]

As Thurman asserts, listeners and critics maintained a "sonic color line" and took such pains to enforce its authority that they assigned aspects of morality to classical music and marked the mastery of this repertoire as the exclusive property of whiteness.[38] As a result of these assertions, the only way to accept Black singers excelling at classical music was to dub them "Negroes with white souls."[39] Nina Sun Eidsheim further discusses how African American singers were often relegated to singing spirituals by critics who deemed that any other repertoire sounded unnatural when performed by Black singers. Eidsheim explains, "Like American reviewers, London critics typically insisted on a connection between African American timbres and spirituals, questioning any black singer's choice to attempt anything but the latter."[40] Thurman's and Eidsheim's work clearly demonstrate the prevalence of perceived limitations that many listeners imposed on Black voices both at home and abroad.

Although these boundaries constrained Black classical singers in some aspects of their careers, Anderson employed tactics of rebellion against these limitations. For instance, Eidsheim describes how Anderson often designed programs that suited her voice and inclinations in spite of outside pressures to do otherwise.[41] In fact, the author includes an anecdote about an occasion "[w]hen [Anderson] was invited to sing a recital at the White House [and] she was asked to sing a set of spirituals only – yet, characteristically, she insisted on including a few pieces by Franz Schubert."[42] As a result, Eidsheim's work provides a model for reading Anderson's repertoire choices as sites of resistance to the constraints others attempted to place on her voice. Anderson's decision to sing Price's arrangement of "My Soul's Been Anchored in the Lord" at her Lincoln Memorial Concert further demonstrated her determination to defy intersectional oppression while supporting her fellow Black woman musician. This choice aligns with a tradition among African American classical singers that involves ending a concert with a spiritual, which was born out of a history that Elektra V. Carter illuminates in Chapter 6. In some ways, this ritual reenacted the marginalization of Black musicians in classical music spaces because it relegated African American composers to the back of the program. Yet, it also designated a specific space for singers to honor the traditions of African American music while normalizing its presence in concert halls. The context of Anderson's performance of "My Soul's Been Anchored in the Lord" displayed a multilayered expression of defiance. In fact, Anderson's decision reveals what Jones describes as a keen sense of "self-awareness" within the singer's programming strategy.[43] First, ending her concert with a spiritual proudly proclaimed Anderson's identity as an African American singer – thus, highlighting the very reason that she was barred from performing at Constitution Hall. Second, Anderson chose a song composed by a Black woman as her final piece. By placing Price's music in this honored section of her program, Anderson not only defied racism but also celebrated Black womanhood. As a result, the acclaim from this concert also benefited Price by putting her music on the national stage.

The Lincoln Memorial Concert is just one example of the collaborations between these women; Anderson often used her celebrated status to promote Price's music. Jones relates that after the famed concert the singer frequently "closed her recitals with 'My Soul's Been Anchored in the Lord,' establishing it as her signature piece."[44] Brown further explains, "Anderson had over 50 of Price's songs in her possession, many of which were premiered by and dedicated to the diva. Two of Price's songs, the spiritual arrangement, 'My Soul's Been Anchored in de Lord,' and 'Songs to the Dark Virgin' were made immediate successes by Anderson's performances of them."[45] In fact, in a concert at Carnegie Hall on January 2, 1940, Anderson sang both of these pieces on the same program. This performance included Price's spiritual arrangement in its customary place at the end of the concert, but the composer's "Songs to the Dark Virgin" appears as the second song in the penultimate set – a placement that interrupts a series of art songs by white men, including Maurice Ravel's "Vocalise."[46] Although Price resides at the end of the program, her work is not confined there. Instead, its placement within this concert disrupts perceptions of whiteness and maleness as a rightful center for the Western art music canon. By making room to include Price's music among other revered composers, Anderson declared her commitment to using her career to resist marginalization while celebrating Black womanhood.

The Mutual Respect between Margaret Bonds and Marian Anderson

> When I was a little girl I never missed a concert of Marian Anderson, Roland Hayes, and Abbie Mitchell. I was always thrilled by their singing of spirituals at the end of each concert. . . . So I felt cheated and wanted some spirituals at the end of my concerts, too.
> —Margaret Bonds on the inspiration behind her *Spiritual Suite for Piano* (1967)[47]

As a girl who grew up surrounded by prominent Black artists, Margaret Bonds developed a keen appreciation for embracing her heritage as a beneficiary of their groundbreaking creativity. In many cases, she was able to meet and work with her heroes, and those interactions allowed Bonds to model some aspects of her work after their innovations. For instance, Bonds created her *Spiritual Suite for Piano*, with three pieces based on specific spiritual melodies, to facilitate her own participation in the aforementioned tradition of including spirituals at the end of concerts. Originally, this tradition applied only to vocal performances. Yet, the depth of Bonds's admiration for the most renowned classical singers of her time inspired her to take ownership of this custom by creating her own version of a final piece based on a spiritual. As a result, Bonds added a new iteration to the existing practice of honoring African American musical traditions at the end of classical concerts.[48] The depth of Bonds's engagement with the people she admired reflects in the influence their work had on her own. This process mirrors Daphne A. Brooks's suggestion to take Black women fans seriously by recognizing their input as listeners and consumers. Taking inspiration from Brooks's methodology, I illustrate how the artistry that Bonds consumed directed her input within broader circles of classical music.

> How often have we asked Black women musicians, critics, and fans about what they've been listening to and why or which records they bought (or downloaded!), which songs set them on a journey to write, perform, and record their own music? How often have we explored the politics as well as the pleasure that women derived from writing about sounds and performances that were meaningful to them? How often have we mapped out and examined the worlds created and inhabited by Black women artists who are also critics and feminist critics whose prose aspired to the level of art? And as to those women who were ensnared in other people's criticism or who were bound – for any number of reasons – to archives that often brutally or carelessly rendered them as objects rather than subjects of their own making, how often have we considered the ways that their music created the conditions for crafting other ways of inhabiting the world?[49]

Although Brooks advocates for using this methodology in popular music studies, I contend that it is also relevant to the study of classical music. Bonds exemplifies this relevance because she not only engrossed herself within the artistic output of the Black Chicago Renaissance, but also used the resulting inspiration to fuel her own creativity while fostering collaborative relationships with her fellow artists.

The text for Bonds's song "The Negro Speaks of Rivers" is a poem with the same title by Langston Hughes – a choice that reflects the significance of his work within her personal and professional life. Bonds originally encountered Hughes's writing as an undergraduate student at Northwestern University.[50] Although the school accepted Black students, she experienced several instances of racial discrimination throughout her time there. Consequently, Bonds sought comfort in the words of Black poets, and she found "The Negro Speaks of Rivers" (1921) particularly inspiring. According to Bonds, "Because in that poem he tells how great the black man is. And if I had any misgivings, which I would have to have – here you are in a setup where the restaurants won't serve you and you're going to college, you're sacrificing, trying to get through school – and I know that poem helped save me."[51] Bonds's decision to use Hughes's words to fuel her music aligns with Brooks's examination of Black women who constructed different "way[s] of inhabiting the world" beyond the oppressive systems that attempted to govern their everyday lives.[52] The power of this connection expanded when Bonds and Hughes met in 1936, the same year she set "The Negro Speaks of Rivers." The two artists became fast friends, and together they fostered a lifelong artistic partnership, throughout which they collaborated on countless projects – including songs, theatrical shows, and cantatas.[53] Through her status as a fan, Bonds created a new form of celebration for Hughes's poetry, while also establishing an artistic connection that had a significant impact on her career.

Bonds was also an avid fan of Marian Anderson, and as a result this song indicates that Anderson's legacy as a singer helped to shape Bonds's legacy as a composer. The fact that Bonds composed this song with Anderson in mind reflects the extensive Black feminist mentorship that Bonds received in her childhood, which encouraged her to pursue further connections with Black women musicians as an adult. Given the expansive nature of Anderson's career and her history of pushing back against systems that attempted to limit her, it is unsurprising that Bonds chose Anderson to voice her own musical rebellion against the status quo. On the other hand, the connection between Bonds's song and Anderson's voice also reflects the potential tensions between personal agency and public expectations for Black classical musicians. In her essay "A Reminiscence," Bonds relates that one of her teachers criticized "The Negro Speaks for Rivers" because of its "'jazzy augmented chords.'" He encouraged her to remove said chords from the music altogether – she refused. Later, the composer offered the song to Anderson, but the singer declined. Bonds states, "She was very polite, but I think the 'jazzy augmented chords' frightened her." Of course, Anderson had every right to reject Bonds's offer with or without an explanation. Still, the situation invites further questions about the singer's reasons for not aligning herself with this song. Was Bonds right about Anderson being wary of a song with "jazzy augmented chords"? If so, was Anderson's aversion to these chords due to personal taste, or was it related to the pressures and expectations to uphold certain, canonical traditions as a classical singer? Is it possible that she was "frightened" of losing her status as a celebrated artist by pushing things too far?[54] The answers to these questions may never become evident, but their presence certainly evokes the complicated relationship between traditional expectations, professional branding, and personal agency that Anderson, Bonds, and others faced as Black musicians within the classical music industry. Although in this case their choices did not align, each woman maintained the right to make a decision that suited her own needs.

Anderson never performed the song that Bonds wrote for her, but the cycle of Black feminist collaboration continued when Etta Moten, "the singer for whom Gershwin originally composed the role of 'Bess' in

Porgy and Bess," premiered "The Negro Speaks of Rivers."[55] Moten was an intimate friend of the Bonds family, and as such her participation is yet another example of the Black feminist influence that surrounded Bonds her entire life.[56] The roots of these connections ran deep in Bonds's history, and as a result her music reflects a personal dedication to honoring the significance of Black women musicians' artistry.

Continued Legacies

Throughout their careers, each of these women demonstrated a continued interest in supporting their fellow artists. After making history as the first African American woman to have a major orchestra premiere her music, Price continued to disrupt boundaries that prevented Black women from accessing specific professional opportunities. Rae Linda Brown explains that Price used the momentum of her success "to join several music clubs. In the 1930s, when segregated musical organizations were accepted a priori, Price is credited with breaking down racial barriers. In addition to integrating the Chicago Club of Women Organists, she became the first woman of color invited to join the Illinois Federation of Music Clubs and the Musicians Club of Women."[57] Becoming the first Black woman to join these organizations not only broadened Price's network but also created possibilities for other Black women musicians to follow suit.

Bonds followed in her mother's footsteps by building "safe spaces" to serve Black artists.[58] She started a school called the Allied Arts Academy in Chicago during the 1930s to train new generations of dancers, artists, and musicians.[59] Later, in 1956, she established the Margaret Bonds Chamber Music Society in New York City, with the specific aspiration of forming a canon of African American music – a goal that demonstrates her dedication to promoting Black music and musicians.[60] In addition to creating new organizations, Bonds also fostered collaborative relationships with several of her fellow artists; this group included famed soprano Leontyne Price, who performed several of Bonds's arrangements of spirituals.[61] She additionally maintained her ties with Nora Holt, performing her music on Holt's radio programs and developing a friendship that mirrored Holt's closeness with Estella back in Chicago. Margaret Bonds committed her entire career to actively seeking out new ways to foster Black feminist resistance, and the results of her efforts are evident in the array of connections and music that she created along the way.

After an extended career of performing on an international level, Marian Anderson further defied what Jennifer Lynn Stoever calls the "sonic color line" by becoming the first African American singer to perform a leading role at the Metropolitan Opera in 1955.[62] The combination of this historic moment and Anderson's career in performing spirituals alongside classical repertoire paved the way for generations of Black classical singers to follow in her wake. Since Anderson lived for a comparatively long time, she actually witnessed some of the results of her achievements within her lifetime. Notably, the revered singer was present at the now famous concert that Kathleen Battle and Jessye Norman sang at Carnegie Hall on May 18, 1990, titled "Spirituals in Concert."[63] She was ninety-three years old. This event and its organization by two Black women opera singers, whose careers were the direct result of Anderson's artistic labors, exemplifies the depth of Anderson's legacy in cultivating Black feminist fellowship.

The foundational work of the women who cultivated the Black Chicago Renaissance lies at the heart of these events. Through their collective care and labor, Black women weathered the obstacles that stood against them while laying the tracks that would empower others to follow their lead. They set precedents of making multiple ways out of no way, and sowed seeds of resistance to ensure that future generations would reap the rewards. Soon afterwards, the young beneficiaries became the new planters. They carried on the tradition by pushing farther into the field to plant more seeds – thus sustaining the cycle of tending and expanding the precious gardens that they inherited from their foremothers.

Notes

1. Patricia Hill Collins, *Black Feminist Thought: Knowledge, Consciousness, and the Politics of Empowerment* (New York: Routledge, 2000), 101.
2. Elizabeth Durrant, "Chicago Renaissance Women: Black Feminism in the Careers and Songs of Florence Price and Margaret Bonds" (MA thesis, University of North Texas, 2021), 11–12.
3. Collins, *Black Feminist Thought*, 101.
4. Durrant, "Chicago Renaissance Women," 3–4, 5.
5. Collins, *Black Feminist Thought*, 101.
6. Lawrence Schenbeck, *Racial Uplift and American Music, 1878–1943* (Jackson: University of Mississippi Press, 2012), 180–181.
7. As Lucy Caplan explains, Holt also created her own magazine called *Music and Poetry* and most of her editorial staff were women – a rare occurrence at the

time. Lucy Caplan, "'Strange What Cosmopolites Music Makes of Us': Classical Music, the Black Press, and Nora Douglas Holt's Black Feminist Audiotopia," *Journal of the Society for American Music* 14, no. 3 (2020): 321.
8. Schenbeck, *Racial Uplift and American Music*, 196.
9. The dates of this convention, July 29, 1919, to August 1, 1919, coincided with a particularly violent period in US history, known as the Red Summer of 1919 due to "[r]ace riots [that] swept through twenty-six American cities." Robert Bone and Richard A. Courage, *The Muse in Bronzeville: African American Creative Expression in Chicago, 1932–1950*, (New Brunswick: Rutgers University Press, 2011), 46.
10. Originally published in Holt's magazine *Music and Poetry* in 1921. Cheryl A. Wall, "Nora Holt: New Negro Composer and Jazz Age Goddess," in *Women and Migration: Responses in Art and History*, edited by Deborah Willis, Ellyn Toscano, and Kaila Brooks Nelson (Cambridge, UK: Open Book, 2019), 95–96.
11. Wall, "Nora Holt," 96–97.
12. Rae Linda Brown, *The Heart of a Woman: The Life and Music of Florence B. Price*, (Urbana: University of Illinois Press, 2020), 88.
13. Samantha Ege, "Composing a Symphonist: Florence Price and the Hand of Black Women's Fellowship," *Women and Music* 24 (2020): 16.
14. Brown, *The Heart of a Woman*, 88–89.
15. Ege, "Composing a Symphonist," 13.
16. Helen Walker-Hill, *From Spirituals to Symphonies: African-American Women Composers and Their Music* (Westport, CT: Greenwood Press, 2002), 144–145.
17. Collins, *Black Feminist Thought*, 101.
18. Walker-Hill, *From Spirituals to Symphonies*, 145.
19. Collins, *Black Feminist Thought*, 101.
20. Walker-Hill, *From Spirituals to Symphonies*, 148, 161. For more about the Bonds salon, see Elizabeth Durrant and Rebecca Dowd Geoffroy-Schwinden, "The Estella Bonds Salon: A Black Chicago Renaissance Genealogy of American Art Song" in *Four Centuries of Women's Musical Salons: A Cross-Cultural History*, edited by Jacqueline Avila and Rebecca Cypess (Cambridge, UK: Cambridge University Press, 2026), 313–331.
21. Rae Linda Brown, "Lifting the Veil: The Symphonies of Florence B. Price," in *Florence Price Symphonies Nos. 1 and 3*, American Musicological Society Recent Researches in American Music, vol. 66, edited by Rae Linda Brown and Wayne Shirley (Middleton, WI: A-R Editions, 2008), xxxi.
22. Brown, *The Heart of a Woman*, 106.
23. "[Price's first] husband, Thomas, was abusive, and throughout their marriage he became increasingly violent. The couple separated in 1920, and on January 19, 1931, a judge granted Price a divorce and full custody of her daughters." Durrant, "Chicago Renaissance Women," 40–41; Brown, *The Heart of a Woman*, 99–100.

24. Ege, "Composing a Symphonist," 19, 20–21.
25. Margaret Bonds, "A Reminiscence," in *The Negro in Music and Art*, edited by Lindsay Patterson (New York: Publisher's Company, 1967), 192.
26. Collins, *Black Feminist Thought*, 101.
27. During the same program that premiered Price's Symphony No. 1, Bonds also made history by becoming the first African American instrumentalist to play with the Chicago Symphony Orchestra – she was the soloist in John Alden Carpenter's Concertino for Piano and Orchestra.
28. Alexandra Kori Hill, "Make the Familiar New: New Negro Modernism in the Concertos of Florence B. Price" (PhD diss., University of North Carolina at Chapel Hill, 2022), 11.
29. Rae Linda Brown explains that there is a picture of this performance, and the conductor is "often misidentified as Price," but Ebba Sundstrom is the person in the photo. Brown, *The Heart of a Woman*, 259.
30. Ibid., 158.
31. Margaret Bonds's maternal grandmother was a fan of Carrie Jacobs-Bond, and Bonds credited said grandmother with encouraging her to become a songwriter. Helen-Walker Hill, *From Spirituals to Symphonies*, 146.
32. Brown, *The Heart of a Woman*, 159.
33. "Carrie Jacobs-Bond, whom Price had met the year before . . . came behind the curtain at the conclusion of the program. Tilting her head back, Jacobs-Bond remarked, 'Ah, that was beautiful.'" Brown, *The Heart of a Woman*, 160.
34. Ibid., 159.
35. Susan Stamberg, "Denied a Stage, She Sang for a Nation," NPR, April 9, 2014, www.npr.org/2014/04/09/298760473/denied-a-stage-she-sang-for-a-nation.
36. Alisha Lola Jones, "Lift Every Voice: Marian Anderson, Florence B. Price and the Sound of Black Sisterhood," NPR, August 30, 2019, https://tinyurl.com/3y7metwt.
37. Kira Thurman, *Singing Like Germans: Black Musicians in the Land of Bach, Beethoven, and Brahms* (Ithaca, NY: Cornell University Press, 2021), 11.
38. Jennifer Lynn Stoever, *The Sonic Color Line: Race and the Cultural Politics of Listening* (New York: New York University Press, 2016).
39. Thurman, *Singing like Germans*, 11.
40. Nina Sun Eidsheim, "Marian Anderson and 'Sonic Blackness' in American Opera," *American Quarterly* 63 no. 3 (September 2011): 659.
41. For theories about the miscategorization of Anderson as a contralto instead of a soprano with input by the singer herself and mezzo-soprano Denyce Graves, see Rita Coburn, "How Racism Effected Marian Anderson's Billing," American Masters, YouTube, January 20, 2022, https://youtu.be/glTQbzv1lS4.
42. Eidsheim, "Marian Anderson," 660.
43. Jones, "Lift Every Voice."
44. Ibid.
45. Brown, *The Heart of a Woman*, 97, 225.

46. Carnegie Hall Program, Season 1939–1940, Carl Van Vechten Collection, Beinecke Rare Book and Manuscript Library, Yale University.
47. Walker-Hill, *From Spirituals to Symphonies*, 166.
48. The final piece in Bonds's *Spiritual Suite for Piano*, "Troubled Water" (based on the spiritual "Wade in the Water"), is one of her most popular pieces and performances of it remain a staple in classical music concerts to date. Walker-Hill, *From Spirituals to Symphonies*, 168.
49. Daphne A. Brooks, *Liner Notes for the Revolution: The Intellectual Life of Black Feminist Sound* (Cambridge, MA: Harvard University Press, 2021), 81.
50. Anna Celenza, "Margaret Bonds and Langston Hughes: A Musical Friendship," Special Collections Gallery, Georgetown University Library, August 30, 2016–January 24, 2017, https://tinyurl.com/2fwccua9.
51. Ibid.
52. Brooks, *Liner Notes for the Revolution*, 81.
53. Walker-Hill, *From Spirituals to Symphonies*,149.
54. Bonds, "A Reminiscence," 191–192.
55. Celenza, "Margaret Bonds and Langston Hughes."
56. Walker-Hill, *From Spirituals to Symphonies*, 148.
57. Brown, *The Heart of a Woman*, 182–183.
58. Collins, *Black Feminist Thought*, 101.
59. Walker-Hill, *From Spirituals to Symphonies*, 150.
60. Celenza, "Margaret Bonds and Langston Hughes."
61. Anna Celenza, "Margaret Bonds: Composer and Activist," Leo Robin Gallery, Georgetown University Library, August 29, 2016–January 24, 2017, www.library.georgetown.edu/exhibition/margaret-bonds-composer-and-activist.
62. See Stoever, *The Sonic Color Line*.
63. In this production there is a brief discussion of Anderson's legacy, along with footage of her sitting in the audience at the concert. These moments occur between 45:45 and 46:53 in the video. Dag Fryer, "The Magic of Spirituals," Great Performances, PBS, February 24, 2023, www.pbs.org/wnet/gperf/magic-of-spirituals-about/14283/.

13 | The Critical Reception of Florence Price

LUCY CAPLAN

In 1934, the African American opera singer Lillian Evanti immortalized her admiration for fellow musician Florence Price in print. Her remarks, circulated widely via the Associated Negro Press, celebrated that Price was "leading the way for American women composers." Setting herself apart from a "general public," who were "just beginning to know" of Price's achievements, Evanti emphasized the "privilege" of her acquaintance with a woman who "thinks orchestrally."[1] An accompanying image shows the two women smiling toward one another, their mutual fondness and admiration made visible. Even as the article's substance focuses largely on Price's recent pathbreaking accomplishments in white musical spheres – notably, the recent premiere of her Symphony No. 1 in E Minor by the Chicago Symphony Orchestra – its structure emphasizes her revered status among fellow stars of the Black musical world. Evanti is described as an "opera star" whose expertise informs her commentary on Price's achievements, and the article is framed as an extended laudatory quotation in her voice. What may initially read as a well-placed puff piece, then, becomes a window into the overlapping social and musical networks in which Price worked, and how those networks shaped and were shaped by the institution of the Black press.

African American newspapers and magazines offer a meticulous documentary record of Price's musical endeavors. Periodicals including the *Chicago Defender*, *Baltimore Afro-American*, and *Pittsburgh Courier* provide detailed information about premieres of her music and reviews of performances, from the major to the obscure. There are records of her travels and announcements of the prizes and honors she received. Price's involvement in local and national musical organizations is documented. Coverage of Price's work in the white-authored press is less extensive, and often superficial in tone – it tends to focus more on the novelty of her presence in predominantly white musical circles rather than the substance of her work – but it, too, offers crucial information about Price's career. It is easy to see how a vibrant biographical narrative might emerge from these sources: one which documents the trajectory of a figure who distinguished herself by way of her outstanding accomplishments. Understood in this light, the Black press might become a resource for recovery, a goldmine of information about the quotidian activities of an extraordinary figure.

Figure 13.1 This photograph of Lillian Evanti and Florence Price appeared in the *Pittsburgh Courier*, accompanied by a caption that emphasized both women's musical achievements, as well as Evanti's respect for Price: "Mme. Lillian Evanti, famous operatic and concert singer (left), greeting Mrs. Florence B. Price, the foremost woman composer of our group. During a recent visit to 'A Century of Progress' in Chicago, when she was completing plans for a country-wide tour, Mme. Evanti in an interview paid high tribute to the work of Mrs. Price." ("Evanti Praises Woman Composer," *Pittsburgh Courier*, October 13, 1934.)

More than simply a record of Price's exceptionality, though, the Black press also shows how inseparable her story is from those of the communities around her. Press coverage highlights her position within myriad social and cultural networks, many comprised of other Black women musicians and artists. While Price's relationships to other well-known musicians including

Margaret Bonds and Marian Anderson have often been recognized, the press elucidates some of the wider, more diffuse communities of which she was part. The Black press itself was also deeply intertwined with musical life, especially in Chicago, creating a situation in which a single individual might be part of the very artistic scene she documented. Nora Douglas Holt and Maude Roberts George, for instance, were both acclaimed musicians who also served as music critics for the *Defender*. Although Price herself did not contribute to the press as a writer, she maintained close social and personal connections to many of the figures who documented her activities. These overlapping spheres meant that, in the act of documenting the circles in which Price moved, the press also became a manifestation of those networks – itself a locale through which she forged connections to others.

These qualities suggest that the same archival materials often used to set Price apart from others – notices about her status as the first Black woman to have her music performed by a major symphony orchestra, for instance – can also serve to reposition her in relation to her contemporaries. Many Price scholars have emphasized her relationship to broader musical communities, from her earliest years in Little Rock to her adulthood as a composer in Chicago. Samantha Ege, for example, argues that Price should be understood as part of an "artistic cohort" shaped by Black women's fellowship.[2] This framing follows a broader turn in Black feminist music studies, which favors attention to the complex lineages and genealogies of Black women's musical endeavors. Similarly, scholars of the Black press have illuminated the crucial role of artists within this cultural sphere, drawing attention to the importance of the press as a locus of cultural networks in addition to political ones. Building upon these scholarly frameworks, this chapter charts the relationship between Price and the Black press across multiple contexts, from her childhood in Little Rock through the apex of her compositional career to the final years of her life. In doing so, it highlights a perpetual tug-of-war that emerges in her critical reception: namely, a discourse that concomitantly exceptionalizes and de-exceptionalizes Price, emphasizing her distinctiveness as much as her embeddedness within Black institutional life.

The Black Press as a Cultural Institution

Price is but one of many twentieth-century African American musicians whose careers were inextricable from the cultural and social institution of the Black press. The press offers an unparalleled record of African Americans' engagement with Western art music traditions. In its heyday, during the first half of the twentieth century, the press became a fundamental element of the Jim Crow-era Black public sphere, an outlet for discourse and community formation in a period otherwise marked by the repressive constraints of segregation and the diminishment of Black legal and political power. As media historian Anna Everett has written, it became in these years "the only dedicated forum for the mass cultivation, appreciation, and dissemination of African American ideas, culture, values, talent, literature, thought, and analysis."[3] Its rise to prominence overlaps almost perfectly with Price's own, as it flourished beginning in the first years of the twentieth century, continued to grow during the 1920s and 1930s, and played a vital role throughout the early years of the long civil rights movement.

Although the Black press is often discussed primarily in terms of political content, the arts were part of its development from the beginning. Early Black newspapers featured fiction and poetry within their pages and, as literary historian Elizabeth McHenry has detailed, facilitated vigorous debates about Black cultural production.[4] Generalist periodicals like the *Indianapolis Freeman* and *New York Age* devoted extensive space to music, arts, and culture; accordingly, the Black press also provided a vital opportunity to counteract white journalists' tendency to ignore or misrepresent Black musical and cultural life. A handful of periodicals emphasized music specifically. These included the *Musical Messenger*, founded by the vocalist, teacher, and writer Amelia Tilghman in 1886; and the short-lived *Negro Music Journal* (1902–1903), edited by J. Hillary Taylor.

The *Chicago Defender* was a hub for Black classical music criticism, and its immense reach allowed it to exceed the influence of earlier periodicals. Founded in 1905, the newspaper soared in popularity as it became a catalyzing force in the Great Migration, and soon became the nation's most widely read Black newspaper, with a circulation of over 100,000. Its founder, Robert Abbott, was himself a musician who, as a college student, had toured nationally with the Hampton University Choir and Quartet. For Black musicians, the *Defender* became a crucial discursive space. Within its pages there could be found announcements of upcoming concerts; advertisements for lessons, instruments, and instructional materials; profiles of eminent musicians; detailed reviews of individual performances; and essays and opinion pieces about music history. In 1917, the *Defender* became the first Black newspaper to feature a regular column of classical music criticism, penned by the composer-cum-singer-cum-socialite Nora Douglas Holt. Maude Roberts George, a singer, pedagogue, and musical institution-builder, subsequently assumed this role. As key figures in the city's musical scene, Holt and George exemplify how the Black press became a locus of musical life rather than merely a recorder of it. The November 13, 1920, installment of Holt's column, for instance, quoted a London reviewer's glowing assessment of Roland Hayes; previewed soprano Florence Cole-Talbert's upcoming engagement with a Chicago glee club; and noted that Holt herself was to "give a lecture on Negro folk-music and play a group of her compositions" for a women's club in the coming days.[5]

In addition to her work with the *Defender*, Holt was cofounder and editor of *Music and Poetry*. Established in 1921, the magazine epitomized the Black musical press's ability to create, shape, and reflect cultural networks. *Music and Poetry* featured editorials, essays, and sheet music by a distinguished roster of primarily African American contributors, among them composer Clarence Cameron White, violinist Kemper Harreld, pianist Helen Hagan, and musicologist Maud Cuney Hare. In contrast to the male-dominated mastheads of most periodicals, the majority of its editors were Black women. Its focus on the circulation of musical knowledge meant that pianists, violinists, and vocalists were regularly invited to contribute pedagogical advice: For example, the Voice Department, edited by soprano Cleota Collins, offered guidance on subjects from vocal mechanics to proper posture.[6] *Music and Poetry* promoted larger-scale change. Holt asked "each reader to be a collaborator" in contributing relevant material to the magazine and published an "Artist Directory," containing the addresses of eminent musicians across the country, at the conclusion of each issue. A recurring item proclaimed "The Musician's Creed for 1921: ... I Will Use Something of Negro Origin on Every Program," urging performers to adhere to a racial "spirit of loyalty" and program worthy compositions by black composers. Through these efforts, Holt worked toward circumventing the structural barriers that restricted African Americans' engagements with classical music, fostering a culture of mutual support and collaboration that helped build a robust musical infrastructure.

Although *Music and Poetry* disbanded in 1922 and predates the bulk of Price's career, it anticipated some of the currents that would come to characterize her critical reception. It discussed representative and exceptional figures in the same breath: Although it often spotlighted the unusual success of a particular African American musician via a glowing profile, its articles were geared toward a wide audience of amateur musicians and their practices of everyday musical activity. The magazine also centered the work of Black musical institutions – most notably, the National Association of

Negro Musicians (NANM), which Holt had cofounded in 1919. NANM and other musical institutions would come to be fundamental to Price's local success in Chicago, as well as the national reach of her compositions. It was into this milieu that Price's own work came to be critiqued, discussed, and represented; it was among this network of figures that she would ultimately find her community.

Price and the Press

Price's relationship to the press began long before she arrived in Chicago. She spent her childhood in Little Rock, Arkansas, where her parents, dentist Dr. James H. Smith and musician Florence Irene Gulliver Smith, were part of a substantial cohort of middle-class Black families in the city. Such communities – socially tight knit, anchored by institutions like schools and churches, and upwardly mobile – were central to the creation and dissemination of postbellum Black periodicals. Little Rock boasted three separate Black newspapers by 1900, and the state of Arkansas had more than thirty.[7] Arkansas also hosted conventions of Black journalists as early as 1889, reflecting the local vitality of the press in a moment before the repressive power of Jim Crow was fully in effect.[8] Price's family was enmeshed in both local and national networks of prominent African American artists, intellectuals, and musicians. They were friendly with the family of William Grant Still, another Little Rock resident, during Price's childhood. Price also had the opportunity to meet Black musicians who traveled through Little Rock; for instance, she wrote one of her earliest compositions for the pianist John Williams "Blind" Boone, who was touring the city at the time.

One incident dating from Price's early childhood illuminates the formative role of both the Black and white presses in African American Little Rock. When Frederick Douglass visited the city in 1889, he stayed with the Smith family at their home. After giving a lecture at the nearby Capital Theater, he spoke with a reporter from the *Arkansas Gazette*, a mainstream newspaper, from the comfort of the Smith family's living room. The putatively descriptive commentary on the setting did ideological work, as Rae Linda Brown notes: The reporter seemed surprised by the "refinement and taste" of the Smith home and characterized Price's father, Dr. Smith, as a "negro in name only."[9] During the same visit, Douglass was denied entrance to a public dining room, an offense that he mentioned in his comments to the *Gazette*. The national Black press picked up the story, expressing justified outrage at the fact that fame could not protect even so distinguished a figure as Douglass from segregation's insults.[10] The incident served as a stark reminder that under a Jim Crow regime, race could easily trump fame, wealth, and other markers of status in shaping an individual's access to public space.

After departing Arkansas in 1903, Price enrolled at the New England Conservatory in Boston, returned to Little Rock to teach, then moved to Atlanta to join the music faculty at Clark University. In each of these settings, she had the opportunity to forge connections to new personal and musical communities. In Boston, for example, she would have encountered a vibrant scene of music-making among Black women; as Josephine Wright has written, from the late nineteenth century onwards, dozens of women contributed to the city's musical life as singers, instrumentalists, educators, composers, critics, and patrons.[11] Black women also stood at the helm of the city's periodicals. Of particular note was Pauline Hopkins, a musician-turned-writer who founded the *Colored American Magazine* in Boston in 1900. "Devoted to Literature, Science, Music, Art, Religion ... of the Negro Race," as its cover proclaimed, the magazine was a vital site of early Black music journalism and had Hopkins herself as its signature critic.[12] An accomplished singer who established a reputation as "Boston's favorite colored soprano" by the age of twenty, composed works of musical theater, and toured with a family singing troupe during the 1880s, Hopkins also explored musical themes in her journalism and fiction writing.[13] For instance, her November 1901 article "Phenomenal Vocalists" offered glowing praise for those illustrious Black women singers who succeeded on the concert stage. While there is no direct evidence that Price engaged with Hopkins's journalism, the convergence of its publication with her time in Boston suggests myriad possibilities. Perhaps, for instance, she read with interest an article in the magazine's January 1905 issue on the "Afro-American People of Little Rock," which praised the city's thriving Black population (including its "three dentists," who counted Price's father among their number) and immediately preceded an article on Afro-British composer Samuel Coleridge-Taylor.[14]

Price was mentioned in the Black press as early as 1918, but her relationship to the institution deepened in the late 1920s, coinciding with her relocation to Chicago.[15] Two important themes emerged in early coverage of her work: one having to do with her rising profile as a composer, and the other with her centrality to the development and growth of Black musical institutions. Beginning around 1926, Price began to submit her work to a variety of national contests. Often sponsored by

Black organizationally affiliated periodicals, like the NAACP's *Crisis* or the Urban League's *Opportunity*, these contests provided a key means of recognition for aspiring composers. An item in the May 1926 issue of *Opportunity*, for example, noted that Price had been awarded second prize in the Holstein Prizes, sponsored by the Afro-Caribbean businessman Casper Holstein, for her piano suite *In the Land O' Cotton*; the next year, the magazine announced that Price had once again been awarded a prize in the contest for her *Memories of Dixieland*.[16] The language of these announcements retained a gendered tone: While the first prize winner in 1927, Hall Johnson, was characterized as an "organizer" and "director" who led an "active musical life" in New York, Price was described as a daughter, wife, and "mother of two little musical daughters."[17]

In parallel to this increasing (if understated, given her gender) recognition of Price's exceptional talent as a composer, the press also began to note Price's involvement in local and national musical organizations. As Imani Perry has argued, "black associational life" was a key feature of early twentieth-century African American life, through which communities established institutional spaces – schools, churches, clubs – to strengthen cultural identity.[18] Musical organizations were no exception: Groups like NANM and its attendant network of local clubs, such as the Chicago Music Association and the R. Nathaniel Dett Club of Music and Allied Arts, created spaces in which musicians of various professional statures could come together, create performance and pedagogical opportunities, and exchange ideas. Price was involved in NANM almost from its inception: She was listed on its roster of Arkansas-based members as early as 1920 and, upon moving to Chicago in 1927, joined multiple local branches.[19] (In Arkansas, she had also served as president of a music club that had requested membership in NANM.) In Chicago, the organization enjoyed a close, even symbiotic, relationship with the *Defender*, and the newspaper's extensive coverage of NANM's goings-on meant that events like the performance of Price's music at NANM conventions received notice in the newspaper. Accordingly, Price's twin identities as prizewinning composer and representative member of organizations became two key constituent parts of her growing public profile.

These trends intensified in 1932, when Price was awarded a Wanamaker Prize for her Symphony in E Minor. The most elite of the various prizes available to African American composers – it was characterized by the *Defender* as "an event of paramount importance open to all musical composers of the Race"[20] – the contest originated in 1927 after the philanthropist Rodman Wanamaker heard musicians perform at a NANM convention in Philadelphia and was inspired to create a recurring set of awards for Black classical composers.[21] Maude Roberts George reported that "Chicago musicians were thrilled" when local composers, including Price and Margaret Bonds, swept the competition, and she boasted that the "daily press has taken particular notice of the achievements of these two Chicagoans."[22] George further emphasized that Price's accomplishment, while admirable, was not unprecedented: Price had received many previous honors prior to this "major achievement," but tended not to boast about them due to her "retiring" personality.[23] While, on the one hand, such a characterization might be read as extending previous gendered descriptions of Price that separated her from the image of the (white, male) "Great Composer," it could also be understood as demonstrating her fundamental disinterest in that role – her desire not to propagate exceptionalist thinking by means of her achievements.

Indeed, even as the *Defender* lauded Price's award – George mentioned it in virtually every iteration of her "News of the Music World" column during October and November of 1932 – the newspaper also continued to emphasize Price's enduring relationships to existing musical communities. One article reported on a well-attended lecture she gave about "the accomplishments and ambitions of our musicians," for example.[24] Another announced Marian Anderson's attendance at Margaret Bonds's performance of Price's composition "Sinner, Please Don't Let This Harvest Pass."[25] The occasion epitomized the close connections that linked a well-known coterie of Black women musicians; so did its venue, the historic Berean Baptist Church, where Bonds's mother, Estella (who succeeded George as president of the Chicago Musical Association), had long served as organist.

The *Defender* also suggested that Price's social function, like that of other local musicians, extended beyond the role of artist or entertainer. George argued that musicians were "playing an important part as a spiritual factor in these times of financial unrest," offering psychological, if not material, comfort to those struggling during the Great Depression and, in doing so, creating a social impact that extended beyond the ephemeral moment of live performance.[26] Importantly, the newspaper also showed how Price not only assisted others, but also benefited from her communities' assistance. On her birthday on April 9, 1933, she attended a performance by an a cappella group newly named in her honor. George reported that although Price had taken a step back from public life recently in order to prepare the parts for her symphony's upcoming performance, she "was present and acknowledged in a very beautiful way the honor which had been bestowed upon her with the naming of their group ... she said it was indeed the happiest [birthday] she had ever had."[27]

Florence B. Price, Distinguished Composer

The relationship between Price and the press shifted course in 1933, when the Chicago Symphony Orchestra performed her Symphony in E Minor – the first time the orchestra, or any major American orchestra, programmed music by an African American woman. The "firstness" of this event bears further scrutiny. In becoming an exception to the rule of patriarchal, white supremacist exclusion, Price circumvented what she famously described as her "two handicaps – those of sex and race." Yet an outsize focus on this accomplishment threatened to prioritize entrance into segregated white spaces over accomplishments within existing structures of what Imani Perry describes as Black formalism: facets of public culture that do not presume the presence of a white audience, and instead involve the practice of rituals and behaviors essential to creating a sense of dignity and strength.[28] That is, a focus on the CSO premiere risked overshadowing the myriad church musicales, recitals, and other Black formalist settings in which Price's music had long been heard. At the same time, the Black press's emphasis on the premiere served a strategic purpose, in that readers could point to Price's unprecedented accomplishments as evidence not only of her talent but also of the absurdity and injustice of Jim Crow writ large.

Coverage of the premiere in the Black and white presses elucidates complex critical dynamics at play with respect to race, gender, and the politics of recognition. Whereas prior to the premiere the *Defender* consistently identified Price as the "1932 Wanamaker Prize winner," after 1933 she became known in the newspaper's pages as "Florence B. Price, distinguished composer," "recognized composer," or, eventually, "dean of composers of the Middle West" – all terminology suggesting that she had officially "arrived" and attained a heightened level of recognition.[29] Even so, the broader critical reception of the work retained a level of ambivalence. While reviews were almost universally complimentary, they took different approaches to situating Price within an individual educational and creative trajectory, an existing community of performers and musicians, and a historical lineage. Some Black newspapers undercut Price's accomplishment along the lines of gender even as it was celebrated for its racial significance. The Baltimore *Afro-American*, for example, initially announced the performance under the anonymizing headline "Woman's Symphony Heard At Fair."[30] In the white-authored press, the *Chicago Daily Tribune*'s Edward Moore noted that the symphony "displayed high talent" and was based on "racial folk song idioms," yet he also showed an ignorance of Price's extensive past achievements and education with the blithe observation that she "would seem to be well acquainted with the use of orchestral instrumental color."[31] Another critic remarked excitedly that "it is believed that an outstanding composer has been discovered," praise which effectively erased the years of accolades and performance opportunities Price had already received within Black communities.[32]

Other commentators focused on the event's sociopolitical significance. The *Defender*'s editor, Robert Abbott, disclosed a sense of "awe" upon attending the performance and seeing the Chicago Symphony Orchestra sound "the beautiful, harmonious strains of a composition by a Race woman," followed by loud applause from an auditorium "filled to the brim with music lovers of all races." Abbott interpreted the event as a hopeful sign that "in the higher arts, our white brother is growing less and less fractious."[33] Within this framework, Price's artistic individuality was subsumed in order to foreground her status as a "Race woman" who might become a conduit for racial harmony and an exemplar of uplift ideology. Another rich review, by the prominent journalist and editor Nahum Daniel Brascher, located Price's work within a historical trajectory dating back to Samuel Coleridge-Taylor's US appearance several decades earlier, thus connecting Price not only to a contemporaneous community of musicians but also to a global, decades-long lineage. Brascher described the premiere of the symphony as an occasion "pregnant with significance," at which a "representative and brilliant" audience gathered to hear a remarkable event, which had since been "the talk of the town." Like Abbott, he was especially impressed with the presence of a multiracial audience, "the balcony and numerous galleries filled with our own music lovers and musicians" engaged in "unstinted and unending applause." He boldly proclaimed that the event heralded "a new era for us in the world of music."

At the end of the review, Brascher made a curious pivot, offering a sort of metacritical reflection on the fact that "years of contact in the newspaper world [had] given [him] a cordial acquaintance with most of our outstanding musical people."[34] The inextricability of the Black press and Black musical cultures meant that, as a journalist, Brascher had enjoyed the opportunity to interact with elite musicians including Roland Hayes, Will Marion Cook, Paul Robeson, Jules Bledsoe, Marian Anderson, and many others. What Brascher did not mention is that this convergence of cultural spheres extended to the premiere itself: His colleague Maude Roberts George, a longtime advocate for Price's music, had underwritten the performance in her capacity as president of the Chicago Musical

Association. This institutional financial support guaranteed Price the opportunity for this success.[35] Such infrastructural details also blur the line between what were typically understood to be two separate musical public spheres, one focused on cultural autonomy within Black Chicago and one committed to the project of desegregation. Price may have been the composer whose work was ultimately featured on the CSO program, but her path there was literally and symbolically paved by the community of musicians and journalists who had long supported her.

In turn, this additional detail helps explain why the Black press covered Price's reception with such attentiveness to its social and political significance. Rae Linda Brown has argued that the Black press, in its focus on the historical import of Price's work, tended to focus less on its musical and aesthetic details; as a result, Brown writes that, perhaps paradoxically, "it was the white press who, in many ways, validated Price's musical skills."[36] Another interpretation, though, would be that the Black press recognized the inseparability of the historical and the aesthetic in the context of Price's career. In doing so, it honored her status as a composer embedded in myriad musical communities, and as such offered a different model of what made a composer "valid" or "significant." It is worth noting that the Black press also paid particular attention to how African American artists interpreted Price's music, thus describing its musical qualities in response to live performance rather than the manuscript score. One review of Abbie Mitchell's performance of Price's concert spiritual "My Soul's Been Anchored in the Lord," for instance, praised Price's music as "rhythmically interesting" and lauded Mitchell's "velvety" voice, "splendid diction and legato," and dignified stage presence.[37] Another critic commended Mitchell for her decision to sing the music of Price and other Black composers such as Hall Johnson and Camille Nickerson, which was "representative of our own efforts," rather than relying on a stale canon of European art song.[38] Such performances ensured that Price's music would remain alive and dynamic, regardless of the uneven progress of desegregation and thanks to the efforts of African American performers.

The Black Press Revises the Record

The year 1933 would not be the last time that Price was described as a pioneer, "first," or history-maker; nor did other Black composers escape this stultifying terminology. The early 1930s saw a flurry of notable premieres of symphonic and operatic works by Black composers, including William Grant Still's Symphony No. 1, "Afro-American," premiered in 1931 by the Rochester Philharmonic Orchestra; Shirley Graham's opera *Tom-Tom*, premiered in 1932 by the Cleveland Stadium Opera Company; and William Levi Dawson's *Negro Folk Symphony*, premiered in 1934 by the Philadelphia Orchestra. The pattern was clear. Each time a Black composer's work was taken up by a predominantly white institution, it was presumed to be new, unprecedented, or pioneering. This characterization framed Black composers as perpetual outsiders to the (white, Eurocentric) tradition of Western art music, and obscured the anchoring Black formalist traditions in which they worked.

The Black press became a medium through which African American writers and artists could correct the record. In 1934, a brief item in the *Philadelphia Tribune* pointedly noted that William Levi Dawson's recently premiered *Negro Folk Symphony* was not *sui generis*, but rather one in a genre of "racial symphonic literature" that included the prior compositions of William Grant Still and Price.[39] Shirley Graham made a similar claim in her article "Spirituals to Symphonies" in *Etude*, noting that "Dawson's is the third symphony by a Negro, which in the last four years has been played by a reputable orchestra in this country. And one of these symphonists is a woman! Florence B. Price."[40] Notably, Graham refused to subsume Price into the gender-nonspecific category of "African American composers," remaining attentive to the particular structural barriers she faced as a Black woman. The *Defender* followed suit: Perhaps due to the increased visibility of prominent male figures like Still and Dawson, by the late 1930s the newspaper described Price not simply as a "dean of Negro composers," but rather as the "foremost woman composer of the Race."[41] Yet, while Graham's invocation of gender served to emphasize the specificity of Price's accomplishments, the *Defender*'s framing had a different effect, seeming to diminish Price's stature in order to make room for Dawson and Still.

A parallel discursive thread connected Price to Marian Anderson, who often programmed Price's concert spirituals. As Anderson became a global phenomenon during the 1930s, Price's name was often invoked in connection with Anderson's extraordinary talent. One rapturous review linked Anderson's "magnificent voice" to "our own Florence B. Price";[42] another admired Anderson's "amazingly wide range, her unmatched ability in singing sustained high notes in such numbers as Verdi's 'O don fatale' or Florence Price's 'My soul's been anchored in the Lord.'"[43] Through Anderson's voice, Price's music reached the White House, performed in front of the president and the queen of England; and, most famously, the Lincoln Memorial, performed in front of the largest crowds the National Mall had ever seen.

The Black press also continued to emphasize Price's indebtedness to, and involvement in, Black musical institutions, especially NANM. Critic Orrin Suthern observed in 1940 that for Price, along with Anderson, Dawson, and others, "the N.A.N.M. has been the means of their being heard in the artistically sympathetic halls of the leading institutions of music."[44] Other vital sources of financial and logistical support were less reliable. The dissolution of the Wanamaker contest in 1935, for instance, cut out a vital funding source for African American composers, prompting Maude Roberts George to state plainly, "If colored American composers are to reach the heights they should, greater financial encouragement is necessary."[45] Such commentary was an important reminder that Black associational life continued to create the conditions under which individualized achievement was possible.

The press also documented how Price's music circulated beyond the context of attention-grabbing performances by mainstream institutions. Performances of her music occurred among Black musical groups and recitalists in Chicago on a near-constant basis throughout the 1930s and early 1940s, with practically every issue of the *Defender* mentioning a piece by Price to be programmed in an upcoming concert. Often, these performances occurred within celebrations of Black musical composition writ large, as when the esteemed actress and singer Etta Moten (who was, notably, married to Claude Barnett, founder of the Associated Negro Press) included Price's music on an "all race program" in Philadelphia in 1939.[46] The press also documented instances in which Price's compositions traveled further afield: A ten-year-old Bernice Johnson played her piano music in recital in Pittsburgh in 1934, for instance, as did another ten-year-old, Alice Ann Walker, in 1944.[47] The image of Price's music being performed by children offers a poignant example of how generations of African American musicians worked to sustain and preserve her music through performance, even alongside a constant struggle for institutional recognition.[48]

It is also worth considering which elements of Price's life and work remained largely out of sight, despite such varied and extensive coverage of her work. She was regularly described as "retiring" and "modest," terms which suggested a certain reluctance to engage in public life, even a strategic opacity. Indeed, her private life – both its more tumultuous aspects, such as her abusive marriage and financial precarity, and its happier elements, like her enduring friendship with Estella Bonds – is virtually absent from the press, beyond these flattering but imprecise descriptors. Curiously, these absences work against the exceptionalizing force of much of Price's critical reception, placing her firmly in the category of respectable "race woman" and hiding any elements of her biography or personality that might undermine that definition. This absence suggests an important limitation of the Black press, and the *Defender* in particular, as institutions with generally conservative gender politics and deep investments in the politics of respectability.

In the later years of her life, Price was often invoked as a predecessor of other notable figures in Black musical life. For instance, when Dorothy Maynor debuted as the first Black woman to appear as vocal soloist with the Chicago Symphony in 1940, the *Defender* alluded to the ensemble's performance of Price's music just seven years before, and noted the composer herself was in the audience to observe the occasion in which "another star has risen in our firmament."[49] A local Chicago branch of NANM, the Florence B. Price Music Study Guild, was named in her honor. At an event sponsored by the Women's Committee of Chicago, Price interviewed the "young Chicago composer" Janice Johnson in her capacity as "dean of American women composers"; the event attracted such illustrious guests as the novelist and poet Gwendolyn Brooks, who reportedly "praised the two composers."[50] In 1948, an extensive event in Price's honor was organized, consisting of an "entire program covering her major works."[51]

Such accolades were well deserved, yet they did not mean Price's reputation was secure. Like Maude Roberts George, who had long advocated for the financial support of Black composers, critic Nora Holt reminded readers in 1948 that the fight for recognition required continued vigilance. "There has been, we admit, a step-up in bringing Negro composers' work to public hearings," Holt acknowledged, "but not half what they deserve." Price was a prime example: a figure who ultimately had received "not nearly enough attention and encouragement," even as she had outpaced many other aspiring artists in finding opportunities for the hearing of her work.[52] Holt's words were an important reminder that while "firsts" like the CSO premiere of Price's symphony were worth celebrating, they were not necessarily harbingers of systemic transformation or enduring change. That would require more sustained investments of "attention and encouragement," as well as financial support, in Black composers' careers.

Conclusion: Music Criticism and Coverage as Archive

As Price's music has received renewed attention in the twenty-first century, recent media coverage has tended to frame her as a singular figure: the only significant Black woman composer of her era, a lone fighter struggling against the racism and sexism of major musical institutions.[53] Yet this narrative obscures fundamental elements of her life and work. Attention to Price's critical reception reveals a more nuanced story: one which emphasizes both the intensity of her individual striving and the consistency of the communal support that she enjoyed. The Black press offers a vibrant repository of information about the granular details of Price's career: the prizes she won, the recitals at which her music was heard, the concerts she performed in, and so on. Even more crucially, though, the press generates analytical insights about Price's discursive and material relationships to broader artistic communities. Characterized as an unparalleled figure who nevertheless maintained deep roots in Black associational life, the Price of the press refuses one-dimensional representation.

The Black press also offers compelling evidence of how Price was remembered and honored in the years after her passing. The *Defender* published detailed accounts of performances of Price's music, as well as biographical information about her compositional career, regularly during the second half of the twentieth century. In 1963, the newspaper covered the opening of an elementary school named in Price's honor; a 1971 article previewed an upcoming performance of chamber music by Price and praised her as a figure who "vindicated the artistic right to pursue areas of classical styles."[54] In 1988, the paper noted that the Van Nir Chamber Orchestra was to perform Price's Symphony in E Minor in honor of the centennial of her birth.[55] At least in the pages of the *Defender*, then, Price was never a forgotten figure. This abundant archive pushes back against the now prevalent idea that Price is a "lost," "neglected," or "rediscovered" composer. These characterizations do a disservice not only to Price herself, but also to the figures who sustained and supported her during her lifetime – including the myriad critics and journalists who documented her work. In erasing the role of those networks, such coverage risks perpetuating a white savior narrative in which Price is rescued from obscurity by the contemporary musical mainstream. A consideration of past press coverage, then, can be cautionary as well as instructive. Criticism continues to be a vital mode of making meaning from and out of Florence B. Price, and the ethics of this coverage will continue to shape the reception of her work.

Notes

1. "Evanti Praises Woman Composer," *Pittsburgh Courier*, October 13, 1934.
2. Samantha Ege, "Composing a Symphonist: Florence Price and the Hand of Black Women's Fellowship," *Women and Music* 24 (2020): 7. See also Rae Linda Brown, *The Heart of a Woman: The Life and Music of Florence B. Price* (Urbana: University of Illinois Press, 2020); A. Kori Hill, "Florence Price and the Self-Determinist Mission of the National Association of Negro Musicians," paper presented at the American Musicological Society Annual Conference, November 12, 2021.
3. Anna Everett, *Returning the Gaze: A Genealogy of Black Film Criticism, 1909–1949* (Durham, NC: Duke University Press, 2001), 2.
4. Elizabeth McHenry, *Forgotten Readers: Recovering the Lost History of African American Literary Societies* (Durham, NC: Duke University Press, 2002), 85–137.
5. Nora Douglas Holt, "Music," *Chicago Defender*, November 13, 1920.
6. Cleota Collins, "The Practice Period," *Music and Poetry* (June 1921) and "The Singer's Health," *Music and Poetry* (May 1921), James Weldon Johnson Memorial Collection of African American Arts and Letters, Beinecke Rare Book & Manuscript Library, Yale University.
7. Brown, *The Heart of a Woman*, 22. Brown also notes the importance of the press as a characteristic of the Little Rock environment.
8. "Personal," *Indianapolis Freeman*, January 5, 1889.
9. See Brown, *The Heart of a Woman*, 27.
10. "The Race's Doings," *Cleveland Gazette*, March 9, 1889.
11. Josephine Wright, "Black Women in Classical Music in Boston during the Late Nineteenth Century: Profiles of Leadership," in *New Perspectives on Music: Essays in Honor of Eileen Southern*, edited by Josephine Wright with Samuel A. Floyd, Jr. (Warren, MI: Harmonie Park Press, 2003).
12. Several of Hopkins's colleagues at the *Colored American Magazine*, including managing editor Walter Wallace and treasurer Harper S. Fortune, also came to the publication following prior careers as musicians. R. S. Elliott, "The Story of Our Magazine," *Colored American Magazine* (May 1901): 45–46.
13. On Hopkins's music journalism, see Daphne A. Brooks, *Liner Notes for the Revolution: The Intellectual Life of Black Feminist Sound* (Cambridge, MA: Harvard University Press, 2021), 83–89.
14. John E. Bush, "Afro-American People of Little Rock," *Colored American Magazine* (January 1905): 41.
15. See "Mrs. Price Returns Home," *Chicago Defender*, September 7, 1918.
16. "Contest Awards," *Opportunity: Journal of Negro Life* 4 (May 1926): 156; "The Contest Spotlight," *Opportunity: Journal of Negro Life* 5 (July 1927): 209.
17. "The Contest Spotlight," *Opportunity: Journal of Negro Life* 5 (July 1927): 205, 209.

18. Imani Perry, *May We Forever Stand: A History of the Black National Anthem* (Chapel Hill: University of North Carolina Press, 2018), 6–8.
19. As A. Kori Hill has noted, this membership was particularly meaningful given that Price had been denied entrance to the Arkansas Music Teachers Association on segregationist grounds around the same time. See Hill, "Florence Price and the Self-Determinist Mission."
20. "Wanamaker Offers Cash for Prize Musical Compositions," *Chicago Defender*, March 26, 1932.
21. Maude Roberts George, "News of the Music World," *Chicago Defender*, October 1, 1932.
22. Maude Roberts George, "News of the Music World," *Chicago Defender*, October 8, 1932; Maude Roberts George, "News of the Music World," *Chicago Defender*, October 15, 1932.
23. Maude Roberts George, "News of the Music World," *Chicago Defender*, October 15, 1932.
24. Maude Roberts George, "News of the Music World," *Chicago Defender*, March 25, 1933.
25. Maude Roberts George, "News of the Music World," *Chicago Defender*, November 5, 1932.
26. Helen Walker-Hill, "Black Women Composers in Chicago: Then and Now," *Black Music Research Journal* 12, no. 1 (1992): 11.
27. Maude Roberts George, "News of the Music World," *Chicago Defender*, April 22, 1933.
28. Perry, *May We Forever Stand*, 12.
29. See, for example, Maude Roberts George, "News of the Music World," *Chicago Defender*, September 9, 1933. Rae Linda Brown notes that the term "dean of composers of the Middle West" was first used in the *Defender* in 1935. Brown, *The Heart of a Woman*, 237.
30. "Woman's Symphony Heard At Fair," *Baltimore Afro-American*, July 1, 1933.
31. Edward Moore, "City Assured Symphony Season of 28 Weeks for Next Winter," *Chicago Daily Tribune*, June 16, 1933.
32. Untitled review, *Winnetka Talk*, June 16, 1933.
33. [Robert Abbott], "The Week," *Chicago Defender*, June 24, 1933. The column is unsigned, but Rae Linda Brown surmises that Abbott was the author.
34. Nahum Daniel Brascher, "Roland Hayes Concert Shows Progress of Race in Music," *Chicago Defender*, June 24, 1933.
35. See Ege, "Composing a Symphonist," 25. See also "Barbara Wright-Pryor: 'Maude Roberts George . . . President of CMA of Which Price Was a Member, Underwrote the Cost of the June 15, 1933 Concert," *Africlassical*, April 7, 2014, https://africlassical.blogspot.com/2014/04/barbara-wright-pryor-maude-roberts.html.
36. Brown, *The Heart of a Woman*, 117.

37. Carl Diton, "Abbie Mitchell Scores Again in N.Y. Recital," *Pittsburgh Courier*, December 5, 1931.
38. Maude Roberts George, "Abbie Mitchell Wins High Praise in Song Recital Here," *Chicago Defender*, November 7, 1931.
39. "Negroes Have Symphonic Literature," *Philadelphia Tribune*, December 6, 1934.
40. Shirley Graham, "Spirituals to Symphonies," *Etude* 54, no. 5 (1936): 692.
41. Lena Caillout, "Music Notes," *Chicago Defender*, June 10, 1939.
42. Neota McCurdy Dyett, "Miss Anderson Sensational in Chicago Recital," *Chicago Defender*, February 1, 1936.
43. Richard Bowling, "The World's Marian," *New Journal and Guide*, January 25, 1936.
44. Orrin Suthern, "Musical Elite Has Opportunity to Hear Artistry of Own Race," *New Journal and Guide*, August 17, 1940.
45. "Sepia Composers in Need of Funds," *Atlanta Daily World*, August 27, 1935.
46. "Singer Will Popularize Race Music," *Chicago Defender*, February 4, 1939.
47. "Child Prodigy in Recital," *Pittsburgh Courier*, June 16, 1934; "Child Pianist is Highly Acclaimed," *Chicago Defender*, February 26, 1944.
48. In 1942, a selection of Price's piano compositions appeared in the *Oxford Piano Course*, ensuring that her music would reach a wide range of students. See Brown, *The Heart of a Woman*, 180.
49. Grace Tompkins, "Dorothy Maynor Given Ovation in Chicago Debut at Orchestra Hall," *Chicago Defender*, April 13, 1940.
50. "Civic Group Entertains Two Noted Women Composers," *Chicago Defender*, August 24, 1946.
51. "Local Artist to Honor Florence B. Price," *Chicago Defender*, April 3, 1948.
52. Nora Holt, "Music," *New York Amsterdam News*, June 12, 1948.
53. See, for example, Micaela Baranello, "Welcoming a Black Female Composer into the Canon. Finally," *New York Times*, February 9, 2018; or Alex Ross, "New World: The Rediscovery of Florence Price," *The New Yorker*, January 29, 2018. While the content of these articles tells a more nuanced story, the headlines tellingly emphasize the atypicality of Price's work.
54. "Children to Participate in Rites for New School," *Chicago Defender*, April 2, 1963; Earl Calloway, "Florence B. Price Works Featured," *Chicago Defender*, February 4, 1971.
55. Earl Calloway, "Soprano Sharon Hamilton Is Guest for Florence B. Price Anniversary," *Chicago Defender*, October 22, 1988.

14 | When Things Don't Fall Apart: The Myth of Black Cultural Rediscovery and the Afterlife of Florence Price

TAMMY L. KERNODLE

> Things don't fall apart. Things hold. Lines connect in thin ways that last and last, and lives become generations made out of pictures and words just kept.
>
> —Lucille Clifton[1]

> The "rediscovered" Black composer is a tired, damaging trope. It reflects an active process, where certain histories and cultural memories are not considered "relevant" to the mainstream until they prove useful. Black musicians kept the name of Florence Price on their lips, in their minds, and under their fingers. She was not forgotten.
>
> —Alexandra Kori Hill[2]

In the summer of 2020, while in the throes of a global pandemic, the world witnessed the violent death of George Floyd. His death, along with the deaths of Breonna Taylor and Ahmaud Arbery, reawakened the Black Lives Matter movement and ignited a wave of racial and social consciousness that prompted many arts-based organizations to consider the larger implications of their programmatic visions. A number of orchestras, opera companies, and other arts-based organizations moved with greater deliberation in offering more inclusive programming to their audiences and constituents, believing that they had a responsibility to stimulate racial understanding.[3] This period of social action and social consciousness intertwined with a range of intellectual activity that surrounded the music of Florence Price.

Only a few years earlier, Price was being heralded as the "first woman to enter the canon" as mainstream media outlets published articles that outlined her achievements, chronicled the gender and racial politics she navigated, and spotlighted her vast oeuvre. There are two problematic tropes that began to emerge around Florence Price. The first is that of the "exceptional woman." Although generally used as a framework to explain the exclusion of women musicians in jazz, the trope of the exceptional woman underscores the way Price is characterized within the classical music narrative.⁴

Her achievements are not used as a means of illuminating Black female intellectual and cultural labor, but become the rationale for excluding other women composers and musicians. As the work of Samantha Ege, Rae Linda Brown, Helen Walker-Hill, and others have illuminated, Florence Price was part of a larger community of Black women composers and musicians that not only defined the Chicago Renaissance but informed the progression of the Black classical aesthetic during the second half of the twentieth century. Florence Price did not work in a context of gendered isolation and the perpetuation of her as classical music's equivalent of the exceptional woman has supported the culture of invisibility in America's concert halls.⁵

The second, and more troubling, trope in this scripting of Price's legacy in the twenty-first century is the characterization of the ascendance of Price's music onto the global stage through the analytical lens and dyadic terminology of discovery/rediscovery.⁶ The origins of this discovery/rediscovery narrative can be traced back to 2009, when unpublished and personal ephemera believed to have been lost were recovered from an abandoned home in St. Anne, Illinois. Their subsequent addition to the Florence Price Collection housed at the University of Arkansas in Fayetteville generated premiere performances, recordings, performance editions, and new scholarship that marked the beginning of a new Black music epoch or, as scholars Samantha Ege and Douglas W. Shadle recently asserted, a "Florence Price Renaissance."⁷ The idea of a Price Renaissance raises several questions. How do we define this era? Where does the Price Renaissance begin? What language is appropriate in characterizing it?

Many consider 2018 as the beginning of this era due to some key events. First, music publisher G. Schirmer acquired exclusive worldwide rights to the Price catalog, and several recordings of Price's music were released, including one that featured the violin concertos recovered in 2009. Secondly, new scholarly insights on Price's life and music were disseminated through blogs, social media threads, and conferences/symposiums like the three-day celebration at the University of Arkansas, Fayetteville. Despite the global pandemic in 2020, the work did not dissipate. It gained momentum with the release of the late Rae Linda Brown's highly anticipated biography of Florence Price, *The Heart of a Woman: The Life and Music of Florence B. Price*, and the launching of the International Florence Price Festival. Indeed, the afterlife of Florence Price and her music had entered a new stage. But was this intellectual labor one that symbolized cultural rediscovery, or was this part of a larger continuum of activity whose roots extended back to Price's death in 1953?

The notion of discovery/rediscovery that is used to characterize the integration of historically neglected composers in the mainstream classical infrastructure perpetuates a myth of Black cultural discovery that is rooted not only in the "othering" of those composers, but also the negation of a history of cultural engagement that took place outside of the hierarchy of concert halls and performing aggregations that frame America's concert idiom. This mythology not only reflects the supremacy of the classical infrastructure, but is often anchored in the raising of territorial flags of expertise amongst scholars, conductors, and musicians. Historically neglected composers and their music become the equivalent of intellectual provincial outposts destined to be mined for their material wealth. I believe the mythology of cultural rediscovery can be challenged through the documenting of the grassroot intellectual labor that surrounds these composers and their music.

As the Hill epigraph above asserts, Florence Price remained on the lips, minds, and under the fingers of Black musicians long after her death and long before the wave of renewed interest.[8] The afterlife of Price's music was defined by a culture of curation, preservation, and advocacy undertaken by a series of intersecting music ecosystems comprised of composers, educators, scholars, librarians, and musicians. It did not fall into a sphere of cultural obscurity, but lived through a type of "shadow culture," which was rooted in a praxis of manuscript/score sharing that instigated the formation and promotion of a counter canon. The circulation of unpublished, and sometimes published, scores amongst musicians and educators led to the formation of large personal collections that birthed the earliest wave of scholarship on Price and provided deeper understanding of what can be characterized as the "lost" performance history of her oeuvre.

Although not discussed extensively in this chapter, one of the earliest examples of this type of music ecosystem was centered in Chicago and consisted of a collective of musicians and organizations that Price engaged with during her lifetime. Evidence of their curation and advocacy of Price's music following her death is detailed in newspaper accounts, concert programs, and conference proceedings that reference Chicago-area churches and organizations such as the Illinois Federation of Music Clubs, the Chicago Club of Women Organists, and the National Association of Negro Musicians.[9] Music ecosystems such as this one, and their promotion of selected repertoires, formed what scholar Marcia J. Citron describes as a "counter canon" consisting of works of Price as well as other Black and women composers.[10] These counter canons tended to reject the hierarchization of genre that underscored the Western European canon, and reveal the functionality of various repertoires with community-based settings. Solo and chamber repertoire were deemed just as important as larger orchestral works. As a result, a standard repertoire of works formed and was promoted through regional and national infrastructures that consisted of community-based conservatories, regional orchestras, cultural centers, churches, and music departments at Predominately White Institutions (PWI) and Historically Black Colleges and Universities (HBCU). This chapter seeks to unmask this shadow culture as it illuminates the connective threads described in the Clifton epigraph that link the work of the Black and feminist music intelligentsias that emerged during the height of the Black Power and Women's Movements to the current wave of cultural work on Florence Price. In doing so, it challenges the mythology of Black intellectual discovery that frames Price's integration into the canon and the afterlife of her music.

The Mid-Century Black Civil Rights Movement and the Birth of the Music Intelligentsia

To understand the culture of advocacy and preservation that defines the afterlife of Florence Price, we must first consider how significant changes in America's social and political terrain during the mid to late 1960s birthed a new wave of Black intellectual culture. Much of this change was instigated by the emergence of the mid-century Black civil rights movement. However, as the movement progressed into the next decade, its identity and strategy of activism shifted from assimilationist politics to direct action, nonviolent resistance. This transition was initiated by Black and white college students, who coalited under the organizational banners of CORE (Congress on Racial Equality) and SNCC (Student Nonviolent Coordinating Committee). Their engagement in embodied resistance (e.g., sit-ins, pray-ins, Freedom Rides) and promotion of movement culture (e.g., protest music, plays, poetry, photography) propelled the movement onto the global stage. However, by 1965 that coalition had begun to splinter. The rift was precipitated by several factors, which ranged from the increasing influence of Black nationalist ideology in movement organizations, to growing disillusionment with the notion of nonviolent resistance as the violence directed at the movement grew, to increasing dissent with US policies and the advancing war in Vietnam.

Equipped with experience in building organizational infrastructures of resistance and mass mobilization, many of the young activists who departed the Black civil rights struggle formed new, variant social movements (e.g., anti-war movement, women's movement, gay liberation movement), whose cultural impact can still be felt. In the late 1960s and early 1970s the influence of these movements extended to the institutional epicenter of American postwar intellectualism – the liberal arts college/ university. By 1966, calls for a radical restructuring of cultural and intellectual institutions, especially colleges and universities, pervaded the rhetoric of movement leaders, community activists, and public intellectuals.

As an incubator for social consciousness movements and ideologies of social change, the American college/university became the battleground for inclusivity, diversity, and social change. As a result, courses on race, gender, and sexuality began to enter discussions of college curriculums. The offering of these courses, and the subsequent creation of related programs of study and departments, fueled bodies of related scholarship that became the foundation of the disciplinary fields of race, gender, and ethnic studies. By the 1980s, the intersection of this wave of Black and feminist intellectual activity had given birth to the first wave of scholarship on Florence Price.

The work of this generation of intellectuals was fueled in part by Lyndon B. Johnson's establishment of the National Endowment for the Arts (NEA) and National Endowment for the Humanities (NEH) in 1968. The initiation of Black studies and women's studies courses extended to larger discussions about pedagogy and to the building of historiography. These conversations extended beyond the fields of political science, history, and literature as scholarly communities began to strategize as to how these modes of inquiry could apply to other disciplines. In the months that followed the assassination of Dr. Martin Luther King, Jr., these conversations spawned the first iterations of Black music studies and feminist studies in music. Both extended from collectives of educators, composers, conductors, musicians, librarians, and historians who, through seminars, workshops, publications, and organizations, advanced these subdisciplines. Both sought to establish these disciplines as a field of serious inquiry, advance pedagogical approaches that could be implemented at the secondary and college levels, and train the next generation of scholars/educators. Symposiums, workshops, and conferences were important in centralizing these goals.

The modern iteration of the Black music symposium evolved out of the personal and professional experiences of music librarian Dominique-René de Lerma, who, in the hours that followed the assassination of King, was unable to name or locate repertoire written by a Black composer that could be performed at a memorial service on the campus of Indiana University. The impact of this moment stretched beyond de Lerma's personal recognition of the bias that had framed his training and education, as it pointed to the paucity of material culture related to Black music that was cataloged in the university's library.[11] As a result, de Lerma organized a Black music committee, which convened a seminar called "Black Music in College and University Curricula" during the summer of 1969.

Over the course of three days, participants attended roundtable discussions, scholarly presentations, and concert performances that focused on both concert and popular forms of Black music. The event proved to be so popular that the program format would serve as the standard template for future Black music symposiums/conferences.[12] The collective of individuals who gathered at Indiana University in 1969 morphed into larger social and professional networks that extended the cultural and geographic scope of this work. In time, this activity was filtered through and supported by an intellectual infrastructure that came to include the following:

1. Professional organizations such as the National Black Music Caucus, National Association for the Study and Performance of African American Music (NASPAAM), and the Afro American Music Opportunities Association (AAMOA)
2. Black music centers and archives on the campuses of HBCUs like Virginia State College (Black Music Center), Howard University (Center for Ethnic Music), and Fisk (Center for Black Music Research) and PWIs such as Columbia College (Center for Black Music Research) and Indiana University (Black Music Archives)
3. The journals *The Black Perspective in Music* and *The Black Music Research Journal* and a Black music series distributed through Greenwood Press, which included bibliographies, discographies, and encyclopedias focused on Black music and musicians
4. Performing aggregations like the Symphony of the New World, VIDEMUS, and the New Black Music Repertory Ensemble, as well as an array of regional and college-based ensembles.

While a full examination of how this iteration of the Black music intelligentsia engaged historically with Price's music cannot be done in this setting, there were some relevant moments that provide insight into how these symposiums helped shape the afterlife of her music.

Florence Price and the Modern Black Music Symposium

Between 1976 and 1986 there were three symposiums that either focused specifically on Price's music or featured it prominently. Two took place at Clark College in Atlanta (1976, 1986) and the other at the University of Michigan (1985). The conferences held at Clark College (now Clark Atlanta University) are particularly noteworthy given Price's personal history with the institution. She joined the music faculty as head of the music department in 1910, and during the two years she spent there the scope of the music curriculum and the musical life of the campus grew exponentially.[13] Like many of her peers, Price's teaching stints at Black colleges during her early career offered some financial stability, but also access to a musical ecosystem that included institution-based and community-based ensembles. Dominique-René de Lerma noted that in addition to recitals and concerts offered through the music department, some HBCU ensembles also made recordings of the works of Black composers. An early example of this in relation to Florence Price is Morgan State College Band's recording of an arrangement of *Three Little Negro Dances* in the 1950s.[14]

In the case of Clark College, the legacy of Price's advocacy in relation to Black music was exemplified in the 1970s with the establishment of a series of annual workshops that included faculty and students from the music department of the five HBCUs connected through the Atlanta University Center (Clark College, Morris Brown College, Morehouse College, Spelman College, Atlanta University) and the Center for African and African American Studies at Atlanta University.

These workshops ran from 1971 until the early 1990s and ranged in theme and focus. Most centered on the musical contributions of selected Black musicians or specific repertoire – as was the case with the 1973 workshop, which featured a performance of George Gershwin's *Porgy and Bess* that included the Atlanta Symphony Orchestra. Outside of public concerts that coupled guest artists with student musicians selected from each of the consortium colleges, workshop participants also navigated a program that consisted of research presentations and panel discussions. These workshops/symposiums were the brainchild of Drs. Richard A. Long (1927–2013) and Florence Crim Robinson (d. 2008) and reflected their desire to elevate Black history and the Black arts through the Atlanta University Center.

Florence Crim Robinson joined the faculty of Clark's music department in 1971. During her twenty-seven-year tenure she taught piano, but also served as chair of the department and associate dean for Arts and Humanities. An accomplished pianist and accompanist, Robinson earned national distinction as one of the first Black music teachers featured prominently on television. She wrote and hosted several syndicated radio programs, including the "Florence Robinson Show" for the Plough Radio Network and "The Many Sides of Black Music," which was sponsored by the Carnation Corporation. She was also the host of a PBS television special entitled "The Music of Black Composers," which featured the Dallas Symphony Orchestra.[15]

Richard A. Long was a cultural historian who taught at several Black colleges before joining the faculty of Atlanta University in 1968. During his tenure at Atlanta, he taught English and also founded the Center for African and African American Studies (CAAS). The latter tied directly into his scholarly interests in Black traditional dance practices and African art. Through the CAAS, Long organized a series of symposia and workshops that celebrated and promoted all forms of Black art. This was exemplified through his organization of the inaugural Triennial Symposium of African Art in 1968 and later through the launching of the annual conference on African and American Studies, which ran from 1968 until 1987.[16] Extant evidence reveals that the intellectual footprint of the annual conference was widened through the offering of smaller disciplinary workshops. This may account for the initiation of the series of annual workshops on Black music that were also sponsored during this period.

In 1976, Long, Robinson, and Harriette W. Bell, another faculty member at Atlanta University, coordinated the two-day workshop titled "The Role of Black Women in Music," which focused on the life and music of composers Florence Price, Margaret Bonds, Julia Perry, and Dorothy Rudd Moore. In addition to research presentations that outlined their individual contributions to American music, the conference program included a concert that featured selected repertoire from each composer. While the research and scholarly aspects of the program were presented, the concert was canceled due to the unexpected death of Dr. Vivian Henderson, president of Clark College.[17]

A decade later, Robinson organized another workshop, which focused solely on Florence Price. Characterized as a "recital/workshop," this 1985 event included performances by mezzo-soprano Roberta Bowers, baritone Mark Anthony Moore, pianist Mark Boozer, and organist James Jones. In addition to Price's vocal and organ works, the main concert also featured a performance of the two-piano version of the Concerto in One Movement with Florence Robinson as one of the performers.[18]

Price's music also figured significantly in the cultural life of predominantly white universities. Much as in the case of the musical life of HBCUs, this was reflected in a myriad of ways – from performances of repertoire by ensembles to the integration of scholarly research in music appreciation and/or musicology courses. Both were exemplified in the cultural work of Neumon Leighton, a white vocal instructor at Memphis State University (now the University of Memphis), who developed a close friendship with Price and championed her music through his public lectures. Born in Cotton Plant, Arkansas, in 1905, Leighton had a personal interest in Black musicians and composers.

According to scholar Mildred Denby Green, Florence Price met Leighton during one of his public lectures, and "as their friendship grew, he began focusing his talks on her works. When she accompanied him to his lectures, he introduced her at the close of the sessions." During his tenure as an instructor at Memphis State, Leighton promoted Price's art songs through student recitals. His knowledge of Price's catalog and his close relationship with the family provided much-needed information for the first generation of Price scholars who began researching the composer's life in the 1970s.[19] The promotion of Price's music at predominantly white institutions was not undertaken by white musicians/educators only, as the late 1960s and early 1970s marked a period in which a generation of Black musicians and composers joined the faculties of these institutions. Willis Patterson's work at the University of Michigan is emblematic of this phenomenon.

Acclaimed as a bass-baritone soloist, Willis Patterson (1930–2025) joined the voice faculty at the University of Michigan in 1968 after teaching stints at Southern University and Virginia State College (now University). A year later, he founded the Willis C. Patterson Our Own Thing Chorale and became the director of the University of Michigan Men's Glee Club. He also transitioned into various administrative roles within the School of Music and served in leadership roles with the National Black Music Caucus and the National Association of Negro Musicians. However, Patterson's contributions to the shaping of the afterlife of Florence Price's music can be measured through the *Anthology of Art Songs by Black Composers* and his organization of the landmark Black American Music Symposium at the University of Michigan in 1985.

Published in 1977, the *Anthology of Art Songs by Black Composers* embodied Patterson's vision to provide a resource for teachers while simultaneously preserving Black art song repertoire. Price's "Night" and "Songs to the Dark Virgin" were included in the anthology, which by 1981 was augmented to include recording performances featuring vocal students at the University of Michigan and noted musicians George Shirley, Hilda Harris, and Laura English-Robinson. The publication was the first in a series of anthologies that featured the work of contemporary composers alongside pioneering composers such as Price, William Grant Still, and Harry T. Burleigh.

The Black American Music Symposium convened by Patterson at the University of Michigan on August 9–15, 1985, was unprecedented. It featured seventeen panels, four formal lectures, ten formal recitals, seven chamber music recitals, and a final banquet that brought community partners, scholars, performers, teachers, conductors, and industry figures together to discuss the progress that had been made in advancing Black music studies in the intervening years since the first seminar at Indiana University in 1969.[20] Patterson would later describe the event as "the most ambitious and potentially significant series of discussions and performances – designed to emphasize the vitality and importance of the contributions of black American musicians to the musical/cultural development of our country – which has ever been attempted."[21]

Price's music was programmed throughout the conference. A chamber music concert devoted to the works of Black women composers featured a performance of the song "Seagulls," while *In Quiet Mood* was performed during the concert devoted to organ music. Price's *Dance Suite* opened an orchestral concert that included T. J. Anderson's *In Memoriam (Malcolm X)*, Morris Lawrence's *Jazz Trilogy* and Hale Smith's *Mediation in Passage*. Lastly, pianist Althea Waites, who produced the first recording of Price's piano works, closed a concert highlighting the piano works of Black composers with the Sonata in E Minor for solo piano.[22]

Florence Price was also discussed during the many different research presentations and roundtables that took place. These sessions are important in documenting the emergence of the first wave of Price scholarship during the late 1970s and 1980s. Scholars Mildred Denby Green (1938–2019) and Rae Linda Brown (1953–2017) were featured prominently during two sessions dedicated to Black women composers and musicians. Brown, a PhD candidate at Yale at the time, was in the process of completing her dissertation on Price's orchestral works. Green's research, however, drew from her 1983 book, *Black Women Composers: A Genesis*, which consisted of a larger analytical discussion of selected works by Florence Price, Margaret Bonds, Julia Perry, Evelyn Pittman, and Lena McLin. The archival and ethnographic research of Brown and Green, along with that conducted by Barbara Garvey Jackson (who was not in attendance at the

1985 symposium), laid the groundwork for more robust scholarly discussions of Price's life and career, aided in advancing the programming of Price's music, and expanded the scope of the earliest wave of feminist music studies to include the work of Black women composers.

Florence Price and the Feminist Music Intelligentsia

The subdiscipline of feminist music studies evolved out of the expanding theoretical lens of women's studies during the 1980s. Its intellectual footprint was defined by a focus on advanced professional opportunities for women musicians and conductors, championing the music of women composers, and creating a body of scholarship that centered on the contribution of women composers and musicians. Much like its mother discipline, feminist music studies was represented through both institutional and grassroot entities, which created an infrastructure that included organizations like the International Congress on Women in Music, the International League of Women Composers, and the National Federation of Women's Clubs; festivals/conferences such as the National Congress on Women in Music; and performance aggregations like the New England Women's Symphony (NEWS) and the Bay Area Women's Philharmonic, which later became known as The Women's Philharmonic.

As scholars have documented, the earliest form of feminist musicology focused primarily on European and white American women composers and musicians.[23] However, by the 1980s the music and achievements of Black women composers/musicians, most notably Florence Price, began to enter these intellectual conversations. The study of Price's life and music grew exponentially during the late 1970s and early 1980s, as evidenced first in two early dissertations that focused on her music: Raymond Jackson's "The Evolution of Piano Music as Seen in the Works of Four Black Composers" (1973, Julliard) and Mildred Denby Green's "A Study of the Lives and Works of Five Black Women Composers in America" (1975, University of Oklahoma). Green's work is particularly relevant to this conversation as it became the basis of the groundbreaking monograph *Black Women Composers: A Genesis* (1983).

Mildred Denby Green was born in Portsmouth, Virginia, in 1938. After two years of study at Oberlin, she transferred to The Ohio State University, where, in 1959, she received a bachelor's degree in music education. Green went on to earn a master's and doctorate in music education from the University of Oklahoma. She and her husband Ruben Green moved to

Memphis in 1963 and joined the faculty of Owen College, a private Baptist college. Initially, Mildred Green taught music appreciation, humanities courses, and directed the choir. However, when Owen College merged with Lemoyne College in 1968, she became director of the choir and professor of music. She taught courses in the traditional areas of music study, but also taught seminars on Black women composers and Black Memphis musicians. The former drew heavily on the archival and ethnographic research she undertook in writing her dissertation and subsequent monograph *Black Women Composers: A Genesis*.

As one of the earliest book-length studies to focus solely on Black women composers/musicians, *Black Women Composers: A Genesis* outlined an intergenerational continuum of Black female intellectuality, which centered on the lives and music of composers Florence Price, Margaret Bonds, Julia Perry, Evelyn Pittman, and Lena McLin. Following a historical discussion of women's music-making in different cultural contexts, Green devoted a chapter to each composer. Biographical sketches were augmented with analysis of selected works and discussion of the markers of compositional style. The preface substantiates how the culture of manuscript/score-sharing aided in the completion of her work, citing that she "obtained selected scores from several sources, including publishers and the private collections of Carol Brice Carey, Neumon Leighton, Evelyn Pittman, Ruby Clark, Nelmatilda Ritchie Woodward, and Lawrence and Djane Richardson."[24]

The compositions featured in the discussion on Florence Price included the art songs "Songs to the Dark Virgin," *Two Traditional Negro Spirituals*, and "My Soul's Been Anchored in the Lord"; choral works "Song for Snow" and "Moon Bridge"; and the piano étude *Three Little Negro Dances*. Although this would be the only published scholarship of Green that included Florence Price, she continued to promote the music of Price and other Black women composers through the ensembles she directed over the remainder of her decades-long career.

Barbara Garvey Jackson (1929–2022) was one of a number of scholar-musicians who were significant in championing the music of Price in the composer's home state of Arkansas. Jackson received a bachelor's degree in music (violin, composition) from the University of Illinois in 1950 and continued her studies at the Eastman School of Music. After receiving a master of music degree in 1952, she pursued a doctorate in musicology at Stanford University (graduating in 1959). Jackson taught music in the Los Angeles public school system and also at Arkansas Tech before joining the music faculty at the University of Arkansas, Fayetteville (referred to as

UA hereon) in 1961.²⁵ Her scholarship stretched across disciplines, but most germane to this discussion was her interest in women composers and Black composers from Arkansas. It was through this work that Jackson began collaborating with writer/regional historian Mary Dengler Hudgins (1901–1987).

Hudgins was a graduate of the UA and worked as a librarian in her hometown of Hot Springs, Arkansas, for many years before transitioning into the world of professional writing. Through the Arkansas Historical Society, Hudgins researched extensively and wrote on the history and cultural life of Arkansas. This work extended to important musicians from the state, like William Grant Still and Florence Price. Hudgins corresponded extensively with Still and his wife Verna Arvey during the late 1960s and early 1970s. This relationship would prove to be important to her subsequent work on Florence Price, which provided the first extensive genealogical information on the composer's parents. William Grant Still also connected Hudgins with Florence Price's eldest daughter, Florence Robinson, who at one point had tried to promote her mother's music. The extant correspondence reveals that initially Hudgins attempted to work with Robinson, but that their exchanges proved to be fruitless as the two were "simply not on the same wavelength."²⁶ Hudgins in turn passed her work on Price over to Barbara Garvey Jackson, whose communication with the composer's daughters, friends, and former students yielded some biographical information on Price.

Hudgins and Jackson were significant in convincing Florence Robinson to donate her mother's papers, letters, diaries, and manuscripts to the special collections division of the university library at UA in 1974.²⁷ These materials became the basis of the Florence Price Collection, which continued to grow thanks to donations from Hudgins and other individuals who had Price ephemera. Most notable was the addition of instrumental parts of the Symphony No. 1 in E Minor created by the North Arkansas Symphony Orchestra in 1989 and materials recovered in Illinois in 2009. Both significantly contributed to interest in Price's orchestral and chamber works.

Barbara Garvey Jackson's work extended beyond the curation of the Florence Price Collection, however, as she became a strong advocate of the composer's music through her scholarship and collaborations with student musicians and regional performing groups. In 1976, she presented the first iteration of her research on the life of Florence Price during the annual meeting of the American Musicological Society (AMS). That same year, she also made a presentation at the annual convention of the Arkansas State

Music Teachers Association. Unlike the AMS presentation, this one, titled "An Arkansas Woman Composer: Florence Price (1888–1953)," included performances of selected art songs. Jackson's narration on the life and achievements of Price was accompanied by performances of "Night," "Songs to the Dark Virgin," "Fantasy in Purple," and "Out of the South Blew a Wind" by mezzo-soprano Elaine Cencel and pianist Edgar Wiley.[28]

Jackson's extensive genealogical work on Price became the basis of an article published in the journal *The Black Perspective in Music* in 1977 and an entry on Price published in *Notable Black American Women*.[29] Five years later, Jackson started the publishing company ClarNan Editions, which initially concentrated on the music of women composers from the seventeenth and eighteenth centuries but later expanded its operational vision to also include the works of Price. Although she continued to champion Price's music until her death in 2022, Jackson passed her preliminary research on the composer to Rae Linda Brown, who would emerge as the preeminent Price scholar during the 1980s and serve as one of the strongest links between the first wave of Price scholarship and the current of work of Samantha Ege, Alexandra Kori Hill, Elektra V. Carter, Douglas Shadle, Linda Holzer, and many others.

Rae Linda Brown was born in 1953 in Hartford, Connecticut, and earned a bachelor of science degree in music education from the University of Connecticut. She first encountered the music of Florence Price during her graduate studies at Yale, finding the score to Price's Symphony No. 3 in C Minor while cataloging the music located in the James Weldon Johnson Collection. This curation work became the basis of her MA thesis, "Music, Printed and Manuscript, in the James Weldon Johnson Memorial Collection of Negro Arts and Letters" (Yale, 1981), which was published as part of Greenwood Press's Critical Studies in Black Life and Culture series in 1982.

By the time Brown appeared at the 1985 Black American Music Symposium at Michigan, she was well into writing a dissertation that focused on Price's orchestral works. For over three decades, as outlined by Carlene Brown and C. E. Aaron in Chapter 2, Brown curated and edited Price's manuscripts, partnered with collectives of musicians who programmed and recorded these works, and produced some of the foundational scholarship that situated Price's role in the Negro Renaissance Movement. She worked directly with several orchestras, including The Women's Philharmonic (TWP), which in 2001 recorded three of Price's orchestral works, *The Oak*, *Mississippi River Suite*, and Symphony No. 3 in

C Minor. This album represented two decades of engagement with Price's music by The Women's Philharmonic.

Founded in 1980 by Elizabeth Seja Min, Miriam Abrams, and Nan Washburn, The Women's Philharmonic was modeled after the short-lived New England Women's Symphony. Its goals were to provided professional opportunities for women conductors and musicians and promote the music of women composers. Price's music was added to the group's repertoire as early as 1988, when *Dances in the Canebrakes*, featuring Althea Waites as soloist, was programmed (Fig. 14.1). A year later, the orchestra gave the West Coast premiere of Symphony No. 1 in E Minor (Fig. 14.2). Excerpts from this performance were featured in the award-winning radio documentary *From Spirituals to Symphony*, produced by Ernest Lamb and Ben Fry for Arkansas Public Radio in 1994. Although The Women's Philharmonic ceased to operate as an active orchestra in 2004, its advocacy of Price's music continued to underscore its reframed mission of curation and preservation.[30]

Interest in Price's music continued to grow in the last decade of the twentieth century and the first decade of the twenty-first century. It was fueled, in part, by the emergence of new anthologies such as *Art Songs and Spirituals by African American Women Composers* (1995), edited by Vivian Taylor; Helen Walker-Hill's *Black Women Composers: A Century of Piano Music 1983–1990* (1992); and recordings such as Maria Corley's *Soulscapes: Piano Music by African American Women* (2006) and the New Black Music Repertory Ensemble's 2011 recording of Symphony No. 1 in E Minor, which also featured Trevor Weston's restoration of the orchestration of the Concerto in One Movement, with Karen Walwyn as the soloist. This history of intellectual labor, while outlined in a somewhat abbreviated form here, provides some deeper understanding of what has framed the afterlife of Florence Price and her music. It also illuminates the connective fibers that link this activity to the work of the current collective of musicians, educators, and scholars that frames the Price Renaissance.

Conclusion

The term "Renaissance" is often understood to mean "rebirth" or "revival," but it also references the age or epoch of discovery and humanism that commenced in Europe during the fifteenth and sixteenth centuries. The intellectual work that defined the European Renaissance also correlated with what historians refer to as the Age of Exploration or Age of Discovery.

◆ CONCERT PROGRAM

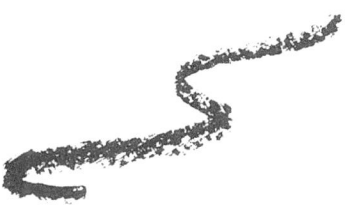

March 11, 1988
First Congregational Church
Berkeley
8:00 P.M.

Althea Waites, piano
Women's Philharmonic String Quartet
Nan Washburn, *Artistic Director*
JoAnn Falletta, *Music Director*
Miriam Abrams, *Executive Director*

Quatuor a cordes (1918)   Germaine Tailleferre
                                                                (1892-1983)

    Modere
    Intermede
    Final—vif

Suite II for Piano
and Strings (1929)   Ruth Crawford Seeger
                                                            (1901-1953)

    Lento
    Leggiero
    Allegro energico

Two Pieces for Viola and Cello (1930)   Rebecca Clark
                                                                (1886-1979)

    Lullaby
    Grotesque

                        INTERMISSION

Dances in the Canebrakes   Florence Price
                                                       (1888-1953)

    Nimble Feet
    Tropical Noon
    Silk Hat and Walking Cane
    Althea Waites, piano

Quintet in F-sharp minor, Op. 67 (1909)   Amy Cheney Beach
                                                                  (1867-1944)

    Adagio—Allegro moderato
    Adagio espressivo
    Allegro agitato

Figure 14.1 Bay Area Women's Philharmonic concert program, March 11, 1988.

It was a time when Europeans began exploring the world in search of knowledge, new trade routes, and material wealth. Their travels would significantly alter the world and render a context to the word "discovery,"

CONCERT PROGRAM

Saturday, February 11, 1989

8:00 P.M.
First Congregational Church
San Francisco

◆ JoAnn Falletta, *Music Director/Conductor*
Sharon Robinson, *Cello*
Nan Washburn, *Artistic Director*
Miriam Abrams, *Executive Director*

Short Piece For Orchestra (1952)

Julia Perry
(1924-1979)

Concerto for Violoncello Op. 107 (1957)

Dmitri Shostakovich
(1906-1975)

Allegretto
Moderato
Cadenza
Allegro con moto

Sharon Robinson, cello

INTERMISSION

***The Violent Bear It Away (1988) (Commissioned by BAWP)

Christine Berl
(b. 1943)

*Symphony in E-minor (1932)

Florence Price
(1888-1953)

Allegro non troppo
Largo maestoso
Juba Dance
Finale: Presto

***World Premiere
*West Coast Premiere

This concert is funded in part by the National Endowment for the Arts, the California Arts Council, SF Grants for the Arts, William and Flora Hewlett Foundation, the Zellerbach Family Fund and the Columbia Foundation.

No photographs or recordings can be made of this concert without the consent of the Bay Area Women's Philharmonic.

Tonight's concert will be broadcast on KKHI AM & FM on April 8th, 1989 at 8:00 p.m.

Figure 14.2 Bay Area Women's Philharmonic concert program, February 11, 1989.

which in time came to signify and promote a narrative of cultural and racial supremacy that led to the erasure of the civilizations and cultures already existing in the space that Europeans later claimed.

In many ways, this historical and cultural context underscores the use of the words discovery and rediscovery, as it relates to the reclaiming of historically neglected artists, writers, musicians, and composers from the intellectual margins. The dyadic language of discovery/rediscovery invokes a context in which the cultural work of these artisans existed in a space of liminality and obscurity – one that is reconciled only through the subjective eye and ear of the cultural elite. However, as this chapter has attempted to show, neither this narrative nor that of the exceptional woman paints the most accurate picture of what defines the afterlife of Florence Price.

The music of Florence Price remained a living artifact, due in part to the intellectual labor of varying generations of scholars, educators, and musicians who exemplified the words of Lucille Clifton invoked at the beginning of this chapter. Things did not fall apart because Price's music was continually rejected by the mainstream classical infrastructure. Things did not fall apart because of Price's sudden death in 1953. Nor did things fall apart because her legacy and that of her peers were excluded from historical narratives. Rather, they thrived through grassroots music ecosystems whose curation, preservation, and advocacy ensured that the words and pictures invoked through Price's life and music would remain for subsequent generations to explore.

Notes

1. This epigraph is taken from Lucille Clifton, *Generations: A Memoir* (New York: Random House, 1976), 86.
2. This epigraph is from a blog that originally appeared on the website associated with the Harry T. Burleigh Society and is now available as A. Kori Hill, "To Be Rediscovered When You Were Never Forgotten: Florence Price and Black Composers in the Mainstream," *Litrary Diversty*, June 11, 2023, https://tinyurl.com/ymymjx7b.
3. For a synopsis of some of this activity, see Sophia Alexandra Hall, "How the murder of George Floyd impacted music-making in Minneapolis and across the globe," Classic FM, July 12, 2022, www.classicfm.com/music-news/george-floyd-murder-music-making-minneapolis/; Heather McDonald, "Classical Music's Suicide Pact (Part 1)," *City Journal*, Summer 2021, www.city-journal.org/article/classical-musics-suicide-pact-part-1.
4. The trope of the exceptional woman has been used to frame the culture of female invisibility in jazz studies. For more information, see Sherrie Tucker, "Big Ears: Listening for Gender in Jazz Studies," *Current Musicology* (Spring 2001/2002): 375–408; Nichol Rustin, "'Mary Lou Williams Plays Like a Man!':

Gender, Genius, and Difference in Black Music Discourse," *South Atlantic Quarterly* 104, no. 3 (2005): 445–462; Tammy L. Kernodle, "Black Women Working Together: Jazz, Gender and the Politics of Validation," *Black Music Research Journal* 34, no. 1 (2014): 27–54.

5. For more information, see Samantha Ege, "Composing a Symphonist: Florence Price and the Hand of Black Women's Fellowship," *Women and Music: A Journal of Gender and Culture* 24 (2020): 7–27; Helen Walker-Hill, "Black Women Composers in Chicago: Then and Now," *Black Music Research Journal* 12, no. 1 (1992): 1–23; Rae Linda Brown, *The Heart of a Woman: The Life and Music of Florence B. Price* (Urbana: University of Illinois Press, 2020).

6. See Micaela Baranello, "Welcoming a Black Female Composer into the Canon. Finally," *New York Times*, February 9, 2018; Nathaniel Meyer, "The Lost World of Florence Price," *Boston Musical Intelligencer*, April 18, 2018, www.classical-scene.com/2018/04/18/florence-price/; Bob McQuiston, "Classical Lost and Found: Florence Price Rediscovered," NPR, February 28, 2012, https://tinyurl.com/2hfrzuh9; Alex Ross, "The Rediscovery of Florence Price," *New Yorker*, January 29, 2018, www.newyorker.com/magazine/2018/02/05/the-rediscovery-of-florence-price.

7. Samantha Ege and Douglas Shadle, "As Her Music Is Reconsidered, a Composer Turns 135. Again," *New York Times*, April 7, 2023, www.nytimes.com/2023/04/07/arts/music/florence-price-music.html.

8. For more information, see Douglas Shadle, "What I Wish Everyone Knew about Florence Price," *The Classical Alternative*, March 19, 2020, https://tinyurl.com/yds2efuk.

9. Correspondence between Dr. Barbara Garvey Jackson and friends of Price reveal this history of programming. Many of these concert programs are in the Florence Price Collection at the University of Arkansas in Fayetteville, Arkansas.

10. Marcia J. Citron, "Gender, Professionalism, and the Musical Canon," *Journal of Musicology* 8, no. 1 (1990): 103.

11. Dominque-René de Lerma, *Reflections on Afro-American Music* (Kent, OH: Kent State University Press, 1973), 1–2.

12. The proceedings of this conference were published in the book Dominque-René de Lerma, *Black Music in Our Culture* (Kent, OH: Kent State University Press, 1970).

13. Brown, The Heart of a Woman, 66.

14. The information is quoted by Dominque-René de Lerma in his review of Althea Waites Performs the Piano Music of Florence Price, which was published in *The Black Perspective in Music* 16, no. 1 (Spring 1988): 117.

15. Special thanks to Tiffany Atwater Lee, head of research services at the Archives Research Center, Robert W. Woodruff Library, Clark Atlanta University, for assisting in locating information on Dr. Robinson and the Black music workshops.

16. Catherine Fox, "In memoriam: Richard A. Long, lion of African American arts and letters, leaves rich legacy," January 9, 2013, www.artsatl.org/memorium-richard-a-long/.
17. The conference and cancellation of the concert are briefly discussed in Raoul Abdul, *Blacks in Classical Music: A Personal History* (New York: Dodd, Mead, 1977), 51.
18. Raoul Abdul, "Florence Price's Huge Untapped Musical Output." *New York Amsterdam News*, April 19, 1986, 26.
19. Mildred Denby Green, *Black Women Composers: A Genesis* (Boston: Twayne, 1983), 32.
20. Special thanks to Jason Imbesi, librarian for music, dance, and theatre in the music library at the University of Michigan for his assistance in accessing materials related to the 1985 Black American Music Symposium.
21. Willis Patterson, as quoted in Georgia A. Ryder, "The Black-American Music Symposium," *The Black Perspective in Music* 14, no. 1 (1986): 85.
22. "Concerts of the Symposium," *The Black Perspective in Music* 14, no. 1 (1986): 66–84.
23. For more information on the emergence of the discipline of feminist music studies, see Elizabeth Wood, "Women in Music," *Signs* 6, no. 2 (1980): 283–297; Susan McClary "Reshaping a Discipline: Musicology and Feminism in the 1990s," *Feminist Studies* 19, no. 2 (1993): 399–423; Susan C. Cook, "Women, Women's Studies, Music and Musicology: Issues of Pedagogy and Scholarship," *College Music Symposium* 29 (1989): 93–100.
24. Green, preface to *Black Women Composers*.
25. Jackson had previously taught at the University of Arkansas for two years (1954–1956).
26. Letter dated February 4, 1974, from Mary Dengler Hudgins to Sam Sizer, curator of Special Collections at the University of Arkansas Library.
27. Barbara Garvey Jackson, "Florence Price, Composer," *The Black Perspective in Music* 5, no. 1 (1977): 41.
28. Program contained in the Barbara Garvey Jackson Collection, Special Collections, University of Arkansas Libraries, Fayetteville.
29. Barbara Garvey Jackson, "Florence Price, Composer," *Black Perspective in Music* 5, no. 1 (1977): 30–43; James Carney Smith, ed., *Notable Black American Women* (Detroit: Gale Research, 1992), 872–874.
30. Special thanks to Nan Washburn for her assistance in understanding the role of The Women's Philharmonic in championing the music of Florence Price and for the photos of the concert programs featured in this chapter.

Select Bibliography

Absher, Amy. *The Black Musician and the White City: Race and Music in Chicago, 1900–1967*. Ann Arbor: University of Michigan Press, 2014.

Barber, Felicia Raphael Marie. *A New Perspective for the Use of Dialect in African American Spirituals: History, Context, and Linguistics*. Lanham, MD: Lexington Books, 2021.

Block, Adrienne Fried and Carol Neuls-Bates. *Women in American Music: A Bibliography of Music and Literature*. Westport, CT: Greenwood Press, 1979.

Bonds, Margaret. "A Reminiscence." In *The Negro in Music and Art*, edited by Lindsay Patterson, 191–193. New York: Publishers Company, 1967.

Bowers, Jane, and Judith Tick, eds. *Women Making Music: The Western Art Tradition, 1150–1950*. Urbana: University of Illinois Press, 1986.

Brown, Rae Linda. "Florence B. Price and Margaret Bonds: The Chicago Years." *Black Music Research Bulletin* 12, no. 2 (Fall 1990): 11–14.

Brown, Rae Linda. *The Heart of a Woman: The Life and Music of Florence B. Price*. Urbana: University of Illinois Press, 2020.

Brown, Rae Linda. "William Grant Still, Florence B. Price, and William Dawson: Echoes of the Harlem Renaissance." In *Black Music and the Harlem Renaissance*, edited by Samuel A. Floyd, Jr., 71–86. Westport, CT: Greenwood Press, 1990. Reprinted by the University of Tennessee Press, 1993.

Brown, Rae Linda. "The Women's Symphony Orchestra of Chicago and Florence B. Price's Concerto in One Movement." *American Music* 11, no. 2 (1993): 185–205.

Brown, Rae Linda, and Wayne Shirley, eds. *Florence Price: Symphonies Nos. 1 and 3*. Middleton, WI: A-R Editions, 2008.

Caplan, Lucy, "'Strange What Cosmopolites Music Makes Us': Classical Music, the Black Press, and Nora Holt's Feminist Audiotopia." *Journal of the Society for American Music* 14, no. 3 (2020): 308–336.

Carter, Elektra V. [formerly known as Marquese Carter]. "The Poet and Her Songs: Analyzing the Art Songs of Florence B. Price." DMA diss., Indiana University, 2018.

Cohen, Aaron I. *International Encyclopedia of Women Composers*. New York: Bowker, 1981.

Collins, Patricia Hill. *Black Feminist Thought: Knowledge, Consciousness, and the Politics of Empowerment*. New York: Routledge, 2009.

Cooper, John M. Foreword to Florence B. Price: Two Traditional Negro Spirituals ("I Am Bound for the Kingdom" and "I'm Workin' on My Buildin'"). New York: G. Schirmer, 2020.

Durrant, Elizabeth. "Chicago Renaissance Women: Black Feminism in the Careers and Songs of Florence Price and Margaret Bonds." MA thesis, University of North Texas, 2021.

Durrant, Elizabeth and Rebecca Dowd Geoffroy-Schwinden. "The Estella Bonds Salon: A Black Chicago Renaissance Genealogy of American Art Song." In *Four Centuries of Women's Musical Salons: A Cross-Cultural History*, edited by Jacqueline Avila and Rebecca Cypess, 313–331. Cambridge, UK: Cambridge University Press, 2026.

Ege, Samantha. "The Aesthetics of Florence Price: Negotiating the Dissonances of a New World Nationalism." PhD diss., University of York, 2020.

Ege, Samantha. "Chicago, the 'City We Love to Call Home!': Intersectionality, Narrativity, and Locale in the Music of Florence Beatrice Price and Theodora Sturkow Ryder." *American Music* 39, no. 1 (2021): 1–40.

Ege, Samantha. "Composing a Symphonist: Florence Price and the Hand of Black Women's Fellowship." *Women and Music: A Journal of Gender and Culture* 24 (2020): 7–27.

Ege, Samantha. "Nora Douglas Holt's Teachings of a Black Classical Canon." In *The Oxford Handbook of Public Music Theory*, edited by J. Daniel Jenkins. New York: Oxford University Press, 2022. http://doi.org/10.1093/oxfordhb/9780197551554.013.21.

Ege, Samantha. *South Side Impresarios: How Race Women Transformed Chicago's Classical Music Scene*. Urbana: University of Illinois Press, 2024.

Floyd, Samuel A., Jr. *The Power of Black Music: Interpreting Its History from Africa to the United States*. New York: Oxford University Press, 1995.

Gallon, Kim. *Pleasure in the News: African American Readership and Sexuality in the Black Press*. Urbana: University of Illinois Press, 2020.

Glasrud, Bruce, and Cary Wintz. *The Harlem Renaissance in the American West*. New York: Routledge, 2012.

Graham, Sandra Jean. *Spirituals and the Birth of a Black Entertainment Industry*. Chicago: University of Illinois Press, 2018.

Graham, Shirley. "Spirituals to Symphonies." *Etude* 54, no. 11 (1936): 691–692, 723, 736.

Green, Mildred Denby. *Black Women Composers: A Genesis*. Boston, MA: Twayne, 1983.

Gross, Rebecca. "Jazz Poetry and Langston Hughes." National Endowment for the Arts Blog. April 11, 2014. www.arts.gov/stories/blog/2014/jazz-poetry-langston-hughes.

Hamm, Charles. *Yesterdays: Popular Song in America*. New York: Norton, 1972.

Hayes Eileen M., and Linda F. Williams, eds. *Black Women and Music: More Than the Blues*. Urbana: University of Illinois Press, 2007.

Hill, Alexandra Kori. "Make the Familiar New: New Negro Modernism in the Concertos of Florence B. Price." PhD diss., University of North Carolina, 2022.

Holly, Ellistine Perkins. "Black Concert Music in Chicago, 1890 to the 1930s." *Black Music Research Journal* 10, no. 1 (1990): 141–149.

Holzer, Linda. "Selected Solo Piano Music of Florence B. Price (1887–1953)." PhD diss., Florida State University, 1995.

Hughes, Langston. "The Negro Artist and the Racial Mountain." In *Within the Circle: An Anthology of African American Literary Criticism from the Harlem Renaissance to the Present*, edited by Angelyn Mitchell, 55–59. Durham: Duke University Press, 1994.

Hutchinson, Kyle. "Pendular Thirds and Pentatonic Parallelisms: Intersecting Black Vernacular and Neo-Romantic Idioms in the Second Movement of Florence Price's Piano Sonata in E Minor." *Intégral* 36 (2023): 163–174.

Jackson, Barbara Garvey. "Florence Price, Composer." *The Black Perspective in Music* 5, no. 1 (1977): 31–43.

Jezic, Diane Peacock. *Women Composers: The Lost Tradition Found*. New York: Feminist Press, 1988.

Jobson, Christine. "Florence Price: An Analysis of Select Art Songs with Text by Female Poets." PhD diss., University of Miami, 2019.

Jones, Alisha. "Lift Every Voice: Marian Anderson, Florence B. Price and the Sound of Black Sisterhood." National Public Radio. August 30, 2019. https://tinyurl.com/3y7metwt.

Karpf, Juanita. "The Early Years of African American Music Periodicals, 1886–1922: History, Ideology, Context." *International Review of the Aesthetics and Sociology of Music* 28, no. 2 (1997): 162–165.

Locke, Alain, ed. *The New Negro: An Interpretation*. New York: Simon & Schuster, 1925.

Marek, Jayne. "Women Editors and Little Magazines in the Harlem Renaissance." In *Little Magazines and Modernism: New Approaches*, edited by Suzanne W. Churchill and Adam McKible, 106–107. Farnham: Ashgate, 2007.

Mashego, Shana. "Music From the Soul of Woman: The Influence of the African American Presbyterian and Methodist Traditions on the Classical Compositions of Florence Price and Dorothy Rudd Moore." PhD diss., University of Arizona, 2010.

Maxile, Horace J., Jr. "Culture and Craft in Florence Price's Piano Sonata in E Minor (First Movement)." In *Analytical Essays on Music by Women Composers: Concert Music 1900–1960*, edited by Laurel Parsons and Brenda Ravenscroft, 139–163. New York: Oxford University Press, 2022.

McGinty, Doris Evans. "'As Large as She Can Make It': The Role of Black Women Activists in Music, 1880–1945." In *Cultivating Music in America: Women Patrons and Activists since 1860*, edited by Ralph P. Locke and Cyrilla Barr, 214–230. Berkeley: University of California Press, 1997.

Ramsey, Guthrie P., Jr. *Who Hears Here?: On Black Music, Pasts and Present*. Oakland: University of California Press, 2022.

Shadle, Douglas. "Plus Ça Change: Florence B. Price in the #BlackLivesMatterEra." *New Music USA*, February 20, 2019. https://tinyurl.com/4x6hjkpd.

Southern, Eileen. *Biographical Dictionary of Afro-American and African Musicians*. Westport, CT: Greenwood Press, 1982.

Southern, Eileen. *The Music of Black Americans: A History*. 3rd ed. New York: Norton, 1997.

Stoever, Jennifer. *The Sonic Color Line: Race and the Cultural Politics of Listening*. New York: New York University Press, 2016.

Teresa, Carrie. *Looking at the Stars: Black Celebrity Journalism in Jim Crow America*. Lincoln: University of Nebraska Press, 2019.

Terry, William E. "*The Negro Music Journal*: An Appraisal." *The Black Perspective in Music* 5, no. 2 (1977): 146–160.

Walker-Hill, Helen, ed. *Black Women Composers: A Century of Piano Music (1893–1990)*. Bryn Mawr, PA: Hildegard Publishing, 1992.

Walker-Hill, Helen. "Black Women Composers in Chicago: Then and Now." *Black Music Research Journal* 12, no. 1 (1992): 1–23.

Walker-Hill, Helen. *From Spirituals to Symphonies: African-American Women Composers and Their Music*. Urbana: University of Illinois Press, 2007.

Zaimont, Judith Lang, Catherine Overhauser, and Jane Gottlieb, eds. *The Musical Woman: An International Perspective, 1983*. Westport, CT: Greenwood Press, 1984.

Select Discography

Burger, Cole. *Beyond the Traveler: Piano Music by Composers from Arkansas*. MSR Classics MS1686, 2019, compact disc.

Cann, Michelle. *Revival: Music of Price & Bonds*. Curtis Studio, 2023, digital.

Catalyst Quartet and Michelle Cann, *Uncovered*, vol. 2: *Florence B. Price*. Azica Records: Azica71346, 2022, compact disc.

Chineke! Orchestra featuring Jeneba Kanneh-Mason. *Florence Price*. Decca, 485 3995, 2023, compact disc.

Corley, Maria. *Soundscapes: Piano Music by African American Women*. Albany, TROY857, 2006, compact disc.

Ege, Samantha. *Black Renaissance Woman: Piano Music by Florence Price, Margaret Bonds, Nora Holt, Betty Jackson King, Helen Hagan*. Lorelt (Lontano Records Ltd.) LNT 145, 2023, compact disc.

Ege, Samantha. *Fantasie Nègre: The Piano Music of Florence Price*. Lorelt (Lontano Records Ltd.) LNT 144, 2021, compact disc.

Ege, Samantha. *Four Women: Music for Solo Piano by Price, Kaprálová, Bilsland and Bonds*. Wave Theory Records WT2018006D, 2018, compact disc.

Goosby, Randall. *Roots*. Decca 485 1664, 2021, compact disc.

Janacek Philharmonic, Er-Gene Kahng, and Ryan Cockerham. *Florence Price: Violin Concertos*. Albany, TROY1706, 2018, compact disc.

Jobson, Christine. *Nearly Lost: Art Songs by Florence Price*. N2A, 2019, digital.

Johnson, Kirsten. *Florence Price: Piano Music*. Guild GM2CD7828, 2022, compact disc.

Lee, Michael. *American Spiritual*. Leaf Music, 2024, digital.

Morrison, Maggie *VOICES*. 2023, digital.

New Black Music Repertory Ensemble, Leslie B. Dunner, and Karen Walwyn. *Florence B. Price: Concerto in One Movement and Symphony in E Minor*. Albany Records, TROY 1295, 2011, compact disc.

New York Youth Symphony, Michelle Cann, and Michael Repper. *Florence Price, Valerie Coleman, Jessie Montgomery*. Avie Records, AV2503, 2022, compact disc.

Philadelphia Orchestra and Yannick Nézet-Séguin. *Florence Price: Symphonies Nos. 1 & 3*. Deutsche Grammophon 486 2029, 2022, compact disc.

Philadelphia Orchestra and Yannick Nézet-Séguin. *Florence Price: Symphony No. 4 – William Dawson: Negro Folk Symphony*. Deutsche Grammophon 486 5137, 2023, compact disc.

Philadelphia Orchestra, Yannick Nézet-Séguin, and Randall Goosby. *Max Bruch & Florence Price: Violin Concertos*. Decca 485 4234, 2023, compact disc.

Slack, Karen and Michelle Cann. *Beyond the Years: Unpublished Songs of Florence Price*. Azica Records 71370, compact disc.

The Women's Philharmonic & Apo Hsu. *Florence Price: Mississippi River (Suite), The Oak, Symphony No. 3*. Alto, ALC1461, 2022, compact disc.

Toppin, Louise, Jay Pierson, and John O'Brien. *Ah! Love, But a Day*. Albany Records, TROY0385, 2000, digital.

Waites, Althea. *Althea Waites Performs the Piano Music of Florence Price*. Cambria Records, C-1027, 1987, vinyl.

Waites, Althea. *Black Diamonds*. Cambria Records, CAMCD–1097, 1993, compact disc.

Walker-Hill, Helen and Gregory T. S. Walker. *Kaleidoscope: Music by African-American Women*. Leonarda, LE339, 1997, compact disc.

Walwyn, Karen. *Florence B. Price*. Kadoro Klassics 13285 77062, 2022, digital.

Württembergische Philharmonie Reutlingen and John Jeter. *Florence Beatrice Price: Song of the Oak*. Naxos, 8559920, 2022, compact disc.

Index

accompaniment, 66, 71, 73, 75, 78, 80, 127, 136, 137, 138, 145, 197, 222, 223, 225
African American harmony, 188
African American history, 34, 37, 38
African American musics, 183
African Methodist Episcopal Church, 57
Africanisms, 108
American Conservatory, 167, 196
American Conservatory of Music, 155
American identity, 144, 145
American Musicological Society (AMS), 39, 278, 279
Anderson, Marian, 5, 10, 56, 59, 206, 207, 224, 225, 228, 231, 232, 234, 236, 237, 238, 239, 241, 243, 249, 255, 257, 259, 260, 275
antiphony, 182
Arkansas State Music Teachers Association, 35, 279
arpeggios, 74, 134, 169, 222
Atlanta University, 272, 273
"Ave Maria," 156, 157

Barmas, Issay, 167
"Beside the Sea," 70, 73, 74, 78
Black American Music Symposium, 272, 274, 275, 279
Black Chicago Renaissance, 11, 17, 28, 36, 57, 176, 220, 228, 229, 233, 234, 240, 243, 267
Black church, 17
Black churches, 1
Black Codes, 53
Black feminism, 228, 229
Black feminist theory, 2, 4
Black feminists, 2, 5, 12, 18, 69, 77, 228, 229, 230, 233, 236, 237, 241, 242, 243, 249
Black folk, 19, 68, 136, 156, 165, 182
Black music studies, 2, 32, 33, 41, 42, 181, 270, 275
Black musicians, 36, 195, 198, 229, 231, 238, 241, 250, 252, 266, 268, 272
  Black, 274
Black nationalism, 269

Black women, 4, 11, 13, 16, 21, 27, 42, 44, 65, 69, 126, 174, 228, 229, 230, 232, 233, 234, 235, 236, 237, 239, 240, 241, 242, 243, 248, 249, 251, 253, 255, 267, 275, 276, 277
Boatner, Edward, 154
Bonds, Estella, 10, 15, 17, 134, 198, 218, 230, 233, 234, 235, 261
Bonds, Margaret, 5, 10, 15, 66, 124, 133, 175, 195, 198, 199, 210, 218, 219, 220, 228, 233, 234, 235, 236, 239, 240, 241, 242, 249, 255, 273, 275, 277
Broadway, 20, 55, 221
Brown, Angela, 94
Brown, Carlene J., 4, 27, 80, 279
Brown, Gwynne Kuhner, 4
Brown, Nellie, 57
Brown, Rae Linda, 10, 22, 41, 42, 138, 209, 236, 238, 242, 267, 275
  and African American history, 38
  and Althea Waites, 39
  and Arkansas State Library, 38
  and Barbara Garvey Jackson, 34, 35
  and Black American Music Symposium, 279
  and Black music, 28, 33, 34
  and Black press, 258
  and Center for Black Music Research, 38
  and *Chicago Defender*, 38
  and Claude Palisca, 37, 40, 41
  and Eileen Southern, 34, 40, 41, 42
  and *Five Negro Folksongs*, 180
  and Florence "Bea" Price, 1, 2, 3, 4, 10, 11, 13, 14, 15, 18, 19, 20, 22, 24, 27, 28, 32, 34, 35, 36, 37, 38, 39, 40, 41, 42, 43, 44, 76, 80, 125, 146, 154, 165, 173, 180, 181, 182, 184, 185, 186, 196, 209, 210, 211, 232, 236, 258, 267, 279, 280, 283
  and Florence Irene Gulliver Smith, 252
  and gender, 3
  and Harry T. Burleigh, 5
  and Hartford (CT), 279
  and juba rhythms, 188
  and Library of Congress, 38
  and Marion Ross, 42

Brown, Rae Linda (cont.)
  and mentees, 41
  and musicology, 33, 38
  and Nora Holt, 231
  and Piano Sonata in E Minor, 39
  and reclamation, 37
  and Samuel Floyd, 41
  and Symphony in E Minor, 39
  and *The Heart of a Woman*, 2, 3, 28
  and University of Arkansas, 38
  and unpublished papers, 36
  and Wayne Shirley, 40
  and William J. Holab, 39
  and Woman's Symphony Orchestra of Chicago, 38, 235
  and Yale University, 34, 209, 275
  death of, 43, 44
  methodology of, 28, 40
  scholarship, 44
  scholarship of, 2, 33, 34, 37, 40, 41, 43, 44, 66, 209
  work of, 38, 43, 44
Brown, Uzee, 90
Bumbry, Grace, 10
Burleigh, Harry T., 5, 51, 55, 139, 217, 218, 219, 220, 221, 222, 223, 225, 226, 275

cakewalk rhythm, 127, 130
call and response, 175, 181, 182, 186, 187, 190
Carter, Elektra V., 4, 68, 69, 147, 182, 190, 197, 224, 238, 279
Carter, Melinda, 147
Catalyst Quartet, 173
Center for Black Music Research, 14, 38, 271
Chadwick, George, 117
chamber music, 20, 66, 175, 176, 190, 200, 217, 262, 275
chamber works, 4, 175, 176, 177, 188, 190, 220, 278
Cheney University, 52
Chicago (IL)
  and Abbie Mitchell, 233
  and Allied Arts Academy, 242
  and Black Belt movie theaters, 92
  and Black concert life, 107
  and Black concert scene, 11
  and Black cultural autonomy, 258
  and Black music scene, 230, 260
  and Black press, 249
  and Century of Progress Exposition, 197
  and churches, 268
  and classical music scene, 194
  and Columbia College, 14
  and composers, 235
  and culture, 37
  and Fannie Carter Woods, 224
  and Florence "Bea" Price, 10, 15, 16, 37, 155, 163, 195, 200, 217, 218, 249, 252, 253
  and Florence Cole-Talbert, 251
  and Florence Louise Robinson, 35
  and Grace Episcopal Church, 131
  and Great Migration, 15
  and Joel Lay, 200
  and music scene, 155, 229, 268
  'and National Association of Negro Musicians (NANM), 56, 231, 232, 254, 261
  and newspapers, 38
  and professional musicians, 220, 255
  and Rae Linda Brown, 196
  and segregation, 16
  and Thomas Orchestra, 167
  and violinists, 155
  Club of Women Organists, 242, 268
  Fine Arts Building, 163
  Historical Society, 38
  Musicians Club of Women, 155
  Nora Holt, 242
  Public Library, 38
  South Side, 16, 175
  Women's Committee, 261
Chicago Civic Theatre, 107
Chicago Daily News, 199
Chicago Daily Tribune, 256
Chicago Defender, 10, 11, 17, 38, 230, 232, 247, 250
Chicago Friends of Music, 198
Chicago Music Association (CMA), 10, 17, 56, 198, 231, 232, 254, 255, 257
Chicago Musical College, 136, 155, 196, 217
Chicago Symphony Orchestra, 1, 10, 135, 167, 193, 202, 209, 217, 234, 247, 256, 257, 261
Chicago Tribune, 193
Chicago Woman's Club, 107
Chicago World's Fair, 234
Chopin, Frédéric, 133, 139
Clark College, 272, 273
class, 2, 11, 15, 48, 49, 53, 65, 67, 70, 124, 125, 126, 129, 203, 210, 252
  upper, 230
classical music
  American, 2, 30, 51
  and antiphony, 182
  and Black composers, 218
  and black experience, 126
  and composers, 28
  and dance forms, 188

and Florence "Bea" Price, 47, 267
and Margaret Bonds, 240
and Marian Anderson, 228
and morality, 237
and possessive investment, 10
and ragtime, 182
and segregation, 200
and white men, 1
Black, 2, 230, 232, 238, 250, 251, 258
culture of, 16, 210, 231
European, 52, 125
history of, 17, 18, 48
in Chicago, 194, 229
industry, 241
making of, 1
narrative of, 267
publishing companies, 39
scholarship on, 2
spaces, 181
study of, 240
Western, 48, 51, 54, 81, 185
Coleridge-Taylor, Samuel, 51, 156, 157, 182, 188, 253, 257
Cole-Talbert, Florence, 251
Colored American Opera Company, 54
community building, 15
Black classical, 1
composers, 33, 50, 54, 65, 69, 81, 138, 140, 163, 166, 167, 174, 175, 180, 181, 190, 191, 193, 194, 195, 196, 200, 202, 204, 207, 209, 210, 217, 218, 219, 220, 233, 234, 235, 237, 238, 239, 251, 253, 254, 256, 258, 259, 260, 261, 267, 268, 270, 275, 277, 283
American, 28, 49
and folk, 2
and race, 57
and repertoires, 1
and spirituals, 236
and trends, 2
Black, 2, 29, 34, 36, 51, 58, 59, 66, 81, 272, 273, 274, 275, 276, 278
European, 124
Germanic, 57
lieder, 91
minoritized, 3
of African descent, 48
of color, 30
studies of, 3
white, 66, 167
women, 276
Concerto in One Movement, 19, 36, 124, 133, 175, 182, 186, 187, 188, 217, 218, 235, 236, 273, 280

concertos, 4, 175, 176, 177, 181, 210
violin, 182
conductors, 155, 194, 206, 207, 268, 270, 275, 276, 280
Cook, Will Marion, 55, 155, 158, 159, 233, 257
and Berlin, 167
culture, 2, 3, 9, 16, 30, 42, 54, 126, 133, 138, 155, 175, 186, 189, 229, 250, 256, 267, 268, 269, 271, 277
of collaboration, 251
Cuney-Hare, Maud, 29, 30, 31, 57, 251

Dances in the Canebrakes, 129, 217, 280
dark virgin, 76, 77
Detroit
Public Library, 38
diversity, 2, 67, 270
domestic work, 53
Du Bois, Shirley Graham, 29
Du Bois, W. E. B., 120
Dunbar, Paul Laurence, 4, 70, 72, 73, 74, 220, 221
Durrant, Elizabeth, 5, 15, 77, 78, 79

Ege, Samantha, xix, 4, 22, 66, 68, 81, 133, 138, 139, 140, 144, 232, 234, 249, 267, 279
Etude, 29, 259
European functional harmony, 135

Fantasie Nègre, 14, 15, 17, 18, 19, 20, 21, 22, 133, 134, 135, 138, 195, 203, 217
Fantasie Nègre No. 1 in E minor, 14, 15, 203
Fantasie Nègre No. 2 in G minor, 15, 134
Fantasie Nègre No. 3 in F minor, 15, 21, 22
Fantasie Nègre No. 4 in B minor, 15, 195
fantasies, 19, 20, 21, 144, 154, 155, 163, 165
"Fantasy in Purple," 279
Federal Music Project, 200, 202, 203, 220
First Sonata for Organ, 136, 138
Floyd, George, 266
Floyd, Samuel A., 38, 40, 41, 181, 182
folk music, 30, 52, 134, 137, 140, 182, 203
Freedmen's Bureau, 52, 53

Gatwood, Darrell, 17
Gatwood, Vicki, 18, 22
gender, 2, 3, 4, 11, 27, 36, 56, 66, 67, 78, 81, 167, 254, 256, 259, 261, 266, 270
gender studies, 2, 5
George Shirley Vocal Competition, 59
George, Maude Roberts, 10, 17, 198, 199, 232, 233, 249, 250, 251, 255, 257, 260, 261, 272, 275

German Romantic tradition, 19
Gershwin, George, 139
Graham, Shirley, 31, 259
Great Depression, 15, 255
Green, Mildred Denby, 2, 3, 28, 32, 33, 76, 274, 275, 276, 277
Greenfield, Elizabeth Taylor, 48
Guilmant, Félix-Alexandre, 136, 137

Hagan, Helen Eugenia, 13, 14, 251
Harlem Renaissance, 57, 176
harmonic relationships, 165
harmonic systems, 188
Harmony and Voice Leading, 66
Hartford (CT), 279
Hartman, Saidiya, 16, 19, 20
Heart of a Woman, The, xvii
heterophony, 186
Hidden Figures, 27
Hill, Alexandra Kori, xix, 4, 81, 155, 158, 165, 235, 266, 268, 279, 280, 286, 288, 289, 290
Historically Black Colleges and Universities (HBCUs), 1, 52, 53, 54, 57, 269, 271, 272, 274
Historically Black Fisk University, 50
"Hold Fast to Dreams," 39, 66, 70, 75, 78
Holstein Prize, 29, 254
Holstein, Casper, 196, 254
Holt, Nora, xxv, xxvi, 56, 229, 230, 231, 232, 233, 242, 249, 250, 251, 252, 261, 286, 287, 289
HOMEMAKER, 9, 11, 13
house*keeping*, 11
Howard University, 38, 50, 53, 155, 236, 271
Hughes, Langston, 4, 70, 72, 73, 75, 76, 77, 78, 206, 220, 229, 233, 240, 241
Hurston, Zora Neale, 12, 21, 69

International Society for Contemporary Music, 155

Jackson, Barbara Garvey, 2, 3, 28, 34, 35, 173, 209, 275, 277, 278, 279
Jackson, Mahalia, 94
Jackson, Mary W., 27
Jackson, Raymond, 276
jazz, 36, 37, 81, 126, 127, 130, 131, 140, 199, 205, 218, 229, 266
Jim Crow, 15, 18, 30, 48, 49, 54, 55, 228, 250, 252, 253, 256
juba, 2, 59, 126, 130, 131, 132, 175, 188, 189, 190, 199, 205
justice, 4, 207

Kernodle, Tammy L., xix, 5, 10, 15, 16
King, Betty Jackson, 87

Lake View Musical Society, 155, 167
Levee Dance, 162, 204
Library of Congress, 38, 40, 202
Little Rock (AR), 1, 35, 37, 47, 57, 58, 217, 249, 252, 253
Locke, Alain, xxvi, 29, 30, 31, 45, 141, 204, 205, 212, 288
London Symphony Orchestra, 135
Long, Richard A., 208, 272, 273

McGill University, 14
Memphis State University, 274
Min, Elizabeth Seja, 280
Mitchell, Abbie, 10, 57, 218, 219, 220, 233, 239, 258
Morehouse College, 272
Morris Brown College, 272
music aesthetics, 3
music historiography, 41
  Black, 28
music history, 36, 40, 44, 66, 80, 81, 250
  Black, 28
music theory, 3, 65, 66, 67, 80, 81
musical cultures, 58, 257
musical intertextuality, 115
musical signatures, 78
musicians, 10, 30, 33, 43, 48, 49, 51, 52, 54, 56, 57, 81, 140, 154, 155, 174, 195, 200, 202, 207, 228, 229, 231, 232, 234, 236, 237, 241, 242, 248, 249, 250, 251, 252, 254, 255, 256, 257, 260, 266, 267, 268, 270, 271, 272, 274, 275, 276, 277, 278, 279, 280, 283
  Black, 230, 240
  Black women, 233
  professional, 220
  white, 217
  women, 277
musicology, 3, 14, 32, 34, 37, 41, 66, 173, 181, 182, 197, 251, 274, 276, 277
musicological research, 1
musicologists, 2, 38, 43, 209
"My Soul's Been Anchored in the Lord," xxviii, 237, 238, 258, 277

National Association of Negro Musicians (NANM), 10, 17, 56, 155, 182, 230, 231, 232, 233, 236, 252, 254, 260, 261
national music, 1, 19
Negro Renaissance Movement, 279

Negro spirituals, 2, 4, 15, 56, 154, 162, 185, 190, 203
New Black Music Repertory Ensemble, 19, 271, 280
New England Conservatory, xxiv, 29, 36, 37, 38, 47, 56, 57, 124, 125, 126, 253
New Negro Movement, 16

Oberlin College, 56, 57, 155, 276
orchestral works, 156, 269, 275, 279
orchestras, 28, 31, 36, 40, 44, 66, 133, 155, 156, 165, 166, 175, 176, 181, 182, 193, 194, 196, 199, 200, 201, 202, 204, 209, 210, 211, 218, 219, 220, 225, 234, 236, 242, 249, 256, 259, 266, 269, 279, 280
   Works Progress Administration, 36
organ, 13, 20, 35, 39, 41, 57, 59, 65, 124, 125, 126, 127, 128, 131, 132, 138, 208, 217, 232, 273, 275

Palisca, Claude, 37, 40, 41
patriarchy, 16
Patterson, Willis, 274, 275
Pennsylvania, 52
"Peter Go Ring dem Bells," 97
Peters, Penelope, 77, 79
Philadelphia Orchestra, 20, 63, 173, 175, 181, 209, 210, 215, 259
pianism, 135
pianists, 14, 19, 29, 36, 39, 49, 56, 58, 66, 76, 124, 128, 133, 135, 138, 139, 140, 144, 167, 198, 235, 251, 252, 273, 275, 279
piano concertos, 14, 20, 133, 135, 176, 186, 190, 200, 201, 203, 204, 220
Piano Sonata No. 1 in E Minor, 68
popular music, 30, 49, 59, 127, 136, 240
Porgy and Bess, 154, 242, 272
Predominantly White Institutions (PWI), 269
Price, Florence "Bea"
   and African American idiom, 4
   and Afrological aesthetic, 118
   and American Musicological Society (AMS), 278
   and antiphony, 182
   and Arkansas, 15, 147
   and Black folk dances, 118
   and Black music culture, 186
   and Black tradition, 183
   and blues, 110
   and Boston Symphony Orchestra, 1
   and call and response, 188
   and Chicago, 10, 15, 16, 155
   and *Chicago Defender*, 10, 11
   and Chicago Music Association (CMA), 10
   and Chicago Musicians Club of Women, 155
   and concert spirituals, 4
   and Concerto in One Movement, 19, 186
   and concertos, 144, 163, 182, 184
   and countermelody, 113
   and Darrell Gatwood, 17, 18
   and diaries, 147
   and domestic work, 116
   and Eleanor Roosevelt, 16
   and Estella Bonds, 15, 17
   and *Etude*, 29
   and Europe, 2
   and extension cords, 72
   and *Fantasie Nègre* No.1, 15
   and fantasies, 14, 19, 20, 21, 22, 145, 155
   and *Five Folksongs in Counterpoint*, 185
   and Florence Price Robinson, 13
   and Great Depression, 15
   and harmonies, 112
   and Helen Eugenia Hagan, 14
   and heterophony, 186
   and homemaker, 11, 22
   and "I'm Going to Lay Down My Heavy Load," 118
   and keyboard, 4
   and labor, 229
   and *Levee Dance*, 163
   and Marian Anderson, 5, 10
   and melodies, 135
   and Montreal, 17
   and musical intertexuality, 115
   and musical landscape, 3
   and musical network, 155
   and musicology, 182
   and National Association of Negro Musicians (NANM), 56, 232
   and national music, 1
   and *Negro Folksongs in Counterpoint* and *Five Folksongs in Counterpoint*, 185
   and Negro Renaissance Movement, 279
   and Negro spirituals, 2
   and piano, 58, 124, 138
   and piano music, 18
   and poetry, 4
   and pseudo-spirituals, 105
   and Pyotr Ilyich Tchaikovsky, 182, 183, 185
   and race, 4, 11
   and "Resignation," 115
   and rhythmic argumentation, 187
   and Serge Koussevitzky, 1, 3
   and Shorter College, 57
   and sonatas, 145

Price, Florence "Bea" (cont.)
  and sorrow songs, 50
  and spirituals, 218
  and String Quartet in A Minor, 187
  and symphonies, 4, 29
  and Symphony No. 1 in E Minor, 40
  and *The Heart of a Woman*, 2, 28, 39, 41, 42, 80, 222, 223, 267
  and *The Oak, Mississippi River Suite*, 279
  and The Women's Philharmonic, 280
  and University of Arkansas, 19
  and vernacularity, 146, 155
  and Vicki Gatwood, 17
  and violin fantasies, 144
  and Violin Fantasy No. 1, mm.83–88, 146
  and violins, 4, 144, 145, 182
  and virtuosity, 155
  and vocal works, 85
  and vocality, 154
  and Western art music, 28
  and Yale University, 279
  archives, 11
  as composer, 2, 20
  as hidden figure, 28
  contemporaries of, 4, 5
  death of, 9, 10, 24, 163, 283
  debut of, 10
  diaries of, 146
  family of, 22
  legacy of, 3, 5, 10
  life of, 1, 3, 4, 9, 10, 11, 13, 37, 58, 283
  manuscripts, 279
  Music Festival, 24
  music of, 1, 2, 4, 10, 13, 14, 15, 18, 19, 20, 22, 35, 36, 38, 39, 40, 154, 181, 182, 184, 185, 186, 210, 280, 283
  orchestral works, 279
  politics of, 11
  reception of, 3, 5, 14, 18
  Renaissance, 280
  research on, 3, 4, 5, 24, 28, 279
  revival of, 10
  scores of, 20
  style of, 2, 3
  writings of, 182
Price, Leontyne, 10
protest music, 269

race, 1, 2, 3, 4, 11, 27, 31, 34, 36, 48, 49, 50, 54, 56, 57, 67, 77, 79, 81, 124, 126, 130, 167, 196, 205, 207, 253, 256, 260, 261, 270
racial identity, 205
racial uplift, 230

racialism, 31, 205
racism, 154, 242
ragtime, 126, 182, 189
Ramsey, Jr., Guthrie P., 14, 30, 41, 44, 80
Reconstruction, 49, 53, 58, 69, 185, 228
rhythmic augmentation, 187, 209
rhythmic diminution, 183, 184
Robinson, Florence, 13, 28, 35, 43, 173, 199, 209, 273, 275, 278
Robinson, Florence Crim, 272, 273
Rochester Philharmonic Orchestra, 259
Ross, Marion, 42, 43

segregation, 2, 16, 36, 43, 56, 77, 189, 200, 221, 236, 242, 256
Shadle, Douglas, 4, 28, 193, 267, 279
shadow culture, 268, 269
sharecropping, 53
sheet music, 19, 251
Shirley, George, 94
signifyin(g), 79, 129, 181, 182
signifying, 76, 175, 181, 182, 183, 184, 185, 189, 190
sonatas, 137, 138, 139, 145, 165, 195, 199, 201, 205, 209
"Songs to the Dark Virgin," 70, 76, 77, 78, 173, 206, 238, 274, 277, 279
"Sorrow Songs," 50
Southern, Eileen, 1, 2, 32, 33, 34, 40, 41, 42, 47, 53, 129, 155, 185, 274
Spelman College, 272
spirituals, 31, 146, 195, 201, 224, 225, 236, 238, 239, 242, 243, 259
  and African American performers, 50, 237
  and Black composers, 51
  and Black concert tradition, 50
  and Florence "Bea" Price, 59, 125
  and pageants, 218
  and Paul Laurence Dunbar, 220
  and pentatonic scale, 99
  and piano, 133
  and racial identity, 205
  and religious services, 112
  and "Sorrow Songs," 50
  and water imagery, 138
  arrangements of, 38, 203, 217, 220
  Black, 160, 163
  commercial, 65
  composers of, 103
  concert, 4, 51, 139, 190
  folk, 105
  function of, 182

impact of, 140
lyricism of, 197
performance of, 187
proliferation of, 106
pseudo-, 110
recorded, 147
textual themes of, 109
traditional, 208
unpublished, 116
St. Anne (IL), 11, 17, 267
stereotypes, 49, 130
String Quartet in A Minor, 175, 187
symphonies, 4, 20, 28, 29, 31, 34, 40, 44, 145, 146, 175, 182, 188, 193, 196, 198, 199, 200, 201, 202, 204, 205, 210, 220, 234, 249, 255, 256, 257, 259, 261
Symphony No. 1 in E Minor, 1, 15, 29, 40, 138, 247, 278, 280
Symphony No. 3 in C Minor, 40, 204, 209, 279, 280

Taylor, Breonna, 266
Taylor, J. Hillary, 250
Taylor, T. Theodore, 124
Taylor, Vivian, 280
Tchaikovsky, Pyotr Ilyich, xiii, 144, 181, 182, 183, 184, 185, 203, 231
The Women's Philharmonic (TWP), 279
Thomas Orchestra, 167
Trip to Coontown, A, 55

universal music, 31
University of Arkansas, 11, 18, 19, 22, 28, 35, 38, 146, 173, 202, 203, 207, 209, 267, 277
University of Michigan, 272, 274, 275

vernacularity, 19, 144, 145, 146, 147, 154, 155, 169
Violin Concerto No. 1 (1939), xiii, xxviii, 173, 175, 182, 183
Violin Concerto No. 2 (1952), 144, 163, 164, 165, 166, 168, 173
Violin Concerto Op. 35 (1878), 144
violin concertos, 144, 175, 180, 181, 194, 267
violin fantasies, 4, 144, 175
Violin Fantasy No. 2 in F♯ minor (1949), 146
violin music, 145, 163
violinists, 48, 49, 51, 58, 127, 144, 145, 155, 156, 158, 163, 166, 180, 182, 196, 251

in Chicago, 155
violins, 2, 4, 66, 144, 145, 155, 156, 161, 163, 165, 166, 167, 168, 169, 173, 175, 180, 181, 182, 186, 187, 189, 190, 193, 194, 197, 200, 201, 206, 208, 267, 277
and vernacularity, 155
and vibrato, 155
German, 158
music for, 155
virtuosity, 19, 124, 133, 134, 135, 144, 145, 155, 161, 163, 166, 167, 169

Waites, Althea, 10, 28, 39, 66, 138, 275, 280
Walker, Alice, 12, 14, 21, 260
Walker, George, 87
Walker, Margaret, 87
Walker-Hill, Helen, 2, 3, 10, 14, 133, 173, 267
Wanamaker competition, xix, 138, 195, 196, 218, 234, 260
Wanamaker prize, 29, 195, 196, 197, 254, 256
Wanamaker, Rodman, 195, 196, 254
white audiences, 79, 256
white savior narrative, 262
white society, 30, 54
white supremacy, 10, 15, 53, 81, 256
and patriarchy, 81
white women, 235
White, Clarence Cameron, 2, 4, 47, 56, 58, 155, 156, 157, 158, 159, 160, 162, 163, 202, 251
and Berlin, 167
and virtuosity, 166
White, George, 50
whiteness, 16, 237, 239
Wiley, Edgar, 279
Williams, Chester W., 4, 38, 81, 124
Woman's Symphony Orchestra of Chicago, 1, 36, 217, 235
Women and Music, 66
women composers, 33, 35, 65, 66, 174, 235, 247, 261, 267, 269, 275, 276, 277, 278, 279, 280
Women's Musical Club of Chicago, 155
Works Progress Administration (WPA), 1, 5, 36, 38, 201, 220

Yale School of Music, 14
Yale University, 33, 209
  music department, 37
Ysaÿe, Eugène, 156

For EU product safety concerns, contact us at Calle de José Abascal, 56–1°, 28003 Madrid, Spain or eugpsr@cambridge.org.

www.ingramcontent.com/pod-product-compliance
Ingram Content Group UK Ltd.
Pitfield, Milton Keynes, MK11 3LW, UK
UKHW050337110426
469783UK00021B/482